Bandit Convex Optimisation

This comprehensive reference brings readers to the frontier of research on bandit or zeroth-order convex optimisation. The focus is on theoretical aspects, with short, self-contained chapters covering all the necessary tools from convex optimisation and online learning, including gradient-based algorithms, interior point methods, cutting plane methods and information-theoretic machinery. The book features a large number of exercises, open problems and pointers to future research directions, making it ideal for students as well as researchers.

TOR LATTIMORE is a researcher at Google DeepMind working on reinforcement learning, bandits, optimisation and the theory of machine learning. He is the co-author of an introductory book on bandit algorithms and has published nearly 100 conference and journal articles. He is an action editor for the *Journal of Machine Learning Research*.

'A landmark text on bandit convex optimisation by an authority in the field, this book develops the full theory of zeroth-order online convex optimisation, which essentially means learning from noisy function values without gradients. Regret bounds are established and elegant algorithms are presented, from gradient descent to cutting planes, multiplicative updates and Newton methods. Touching on all key areas of advanced optimisation, the text is an essential companion for researchers, offering both the conceptual foundations and the algorithmic toolkit that together continue to drive progress in online convex optimisation and mathematical optimisation more broadly.'

Elad Hazan, Princeton University

Bandit Convex Optimisation

TOR LATTIMORE
Google DeepMind, London

Shaftesbury Road, Cambridge CB2 8EA, United Kingdom

One Liberty Plaza, 20th Floor, New York, NY 10006, USA

477 Williamstown Road, Port Melbourne, VIC 3207, Australia

314321, 3rd Floor, Plot 3, Splendor Forum, Jasola District Centre, New Delhi 110025, India

Cambridge University Press is part of Cambridge University Press & Assessment, a department of the University of Cambridge.

We share the Universitys mission to contribute to society through the pursuit of education, learning and research at the highest international levels of excellence.

www.cambridge.org
Information on this title: www.cambridge.org/9781009607599
DOI: 10.1017/9781009607551

© Tor Lattimore 2026

This publication is in copyright. Subject to statutory exception and to the provisions of relevant collective licensing agreements, no reproduction of any part may take place without the written permission of Cambridge University Press & Assessment.

When citing this work, please include a reference to the DOI 10.1017/9781009607551

First published 2026

Image credit: Author

A catalogue record for this publication is available from the British Library

A Cataloging-in-Publication data record for this book is available from the Library of Congress

ISBN 978-1-009-60759-9 Hardback

Cambridge University Press & Assessment has no responsibility for the persistence or accuracy of URLs for external or third-party internet websites referred to in this publication and does not guarantee that any content on such websites is, or will remain, accurate or appropriate.

For EU product safety concerns, contact us at Calle de José Abascal, 56, 1°, 28003 Madrid, Spain, or email eugpsr@cambridge.org

Contents

	Preface	*page* ix
1	**Introduction and Problem Statement**	1
	1.1 Methods and Challenges	3
	1.2 Prerequisites	4
	1.3 Bandit Convex Optimisation	4
	1.4 Notation	9
	1.5 Notes	12
2	**Overview of Methods and History**	14
	2.1 Methods for Bandit Convex Optimisation	14
	2.2 History	15
	2.3 Classical Stochastic Optimisation Methods	17
	2.4 Lower Bounds Summarised	20
	2.5 Upper Bounds Summarised	22
	2.6 Notes	24
3	**Mathematical Tools**	26
	3.1 Convex Bodies	26
	3.2 Smoothness and Strong Convexity	29
	3.3 Scaling Properties	30
	3.4 Convex Functions are Nearly Lipschitz	30
	3.5 Near-Optimality on the Interior	31
	3.6 Classical Positions and Rounding	32
	3.7 Extension	34
	3.8 Smoothing	38
	3.9 Computation	39
	3.10 Notes	40
4	**Bisection in One Dimension**	42
	4.1 Bisection Method without Noise	42

	4.2	Bisection Method with Noise	43
	4.3	Notes	49
5	**Online Gradient Descent**		50
	5.1	Gradient Descent	50
	5.2	Spherical Smoothing	53
	5.3	Algorithm and Regret Analysis	54
	5.4	Smoothness and Strong Convexity	56
	5.5	Notes	59
6	**Self-Concordant Regularisation**		61
	6.1	Self-Concordant Barriers	62
	6.2	Follow-the-Regularised-Leader	64
	6.3	Optimistic Ellipsoidal Smoothing	65
	6.4	Algorithms and Regret Analysis	67
	6.5	Smoothness and Strong Convexity	71
	6.6	Stochastic Setting and Variance	74
	6.7	Notes	76
7	**Linear and Quadratic Bandits**		79
	7.1	Covering Numbers	79
	7.2	Optimal Design	80
	7.3	Exponential Weights	81
	7.4	Continuous Exponential Weights	83
	7.5	Linear Bandits	85
	7.6	Quadratic Bandits	89
	7.7	Notes	91
8	**Exponential Weights**		94
	8.1	Exponential Weights for Convex Bandits	94
	8.2	Exponential Weights in One Dimension	95
	8.3	The Bregman Divergence	102
	8.4	Exponential Weights and Regularisation	104
	8.5	Exploration by Optimisation	107
	8.6	Bayesian Convex Bandits	110
	8.7	Duality and the Information Ratio	111
	8.8	Notes	116
9	**Cutting Plane Methods**		118
	9.1	High-Level Idea	119
	9.2	Infinite-Armed Bandits	123
	9.3	Best Arm Identification	127
	9.4	Finding a Cutting Plane	128

	9.5 Centre of Gravity Method	133
	9.6 Method of the Inscribed Ellipsoid	137
	9.7 Ellipsoid Method	139
	9.8 Proof of Proposition 9.24	140
	9.9 Notes	142
10	**Online Newton Step**	**145**
	10.1 The Blessing and Curse of Curvature	146
	10.2 Introducing Online Newton Step	147
	10.3 Regularity	149
	10.4 Extension and Surrogate Losses	153
	10.5 Algorithm and Analysis	156
	10.6 Proof of Theorem 10.8	161
	10.7 Proof of Lemma 10.12	169
	10.8 Constraints	171
	10.9 Notes	171
11	**Online Newton Step for Adversarial Losses**	**175**
	11.1 Approximate Convex Minimisation	175
	11.2 Decaying Online Newton Step	177
	11.3 Regularity and Extensions	179
	11.4 Algorithm	180
	11.5 Analysis	182
	11.6 Decay Analysis	191
	11.7 Approximate Optimisation	194
	11.8 Constraints	195
	11.9 Notes	196
12	**Gaussian Optimistic Smoothing**	**198**
	12.1 Smoothing	201
	12.2 Elementary Properties	201
	12.3 Properties of the Hessian	202
	12.4 Properties of the Quadratic Surrogate	206
	12.5 Lower Bound on the Surrogate	207
	12.6 Estimation	210
	12.7 Concentration	212
	12.8 Sequential Concentration	214
	12.9 Summary	224
	12.10 Notes	226
13	**Submodular Minimisation**	**227**
	13.1 Lovász Extension	228
	13.2 Bandit Submodular Minimisation	232

	13.3	Gradient Descent for Submodular Minimisation	234
	13.4	Notes	237
14	**Outlook**		239
	Appendix A	Miscellaneous	242
	Appendix B	Concentration	246
	Appendix C	Notation	255
	References		258
	Index		267

Preface

This book is about zeroth-order convex optimisation; that is, approximately solving

$$\arg\min_{x \in K} f(x),$$

where $f: K \to \mathbb{R}$ is convex, $K \subset \mathbb{R}^d$ is a convex body and the learning system can only observe noisy function values and not gradients or higher-order derivatives. The focus is on finite-time minimax bounds on the regret or sample complexity that is standard in the multi-armed bandit literature. The book covers all the algorithmic ideas, including gradient descent, barrier methods, cutting plane methods, exponential weights, information-theoretic arguments and second-order methods. The penultimate chapter is devoted to bandit submodular minimisation and its relation to bandit convex optimisation via the Lovász extension. The book is more or less self-contained, though a little background in optimisation and online learning will go a long way. The content is almost entirely theoretical.

Acknowledgements

This work would not have been possible without my many wonderful collaborators, especially Alireza Bakhtiari, Hidde Fokkema, András György, Dirk van der Hoeven, Jack Mayo and Csaba Szepesvári. For at least the second time I am in debt to Marcus Hutter, who read almost the entire book and made a huge number of thoughtful suggestions. Finally, thank you Rosina for your endless love and support; and Phoebe for your love and smiles.

1
Introduction and Problem Statement

This book is about approximately solving problems of the form

$$\arg\min_{x \in K} f(x), \qquad (1.1)$$

where K is a convex body in $\mathbb{R}^d$ (convex, compact and nonempty interior) and $f : K \to \mathbb{R}$ is a convex function. Problems of this kind are ubiquitous in machine learning, operations research, economics and beyond. The difficulty of this problem depends on many factors; for example, the dimension and smoothness properties of f. Most important, however, is the representation of the function f and constraint set K. Our focus is on zeroth-order stochastic optimisation, where you can query f at any $x \in K$ and observe $y = f(x) + \text{noise}$. By contrast, the vast majority of the literature on mathematical programming allows both the value of f and its derivatives to be computed at any $x \in K$, either exactly or with additive noise. This is not a book about applications, but for the sake of inspiration and motivation we list a few situations where zeroth-order optimisation is a natural fit.

○ *Real-world experiments:* A chef wants to optimise the temperature and baking time when baking a soufflé. The constraint set K is some reasonable subset of the possible temperature/time pairings and $f(x)$ is the expected negative quality of the finished product. Noise arises here from exogenous factors, such as unintentional variation in recipe preparation.
○ *Adversarial attacks in machine learning:* A company releases an image recognition system. Can you find an image that looks to the human eye like a stop sign but is classified by the system as something else? Unless the company has released the code and weights, you can only interact with a black-box function C that accepts images as input and returns a classification, possibly at some cost. A simple idea is to take an image $x_\circ$ and let K be a set of images that are visually indistinguishable from $x_\circ$. Then approximately

solve the following optimisation problem:

$$\arg\min_{x \in K} S(C(x), C(x_\circ)),$$

where $S(C(x), C(y))$ is some measure of similarity between the classifications $C(x)$ and $C(y)$. That is, the problem is to find an image x that looks similar to $x_\circ$ but with $C(x)$ maximally different from $C(x_\circ)$.

- *Reinforcement learning and control:* There are many ways to do reinforcement learning. Suppose that π_θ is a policy parameterised by $\theta \in K$ and $f(\theta)$ is the (expected) loss when implementing policy π_θ. Then solving (1.1) corresponds to finding the optimal policy in $\{\pi_\theta : \theta \in K\}$.
- *Hyperparameter tuning:* Most machine learning systems have a range of parameters; for example, the width, depth and structure of a neural network or learning rates (schedules) for the training algorithm. You may want to automate the process of finding the best architecture and training parameters. The loss in this case could be the performance of the resulting system after training. So computing $f(x)$ requires running an entire training process, which is enormously expensive and possibly random. Generally speaking f cannot be differentiated.
- *Dynamic pricing:* In dynamic pricing a retailer interacts sequentially with an environment. Customers arrive in the system and the retailer suggests a price $X_t \in K \subset \mathbb{R}$. The loss $f(X_t)$ is the (expected) negative profit. When the price is too high the customer will not purchase and some loss is incurred (operating costs). On the other hand, when the price is too low there is also a loss. The function f is not known *a priori* to the retailer and variability in customers introduces noise in the observations.

The last application reveals another consideration. Approximately minimising the loss f as in (1.1) is not the only possible objective. In dynamic pricing every query to the loss function (decision) entails an actual cost (or profit). In this situation a more natural objective is to minimise the cumulative loss over all interactions. Most of this book is about

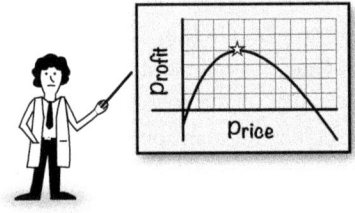

this objective, which is most often seen in the literature on multi-armed bandits. As we shall soon see, an algorithm that approximately minimises the cumulative loss can be used to solve the optimisation problem (1.1), but the reverse does not hold. Note that many practical problems are not convex. Nevertheless, enormous practical experience with first-order methods suggests this is less of a problem than it seems. The same may be true in the zeroth-order setting.

Many of the proposed applications in this book are aspirational rather than truly practical. Automatic hyperparameter tuning is used everywhere, but the algorithms employed are usually based on other methods, such as Gaussian process bandits. Presumably the reason for this is because convex bandit algorithms are not quite ready for the big stage yet. The simple methods converge slowly, while the complicated methods are challenging to implement and tune. Hopefully in the coming years new and better algorithms will be developed.

1.1 Methods and Challenges

In spite of its simplicity, bandit (and zeroth-order) convex optimisation is still not fully understood; and certainly much less so than first-order optimisation where the gradients of f are available. Nearly every method for bandit convex optimisation is based on estimating the gradient (and maybe higher-order derivatives) of a surrogate loss and combining this with a classical gradient-based optimisation method. This approach leads to a pernicious bias/variance trade-off, which is particularly exacerbated when the loss function is non-smooth. Unsurprisingly, then, the primary focus of the classical literature on stochastic zeroth-order optimisation is on smooth settings.

This book explores the full range of methods, including the most classical online projected gradient descent (Chapter 5), cutting plane methods (Chapter 9) and more exotic methods based on information theory and minimax duality (Chapter 8). Buried somewhere in nearly every approach is some kind of bias/variance trade-off. Optimising for the regret also introduces complications. The learner cannot freely query the loss at any point they might like without consideration for the loss suffered. This is known as the exploration/exploitation dilemma for which reinforcement learning is famous. We will see, in fact, that in certain settings optimising for the regret is (provably) harder than merely finding a near-optimiser of the loss. Another theme that raises its head in many chapters is the need to balance statistical and computational efficiency, both of the theoretical kind (poly time or not) and the practical kind. At present, those algorithms with the best statistical guarantees do not have known efficient implementations.

So, let us begin. The next section explains what prerequisites you may find useful. After that, the rest of the chapter is devoted to the formal problem settings studied later. Chapter 2 covers the history and includes large reference tables of known results. Chapter 3 covers the necessary mathematical tools. Nearly every chapter thereafter is based on what can be achieved with some algorithmic idea.

1.2 Prerequisites

Most readers will benefit from a reasonable knowledge of online learning (Cesa-Bianchi and Lugosi, 2006; Hazan, 2016; Orabona, 2019) and bandits (Bubeck and Cesa-Bianchi, 2012; Slivkins, 2019; Lattimore and Szepesvári, 2020). We use some theory from interior point methods, which you could refresh by reading the lecture notes by Nemirovski (1996). None of this is essential, however, if you are prepared to take a few results on faith. Similarly, we use a few simple results from concentration of measure. Our reference was the book by Vershynin (2018) but Boucheron et al. (2013) also covers the material needed. We do use martingale versions of these results, which sadly do not appear in these books but are more or less trivial extensions. The standard reference for convex analysis is the book by Rockafellar (1970) to which we occasionally refer. No deep results are needed, however. Similarly, we make use of certain elementary results in convex geometry. Our reference for these is mostly the book by Artstein-Avidan et al. (2015). The symbol (✦) on a proof, section or chapter means that you could (should?) skip this part on your first pass. The book contains a number of exercises, which are assigned a difficulty based on a star rating. Problems with one ★ are straightforward, requiring limited ingenuity or mathematical sophistication. Problems with two ★★ are moderately difficult and may require considerable ingenuity. Problems with three ★★★ will probably take several days of work. Problems marked with 📕 may require extensive literature searches and problems marked with ? have not been solved yet. All difficulty assessments are subjective estimates only.

1.3 Bandit Convex Optimisation

Let $K \subset \mathbb{R}^d$ be convex and $f_1, \ldots, f_n : K \to \mathbb{R}$ be an unknown sequence of convex functions. A learner interacts with the environment over n rounds. In round t the learner chooses an action $X_t \in K$. They then observe a noisy loss $Y_t = f_t(X_t) + \varepsilon_t$, where $(\varepsilon_t)_{t=1}^n$ is a sequence of noise random variables. The precise conditions on the noise are given in (1.2) below, but for now you could think of the noise as a sequence of independent standard Gaussian random variables. The learner's decision X_t is allowed to depend on an exogenous source of randomness and the data observed already, which is $X_1, Y_1, \ldots, X_{t-1}, Y_{t-1}$.

1.3 Bandit Convex Optimisation

The main performance metric in this book is the regret, which is

$$\text{Reg}_n = \sup_{x \in K} \sum_{t=1}^{n} (f_t(X_t) - f_t(x)).$$

The regret is a random variable with the randomness coming from both the noise and the learner's decisions. Normally the regret will be bounded in expectation or with high probability, depending on what is most convenient. Of course, the regret also depends on the loss functions. In general we will argue that our algorithms have small regret for any convex losses within some class. Stronger assumptions (smaller classes) lead to stronger results and/or simpler and/or more efficient algorithms. The following definition and notation are sufficient for our purposes.

Definition 1.1 Let $\mathscr{F}$ be the space of convex functions from K to $\mathbb{R}$, and with $\|\cdot\|$ the standard euclidean norm define the following properties of a function $f \in \mathscr{F}$:

Prop (b) f is bounded: $f(x) \in [0, 1]$ for all $x \in K$.
Prop (l) f is Lipschitz: $f(x) - f(y) \leq \|x - y\|$ for all $x, y \in K$.
Prop (sm) f is β-smooth: $f(x) - \frac{\beta}{2}\|x\|^2$ is concave on K.
Prop (sc) f is α-strongly convex: $f(x) - \frac{\alpha}{2}\|x\|^2$ is convex on K.
Prop (lin) f is linear: $f(x) = x^\top b + c$.
Prop (quad) f is quadratic: $f(x) = x^\top A x + x^\top b + c$.

We use the property symbols to define subsets of $\mathscr{F}$. For example:

◦ $\mathscr{F}_{\text{b}} = \{f \in \mathscr{F} : f(x) \in [0, 1] \text{ for all } x \in K\}$.
◦ $\mathscr{F}_{\text{b,sm,sc}}$ is the set of bounded convex functions that are smooth and strongly convex.

When smoothness and strong convexity are involved, our bounds will depend on the parameters $\alpha > 0$ and $0 \leq \beta < \infty$, which we assume are known constants.

1.3.1 Constraint Set

The set K is called the constraint set and its geometry also plays a role in the hardness of bandit convex optimisation. We make the following assumption throughout the entire book:

Assumption 1.2 The constraint set $K \subset \mathbb{R}^d$ is a convex body, which means that:

(1) K is convex;

(2) K has a nonempty interior; and
(3) K is compact.

Only convexity and the boundedness part of compactness are really essential for most results. Every nonempty convex set has a nonempty interior when embedded in a suitable affine subset of $\mathbb{R}^d$. Properties of K that influence the regret of various algorithms include its diameter and how well-rounded it is (Section 3.6). Mathematically speaking, nothing more is needed from the constraint set. Computationally the representation of K is very important. Standard options are as a polytope, the convex hull of a point cloud or as given by a separation/membership oracle. Matters involving computation and the constraint set are discussed in Section 3.9.

Remark 1.3 You may be interested to know what happens when K is not bounded; for example, when $K = \mathbb{R}^d$. We discuss this and other possible assumptions on the constraint set in Note 1.ii at the end of the chapter.

1.3.2 Noise

Our assumption on the noise is that the sequence $(\varepsilon_t)_{t=1}^n$ is conditionally subgaussian. By this we mean:

Assumption 1.4 The noise random variables $\varepsilon_1, \ldots, \varepsilon_n$ are conditionally subgaussian:

$$\mathbb{E}\left[\varepsilon_t \mid X_1, Y_1, \ldots, X_{t-1}, Y_{t-1}, X_t\right] = 0 \text{; and}$$
$$\mathbb{E}\left[\exp(\varepsilon_t^2) \mid X_1, Y_1, \ldots, X_{t-1}, Y_{t-1}, X_t\right] \leq 2 \,. \quad (1.2)$$

Assumption 1.4 is considered global and will not be referred to subsequently. Note that (1.2) together with the fact that $x^2 \leq \exp(x^2) - 1$ for all x guarantees that the conditional variance of ε_t satisfies

$$\mathbb{E}[\varepsilon_t^2 \mid X_1, Y_1, \ldots, X_{t-1}, Y_{t-1}, X_t] \leq 1 \,. \quad (1.3)$$

This definition of subgaussianity is based on the Orlicz norm definitions. We give a brief summary in Appendix B, or you can read the wonderful book by Vershynin (2018). Sometimes we work in the noise-free setting where $\varepsilon_t = 0$. The assumption of subgaussian noise is rather standard in the bandit literature. The Gaussian distribution $\mathcal{N}(0, 3/8)$ is subgaussian, and so is any distribution that is suitably bounded almost surely. All that is really needed is a suitable concentration of measure phenomenon, and hence all results in this book could be generalised to considerably larger classes of noise distribution without too much effort. We keep things simple, however.

1.3.3 Adversarial and Stochastic Convex Bandits

We have already outlined some of the assumptions on the function class to which the losses belong. The other major classification is whether or not the problem is adversarial or stochastic.

Adversarial Bandit Convex Optimisation

In the adversarial setting the most common assumption is that the noise $\varepsilon_t = 0$ while the functions $f_1, \ldots, f_n$ are chosen in an arbitrary way by the adversary. Sometimes the adversary is allowed to choose f_t at the same time as the learner chooses X_t, in which case we say the adversary is non-oblivious. Perhaps more commonly, however, the adversary is obliged to choose all loss functions $f_1, \ldots, f_n$ before the interaction starts. Adversaries of this kind are called oblivious. For our purposes it is convenient to allow nonzero noise even in the adversarial case. This is sometimes essential in applications; for example, in bandit submodular minimisation (Chapter 13). And besides, it feels natural that the adversarial setting should generalise the stochastic one.

Remark 1.5 In the adversarial setting you might be tempted to combine the noise and losses by defining the loss function to be $f_t + \varepsilon_t$. But this would prevent the noise distribution from depending on the action of the learner, which is permitted by Assumption 1.4 and is essential in certain applications, such as submodular bandits (Chapter 13).

Stochastic Bandit Convex Optimisation

The stochastic setting is more classical. The loss function is now constant over time: $f_t = f$ for all rounds t and unknown f. The standard performance metric in bandit problems is the regret, but in the stochastic setting it also makes sense to consider the simple regret. At the end of the interaction the learner is expected to output one last point $\widehat{X} \in K$ and the simple regret is

$$\mathrm{sReg}_n = f(\widehat{X}) - \inf_{x \in K} f(x).$$

Thanks to convexity, there is a straightforward reduction from cumulative regret to simple regret: simply let $\widehat{X} = \frac{1}{n} \sum_{t=1}^n X_t$. Then by convexity,

$$\mathrm{sReg}_n \leq \frac{1}{n} \mathrm{Reg}_n. \tag{1.4}$$

Another standard measure of performance in the stochastic setting is the sample complexity, which is the number of interactions needed before the simple regret is at most $\varepsilon > 0$ with high probability. The following fact provides a conversion from a high probability bound on the cumulative regret to sample complexity:

Fact 1.6 Suppose that with probability at least $1 - \delta$ the regret of some algorithm is bounded by $\text{Reg}_n \leq R(n)$. Then, by the above conversion, the sample complexity can be bounded by the smallest n such that $R(n)/n \leq \varepsilon$. Concretely, if $R(n) = An^p$ for $p \in (0, 1)$ and $A > 0$, then the sample complexity is at most $1 + (A/\varepsilon)^{1/(1-p)}$.

There is also a simple reduction from a bound on the expected regret to a (high probability) sample complexity bound. The idea is to run the regret-minimising algorithm $k_{\max} = O(\log(1/\delta))$ times with horizon n large enough that $\mathbb{E}[\frac{1}{n}\text{Reg}_n] \leq \frac{\varepsilon}{4}$. By Markov's inequality and (1.4), with constant probability the average iterate over any run is nearly optimal, which means that one of the $k_{\max}$ average iterates is nearly optimal with high probability. Lastly, a best arm identification procedure is applied to select a near minimiser among the $k_{\max}$ candidates. The full procedure and its analysis follow.

```
1  args: base algorithm ALG, R(·), ε > 0, δ ∈ (0, 1)
2  let n = min{s: R(s)/s ≤ ε/4}
3  for k = 1 to k_max ≜ ⌈log(2/δ)/log(2)⌉:
4      run ALG over n rounds
5      observe iterates X_1,...,X_n
6      let x̂_k = (1/n) Σ_{s=1}^n X_s
7  return BAI(ε/2, δ/2, x̂_1,...,x̂_{k_max})      # Algorithm 9.2
```

Algorithm 1.1 A master algorithm for obtaining high probability sample complexity bounds from a base algorithm with expected regret. See Section 9.3 for a detailed explanation of the BAI subroutine (Algorithm 9.2).

Proposition 1.7 *Suppose that $\mathbb{E}[\text{Reg}_n] \leq R(n)$. Then*

(1) Algorithm 1.1 queries the loss at most

$$O\left(\left(\min\left\{n: \frac{R(n)}{n} \leq \frac{\varepsilon}{4}\right\} + \frac{\log(1/\delta)}{\varepsilon^2}\right) \log(1/\delta)\right)$$

times; and

(2) With probability at least $1 - \delta$, Algorithm 1.1 returns an $\widehat{X} \in K$ such that

$$f(\widehat{X}) \leq \inf_{x \in K} f(x) + \varepsilon.$$

Proof Let $f_\star = \inf_{x \in K} f(x)$. By (1.4), $\mathbb{E}[f(\widehat{x}_k)] - f_\star \leq \frac{\varepsilon}{4}$. Since $f(x) - f_\star \geq 0$

for all $x \in K$, by Markov's inequality,
$$\mathbb{P}\left(f(\widehat{x}_k) - f_\star \geq \frac{\varepsilon}{2}\right) \leq \frac{1}{2}.$$
Hence, by the definition of $k_{\max}$, with probability at least $1 - \delta/2$ there exists a $k \in \{1, \ldots, k_{\max}\}$ such that
$$f(\widehat{x}_k) - f_\star \leq \frac{\varepsilon}{2}.$$
Finally, referring to Section 9.3, by Theorem 9.10 the call to Algorithm 9.2 uses
$$O\left(\frac{k_{\max}}{\varepsilon^2} \log\left(\frac{k_{\max}}{\delta}\right)\right)$$
queries to the loss function and with probability at least $1 - \delta/2$ returns an $\widehat{X} \in \{\widehat{x}_1, \ldots, \widehat{x}_{k_{\max}}\}$ with
$$f(\widehat{X}) \leq \min_{1 \leq k \leq k_{\max}} f(\widehat{x}_k) + \frac{\varepsilon}{2}.$$
Combining everything with a union bound completes the proof. □

Our focus for the remainder of the book is primarily on the cumulative regret, but we occasionally highlight the sample complexity of algorithms in order to compare to the literature. The arguments above show that bounds on the cumulative regret imply bounds on the simple regret and sample complexity. The converse is not true.

Regret is Random

You should note that Reg_n and sReg_n are random variables with the randomness arising from both the algorithm and the noise. Most of our results either control $\mathbb{E}[\text{Reg}_n]$ or prove that Reg_n is bounded by such-and-such with high probability. Bounds that hold with high probability are generally preferred since they can be integrated to obtain bounds in expectation. But we will not be too dogmatic about this. Indeed, we mostly prove bounds in expectation to avoid tedious concentration of measure calculations. As far as we know, these always work out if you try hard enough.

1.4 Notation

A full list of notation is available in Appendix C.

Norms

The norm $\|\cdot\|$ is the euclidean norm for vectors and the spectral norm for matrices. For positive definite A, $\langle x, y\rangle_A = x^\top A y$ and $\|x\|_A^2 = \langle x, x\rangle_A$. Given a random variable X, $\|X\|_{\psi_k} = \inf\{t > 0 \colon \mathbb{E}[\exp(|X/t|^k)] \leq 2\}$ for $k \in \{1, 2\}$ are the Orlicz norms. Remember, X is subgaussian if $\|X\|_{\psi_2} < \infty$ and subexponential if $\|X\|_{\psi_1} < \infty$. You can read more about the Orlicz norms in Appendix B.

Sets

$\mathbb{R}$ and $\mathbb{Z}$ are the sets of real values and integers. The restriction of the reals to the (strictly) positive real line are $\mathbb{R}_+ = [0, \infty)$ and $\mathbb{R}_{++} = (0, \infty)$. The euclidean ball and sphere of radius r are denoted by $\mathbb{B}_r^d = \{x \in \mathbb{R}^d \colon \|x\| \leq r\}$ and $\mathbb{S}_r^{d-1} = \{x \in \mathbb{R}^d \colon \|x\| = r\}$. Hopefully the latter will not be confused with the space of positive (semi-)definite matrices on $\mathbb{R}^d$, which we denote by $(\mathbb{S}_+^d)$ $\mathbb{S}_{++}^d$. Given $x \in \mathbb{R}^d$ and $0 \neq \eta \in \mathbb{R}^d$ we let $H(x, \eta) = \{y \colon \langle y - x, \eta\rangle \leq 0\}$, which is a closed half-space passing through x with outwards-facing normal η. Given $x \in \mathbb{R}^d$ and positive definite matrix A, $E(x, A) = \{y \in \mathbb{R}^d \colon \|x - y\|_{A^{-1}} \leq 1\}$, which is an ellipsoid centred at x. When $E = E(x, A)$ is an ellipsoid, $E(r) = E(x, \sqrt{r}A)$ denotes the same ellipsoid scaled by a factor of r. The space of probability measures on $K \subset \mathbb{R}^d$ is $\Delta(K)$ where we always take the Borel σ-algebra $\mathscr{B}(K)$. Given a natural number m, $\Delta_m = \{p \in \mathbb{R}_+^m \colon \|p\|_1 = 1\}$ and $\Delta_m^+ = \Delta_m \cap \mathbb{R}_{++}^m$. For $x, y \in \mathbb{R}^d$ we let $[x, y] = \{(1 - \lambda)x + \lambda y \colon \lambda \in [0, 1]\}$, which is the chord connecting x and y.

Elementary Notation

We define arithmetic operations on sets in the Minkowski fashion. Concretely, given $A, B \subset \mathbb{R}^d$ the Minkowski sum is $A + B = \{x + y \colon x \in A, y \in B\}$. When $u \in \mathbb{R}$ we let $uA = \{ux \colon x \in A\}$ and of course $-A = (-1)A$ and $A - A = A + (-A)$. Occasionally for $x \in \mathbb{R}^d$ we abbreviate $\{x\} + A = x + A$. The closure of A is $\mathrm{cl}(A)$, its interior is $\mathrm{int}(A) = \{x \in A \colon \exists \epsilon > 0, x + \mathbb{B}_\epsilon^d \subset A\}$ and its boundary is $\partial A = \mathrm{cl}(A) \setminus \mathrm{int}(A)$. When A is convex, the relative interior of A is $\mathrm{ri}(A) = \{x \in A \colon \exists \varepsilon > 0, (x + \mathbb{B}_\varepsilon^d) \cap \mathrm{aff}(A) \subset A\}$ where $\mathrm{aff}(A)$ is the affine hull of A. The polar of A is $A^\circ = \{u \colon \sup_{x \in A} \langle x, u\rangle \leq 1\}$. We use $\mathbb{1}$ for the identity matrix and $\mathbf{0}$ for the zero matrix or zero vector. Dimensions and types will always be self-evident from the context. The euclidean projection onto K is $\Pi_K(x) = \arg\min_{y \in K} \|x - y\|$. Suppose that $f \colon \mathbb{R}^d \supset A \to \mathbb{R}$ is differentiable at $x \in A$; then we write $f'(x)$ for its gradient and $f''(x)$ for its Hessian. When f is convex we write $\partial f(x)$ for the set of subderivatives of f at x. More generally, $Df(x)[h]$ is the directional derivative of f at x in the direction h. Higher-order directional derivatives are denoted by $D^k f(x)[h_1, \ldots, h_k]$. Note that for convex f, $Df(x)[h]$ is defined for all $x \in \mathrm{int}(\mathrm{dom}(f))$ and $h \in \mathbb{R}^d$ but the mapping

1.4 Notation

$h \mapsto Df(x)[h]$ need not be linear, as the convex function $\mathbb{R}: x \mapsto |x|$ shows. Densities are always with respect to the Lebesgue measure. The diameter of a nonempty set K is

$$\mathrm{diam}(K) = \sup_{x,y \in K} \|x - y\|.$$

The Lipschitz constant of a function $f: K \to \mathbb{R}$ is

$$\mathrm{lip}_K(f) = \sup\left\{\frac{f(x) - f(y)}{\|x - y\|} : x, y \in K, x \neq y\right\}.$$

When $f: \mathbb{R}^d \to \mathbb{R} \cup \{\infty\}$ is convex we write $\mathrm{lip}(f)$ to mean $\mathrm{lip}_{\mathrm{dom}(f)}(f)$ where $\mathrm{dom}(f) = \{x: f(x) < \infty\}$. Suppose that $A, B \in \mathbb{S}_+^d$. Then $A \preceq B$ if $B - A \in \mathbb{S}_+^d$ and $A \succeq B$ if $A - B \in \mathbb{S}_+^d$. $A \prec B$ and $A \succ B$ are defined similarly but with $\mathbb{S}_+^d$ replaced by $\mathbb{S}_{++}^d$.

Probability Spaces

We will not formally define the probability space on which the essential random variables $X_1, Y_1, \ldots, X_n, Y_n$ live. You can see how this should be done in the book by Lattimore and Szepesvári (2020). In general $\mathbb{P}$ is the probability measure on some space carrying these random variables and we let $\mathscr{F}_t = \sigma(X_1, Y_1, \ldots, X_t, Y_t)$ be the σ-algebra generated by the first t rounds of interaction. Events are often defined as {condition}. For example, $\{f(X_t) > \varepsilon\}$ is the event that $f(X_t) > \varepsilon$. We abbreviate $\mathbb{P}_t(\cdot) = \mathbb{P}(\cdot|\mathscr{F}_t)$ and $\mathbb{E}_t[\cdot] = \mathbb{E}[\cdot|\mathscr{F}_t]$. The multivariate Gaussian distribution with mean μ and covariance Σ is $\mathscr{N}(\mu, \Sigma)$. Given $A \subset \mathbb{R}^d$ we let $\mathscr{U}(A)$ be the uniform probability measure on A, which can be defined in multiple ways. We only need it when A is finite or $A \in \{\mathbb{B}_r^d, \mathbb{S}_r^{d-1}\}$, where the definition is obvious.

Regret

Recall the regret is defined by

$$\mathrm{Reg}_n = \sup_{x \in K} \sum_{t=1}^n (f_t(X_t) - f_t(x)).$$

The sup cannot always be replaced by a max because even for compact K the loss functions may not be continuous. For example, when $K = [0, 1]$ and $f: K \to [0, 1]$ is defined by $f(0) = 1$ and $f(x) = x$ for $x > 0$, then f is convex and does not have a minimiser on K. We occasionally need the regret relative to a specific $x \in K$, which is

$$\mathrm{Reg}_n(x) = \sum_{t=1}^n (f_t(X_t) - f_t(x)).$$

1.5 Notes

1.i The function classes outlined in Definition 1.1 are by no means the only ones considered. For example, the definition of smoothness can be generalised beyond the second-order smoothness. There are multiple ways to do this, but one is to call a function $f: \mathbb{R}^d \to \mathbb{R}$ smooth of order $p \in [2, \infty)$ on $\mathbb{R}^d$ if for all $x, y \in \mathbb{R}^d$,

$$\|D^q f(x) - D^q f(y)\| \leq \beta \|x - y\|^{p-q},$$

where q is the largest integer strictly smaller than p and the norm of the left-hand side is the operator norm. When $p = 2$ and f is convex this definition is equivalent to what appears in Definition 1.1 (Nesterov, 2018, Theorem 2.1.5). Zeroth-order convex optimisation has been studied for highly smooth functions with slightly varying definitions of smoothness by Polyak and Tsybakov (1990); Bach and Perchet (2016); Akhavan et al. (2020, 2024b) and others. This line of work is briefly discussed in the notes of Chapter 6.

1.ii The focus of this book is on a particular kind of *constrained* optimisation where the learner must play in a convex body K, which by definition is compact, convex and has a nonempty interior. As mentioned, only boundedness and convexity are really important for the results in this book. But assuming boundedness discards many interesting settings. Most fundamentally, it prohibits the *unconstrained* setting where $K = \mathbb{R}^d$. Similarly, K cannot be a half-space or other unbounded subset of $\mathbb{R}^d$. Practically speaking, unbounded domains can often be reduced to bounded ones with prior knowledge that the minimiser must lie in a bounded convex set. But such reductions do not always play well with the other assumptions; for example, that the loss is bounded on K.

1.iii Another situation related to the constraint set that arises often is that the losses are defined on all of $\mathbb{R}^d$ and the learner can query any point in $\mathbb{R}^d$ but is only evaluated against the best point in K. This setting is sometimes referred to as the *improper* setting. The definition ensures that the improper setting is easier than both the constrained setting (the learner has more power) and the unconstrained setting (the adversary has less power).

1.iv Other performance criteria also exist in the literature. For example, both the distance to the minimiser and the gradient of the loss are potentially sensible measures of quality. Neither of these is considered in this book.

1.v We assume throughout that the noise either vanishes completely or is 1-subgaussian: $\mathbb{E}_{t-1}[\exp(\varepsilon_t^2)|X_t] \leq 2$ and $\mathbb{E}_{t-1}[\varepsilon_t] = 0$. At the same time, we often assume that the range of the losses is in $[0, 1]$. This means the scale of the

1.5 Notes

noise is the same as the scale of the losses and makes it hard to know how the range or variance of the noise might affect the regret bound if either of these quantities were scaled individually. One analysis that decouples these quantities is given in Section 6.6; occasionally we give pointers to the literature or suggest exercises/open problems.

1.vi More exotic interaction protocols have also been investigated. Consider for a moment adversarial setting without noise. A number of authors have explored what changes if the learner is allowed to choose *two* points $X_{t,1}, X_{t,2} \in K$ and observes $f_t(X_{t,1})$ and $f_t(X_{t,2})$. One might believe that such a modification would have only a mild effect but this is not at all the case. Having access to two evaluations makes the bandit setup behave more like the full information setting (Agarwal et al., 2010; Nesterov and Spokoiny, 2017; Duchi et al., 2015). Essentially the learner can compute directional derivatives to arbitrary precision, which is not possible in the standard setting. Note that in the stochastic setting the noise is what makes it impossible to compute directional derivatives, while in the adversarial setting there need not be any relation from one loss to the next.

1.vii At the end of the day, the number of settings and possible assumptions is *enormous*. We have naturally selected a subset most aligned with our interest and expertise. Many of the algorithms and analysis presented can be generalised straightforwardly to other settings. But sometimes the conditions and modifications are subtle. As much as possible we try to give pointers to the literature, but no doubt much has been missed.

2
Overview of Methods and History

This chapter briefly outlines the key algorithmic ideas and history of bandit convex optimisation. There follow in Section 2.4 and Section 2.5 summary tables of known lower and upper bounds for the various settings studied in this book.

2.1 Methods for Bandit Convex Optimisation

Methods for bandit convex optimisation can be characterised into five classes:

- *Cutting plane methods* are important theoretical tools for linear programming and non-smooth convex optimisation. The high-level idea is to iteratively cut away pieces of K that have large volume while ensuring that the minimiser stays inside the active set. Cutting plane methods are the geometric version of elimination algorithms for bandits and consequentially are typically analysed in the stochastic setting. At least three works have adapted these ideas to stochastic convex bandits. Agarwal et al. (2011) and Lattimore and György (2021a) both use the ellipsoid method, while Carpentier (2025) uses the centre of gravity method. A simple bisection algorithm is discussed in Chapter 4 for one-dimensional convex bandits while in Chapter 9 the approach is generalised to higher dimensions using the centre of gravity method, the ellipsoid method or the method of the inscribed ellipsoid.
- *Gradient descent* is the fundamental algorithm for (convex) optimisation and a large proportion of algorithms for convex bandits use it as a building block (Kleinberg, 2005; Flaxman et al., 2005; Saha and Tewari, 2011; Hazan and Levy, 2014, and more). At a high level the idea is to estimate gradients of a smoothed version of the loss and use these in gradient descent in place of the real unknown gradients. We explore this idea in depth in Chapters 5 and 6.

○ *Newton's method* is a second-order method that uses curvature information as well as the gradient. One of the challenges in bandit convex optimisation is that algorithms achieving optimal regret need to behave in a way that depends on the curvature. Second-order methods that estimate the Hessian of the actual loss or a surrogate have been used for bandit convex optimisation (Suggala et al., 2021; Lattimore and György, 2023; Suggala et al., 2024; Fokkema et al., 2024) and are the topic of Chapter 10.

○ *Continuous exponential weights* is a powerful algorithm for full information online learning and has been used for convex bandits by Bubeck et al. (2017), who combined it with the surrogate loss function described in Chapter 12 along with many tricks to construct the first polynomial-time algorithm for bandit convex optimisation in the adversarial setting with $O(\sqrt{n})$ regret and without any assumptions beyond boundedness. Their algorithm is more complex than one might like and is not discussed here except for the special case when $d = 1$ where many details simplify and the approach yields a reasonably practical algorithm. More details are in Chapter 8.

○ *Information-directed sampling* is a principled Bayesian algorithm for sequential decision making (Russo and Van Roy, 2014). Bubeck et al. (2015) showed how to use information-directed sampling to bound the Bayesian regret for one-dimensional convex bandits and then applied minimax duality to argue that the minimax Bayesian regret is the same as the adversarial regret. This idea was later extended by Bubeck and Eldan (2018) and Lattimore (2020). Although these methods still yield the best bounds currently known for the adversarial setting, they are entirely non-constructive thanks to the application of minimax duality. We explain how these ideas relate to continuous exponential weights and mirror descent in Chapter 8.

2.2 History

Bandit convex optimisation is a relative newcomer in the bandit literature, with the earliest work by Kleinberg (2005) and Flaxman et al. (2005), both of whom use gradient-based methods in combination with gradient estimates of the smoothed losses (explained in Chapter 5). At least for losses in $\mathscr{F}_{b,1}$ they showed that the regret is at most $O(n^{3/4})$. While these works seem to be the first to have considered the regret criterion for zeroth-order convex optimisation, their algorithms strongly resemble those algorithms designed for zeroth-order stochastic approximation, which we briefly summarise in Section 2.3.

Agarwal et al. (2010) showed that by assuming strong convexity and smoothness the regret of these algorithms could be improved to $\tilde{O}(\sqrt{n})$ in the improper setting where the learner is allowed to query outside K (see Note 1.iii). The big question was whether or not $\tilde{O}(\sqrt{n})$ regret is possible without assuming smoothness and strong convexity. A resolution in the stochastic setting was provided by Agarwal et al. (2013), who used the ellipsoid method in combination with the pyramid construction of Nemirovsky and Yudin (1983), which is classically used for deterministic zeroth-order optimisation. They established $\tilde{O}(d^{16}\sqrt{n})$ regret while assuming only that the loss is bounded and Lipschitz. Because their algorithm is essentially an elimination method, the idea does not generalise to the adversarial setting, where the minimiser may appear to be in one location for a long time before moving elsewhere.

Meanwhile, back in the adversarial setting Hazan and Levy (2014) assumed strong convexity and smoothness to prove that a version of follow-the-regularised-leader achieves $\tilde{O}(\sqrt{n})$ regret without the assumption that the learner can play outside the constraint set, thus improving the results of Agarwal et al. (2010). The observation is that the increased variance of certain estimators when the learner is playing close to the boundary can be mitigated by additional regularisation at the boundary using a self-concordant barrier (Chapter 6).

One fundamental question remained, which is whether or not $\tilde{O}(\sqrt{n})$ regret was possible in the adversarial setting without strong convexity or smoothness. The first breakthrough in this regard came when Bubeck et al. (2015) proved that $\tilde{O}(\sqrt{n})$ regret *is* possible in the adversarial setting with no assumptions beyond convexity and boundedness, but only when $d = 1$. Strikingly, their analysis was entirely non-constructive, with the argument relying on minimax duality to relate the Bayesian regret to the adversarial regret and on information-theoretic means to bound the Bayesian regret (Russo and Van Roy, 2014).

Bubeck and Eldan (2018) subsequently extended the information-theoretic tools to $d > 1$, showing for the first time that $\text{poly}(d)\sqrt{n}$ regret is possible in the adversarial setting. Later, Lattimore (2020) refined these arguments to prove that the minimax regret for adversarial bandit convex optimisation with no assumptions beyond boundedness and convexity is at most $d^{2.5}\sqrt{n}$. This remains the best result known in the adversarial setting with losses in $\mathscr{F}_b$. One last chapter in the information-theoretic story is a duality between the information-theoretic means and classical approaches based on mirror descent. Lattimore and György (2021b) have shown that any bound obtainable with the information-theoretic machinery of Russo and Van Roy (2014) can also be obtained using mirror descent. Their argument is still non-constructive since the mirror descent algorithm needs to solve an infinite-dimensional convex optimisation problem. Nevertheless, we believe this is a promising area for further exploration (Chapter 8).

The most obvious remaining challenge was to find an efficient algorithm with

$\tilde{O}(\sqrt{n})$ regret for the adversarial setting and losses in $\mathscr{F}_b$. An interesting step in this direction was given by Hazan and Li (2016) who proposed an algorithm with $\tilde{O}(\sqrt{n})$ regret but super-exponential dependence on the dimension. Their algorithm has a running time of $O(\log(n)^{\text{poly}(d)})$.

Finally, Bubeck et al. (2017) constructed an algorithm based on continuous exponential weights for which the regret in the adversarial setting with losses in $\mathscr{F}_b$ is bounded by $\tilde{O}(d^{10.5}\sqrt{n})$. Furthermore, the algorithm can be implemented in polynomial time. Although a theoretical breakthrough, this algorithm has several serious limitations. For one, the dimension-dependence is so large that in practically all normal situations one of the earliest algorithms would have better regret. Furthermore, although the algorithm can be implemented in polynomial time, it relies on approximate log-concave sampling and approximate convex optimisation in every round. Practically speaking the algorithm is nearly impossible to implement. The exception is when $d = 1$ where many aspects of the algorithm simplify (Chapter 8).

The remaining challenge at this point was (and still is) to improve the practicality of the algorithms and reduce the dimension-dependence in the regret. Lattimore and György (2021a) used the ellipsoid method in the stochastic setting in combination with the surrogate loss introduced by Bubeck et al. (2017) to show that $\tilde{O}(d^{4.5}\sqrt{n})$ regret is possible in that setting with a semi-practical algorithm. Recently Lattimore and György (2023) showed that $O(d^{1.5}\sqrt{n})$ regret is possible in the improper stochastic setting when the loss is Lipschitz and $K = \mathbb{B}_1^d$, a result that was extended to the constrained setting without the Lipschitz assumption by Fokkema et al. (2024). This last algorithm is detailed in Chapter 10.

2.3 Classical Stochastic Optimisation Methods

This book has a particular focus on constrained optimisation with finite-time bounds on the regret as a measure of performance. You will surely not be surprised to know that stochastic zeroth-order optimisation (often called stochastic approximation) has a long history. One of the earliest works is by Kiefer and Wolfowitz (1952),[1] who studied the one-dimensional problem and constructed an iterative algorithm based on the Robbins–Monro algorithm for root finding (Robbins and Monro, 1951). The same idea was generalised to the multidimensional setting by Blum (1954).

The stochastic approximation literature is now enormous. A short and readable

---

[1] This paper is just five pages long. You should go and read it right now and come back.

summary of the earlier developments is by Spall (1994) while the modern literature is covered in detail by Prashanth and Bhatnagar (2025). The algorithms developed by this community have a similar flavour to the gradient-based methods used in bandit convex optimisation. Concretely, they propose iterative schemes based on gradient descent or Newton's method with a huge array of methods for estimating the gradient and Hessian using zeroth-order oracles.

The fundamental difference between stochastic approximation and bandit convex optimisation is in the assumptions and analysis. The stochastic optimisation community has largely avoided assuming global convexity but is quite satisfied to make assumptions on smoothness and prove asymptotic convergence bounds, often to a local minimum. Because of this, the results have a different flavour and can be hard to compare. For example, Kiefer and Wolfowitz (1952) prove their scheme converges to the minimiser of f in probability under mild assumptions on the noise and assuming that

(1) f is unimodal and has a global minimiser $x_\star \in \mathbb{R}$;
(2) f is bounded and Lipschitz on an interval containing $x_\star$; and
(3) f is not arbitrarily flat away from the minimiser. Formally, there exists a function $\varrho \colon (0, \infty) \to (0, \infty)$ such that

$$|x - x_\star| \geq \varepsilon \text{ implies } \inf_{\delta \in (0, \varepsilon/2)} \frac{|f(x + \delta) - f(x - \delta)|}{\delta} > \varrho(\varepsilon).$$

Convergence in probability is rather a weak notion and later work has strengthened this considerably, for example by proving asymptotic normality (Spall, 1992).

There are also considerable differences in methods of analysis. The standard method in the stochastic approximation community is to view the iterates of a gradient-based method as an approximation of a differential equation, while in bandit convex optimisation the workhorse is the theory of online convex optimisation (i.e. online learning). At the moment there seems to be a regrettable divide between the bandit convex optimisation literature and the classical stochastic optimisation literature. The two communities focus on different aspects of related problems, with the former intent on finite-time bounds in the convex setting with limited assumptions beyond global convexity. The latter lean more towards asymptotic analysis with more local assumptions. It seems there is some scope for unification, which we do not address at all here.

Dependent Noise Model

In many works on zeroth-order stochastic optimisation there is some unknown convex function $f \colon K \to \mathbb{R}$ to be minimised. The learner has oracle access to some function $F \colon K \times \Omega \to \mathbb{R}$ and a probability measure ρ on a measurable

2.3 Classical Stochastic Optimisation Methods

space $(\Omega, \mathcal{G})$ such that $\int_\Omega F(x, \xi) \, d\rho(\xi) = f(x)$ for all $x \in K$. Equivalently, $f(x) = \mathbb{E}[F(x, \xi)]$ when ξ has law ρ. The learner can sample freely from ρ and query F at any point $x \in K$ and $\xi \in \Omega$. Structural assumptions are then made on F, f or both. For example, Nesterov and Spokoiny (2017) assume that f is convex and $x \mapsto F(x, \xi)$ is Lipschitz ρ-almost surely. The big difference relative to the setting we study is that the learner can query $x \mapsto F(x, \xi)$ at multiple points with the same $\xi \in \Omega$. Our stochastic setting can more or less be modelled in this setting but with the only assumption on F being that for all $x \in K$ the random variable $F(x, \xi)$ has well-behaved moments. Our setting is slightly more generic because we allow the noise to depend on the history as well as the decision. Whether or not you want to make continuity/Lipschitz/smoothness assumptions on F depends on how your problem is modelled. Here are two real-world examples.

○ You are crafting a new fizzy beverage and are deciding the sugar content. A focus group has been arranged and with each person you can give a few samples and obtain their scores. You want to find the amount of sugar that maximises the expected score over the entire population. This problem fits the stochastic optimisation viewpoint because you can trial multiple recipes with each person in your focus group. Connecting this formally to the notation, Ω is the space of potential customers and ρ is some reasonable distribution over customers. K is the space of parameters for the fizzy beverage (the amount of sugar) and $F(x, \xi)$ is the loss suffered by person ξ on the beverage with sugar content x.

○ You operate a postal service using donkeys to transport mail between Sheffield and Hathersage. Donkeys are stoic creatures and do not give away how tired they are. Every day you decide how much to load your donkey. Overload and they might have a nap along the way but obviously you want to transport as much post as possible. The success of a journey is a function of how much mail was delivered  and how long it took. You'll get a telegraph with this information at the end of the day. This problem is best modelled using the bandit framework because the tiredness of the donkey varies from day to day unpredictably and you only get one try per day. Formally in this setting K is the set of possible loads for the donkey and ρ is a distribution on unobservable states.

There is too much material to do justice to this literature here. Some influential papers are by Ghadimi and Lan (2013) and Nemirovski et al. (2009).

2.4 Lower Bounds Summarised

The best lower bound known when the losses are in $\mathscr{F}_b$ is that the minimax regret is at least $\Omega(d\sqrt{n})$. Interestingly, the lower bound was established using linear losses where the upper bound is $\tilde{O}(d\sqrt{n})$. Can it really be that the hardest examples in the enormous non-parametric class of bounded convex functions $\mathscr{F}_b$ lie in the tiny subset of linear functions? Our intuition from the full information setting says it could be like this. Curvature always helps in the full information setting. We discuss in Chapter 10 why, in bandit convex optimisation, curvature both helps and hinders in a complicated way. There also exist lower bounds for more structured classes of convex losses, which are summarised in Table 2.1.

Reading the Table

In the class column we use an (s) superscript to indicate that the lower bound holds in the stochastic setting and (i) to show that it holds in the improper setting explained in Note 1.iii. In the improper setting, Lipschitzness and boundedness only hold inside K while smoothness and strong convexity hold everywhere.

AUTHOR	REGRET	CLASS	K
Dani et al. 2008[1]	$\Omega(d\sqrt{n})$	$\mathscr{F}^s_{b,\mathrm{lin}}$	$\prod_{k=1}^{d/2} \mathbb{S}^1_1$
Shamir 2013	$\Omega(d\sqrt{n})$	$\mathscr{F}^{s,i}_{b,1,\mathrm{sc,sm}}, \alpha = \frac{1}{2}, \beta = \frac{7}{2}$	$\mathbb{B}^d_1$
Shamir 2013	$\Omega(d\sqrt{n})$	$\mathscr{F}^s_{b,1,\mathrm{quad,sc,sm}}, \alpha = \beta = 1$	$\mathbb{B}^d_1$
Akhavan et al. 2024b[2]	$\Omega\left(\frac{d\sqrt{n}}{\max(1,\alpha)}\right)$	$\mathscr{F}^{s,i}_{b,1,\mathrm{sc,sm}}, \beta = O(\alpha)$	$\mathbb{B}^d_1$

(a) Lower bounds on the regret. [1]The product of spheres is not convex. As Shamir (2015) argues, in the linear setting lower bounds for non-convex sets imply lower bounds on $\mathrm{conv}(K)$ via a simple reduction. [2]These authors also prove a more general result for function classes with more smoothness and their results hold for a large class of noise models.

AUTHOR	SIMPLE REGRET	CLASS	K
Shamir 2013	$\Omega(d/\sqrt{n})$	$\mathscr{F}^{s,i}_{b,1,\mathrm{sc,sm}}, \alpha = \frac{1}{2}, \beta = \frac{7}{2}$	$\mathbb{B}^d_1$
Akhavan et al. 2024b[2]	$\Omega\left(\frac{d}{\max(1,\alpha)\sqrt{n}}\right)$	$\mathscr{F}^{s,i}_{b,1,\mathrm{sc,sm}}, \beta = O(\alpha)$	$\mathbb{B}^d_1$

(b) Lower bounds on the simple regret. [2]See the footnote for table above.

Table 2.1 Summary of lower bounds.

Let us make some comments on the lower bounds and how they relate to each other:

○ The unconstrained (Note 1.ii) and constrained settings are both harder than

2.4 Lower Bounds Summarised

the improper setting (Note 1.iii). Hence, lower bounds that hold in the latter also hold in the unconstrained/constrained settings.

○ The reduction in (1.4) shows that lower bounds on the simple regret imply lower bounds on the cumulative regret.

○ Lower bounds that are proven with Gaussian noise can be generalised to lower bounds with bounded noise at the price of at most logarithmic factors, which follows by a scaling and truncation argument (Shamir, 2015).

○ The adversarial setting as defined here is strictly harder than the stochastic setting, which means that all the bounds in Table 2.1 also apply to the adversarial setting. Many authors focus on the adversarial setting without noise and where the losses are assumed to be bounded. The scaling and truncation argument by Shamir (2015) shows that lower bounds proven with Gaussian noise also apply in this case except for logarithmic factors.

○ As far as we know, no one has written a minimax simple regret lower bound for linear losses. At least when $K = [-1, 1]^d$, the technique for bounding the cumulative regret by Lattimore and Szepesvári (2020) also yields a bound on the simple regret of $\Omega(d/\sqrt{n})$.

○ The quadratic case with smoothness and strong convexity ($\alpha, \beta = \Theta(1)$) is quite interesting. The lower bound on the cumulative regret is $\Omega(d\sqrt{n})$, which is matched by upper bounds in the unconstrained and improper settings (Akhavan et al., 2020) and nearly so in the constrained setting (Hazan and Levy, 2014). In the unconstrained and improper settings, however, the upper bound on the simple regret improves to $O(d^2/n)$. This shows that the reduction in (1.4) is not guaranteed to be tight.

○ Many of the algorithms in this book are based on combining gradient descent with noisy gradient estimates of some surrogate loss function. Hu et al. (2016) explore the limitations of this argument. Their idea is to modify the information available to the learner. Rather than observing the loss directly, the learner observes a noisy gradient estimate from an oracle that satisfies certain conditions on its bias and variance. This allows the authors to prove a lower bound in terms of the bias and variance of the oracle that holds for any algorithm. The main application is to argue that any analysis using the spherical smoothing estimates explained in Chapter 5 either cannot achieve $O(\sqrt{n})$ regret or must use some more fine-grained properties of the specific estimator than its bias and variance alone.

2.5 Upper Bounds Summarised

Table 2.2 summarises the past and current situation. Those bounds that depend on n are regret bounds while those that depend on ε are sample complexity bounds. Remember, you can use Fact 1.6 or Proposition 1.7 to convert a regret bound into a sample complexity bound. The superscript (s) in the function classes indicate whether or not the work only considers the stochastic setting, while the superscript (i) is used when the algorithm needs to query outside K (the improper setting of Note 1.iii). In some cases the subscript $d = 1$ in the function class indicates that the algorithm assumes the dimension is one. The quantity ϑ is the parameter associated with a self-concordant barrier on K (see Chapter 6) and D is an abbreviation for the diameter $D = \text{diam}(K)$. The COMPUTE column gives the per-round complexity of each algorithm, which is ∞ in the few cases that the regret bound was established non-constructively. Some algorithms need to position K into Löwner's position or isotropic position, marked in the COMPUTE column by LÖW and ISO, respectively. The COMPUTE column also indicates whether the algorithm uses one of the classical cutting plane methods: ellipsoid method (ELLIPSOID), centre of gravity method (COG) or the method of inscribed ellipsoid (INSCRIBED). The symbol Π refers to the complexity of a euclidean projection onto K, which depends on how K is represented, and SVD refers to the complexity of a singular value decomposition, which is generally $O(d^3)$. Those algorithms that use $O(1)$ computation per round all query the same point for many rounds in a row. In many implementations this could take $O(d)$ computation, since storing/copying the iterate generally has this complexity. We offload this aspect to the oracle computing the loss function. The last column refers to the chapter where we analyse the relevant algorithm, if applicable.

2.5 Upper Bounds Summarised

AUTHOR	REGRET/COMP	CLASS	COMPUTE	CH
Flaxman et al. (2005)	$O(d^{1/2}D^{1/2}n^{3/4})$	$\mathscr{F}_{b,1}$	$O(d), \Pi$	5
Flaxman et al. (2005)	$O(dn^{5/6})$	$\mathscr{F}_b$	$O(d), \Pi, \text{ISO}$	–
This book	$\tilde{O}(d^{1/2}\vartheta^{1/4}n^{3/4})$	$\mathscr{F}_b$	$O(d^2), \text{OPT}, \text{SVD}$	6
Agarwal et al. (2010)[1]	$\tilde{O}(d\sqrt{\beta n/\alpha})$	$\mathscr{F}^i_{b,\text{sm,sc}}$	$O(d), \Pi$	–
This book	$O(d\sqrt{\beta n/\alpha})$	$\mathscr{F}^i_{b,\text{sm,sc}}$	$O(d), \Pi$	5
Saha and Tewari (2011)	$\tilde{O}([\vartheta\beta]^{1/3}[Ddn]^{2/3})$	$\mathscr{F}_{b,\text{sm}}$	$O(d^2), \text{OPT}, \text{SVD}$	6
Bubeck et al. (2012)	$\tilde{O}(d\sqrt{n})$	$\mathscr{F}_{b,\text{lin}}$	$O(\exp(d))$	7
Agarwal et al. (2013)	$\tilde{O}(\sqrt{n})$	$\mathscr{F}^s_{1,d=1}$	$O(1)$	4
Agarwal et al. (2013)	$\tilde{O}(d^{16}\sqrt{n})$	$\mathscr{F}^s_1$	$O(1), \text{ELLIPSOID}$	–
Hazan and Levy (2014)	$\tilde{O}(d\sqrt{(\vartheta+\beta/\alpha)n})$	$\mathscr{F}_{b,\text{sm,sc}}$	$O(d^2), \text{OPT}, \text{SVD}$	6
Belloni et al. (2015)	$\tilde{O}(d^{7.5}/\varepsilon^2)$	$\mathscr{F}^s$	$O(1)$	–
Bubeck et al. (2015)	$\tilde{O}(\sqrt{n})$	$\mathscr{F}_{b,d=1}$	∞	–
Hazan and Li (2016)	$\tilde{O}(2^{(d^4)}\sqrt{n})$	$\mathscr{F}_b$	$O(\log(n)^{\text{poly}(d)})$	–
Bubeck et al. (2017)	$\tilde{O}(d^{10.5}\sqrt{n})$	$\mathscr{F}_b$	$\text{poly}(d,n)$	–
Bubeck et al. (2017)	$\tilde{O}(\sqrt{n})$	$\mathscr{F}_{b,d=1}$	$O(\sqrt{n})$	8
Bubeck et al. (2018)	$\tilde{O}(d^{18}\sqrt{n})$	$\mathscr{F}_b$	∞	–
Akhavan et al. (2020)[2]	$O(d\sqrt{\beta n/\alpha})$	$\mathscr{F}^{s,i}_{1,\text{sm,sc}}$	$O(d)$	–
Lattimore (2020)	$\tilde{O}(d^{2.5}\sqrt{n})$	$\mathscr{F}_b$	∞	–
Ito (2020)[3]	$\tilde{O}(d\sqrt{\beta n/\alpha})$	$\mathscr{F}_{b,\text{sm,sc}}$	$\text{poly}(d)$	–
Ito (2020)	$\tilde{O}(d^{1.5}\sqrt{\beta n/\alpha})$	$\mathscr{F}_{b,\text{sm,sc}}$	$\text{poly}(d)$	–
Suggala et al. (2021)	$\tilde{O}(d^{16}\sqrt{n})$	$\mathscr{F}_{b,\text{quad}}$	$\text{poly}(d)$	–
Lattimore and György (2021a)	$\tilde{O}(d^{4.5}\sqrt{n})$	$\mathscr{F}^s_b$	$O(d^2), \text{ELLIPSOID}$	–
Lattimore and György (2023)	$\tilde{O}(d^{1.5}\sqrt{n})$	$\mathscr{F}^{s,i}_1$	$O(d^2), \text{SVD}$	–
Fokkema et al. (2024)[4]	$\tilde{O}(d^{1.5}\sqrt{n})$	$\mathscr{F}^s_b$	$O(d^2), \Pi, \text{SVD}, \text{LÖW}$	10
Fokkema et al. (2024)	$\tilde{O}(d^2\sqrt{n})$	$\mathscr{F}^s_b$	$O(d^2), \Pi, \text{SVD}, \text{ISO}$	10
Fokkema et al. (2024)	$\tilde{O}(d^{2.5}\sqrt{n})$	$\mathscr{F}_b$	$\text{poly}(d,n), \text{ISO}$	11
Carpentier (2025)	$\tilde{O}(d^4/\varepsilon^2)$	$\mathscr{F}^s_b$	$O(d^2), \text{COG}$	9
This book	$\tilde{O}(d^5/\varepsilon^2)$	$\mathscr{F}^s_b$	$O(d^2), \text{ELLIPSOID}$	9
This book	$\tilde{O}(d^4/\varepsilon^2)$	$\mathscr{F}^s_b$	$O(d^2), \text{INSCRIBED}$	9

[1] The proof of this result is only sketched and both the theorem statement and proof contain minor issues. These are corrected in Section 5.4 where we take the opportunity to incorporate an idea by Akhavan et al. (2020) to remove the logarithmic factor.
[2] These authors also show how to exploit the case where the noise is small as well as higher-order smoothness.
[3] This result holds when the minimiser lies deep inside K.
[4] This also holds if K is symmetric and either in John's position or its polar is isotropic.

Table 2.2 Summary of upper bounds

2.6 Notes

2.i There are some books on zeroth-order optimisation (Larson et al., 2019; Conn et al., 2009, for example). These works focus most of their attention on noise-free settings and without a special focus on convexity. Nemirovsky and Yudin (1983) is a more theoretically focused book with one chapter on zeroth-order methods. Bhatnagar et al. (2012) and Prashanth and Bhatnagar (2025) take the stochastic optimisation viewpoint and focus primarily on gradient-based methods in both convex and non-convex settings. There is also a short survey by Liu et al. (2020).

2.ii Speaking of non-convexity, zeroth-order methods are also analysed in non-convex settings. Sometimes the objective is still to find the global minimum, but for many non-convex problems this cannot be done efficiently. In such cases one often tries to find a point $x \in K$ such that $\|f'(x)\|$ is small or even a local minimum. We only study convex problems here. A recent reference for the non-convex case is the work by Balasubramanian and Ghadimi (2022).

2.iii There are esoteric settings that are quite interesting and may suit some applications. For example, Bach and Perchet (2016) study a problem where the learner chooses two actions in each round. The learner receives information for only the first action but is evaluated based on the quality of the second. They also study higher levels of smoothness than we consider here.

2.iv Online learning has for a long time made considerable effort to prove adaptive bounds that yield stronger results when the loss functions are somehow nice or show that the learner adapts to non-stationary environments. Such results have also been commonplace in the standard bandit literature and are starting to appear in the convex bandit literature as well (Zhao et al., 2021; Luo et al., 2022; Wang, 2023; Liu et al., 2025)

2.v We have not talked much about the efforts focused on sample complexity or simple regret for the stochastic setting. Jamieson et al. (2012) consider functions in $\mathcal{F}_{\text{sm,sc}}$ and $K = \mathbb{R}^d$ and prove a sample complexity bound of $O(\frac{d^3}{\varepsilon^2})$ for an algorithm based on coordinate descent with polynomial dependence on the smoothness and strong convexity parameters hidden. Belloni et al. (2015) use an algorithm based on simulated annealing to prove a sample complexity bound of $O(\frac{d^{7.5}}{\varepsilon^2})$ for losses in $\mathcal{F}_b$. In its current form their algorithm is not suitable for regret minimisation though this minor deficiency may be correctable. Another thing to mention about that work is that the algorithm is robust in the sense that it can (approximately) find minima of functions that are only approximately convex. Slightly earlier, Liang et al. (2014) also used a method based on random walks but obtained a worse rate of $O(\frac{d^{14}}{\varepsilon^2})$.

3
Mathematical Tools (🦘)

The purpose of this chapter is to introduce the necessary tools from optimisation, convex geometry and convex analysis. You can safely skip this chapter, referring back as needed. The main concepts introduced are as follows:

- Convex bodies, the Minkowski and support functions and basic theory of polarity.
- Basic properties associated with smoothness and strong convexity.
- The near-Lipschitzness of convex functions and the implications of this for the location of near-minimisers of convex functions.
- Rounding procedures for convex bodies, including the classical John's and isotropic positions of convex bodies.
- Smoothing operators and mechanisms for extending the domain of a convex function $f \colon K \to \mathbb{R}$ to all of $\mathbb{R}^d$.
- Methods for computing various operations on convex bodies, such as projection and optimisation.

3.1 Convex Bodies

A convex set $K \subset \mathbb{R}^d$ is a convex body if it is compact and has a nonempty interior. The latter corresponds to the existence of an $x \in \mathbb{R}^d$ and $\varepsilon > 0$ such that $x + \mathbb{B}^d_\varepsilon \subset K$. The Minkowski functional of K is the function $\pi \colon \mathbb{R}^d \to \mathbb{R}$ defined by

$$\pi(x) = \inf \{t > 0 \colon x \in tK\}.$$

A top-down illustration is provided in Figure 3.1a. Another way to visualise the Minkowski functional is via the suspension cone, which is the set

$$S(K) = \{(x, y) \colon x \in \mathbb{R}^d, y \in \mathbb{R}, \pi(x) \le y, y \ge 0\}.$$

3.1 Convex Bodies

The set $S(K)$ is a cone with tip $(0,0)$ and $\{x\colon (x,1) \in S\} = K$. In most of our applications $\mathbf{0} \in \text{int}(K)$ and K is a convex body (hence closed). In this case $1_K(x) = 1(\pi(x) \leq 1)$. Moreover, when K is a symmetric convex body, then π is a norm and K is its unit ball. The support function is

$$h(u) = \sup_{x \in K} \langle u, x \rangle .$$

The support function is defined so that for any $\mathbb{R}^d \ni u \neq \mathbf{0}$, the hyperplane $\{x\colon \langle u, x \rangle = h(u)\}$ is a supporting hyperplane of K (Figure 3.1b). Of course the Minkowski functional and support function both depend on K as well as x. When necessary we explicitly write π_K or h_K but in general the set will be K and is omitted from the notation.

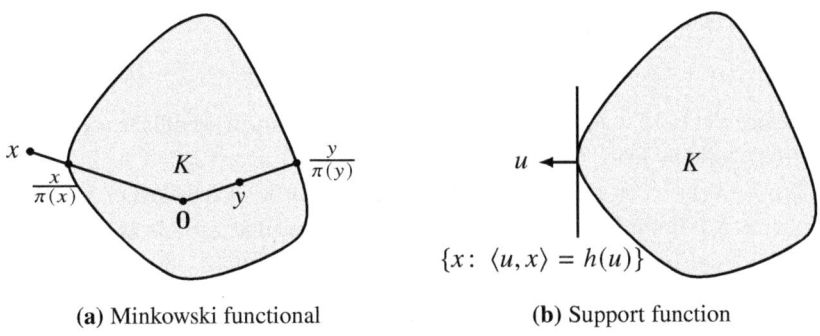

(a) Minkowski functional   (b) Support function

Figure 3.1 The Minkowski and support functions.

The polar is $K^\circ = \{u \in \mathbb{R}^d \colon h(u) \leq 1\}$. The polar is not easy to visualise and for our purposes an in-depth understanding of this concept is rarely needed. Readers looking for more intuition and theory should read the classic text by Rockafellar (1970, §14).

Proposition 3.1 *The following hold:*
(1) *Given convex bodies $K \subset J$, polarity reverses inclusion: $J^\circ \subset K^\circ$.*
(2) *Given a convex body K with $\mathbf{0} \in \text{int}(K)$, the polar K° is a convex body with $\mathbf{0} \in \text{int}(K^\circ)$.*
(3) *The polar body of a nonempty ball $K = \mathbb{B}_r^d$ is $K^\circ = \mathbb{B}_{1/r}^d$.*
(4) *For a symmetric convex body K, $\|\cdot\|_K \triangleq \pi_K(\cdot)$ is a norm.*
(5) *For a symmetric convex body K, the dual of $\|\cdot\|_K$ is $\|\cdot\|_{K^\circ}$:*

$$\|u\|_{K^\circ} = \max\{\langle u, x \rangle \colon \|x\|_K \leq 1, x \in \mathbb{R}^d\} .$$

Exercise 3.2 ★ Prove Proposition 3.1.

The Minkowski functional has many properties:

Lemma 3.3 *Let K be a convex body with $\mathbf{0} \in \text{int}(K)$ and π the associated Minkowski functional. The following hold:*
(1) $\pi(\alpha x) = \alpha \pi(x)$ *for all* $\alpha > 0$.
(2) π *is convex.*
(3) $\pi(x + y) \leq \pi(x) + \pi(y)$ *for all* $x, y \in \mathbb{R}^d$.
(4) $x/\pi(x) \in \partial K$ *whenever* $\pi(x) > 0$.
(5) π *is the support function of the polar body:* $\pi(x) = \sup_{u \in K^\circ} \langle x, u \rangle$.
(6) $D\pi(x)[h] = \langle u, h \rangle$ *for some* $u \in K^\circ$.
(7) $\text{lip}(\pi) \leq 1/r$ *whenever* $\mathbb{B}_r^d \subset K$.

Proof Part (1) is immediate from the definitions. For part (2), by definition, $x \in \pi(x)K$ and $y \in \pi(y)K$. Hence, for any $\lambda \in [0, 1]$,

$$(1 - \lambda)x + \lambda y \in (1 - \lambda)\pi(x)K + \lambda\pi(y)K = ((1 - \lambda)\pi(x) + \lambda\pi(y))K.$$

Therefore $\pi((1-\lambda)x + \lambda y) \leq (1-\lambda)\pi(x) + \lambda\pi(y)$, which establishes convexity. Part (3) follows from (1) and (2) since $\pi(x + y) = \pi((2x)/2 + (2y)/2) \leq \pi(2x)/2 + \pi(2y)/2 = \pi(x) + \pi(y)$. For part (4), let x be such that $\pi(x) > 0$. That $x/\pi(x) \in K$ is immediate from the definition. Suppose that $y = x/\pi(x) \in \text{int}(K)$; then there exists an $\epsilon > 0$ such that $y + \mathbb{B}_\epsilon^d \subset K$. A simple calculation shows there exists a $\delta \in (0, \pi(x))$ such that $x/(\pi(x) - \delta) \in K$, which contradicts the definition of $\pi(x)$. Part (5) is given by Rockafellar (1970, Theorem 14.5) and part (6) follows from part (5) and Rockafellar (1970, Corollary 23.5.3). Part (7) follows because the Minkowski functional is the support function of the polar body K° and polarity reverses inclusion, $K^\circ \subset \mathbb{B}_{1/r}^d$. Finally, the subgradients of the support function are in K° and the result follows (Rockafellar, 1970, Corollary 23.5.3). □

Convex functions $f: K \to [0, 1]$ are often not well behaved near the boundary (see Section 3.4). For this reason we often shrink K towards the origin. Given $\varepsilon > 0$, let

$$K_\varepsilon = \{(1 - \varepsilon)x : x \in K\} = \{x \in K : \pi(x) \leq 1 - \varepsilon\}.$$

Lemma 3.4 *Suppose that $\mathbb{B}_r^d \subset K$ and $x \in K_\varepsilon$. Then $x + \mathbb{B}_{r\varepsilon}^d \subset K$.*

Proof Let $x \in K_\varepsilon$. By the definition of the Minkowski functional there exists a $y \in K$ such that $x = (1 - \varepsilon)y$. Since K is convex and $\mathbb{B}_r^d \subset K$, it follows that

$$K \supset \varepsilon \mathbb{B}_r^d + (1 - \varepsilon)y = x + \mathbb{B}_{\varepsilon r}^d.$$

□

3.2 Smoothness and Strong Convexity

For your own understanding, you should solve the following:

Exercise 3.5 ★ Suppose that $f \in \mathcal{F}_{\text{sm,sc}}$ and f is twice differentiable. Show that

$$\alpha \mathbb{1} \preceq f''(x) \preceq \beta \mathbb{1} \text{ for all } x \in \text{int}(K).$$

Besides this, the only properties of smoothness and strong convexity that we need are as follows:

Lemma 3.6 *If $f \in \mathcal{F}$ is α-strongly convex, then for all $y \in \text{int}(\text{dom}(f))$,*

$$f(x) \geq f(y) + Df(y)[x-y] + \frac{\alpha}{2} \|x-y\|^2.$$

Proof Let $g(x) = f(x) - \frac{\alpha}{2} \|x\|^2$, which by assumption is convex. By convexity,

$$f(x) - \frac{\alpha}{2} \|x\|^2 = g(x)$$
$$\geq g(y) + Dg(y)[x-y]$$
$$= f(y) - \frac{\alpha}{2} \|y\|^2 + Df(y)[x-y] - \alpha \langle y, x-y \rangle.$$

Rearranging shows that

$$f(x) \geq f(y) + Df(y)[x-y] + \frac{\alpha}{2} \|x\|^2 - \frac{\alpha}{2} \|y\|^2 - \alpha \langle y, x-y \rangle$$
$$= f(y) + Df(y)[x-y] + \frac{\alpha}{2} \|x-y\|^2. \qquad \square$$

Lemma 3.7 *If $f \in \mathcal{F}$ is β-smooth and X is a random variable supported in K and $x = \mathbb{E}[X]$. Then,*

$$\mathbb{E}[f(X) - f(x)] \leq \frac{\beta}{2} \mathbb{E}\left[\|X-x\|^2\right].$$

Proof Let $g(x) = f(x) - \frac{\beta}{2} \|x\|^2$, which by assumption is concave. Then,

$$\mathbb{E}[f(X) - f(x)] = \mathbb{E}[g(X) - g(x)] + \frac{\beta}{2} \mathbb{E}\left[\|X\|^2 - \|x\|^2\right]$$
$$\leq \frac{\beta}{2} \mathbb{E}\left[\|X\|^2 - \|x\|^2\right] \qquad \text{since } g \text{ is concave}$$
$$= \frac{\beta}{2} \mathbb{E}\left[\|X-x\|^2\right] \qquad \text{since } \mathbb{E}[X] = x.$$

$\square$

3.3 Scaling Properties

A class of problems is defined by the constraint set K and the function class in which the losses lie (see Definition 1.1) as well as constraints on the adversary (stochastic/non-stochastic) or the noise. Regardless, we hope you agree that simply changing the scale of the coordinates should not affect the achievable regret. The following proposition describes how the various constants change when the coordinates are scaled.

Proposition 3.8 *Let $f: K \to [0, 1]$ be convex and twice differentiable. Define $g(y) = f(x/\gamma)$ and $J = \{\gamma x: x \in K\}$. The following hold:*
(1) $g: J \to [0, 1]$ is convex and twice differentiable.
(2) $g'(y) = f'(x/\gamma)/\gamma$.
(3) $g''(y) = f''(x/\gamma)/\gamma^2$.
(4) $\mathrm{diam}(J) = \gamma \, \mathrm{diam}(K)$.

From this we see that the product of the Lipschitz constant and the diameter is invariant under scaling, as is the ratio of strong convexity and smoothness parameters. You should always check that various results are compatible with these scaling results in the sense that the regret bound should be invariant to scale if the assumptions permit scaling.

3.4 Convex Functions are Nearly Lipschitz

Let $f: K \to [0, 1]$ be a convex function. The example $K = [0, 1]$ and $f(x) = 1 - \sqrt{x}$ shows that such functions are not always Lipschitz. What is true is that f must be Lipschitz on the interior of K in some sense. You should start by solving the following exercise:

Exercise 3.9 ★ Suppose that $f: \mathbb{R}^d \to \mathbb{R} \cup \{\infty\}$ is convex. Show the following:
(1) Suppose that $A \subset \mathrm{int}(\mathrm{dom}(f))$. Then
$$\mathrm{lip}_A(f) \leq \sup_{x \in A} \sup_{\eta \in \mathbb{S}_1^{d-1}} Df(x)[\eta].$$

(2) Suppose that A is a bounded subset of $\mathbb{R}^d$ and $\mathrm{dom}(f) = \mathbb{R}^d$. Then
$$\mathrm{lip}(f) \leq \sup_{x \notin A} \sup_{\eta \in \mathbb{S}_1^{d-1}} Df(x)[\eta].$$

Proposition 3.10 *Suppose that $f \in \mathcal{F}_b$ and $r > 0$ and $x + \mathbb{B}_r^d \subset K$. Then*

$$\max_{\eta \in \mathbb{S}_1^{d-1}} Df(x)[\eta] \leq \frac{1}{r}.$$

Proof The assumption that f is convex and bounded in $[0, 1]$ on K shows that for any $\eta \in \mathbb{S}_1^{d-1}$,

$$1 \geq f(x + r\eta) \geq f(x) + Df(x)[r\eta] \geq Df(x)[r\eta] = rDf(x)[\eta].$$

Therefore $Df(x)[\eta] \leq \frac{1}{r}$. □

Combining Proposition 3.10 and the solution to Exercise 3.9 yields the following:

Corollary 3.11 *Let $f \in \mathcal{F}_b$ be convex and suppose that A is convex and $A + \mathbb{B}_r^d \subset K$. Then $\text{lip}_A(f) \leq \frac{1}{r}$.*

Corollary 3.12 *Suppose that $f: K \to [0, 1]$ is convex and $\mathbb{B}_r^d \subset K$ and $K_\varepsilon = (1 - \varepsilon)K$. Then $\text{lip}_{K_\varepsilon}(f) \leq \frac{1}{\varepsilon r}$.*

3.5 Near-Optimality on the Interior

The observation that convex functions are Lipschitz on a suitable subset of the interior of K suggests that if we want to restrict our attention to Lipschitz functions, then we might pretend that the domain of f is not K but rather a subset. This idea is only fruitful because bounded convex functions are always nearly minimised somewhere in the interior, in the following sense. Recall the definition of K_ε from Section 3.1.

Proposition 3.13 *Let K be a convex body with $\mathbf{0} \in \text{int}(K)$ and $\varepsilon \in (0, 1)$ and $f \in \mathcal{F}_b$. Then*

$$\min_{y \in K_\varepsilon} f(y) \leq \inf_{y \in K} f(y) + \varepsilon.$$

Proof K_ε is a closed subset of $\text{int}(K)$, hence compact. Convex functions are continuous on the interior of their domain, which means that f is continuous on $K_\varepsilon \subset \text{int}(K)$ and hence has a minimiser. Let $y \in K$. Then $z = (1 - \varepsilon)y \in K_\varepsilon$ and by convexity, $f(z) \leq (1 - \varepsilon)f(y) + \varepsilon f(0) \leq f(y) + \varepsilon$. Taking the infimum over all $y \in K$ completes the proof. □

3.6 Classical Positions and Rounding

We make frequent use of certain classical positions of convex bodies.

- A convex body K is in John's position if $\mathbb{B}_1^d$ is the ellipsoid of largest volume contained in K.
- A convex body K is in Löwner's position if $\mathbb{B}_1^d$ is the ellipsoid of smallest volume that contains K.
- A convex body K is in isotropic position if $\frac{1}{\text{vol}(K)} \int_K xx^\top \, dx = \mathbb{1}$ and $\int_K x \, dx = \mathbf{0}$.

The unifying characteristic of these positions is that for every convex body K there exists an affine map $T \colon \mathbb{R}^d \to \mathbb{R}^d$ such that the image $T(K)$ is in the relevant position:

Theorem 3.14 *Given $X \in \{\textit{John's}, \textit{Löwner's}, \textit{isotropic}\}$ and convex body K, there exists an affine transformation $T \colon \mathbb{R}^d \to \mathbb{R}^d$ such that $T(K)$ is in X position.*

Some of our analysis depends on the constraint set K being well rounded. By this we mean that

$$\mathbb{B}_r^d \subset K \subset \mathbb{B}_R^d,$$

where R/r is not too large. The following shows that convex bodies in John's position are well rounded:

Theorem 3.15 *Suppose that K is in John's position. Then*

$$\mathbb{B}_1^d \subset K \subset \mathbb{B}_d^d.$$

Theorem 3.15 is an immediate consequence of John's theorem (Artstein-Avidan et al., 2015, Remark 2.1.17). Combining Theorem 3.15 with Theorem 3.14 shows that for any convex body K there exists an affine map T such that

$$\mathbb{B}_1^d \subset T(K) \subset \mathbb{B}_d^d. \tag{3.1}$$

This is less constructive than we would like because even when K is represented by a separation oracle, there is no known procedure for efficiently computing John's position. In a moment we discuss how to algorithmically find an affine mapping T such that (3.1) holds approximately. First though, we explain how such a mapping can be used. Any affine T for which (3.1) holds must be invertible. A learning algorithm designed for rounded constraint sets can be used on arbitrary constraint sets by first finding a T such that (3.1) approximately

3.6 Classical Positions and Rounding

holds. The learner is then instantiated with $T(K)$ as a constraint set and proposes actions $(X'_t)_{t=1}^n$ with $X'_t \in T(K)$. The response is $Y_t = f_t(T^{-1}(X'_t)) + \varepsilon_t$. Letting $g_t = f_t \circ T^{-1}$, we have

$$\begin{aligned}
\text{Reg}_n &= \sup_{x \in K} \sum_{t=1}^n (f_t(X_t) - f_t(x)) \\
&= \sup_{x' \in T(K)} \sum_{t=1}^n (f_t(T^{-1}(X'_t)) - f_t(T^{-1}(x'))) \\
&= \sup_{x' \in T(K)} \sum_{t=1}^n (g_t(X'_t) - g_t(x')).
\end{aligned}$$

The Lipschitz and smoothness properties of g_t may be different from f_t, but if f_t is bounded on K, then g_t is similarly bounded on $T(K)$. Therefore when assuming losses are in $\mathscr{F}_b$ and you are indifferent to computation cost you can assume that $\mathbb{B}_1^d \subset K \subset \mathbb{B}_d^d$. Next we discuss what is possible using a computationally efficient algorithm.

Rounding Algorithms

In order to implement the translation we need a procedure for finding T. Let ν_K be the uniform probability measure on K and $\mu = \int_K x \, d\nu_K(x)$ be the centre of mass and $\Sigma = \int_K (x - \mu)(x - \mu)^\top d\nu_K(x)$ the moment of inertia of K. Let $\text{iso}_K(x) = \Sigma^{-1/2}(x - \mu)$ and $J = \text{iso}_K(K)$. A simple calculation shows that $\int_J x \, d\nu_J(x) = 0$ and $\int_J xx^\top d\nu_J(x) = \mathbb{1}$. That is, J is in isotropic position.

Theorem 3.16 (Theorem 4.1, Kannan et al. 1995) *Suppose that J is in isotropic position. Then*

$$\mathbb{B}_1^d \subset J \subset \mathbb{B}_{1+d}^d.$$

Remark 3.17 Be careful. Our definition of isotropic position is standard in probability theory while in geometric analysis it is normal to say that K is in isotropic position if $\int_K x \, dx = 0$, $\text{vol}(K) = 1$ and $\int_K xx^\top dx = L_K \mathbb{1}$ for some L_K. The recent resolution to the 'slicing conjecture' shows that L_K is upper- and lower-bound by universal constant, which means that up to constant scaling factors the two definitions of isotropic position are the same (Klartag and Lehec, 2024).

Provided that K is suitably represented, then there exist algorithms that find an affine map T in polynomial time such that $J = T(K)$ is close enough to isotropic position that $\mathbb{B}_1^d \subset K \subset \mathbb{B}_{2d}^d$. The procedure is based on estimating the centre of mass and moment of inertia of K using uniform samples and estimating the corresponding affine map T defined above (Lovász and Vempala, 2006).

3.7 Extension

Some of the algorithms presented in this book are only defined for unconstrained problems where $K = \mathbb{R}^d$. Furthermore, techniques designed for handling constraints such as self-concordant barriers introduce complexity and dimension-dependent constants into the analysis. One way to mitigate these problems is to use an algorithm designed for unconstrained bandit convex optimisation on an extension of the loss function(s). An extension of a convex function $f \colon \mathbb{R}^d \to \mathbb{R} \cup \{\infty\}$ with $K \subset \mathrm{dom}(f)$ is another convex function $e \colon \mathbb{R}^d \to \mathbb{R}$ such that

$$e(x) = f(x) \text{ for all } x \in K.$$

Sometimes no such extension exists. For example, the function defined by

$$f(x) = \begin{cases} 1 - \sqrt{x} & \text{if } x \geq 0 \\ \infty & \text{if } x < 0 \end{cases}$$

cannot be extended from $K = \mathrm{dom}(f)$ to a convex function with domain $\mathbb{R}$. When f is Lipschitz on its domain then an extension to $\mathbb{R}^d$ is always possible.

Proposition 3.18 *Suppose that $f \colon \mathbb{R}^d \to \mathbb{R} \cup \{\infty\}$ is convex and $\mathrm{lip}(f) < \infty$. Then there exists a convex function $e \colon \mathbb{R}^d \to \mathbb{R}$ such that*
(1) $e(x) = f(x)$ *for all* $x \in \mathrm{dom}(f)$; *and*
(2) $\mathrm{lip}(e) = \mathrm{lip}(f)$.

Proof (✦) To keep things simple, let us assume that $\mathrm{dom}(f)$ has nonempty interior (but see Exercise 3.19). The idea is to define e as the supremum of all tangent hyperplanes to f in $\mathrm{int}(\mathrm{dom}(f))$. Define

$$e(x) = \sup_{y \in \mathrm{int}(\mathrm{dom}(f))} (f(y) + Df(y)[x - y]).$$

Note that no convex extension can take a smaller value than this by convexity, so this e is the minimal extension. We leave it as an exercise to establish the claimed properties of e. □

Exercise 3.19 (✦) ★▰ Prove Proposition 3.18. We suggest you start by assuming $\mathrm{dom}(f)$ has nonempty interior. In case $\mathrm{dom}(f)$ has no interior you should first extend f to the affine hull of the relative interior and then extend the extension to the whole space. You may find it useful to use the fact that for $y \in \mathrm{int}(\mathrm{dom}(f))$, $Df(y)[h] = \sup_{g \in \partial f(y)} \langle g, h \rangle$.

The extension in Proposition 3.18 has the limitation that it cannot be evaluated in an unbiased way with stochastic oracle access to f. The reason is that to even

3.7 Extension

approximate e at some point $x \notin \text{dom}(f)$ you need to solve an optimisation problem that may require you to evaluate f at many points in $\text{dom}(f)$. The next proposition shows there exists an extension that can be evaluated at $x \notin \text{dom}(f)$ using only a single evaluation of f.

Proposition 3.20 *Suppose that $r > 0$ and $f : \mathbb{R}^d \to \mathbb{R} \cup \{\infty\}$ is a convex function such that $\mathbb{B}_r^d \subset K \subset \text{int}(\text{dom}(f))$, $f(K) \subset [0, 1]$ and $\text{lip}(f) < \infty$. Let $m \in \mathbb{R}_+$ be such that $Df(y)[y] - f(y) \leq m$ for all $y \in K$. Let π be the Minkowski functional of K and*

$$e(x) = \max(1, \pi(x)) f\left(\frac{x}{\max(1, \pi(x))}\right) + m(\max(1, \pi(x)) - 1).$$

The function e satisfies the following:

(1) $e(x) = f(x)$ for all $x \in K$.
(2) e is convex.
(3) $\text{lip}(e) \leq \frac{m}{r} + \frac{1}{r} + \text{lip}(f)$.
(4) For all $x \notin K$, $e(x/\pi(x)) \leq e(x)$.

Remark 3.21 The condition that $K \subset \text{int}(\text{dom}(f))$ ensures that $Df(y)[y]$ is real-valued for all $y \in K$. You could replace this condition with $\text{dom}(f) = K$ and define $Df(y)[y]$ for $y \in \partial K$ via the extension in Proposition 3.18. Note, it can happen in this case that $Df(y)[y] \neq -Df(y)[-y]$.

Compared to the extension in Proposition 3.18, the extension above has the drawback that $\text{lip}(e)$ can be much larger than $\text{lip}(f)$. More positively, however, the extension above can be evaluated at x by computing $\pi(x)$ and evaluating f at $x/\max(1, \pi(x))$, which means the extension can be evaluated at x using a single query to f.

Remark 3.22 Let $x \in \partial K$. By Lemma 3.3(1), the Minkowski functional is homogeneous, which means that for $t \geq 1$ $e(tx) = tf(x) + m(t - 1)$ is a linear function. So e is defined outside of K by glueing together rays emanating from points $x \in \partial K$. The most challenging part of the proof of Proposition 3.20 is establishing convexity.

Proof of Proposition 3.20 Abbreviate $\pi_\wedge(x) = \max(1, \pi(x))$. Recall that for $x \in \text{int}(\text{dom}(f))$, $h \mapsto Df(x)[h]$ is convex and positively homogeneous, and hence subadditive. Part (1) follows immediately from the fact that for $x \in K$, $\pi(x) \leq 1$ and therefore $\pi_\wedge(x) = 1$. Moving to part (2), define $g(z, \lambda) = \lambda f(z/\lambda)$, which is called the perspective of f and according to Boyd and Vandenberghe

(2004, §2.3.3) is jointly convex on $\mathbb{R}^d \times (0, \infty)$. Let $z \in \mathbb{R}^d$ and $\lambda \geq \pi_\wedge(z)$. Then

$$g(z, \lambda) \stackrel{(a)}{\geq} g(z, \pi_\wedge(z)) + \frac{dg(z, \theta)}{d\theta}\bigg|_{\theta=\pi_\wedge(z)} (\lambda - \pi_\wedge(z))$$

$$\stackrel{(b)}{=} g(z, \pi_\wedge(z)) + \left(f\left(\frac{z}{\pi_\wedge(z)}\right) + Df\left(\frac{z}{\pi_\wedge(z)}\right)\left[\frac{-z}{\pi_\wedge(z)}\right] \right) (\lambda - \pi_\wedge(z))$$

$$\stackrel{(c)}{\geq} g(z, \pi_\wedge(z)) - m(\lambda - \pi_\wedge(z)), \qquad (3.2)$$

where in (a) the derivative is the right-derivative and the inequality follows from convexity of g, (b) follows by the chain rule and the definition of g and (c) by the assumptions on m in the proposition statement so that with $w = z/\pi_\wedge(z) \in K$ by subadditivity of $Df(w)[\cdot]$, $f(w) + Df(w)[-w] \geq f(w) - Df(w)[w] \geq -m$. Let $x, y \in \mathbb{R}^d$ and $p \in (0, 1)$ and $z = px + (1-p)y$. By definition,

$$e(z) = \pi_\wedge(z) f\left(\frac{z}{\pi_\wedge(z)}\right) + m(\pi_\wedge(z) - 1)$$

$$= g(z, \pi_\wedge(z)) + m(\pi_\wedge(z) - 1)$$

$$\stackrel{(a)}{\leq} g(z, p\pi_\wedge(x) + (1-p)\pi_\wedge(y)) + m[p\pi_\wedge(x) + (1-p)\pi_\wedge(y) - 1]$$

$$\stackrel{(b)}{\leq} pg(x, \pi_\wedge(x)) + (1-p)g(y, \pi_\wedge(y)) + m[p\pi_\wedge(x) + (1-p)\pi_\wedge(y) - 1]$$

$$= pe(x) + (1-p)e(y),$$

where (a) follows from (3.2) with $\lambda = p\pi_\wedge(x) + (1-p)\pi_\wedge(y) \geq \pi_\wedge(z)$ by convexity of $\pi_\wedge$, and (b) follows from joint convexity of g and because $z = px + (1-p)y$. Therefore e is convex. Next we prove part (3). Let $h \in \mathbb{S}_1^{d-1}$ and $x \notin K$, which means that $\pi_\wedge(x) = \pi(x) > 1$. By Lemma 3.3(6), $D\pi(x)[h] = \langle \theta, h \rangle$ for some $\theta \in K^\circ$. Because polarity reverses inclusion (Proposition 3.1) and $\mathbb{B}_r^d \subset K$, $K^\circ \subset \mathbb{B}_{1/r}^d$ and therefore $\|\theta\| \leq 1/r$. Letting $w = x/\pi(x) \in K$,

$$De(x)[h] = \langle \theta, h \rangle (m + f(w)) + Df(w)[h - \langle \theta, h \rangle w]$$

$$\leq \langle \theta, h \rangle (m + f(w)) + Df(w)[-\langle \theta, h \rangle w] + \mathrm{lip}(f), \qquad (3.3)$$

where the inequality follows because $Df(w)[\cdot]$ is subadditive and $Df(w)[h] \leq \mathrm{lip}(f)$ since $w \in \mathrm{int}(\mathrm{dom}(f))$. When $\langle \theta, h \rangle \geq 0$; then by convexity

$$\langle \theta, h \rangle (m + f(w)) + Df(w)[-\langle \theta, h \rangle w] = \langle \theta, h \rangle (m + f(w) + Df(w)[-w])$$

$$\leq \langle \theta, h \rangle (m + f(\mathbf{0})) \leq \frac{m+1}{r}.$$

Alternatively, if $\langle \theta, h \rangle < 0$, then by the assumption that $Df(w)[w] - f(w) \leq m$,

$$\langle \theta, h \rangle (m + f(w)) + Df(w)[-\langle \theta, h \rangle w] = \langle \theta, h \rangle (m + f(w) - Df(w)[w])$$

$$\leq 0.$$

Combining the previous two displays with (3.3) shows that $De(x)[h] \leq (m + 1)/r + \text{lip}(f)$ for all $h \in \mathbb{S}_1^{d-1}$ and $x \notin K$. The claim now follows from Exercise 3.9 and the fact that K is bounded. For part (4), since $x \notin K$ we have

$$e(x) = \pi(x)f\left(\frac{x}{\pi(x)}\right) + m(\pi(x) - 1) \geq f\left(\frac{x}{\pi(x)}\right) = e\left(\frac{x}{\pi(x)}\right),$$

where we used the fact that $x/\pi(x) \in K$ so that $e(x/\pi(x)) = f(x/\pi(x))$. □

The next proposition uses the results from Section 3.4 to refine the Lipschitz constant of the extension in Proposition 3.20 when f is extended from a suitable subset of its domain.

Proposition 3.23 *Suppose that $f \in \mathcal{F}_\flat$ and $\mathbb{B}_r^d \subset K$. Let π be the Minkowski functional of K and $\varepsilon \in (0, 1)$, and let $\pi_\wedge(x) = \max(1, \pi(x)/(1 - \varepsilon))$ and*

$$e(x) = \pi_\wedge(x)f\left(\frac{x}{\pi_\wedge(x)}\right) + \frac{1-\varepsilon}{\varepsilon}(\pi_\wedge(x) - 1).$$

Then, the following hold:
(1) $e(x) = f(x)$ for all $x \in K_\varepsilon = \{x \in K : \pi(x) \leq 1 - \varepsilon\}$.
(2) e is convex.
(3) $\text{lip}(e) \leq \frac{2}{\varepsilon(1-\varepsilon)r}$.
(4) For all $x \notin K_\varepsilon$, $e(x/\pi_\wedge(x)) \leq e(x)$.

Proof Let $y \in K_\varepsilon$ and $z = y/(1 - \varepsilon) \in K$, which means that $z - y = \frac{\varepsilon}{1-\varepsilon}y$. Combining this with the fact that $f \in \mathcal{F}_\flat$ yields

$$\begin{aligned}
1 &\geq f(z) & f \in \mathcal{F}_\flat \\
&\geq f(y) + Df(y)[z - y] & f \text{ convex} \\
&= f(y) + \frac{\varepsilon}{1-\varepsilon}Df(y)[y] & \text{def. of } z \\
&\geq \frac{\varepsilon}{1-\varepsilon}(Df(y)[y] - f(y)). & f \in \mathcal{F}_\flat
\end{aligned}$$

Rearranging shows that for all $y \in K_\varepsilon$, $Df(y)[y] - f(y) \leq \frac{1-\varepsilon}{\varepsilon} \triangleq m$. The claim now follows by applying Proposition 3.20 to K_ε, which by definition has $\mathbb{B}_{(1-\varepsilon)r} \subset K_\varepsilon$. Hence, by Corollary 3.12, $\text{lip}_{K_\varepsilon}(f) \leq \frac{1}{\varepsilon r}$, which by Proposition 3.20 means the Lipschitz constant $\text{lip}(e)$ is bounded by

$$\begin{aligned}
\text{lip}(e) &\leq \frac{m+1}{(1-\varepsilon)r} + \text{lip}_{K_\varepsilon}(f) \\
&\leq \frac{\frac{1-\varepsilon}{\varepsilon} + 1}{(1-\varepsilon)r} + \frac{1}{r\varepsilon} \\
&\leq \frac{2}{\varepsilon(1-\varepsilon)r}.
\end{aligned}$$

□

3.8 Smoothing

Let $\phi: \mathbb{R}^d \to \mathbb{R}$ be the twice-differentiable function given by

$$\phi(x) = \frac{1}{C}\left(1 - \|x\|^2\right)^3 \mathbf{1}_{\mathbb{B}_1^d}(x) \quad \text{with}$$

$$C = \int_{\mathbb{B}_1^d}\left(1 - \|x\|^2\right)^3 dx.$$

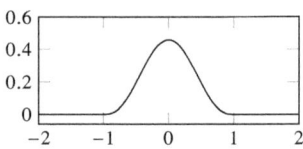

Figure 3.2 ϕ in dimension one.

Note that ϕ is the density of a probability measure on $\mathbb{R}^d$ that is supported on $\mathbb{B}_1^d$ (see Figure 3.2). Given $\varepsilon > 0$, let

$$\phi_\varepsilon(x) = \varepsilon^{-d}\phi(x/\varepsilon),$$

which by a change of measure is also a probability density, this time supported on $\mathbb{B}_\varepsilon^d$.

Proposition 3.24 *Suppose that $f: \mathbb{R}^d \to \mathbb{R} \cup \{\infty\}$ is convex and $\mathrm{lip}(f) < \infty$ and let $g = f * \phi_\varepsilon$ with $*$ the convolution, which is defined on $\mathrm{dom}(g) = \{x \in \mathbb{R}^d : x + \mathbb{B}_\varepsilon^d \subset \mathrm{cl}(\mathrm{dom}(f))\}$. Then the following hold:*

(1) *g is twice differentiable on $\mathrm{int}(\mathrm{dom}(g))$.*

(2) *$\mathrm{lip}(g) \leq \mathrm{lip}(f)$.*

(3) *g is smooth: $\|g''(x)\| \leq \frac{(d+1)(d+6)\,\mathrm{lip}(f)}{\varepsilon}$ for all $x \in \mathrm{int}(\mathrm{dom}(g))$.*

(4) *$\max_{x \in \mathrm{dom}(g)} |f(x) - g(x)| \leq \varepsilon\,\mathrm{lip}(f)$.*

Proof Part (1) follows by writing out the definition, making a change of variables and exchanging limits and integrals. This is a good technical exercise. Part (2) is also left as an (easy) exercise. For part (3), the constant C can be calculated by integrating in polar coordinates:

$$\begin{aligned}
C &= \int_{\mathbb{B}_1^d}\left(1 - \|x\|^2\right)^3 dx \\
&= d\,\mathrm{vol}(\mathbb{B}_1^d)\int_0^1 r^{d-1}\left(1 - r^2\right)^3 dr \qquad \text{Proposition A.2} \\
&= \frac{48\,\mathrm{vol}(\mathbb{B}_1^d)}{(d+2)(d+4)(d+6)}.
\end{aligned}$$

3.9 Computation

By convexity of the spectral norm and naive calculation,

$$\|g''(x)\| = \left\| \int_{\mathbb{B}_\varepsilon^d} f(x+u)\phi_\varepsilon''(u)\,du \right\|$$

$$\stackrel{(a)}{=} \left\| \int_{\mathbb{B}_\varepsilon^d} (f(x+u) - f(x))\phi_\varepsilon''(u)\,du \right\|$$

$$\stackrel{(b)}{\leq} \varepsilon \operatorname{lip}(f) \int_{\mathbb{B}_\varepsilon^d} \|\phi_\varepsilon''(u)\|\,du$$

$$\stackrel{(c)}{=} \frac{\operatorname{lip}(f)}{\varepsilon} \int_{\mathbb{B}_1^d} \|\phi''(u)\|\,du$$

$$\stackrel{(d)}{=} \frac{\operatorname{lip}(f)}{C\varepsilon} \int_{\mathbb{B}_1^d} \left\| 24uu^\top(1-\|u\|^2) - 6\mathbb{1}(1-\|u\|^2)^2 \right\|\,du$$

$$\stackrel{(e)}{\leq} \frac{\operatorname{lip}(f)}{C\varepsilon} \int_{\mathbb{B}_1^d} \left(\|24uu^\top(1-\|u\|^2)\| + 6\|\mathbb{1}(1-\|u\|^2)^2\| \right)\,du$$

$$\stackrel{(f)}{=} \frac{d\operatorname{vol}(\mathbb{B}_1^d)\operatorname{lip}(f)}{C\varepsilon} \int_0^1 r^{d-1} \left[24r^2(1-r^2) + 6(1-r^2)^2 \right]\,dr$$

$$= \frac{(d+1)(d+6)\operatorname{lip}(f)}{\varepsilon},$$

where (a) follows because $\int_{\mathbb{B}_\varepsilon^d} \phi_\varepsilon''(u)\,du = 0$; (b) since f is Lipschitz and the spectral norm is convex (or triangle inequality); (c) and (d) by a change of measure and differentiating; (e) by the triangle inequality; and (f) by Proposition A.2 and because $\|uu^\top\| = \|u\|^2$. For part (4), since f is Lipschitz,

$$|g(x) - f(x)| = \left| \int_{\mathbb{B}_\varepsilon^d} (f(x+u) - f(x))\phi_\varepsilon(u)\,du \right|$$

$$\leq \operatorname{lip}(f) \int_{\mathbb{B}_\varepsilon^d} \|u\|\phi_\varepsilon(u)\,du$$

$$\leq \varepsilon \operatorname{lip}(f). \qquad \square$$

Exercise 3.25 ★ Prove Proposition 3.24(1) and (2).

3.9 Computation

There are a variety of standard operations that are components in (bandit) convex optimisation algorithms; for example, projections and positioning a convex body K into isotropic/John's position.

Standard operations

We are interested in the following operations:

- MEM$_K$ is the membership oracle: MEM$_K(x) = \mathbf{1}_K(x)$.
- SEP$_K$ is a separation oracle: SEP$_K(x) = \bot$ if $x \in K$ and otherwise SEP$_K(x) = H$ for some half-space H with $K \subset H$.
- LIN$_K$ is the linear optimisation oracle: LIN$_K(c) = \arg\min_{x \in K} \langle c, x \rangle$.
- CVX$_K$ is the function with CVX$_K(f) = \arg\min_{x \in K} f(x)$.
- PROJ$_{K,N}$ is the function PROJ$_{K,N}(y) = \arg\min_{x \in K} N(x-y)$ where N is a norm.
- ISO$_K$ is the affine map such that $\{\text{ISO}_K(x): x \in K\}$ is istropic.
- JOHN$_K$ is the affine map such that $\{\text{JOHN}_K(x): x \in K\}$ is in John's position.
- SAMP$_K$ is the oracle that returns a point sampled from the uniform distribution on K.
- GRAD$_f$ returns the gradient of a function $f: \mathbb{R}^d \to \mathbb{R}$.

Table 3.1 provides complexity bounds for computing one oracle from others. The bounds ignore logarithmic factors and are given in terms of the number of arithmetic operations as well as calls to other oracles. For example, Table 3.1 claims that linear optimisation can be computed in $\tilde{O}(d^3)$ arithmetic operations and $\tilde{O}(d)$ calls to a separation oracle for K. More importantly, we are only claiming the relevant quantity can be computed *approximately*. Moreover, the oracles used as inputs are permitted to be approximate as well. We badly want to avoid handling approximation errors for computations in this book. We will assume exact computation in our analysis and leave it to you to carefully consider the approximation error if this concerns you. For some of the oracles it is not even obvious what metric should be used to define the approximation error. That too, we leave to you to figure out. Usually the reference in Table 3.1 contains what you need to know.

Exercise 3.26 ★ Prove the complexity bound for all entries in Table 3.1 without a reference.

3.10 Notes

3.i Versions of some or all the properties used here have been exploited in a similar fashion by Flaxman et al. (2005); Bubeck et al. (2017); Lattimore (2020) and others.

3.ii Occasionally it would be convenient to be able to extend β-smooth functions while preserving β-smoothness to all of $\mathbb{R}^d$. Curiously, this is not always possible (Drori, 2018).

OP.	COMPLEXITY	REFERENCE
MEM_K	md	–
MEM_K	$v^{2.37}$†	Jiang et al. 2021
MEM_{K°	$1 + \text{LIN}_K$	–
SEP_K	md	–
SEP_K	$d\,\text{MEM}_K$	Lee et al. 2018
LIN_K	$d^3 + d^2\,\text{MEM}_K$	Lee et al. 2015, Lee et al. 2018
LIN_K	$d^3 + d\,\text{SEP}_K$	Lee et al. 2015
LIN_K	$m^{2.37}$†	Jiang et al. 2021
LIN_K	vd	–
CVX_K	$d^3 + d\,\text{GRAD}_f + d^2\,\text{MEM}_K$	Lee et al. 2015, Lee et al. 2018
CVX_K	$d^3 + d\,\text{GRAD}_f + d\,\text{SEP}_K$	Lee et al. 2015
CVX_K	$d^3 + d\,\text{GRAD}_f + md^2$	Lee et al. 2015
$\text{PROJ}_{K,N}$	$d^3 + d\,\text{GRAD}_N + d^2\,\text{MEM}_K$	–
$\text{PROJ}_{K,N}$	$d^3 + d\,\text{GRAD}_N + d\,\text{SEP}_K$	–
$\text{PROJ}_{K,N}$	$d^3 + d\,\text{GRAD}_N + md^2$	–
ISO_K	$d^4 + d^4\,\text{MEM}_K$	Lovász and Vempala 2006
ISO_K	$d^3 + d\,\text{SAMP}_K$	Lovász and Vempala 2006
JOHN_K	$m^{3.5}$	Khachiyan and Todd 1993
JOHN_{K°	$v^{3.5}$	Khachiyan and Todd 1993

† these bounds would improve to $m^{2.055}$ and $v^{2.055}$ if matrix multiplication algorithms improved to their theoretical limits (Jiang et al., 2021).

Table 3.1 Computation costs for standard operations. In rows where m appears we assume that $K = \{x : Ax \leq b\}$ with $A \in \mathbb{R}^{m \times d}$. In rows where v appears we assume that $K = \text{conv}(x_1, \ldots, x_v)$. Since K is assumed to be a convex body, $m = \Omega(d)$ and $v = \Omega(d)$.

3.iii The extension in Proposition 3.20 is due to Fokkema et al. (2024). A related extension was proposed by Mhammedi (2022), who also use an extension based on the 'projection' $x/\pi(x)$ but assume knowledge of the gradient of f at this point.

4
Bisection in One Dimension

We start with a simple but instructive algorithm for the one-dimensional stochastic setting. The next assumption is considered global throughout the chapter:

Assumption 4.1 The following hold:
(1) $d = 1$ and K is a nonempty interval;
(2) the setting is stochastic: $f_t = f$ for all t; and
(3) the loss function is Lipschitz: $f \in \mathscr{F}_1$.

Like many algorithms for convex bandits, the bisection method is based on a classical technique for deterministic convex optimisation. The algorithm in this chapter only works in the stochastic one-dimensional setting but has the advantages that it can be implemented trivially and is nearly minimax optimal. The ideas are also quite instructive and highlight some of the challenges when moving from deterministic to noisy zeroth-order optimisation. The main theoretical result is a proof that under Assumption 4.1 the regret of Algorithm 4.3 is bounded with high probability by $\tilde{O}(\sqrt{n})$.

4.1 Bisection Method without Noise

We start by considering the noise-free setting, which illustrates the main idea. The bisection method for deterministic zeroth-order convex optimisation is very simple.

Theorem 4.2 *Let $(K_k)_{k=1}^{\infty}$ be the sequence of sets produced by Algorithm 4.1. Then*

$$\max_{x \in K_k} f(x) \leq \min_{y \in K} f(y) + \left(\frac{2}{3}\right)^{k-1} \mathrm{vol}(K) \text{ for all } k \geq 1,$$

4.2 Bisection Method with Noise

```
1  let K₁ = K
2  for k = 1 to ∞:
3      let x = min Kₖ and y = max Kₖ
4      let x₀ = ⅔x + ⅓y,  x₁ = ⅓x + ⅔y
5      if f(x₁) ≥ f(x₀): then Kₖ₊₁ = [x, x₁]
6      else: Kₖ₊₁ = [x₀, y]
```

Algorithm 4.1   Bisection method without noise

where $\mathrm{vol}(K)$ is the width of the interval K.

Proof Suppose that $x \in K_k$ and $x \notin K_{k+1}$. By convexity you immediately have that $f(x) \geq \min_{y \in K_{k+1}} f(y)$. Therefore by induction, $\min_{x \in K_k} f(x) = \min_{x \in K} f(x)$ for all k. By construction of the algorithm, $\mathrm{vol}(K_k) = (2/3)^{k-1} \mathrm{vol}(K)$. Since f is Lipschitz by assumption, it follows that

$$\max_{x \in K_k} f(x) \leq \max_{x \in K_k} \min_{y \in K_k} (f(y) + |x - y|)$$
$$\leq \min_{y \in K_k} f(y) + \mathrm{vol}(K_k)$$
$$= \min_{y \in K} f(y) + \left(\frac{2}{3}\right)^{k-1} \mathrm{vol}(K),$$

which completes the proof. □

4.2 Bisection Method with Noise

The generalisation of the bisection method to noisy optimisation is surprisingly subtle. While Algorithm 4.1 divides the current interval into three blocks, in the noisy setting it turns out that four blocks are necessary. The situation is best illustrated by the example in Figure 4.1. Suppose you have noisy (and therefore only approximate) estimates of the loss at all of $x \in \{0, 1, 2, 3\}$. Notice how all three convex functions f, g and h have very similar values at these points but the minimiser could be in any of $(0, 1)$, $(1, 2)$ or $(2, 3)$. Hence it will take many samples to

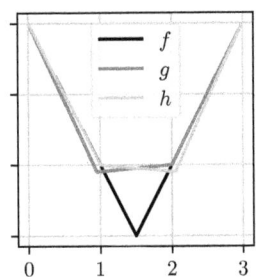

Figure 4.1   Three convex functions

identify which function is the truth. Even worse, if the real function is f, then you are paying considerable regret while trying to identify the region where the minimiser lies. The example illustrates the problem of exploring efficiently. A good exploration strategy will ensure that if the regret is large, then the information gain about the identity/location of a near-minimiser is also large. The exploration strategy in Figure 4.1 is not good. The example also illustrates the challenges of generalising methods designed for deterministic zeroth-order optimisation to stochastic zeroth-order optimisation. Fundamentally the problem is one of stability. Algorithm 4.1 is not a stable algorithm because small perturbations of its observations can dramatically change its behaviour.

We decompose the bisection method for stochastic convex optimisation into two algorithms. The first accepts as input an interval and interacts with the loss for a number of rounds. Eventually it outputs a new interval such that with high probability all of the following hold:

○ The minimiser of the loss is contained in the output interval.
○ The new interval is three quarters as large as the input interval.
○ The regret suffered during the interaction is controlled.

```
1  def BISECT(K = [x, y], n, δ ∈ (0, 1)):
2      x_0 = 3/4 x + 1/4 y,  x_1 = 1/2 x + 1/2 y,  x_2 = 1/4 x + 3/4 y
3      for t = 1 to n:
4          c_t = sqrt( 24/t log(4n/3δ) )
5          let X_t = x_{t mod 3} and observe Y_t = f(X_t) + ε_t
6          if t ≡ 0 mod 3:
7              let f̂_t(x_k) = 3/t ∑_{u=1}^{t} 1(u ≡ k mod 3) Y_u with k ∈ {0, 1, 2}
8              if f̂_t(x_2) − f̂_t(x_1) ≥ c_t:  return [x, x_2]
9              if f̂_t(x_0) − f̂_t(x_1) ≥ c_t:  return [x_0, y]
10     return [x, y]
```

Algorithm 4.2 Bisection episode

Proposition 4.3 *Let $[z, w]$ be the interval returned by Algorithm 4.2 with inputs K, n and $\delta \in (0, 1)$, and let*

$$\Delta = \frac{1}{3} [f(x_0) + f(x_1) + f(x_2)] - \min_{x \in K} f(x).$$

Suppose that $\Delta > 0$. Then, with probability at least $1 - \delta$ the following both hold:

(1) *The interval $[z, w]$ returned by the algorithm satisfies*

$$\min_{x \in [z,w]} f(x) = \min_{x \in K} f(x).$$

(2) *The number of queries to the zeroth-order oracle is at most*

$$3 + \frac{384}{\Delta^2} \log\left(\frac{4n}{3\delta}\right).$$

Proof By convexity, $\max(f(x_0), f(x_2)) \geq f(x_1)$. Assume without loss of generality for the remainder of the proof that $f(x_2) \geq f(x_0)$ and let $\theta = f(x_2) - f(x_1)$. Let $G = G_{01} \cap G_{21}$ with

$$G_{01} = \bigcap_{t \in I} \{|\hat{f}_t(x_0) - \hat{f}_t(x_1) - f(x_0) + f(x_1)| \leq c_t\} \quad \text{and}$$

$$G_{21} = \bigcap_{t \in I} \{|\hat{f}_t(x_2) - \hat{f}_t(x_1) - f(x_2) + f(x_1)| \leq c_t\},$$

where $I = \{1 \leq t \leq n : t \equiv 0 \mod 3\}$. These are the events that $\hat{f}_t(x_0) - \hat{f}_t(x_1)$ is a reasonable approximation of $f(x_0) - f(x_1)$ for all rounds $t \in I$ and similarly for $\hat{f}_t(x_2) - \hat{f}_t(x_1)$.

Exercise 4.4 ★ Use Theorem B.17 and a union bound to show that $\mathbb{P}(G) \geq 1 - \delta$.

Suppose now that G holds. We claim that $\theta \geq \frac{1}{2}\Delta$. To reduce clutter, assume without loss of generality that $f(x_\star) = 0$. Suppose we can show that $f(x_0) + f(x_1) + f(x_2) \leq 6\theta$. Then

$$\Delta = \frac{1}{3}[f(x_0) + f(x_1) + f(x_2)] - f(x_\star) \leq 2\theta,$$

which shows that $\theta \geq \frac{1}{2}\Delta$ as required. Proving that $f(x_0) + f(x_1) + f(x_2) \leq 6\theta$ is a tedious case-based analysis depending on the interval containing $x_\star$. To begin, convexity of f and the assumption that $f(x_2) \geq f(x_0)$ implies that $x_\star$ can be chosen in $[x, x_2]$.

<u>Case 1</u>: $[x_\star \in [x, x_0]]$. Let $\lambda \in [0, 1]$ be such that $x_1 = \lambda x_2 + (1 - \lambda)x_\star$. Then $x_1 = \lambda x_2 + (1 - \lambda)x_\star \geq \lambda x_2 + (1 - \lambda)x$ and therefore $\lambda \leq (x_1 - x)/(x_2 - x) = \frac{2}{3}$.

By convexity of f,

$$\begin{align}
f(x_1) &= f(\lambda x_2 + (1-\lambda)x_\star) & \text{Definition of } \lambda \\
&\leq \lambda f(x_2) + (1-\lambda) f(x_\star) & \text{Convexity of } f \\
&= \lambda f(x_2) & \text{Since } f(x_\star) = 0 \\
&\leq \frac{2}{3} f(x_2) & \text{Since } \lambda \leq \frac{2}{3} \\
&= \frac{2}{3} f(x_1) + \frac{2}{3} \theta. & \text{Definition of } \theta
\end{align}$$

Rearranging shows that $f(x_1) \leq 2\theta$. Similarly, $f(x_0) \leq \frac{1}{2} f(x_1) \leq \theta$. Finally, by definition, $f(x_2) = f(x_1) + \theta \leq 3\theta$. Summing the bounds we have $f(x_0) + f(x_1) + f(x_2) \leq \theta + 2\theta + 3\theta = 6\theta$.

Case 2: $[x_\star \in [x_0, x_1]]$. The argument follows a similar pattern. Let $\lambda \in [0, 1]$ be such that $x_1 = \lambda x_2 + (1-\lambda) x_\star$. Then $x_1 = \lambda x_2 + (1-\lambda) x_\star \geq \lambda x_2 + (1-\lambda) x_0$ and hence $\lambda \leq (x_1 - x_0)/(x_2 - x_0) = \frac{1}{2}$. By convexity, $f(x_1) \leq \frac{1}{2} f(x_2) = \frac{1}{2} f(x_1) + \frac{1}{2} \theta$ and hence $f(x_1) \leq \theta$. As before, $f(x_2) = f(x_1) + \theta \leq 2\theta$, and by assumption $f(x_0) \leq f(x_2) \leq 2\theta$. Summing shows that $f(x_0) + f(x_1) + f(x_2) \leq 2\theta + \theta + 2\theta = 5\theta$.

Case 3: $[x_\star \in [x_1, x_2]]$. Let $\lambda \in [0, 1]$ be such that $x_1 = \lambda x_0 + (1-\lambda) x_\star$. Then $x_1 = \lambda x_0 + (1-\lambda) x_\star \leq \lambda x_0 + (1-\lambda) x_2$. Therefore $\lambda \leq (x_2 - x_1)/(x_2 - x_0) = \frac{1}{2}$. Hence $f(x_1) \leq \frac{1}{2} f(x_0) \leq \frac{1}{2} f(x_2) = \frac{1}{2} f(x_1) + \frac{1}{2} \theta$ and so $f(x_1) \leq \theta$. As before, $f(x_0) \leq f(x_2) = f(x_1) + \theta \leq 2\theta$, which also shows $f(x_2) \leq 2\theta$. Therefore $f(x_0) + f(x_1) + f(x_2) \leq 5\theta$.

We are now in a position to establish the claims of the theorem, starting with part (1). By assumption $f(x_2) \geq f(x_1)$ and hence $x_\star$ cannot be in $[x_2, y]$. The algorithm cannot do any wrong if $x_\star \in [x_0, x_2]$. Suppose that $x_\star \in [x, x_0]$. By convexity $f(x_0) \leq f(x_1)$ and hence on G,

$$\hat{f}_t(x_0) - \hat{f}_t(x_1) < f(x_0) - f(x_1) + c_t \leq c_t,$$

which means the algorithm does not return $[x_0, y]$. For part (2), suppose that $c_t \leq \frac{1}{2} \theta$. Then, on event G,

$$\hat{f}_t(x_2) - \hat{f}_t(x_1) \geq f(x_2) - f(x_1) - c_t = \theta - c_t \geq c_t,$$

which means the algorithm halts. Since $\theta \geq \frac{1}{2} \Delta$, it follows that on G the algorithm halts once t is a multiple of three and

$$\frac{1}{4} \Delta \geq c_t = \sqrt{\frac{24}{t} \log\left(\frac{4n}{3\delta}\right)}.$$

Solving shows the algorithm halts after at most

$$3 + \frac{384}{\Delta^2} \log\left(\frac{4n}{3\delta}\right)$$

queries to the loss function. □

Exercise 4.5 ★★❷ Find a slick proof to replace the ugly case-by-case analysis in the proof of Proposition 4.3.

The main algorithm runs Algorithm 4.2 iteratively on a shrinking interval and decreasing confidence parameter δ to ensure that with high probability the returned interval contains a minimiser of f.

```
1   args: K = [x, y], n, δ ∈ (0, 1)
2   let K₁ = [x, y] and kmax = 1 + ⌈log(n)/log(4/3)⌉.
3   for k = 1 to ∞:
4       let t be the current round
5       if t = n + 1: exit
6       K_{k+1} = BISECT(K_k, n − t + 1, δ/kmax)      # Algorithm 4.2
```

Algorithm 4.3 Bisection method

The main theorem of this chapter is the following theorem bounding the regret of Algorithm 4.3.

Theorem 4.6 *Under Assumption 4.1, with probability at least $1 − \delta$, the regret of Algorithm 4.3 is bounded by*

$$\text{Reg}_n = O\left(\text{vol}(K) + \sqrt{n \log\left(\frac{n}{\delta}\right) \log(n)}\right).$$

Proof Algorithm 4.3 runs until the time horizon is reached, repeatedly calling Algorithm 4.2. Let n_k be the number of queries made to the loss function in episode k of Algorithm 4.3 and before the time horizon n has been reached. Hence $\sum_{k=1}^{\infty} n_k = n$. Let $K_k = [x_k, y_k]$ and

$$\Delta_k = \frac{1}{3}\left[f\left(\frac{1}{4}x_k + \frac{3}{4}y_k\right) + f\left(\frac{1}{2}x_k + \frac{1}{2}y_k\right) + f\left(\frac{3}{4}x_k + \frac{1}{4}y_k\right)\right] - f(x_\star).$$

Since f is Lipschitz, provided that $x_\star \in K_k$ it holds that

$$\Delta_k \leq \max_{x \in K_k}(f(x) - f(x_\star)) \leq \text{vol}(K_k) = \left(\frac{3}{4}\right)^{k-1} \text{vol}(K). \quad (4.1)$$

A union bound and Proposition 4.3 show that with probability at least $1-\delta$ every call made to Algorithm 4.2 in iterations $k \leq k_{\max}$ either ends with the horizon being reached or returns a new interval containing the optimum after at most n_k queries with

$$n_k \leq 3 + \frac{384}{\Delta_k^2} \log\left(\frac{4nk_{\max}}{3\delta}\right). \tag{4.2}$$

Assume this good event occurs. We claim that

$$\text{Reg}_n = \sum_{t=1}^n (f(X_t) - f(x_\star)) \leq 2\,\text{vol}(K) + \sum_{k=1}^\infty \mathbf{1}(k < k_{\max}) n_k \Delta_k. \tag{4.3}$$

There are two cases.

<u>Case 1</u>: $[n_{k_{\max}} > 0]$. This means that all calls to BISECT in episodes $k < k_{\max}$ resulted in a smaller interval being returned. Hence, for $k < k_{\max}$, n_k is a multiple of 3 and the regret is $n_k \Delta_k$. The regret in the remaining episodes is bounded by $n(3/4)^{k_{\max}-1} \leq \text{vol}(K)$ by (4.1).

<u>Case 2</u>: $[n_{k_{\max}} = 0]$. In this case the final episode ends before a smaller interval could be returned. Since for this k it may not hold that n_k is a multiple of 3, we naively bound the regret by $n_k \Delta_k + 2\,\text{vol}(K)$.

Together the two cases establish (4.3). By (4.2), for $k < k_{\max}$,

$$n_k \Delta_k \leq 6\Delta_k + \sqrt{768 n_k \log\left(\frac{4nk_{\max}}{3\delta}\right)}.$$

Hence, by (4.3),

$$\text{Reg}_n \leq 2\,\text{vol}(K) + \sum_{k=1}^\infty \mathbf{1}(k < k_{\max}) \left[6\Delta_k + \sqrt{768 n_k \log\left(\frac{4nk_{\max}}{3\delta}\right)} \right]$$

$$\leq 2\,\text{vol}(K) + 6 \sum_{k=1}^\infty \left(\frac{3}{4}\right)^{k-1} \text{vol}(K) + \sqrt{768 k_{\max} \sum_{k=1}^\infty n_k \log\left(\frac{4nk_{\max}}{3\delta}\right)}$$

$$\leq 26\,\text{vol}(K) + \sqrt{768 k_{\max} n \log\left(\frac{4nk_{\max}}{3\delta}\right)}$$

$$= O\left(\text{vol}(K) + \sqrt{n \log(n/\delta) \log(n)}\right),$$

where we used Cauchy–Schwarz along with the fact that $\sum_{k=1}^\infty n_k = n$ and the formula for the geometric sum. $\square$

4.3 Notes

4.i Algorithm 4.2 is due to Agarwal et al. (2011). The basic principle behind the bisection method is that the volume of K_k is guaranteed to decrease rapidly with the number of iterations. Generalising this method to higher dimensions is rather non-trivial. Agarwal et al. (2011) and Lattimore and György (2021a) both used algorithms based on the ellipsoid method while Carpentier (2025) used the centre of gravity method. These methods are covered in Chapter 9.

4.ii Algorithm 4.2 works with no assumptions on f beyond convexity and Lipschitzness and ensures $O(\sqrt{n}\log(n))$ regret in the stochastic setting. The algorithm is distinct from all others in this book because its regret depends only very weakly on the range of the loss function. This is what one should expect from algorithms in the stochastic setting where the magnitude of the noise rather than the losses should determine the regret, as it does for finite-armed bandits.

4.iii There are various ways to refine Algorithm 4.1 for the deterministic case that better exploit convexity (Orseau and Hutter, 2023). These ideas have not yet been exploited in the noisy (bandit) setting. Bisection-based methods for the deterministic setting seem fast and require just $O(\log(1/\varepsilon))$ queries to the zeroth-order oracle to find an ε-optimal point. Remarkably, for suitably well-behaved functions Newton's method is exponentially faster with sample complexity $O(\log\log(1/\varepsilon))$.

4.iv Algorithm 4.1 can be improved with a simple modification. The algorithm evaluates f at two points in each iteration, but by reusing data from previous iterations you can implement almost the same algorithm using only one evaluation in each iteration. The algorithm is called the golden section search, and is usually analysed for unimodal function minimisation (Kiefer, 1953).

4.v There is an interesting generalisation of the bisection search to a different model where the noise is a bit more adversarial (Bachoc et al., 2024, 2022). In the setting of this chapter these algorithms have about the same regret as Algorithm 4.3 but are careful to reuse data as we hinted at in Note 4.iv above.

4.vi The confidence intervals used by Algorithm 4.2 are generally quite conservative. In practice you may prefer to use standard statistical tests. This will generally improve performance (quite dramatically). The price is that in extreme cases your confidence intervals will be invalid and the algorithm could suffer linear regret.

5
Online Gradient Descent

In this chapter we introduce an idea that is ubiquitous in zeroth-order optimisation, which is to use a gradient-based algorithm but replace the true gradients with estimated gradients of a smoothed loss. Except for Section 5.4, we assume throughout this chapter that the constraint set contains a euclidean ball of unit radius, the losses are bounded, Lipschitz and there is no noise:

Assumption 5.1 The following hold:
(1) $\mathbb{B}_1^d \subset K$;
(2) the loss functions $(f_t)_{t=1}^n$ are in $\mathscr{F}_{b,1}$; and
(3) there is no noise: $\varepsilon_t = 0$ for all t.

The long steady slog to the top. Hope the view is nice.

In contrast to the previous chapter, the setting is now adversarial. The most well-known optimisation algorithm is gradient descent. By default this algorithm needs access to the gradient of the loss. We start by explaining the standard analysis of online gradient descent and then introduce spherical smoothing. These ideas are then combined to yield a simple algorithm and analysis. At the end of the chapter we explain how smoothness and strong convexity can be exploited to improve the bound, but only in the improper setting where the learner is allowed to play outside of K.

5.1 Gradient Descent

Gradient descent incrementally computes a sequence of iterates $(x_t)_{t=1}^n$ with x_{t+1} computed by taking a gradient step from x_t. Let $\Pi_K(x) = \arg\min_{y \in K} \|x - y\|$ be the euclidean projection onto K. An abstract version of gradient descent for bandit convex optimisation is given below.

5.1 Gradient Descent

```
1  args: learning rate η > 0
2  initialise x₁ ∈ K
3  for t = 1 to n
4     sample Xₜ from some distribution based on xₜ
5     observe Yₜ = fₜ(Xₜ)
6     compute gradient estimate gₜ using xₜ, Xₜ and Yₜ
7     update xₜ₊₁ = Π_K(xₜ − ηgₜ)
```

Algorithm 5.1 Abstract gradient descent

Importantly, the algorithm does not evaluate the loss function at x_t but rather at some random point X_t whose distribution has not been specified yet. We have rather informally written that the (conditional) law of X_t should be based on x_t, by which we mean that

$$\mathbb{P}(X_t \in A | \mathscr{F}_{t-1}) = \nu(A|x_t)$$

for some probability kernel $\nu: \mathscr{B}(K) \times K \to [0, 1]$. The kernel ν determines how the algorithm explores. The gradient estimate g_t is usually not an estimate of $f'_t(x)$, which may not even exist. Instead it is an estimate of the gradient of some surrogate loss function s_t that is close to f_t. We return to the problem of defining the exploration kernel, surrogate and gradient estimates momentarily. Before that we give some details about gradient descent. The analysis of gradient descent at our disposal from the online learning literature yields a bound on the regret relative to the linear losses defined by the gradient estimates g_t. Specifically, we have the following theorem:

Theorem 5.2 Let $(x_t)_{t=1}^n$ be the iterates produced by Algorithm 5.1. Then, for any $x \in K$,

$$\widehat{\text{Reg}}_n(x) \triangleq \sum_{t=1}^{n} \langle g_t, x_t - x \rangle \leq \frac{\text{diam}(K)^2}{2\eta} + \frac{\eta}{2} \sum_{t=1}^{n} \|g_t\|^2 .$$

Remark 5.3 In most applications of Theorem 5.2, $g_t = f'_t(x_t)$. By convexity one has $f_t(x_t) - f_t(x) \leq \langle g_t, x_t - x \rangle$ and Theorem 5.2 provides an upper bound on the regret of gradient descent with respect to the losses (f_t). As mentioned above, in the bandit setting the gradient $f'_t(x_t)$ is not available and we will let g_t be an estimate of the gradient of a suitable surrogate.

Proof Let $x \in K$. The idea is quite simple. Suppose the instantaneous regret $r_t = \langle g_t, x_t - x \rangle$ is large. Then, provided that $\eta \|g_t\|$ is not too large, the algorithm takes a step such that $\|x_{t+1} - x\| \le \|x_t - x\|$. And indeed, the decrease can be written as a function of r_t. Since the distance to x is always non-negative, the cumulative change in distance to x cannot be large. This suggests a potential argument, which mathematically uses the squared norms as follows:

$$\begin{aligned}
\frac{1}{2}\|x_{t+1} - x\|^2 &= \frac{1}{2}\|\Pi_K(x_t - \eta g_t) - x\|^2 \\
&\le \frac{1}{2}\|x_t - x - \eta g_t\|^2 \\
&= \frac{1}{2}\|x_t - x\|^2 + \frac{\eta^2}{2}\|g_t\|^2 - \eta \langle g_t, x_t - x \rangle,
\end{aligned}$$

where in the inequality we used the fact that $\|z - \Pi_K(y)\| \le \|z - y\|$ for all $z \in K$ and $y \in \mathbb{R}^d$. Rearranging shows that

$$\begin{aligned}
\widehat{\mathrm{Reg}}_n(x) &= \sum_{t=1}^n \langle g_t, x_t - x \rangle \\
&\le \sum_{t=1}^n \left[\frac{\eta}{2}\|g_t\|^2 + \frac{1}{2\eta}\|x_t - x\|^2 - \frac{1}{2\eta}\|x_{t+1} - x\|^2 \right] \\
&\le \frac{1}{2\eta}\|x_1 - x\|^2 + \frac{\eta}{2}\sum_{t=1}^n \|g_t\|^2 \\
&\le \frac{\mathrm{diam}(K)^2}{2\eta} + \frac{\eta}{2}\sum_{t=1}^n \|g_t\|^2.
\end{aligned}$$

$\square$

What conditions are needed on the gradients $(g_t)_{t=1}^n$ if we want to bound the actual regret in terms of $\widehat{\mathrm{Reg}}_n$? Let $x_\star = \arg\min_{x \in K} \sum_{t=1}^n f_t(x)$. We have

$$\begin{aligned}
\mathbb{E}[\mathrm{Reg}_n] &= \mathbb{E}\left[\sum_{t=1}^n (f_t(X_t) - f_t(x_\star))\right] \\
&= \mathbb{E}\left[\sum_{t=1}^n (\mathbb{E}_{t-1}[f_t(X_t)] - f_t(x_\star))\right] \\
&\stackrel{(\dagger)}{\le} \mathbb{E}\left[\sum_{t=1}^n \langle \mathbb{E}_{t-1}[g_t], x_t - x_\star \rangle\right] \\
&= \mathbb{E}\left[\sum_{t=1}^n \langle g_t, x_t - x_\star \rangle\right] = \mathbb{E}\left[\widehat{\mathrm{Reg}}_n(x_\star)\right]
\end{aligned}$$

Can we ensure that (†) holds? Remember that $\mathbb{P}_{t-1}(X_t = \cdot) = \nu(\cdot | x_t)$ and we get to choose the kernel ν and the gradient estimator g_t. Since $x_\star$ is not known, the most natural objective is to try and select the kernel and gradient estimate in

such a way that for all $x \in K$,
$$\mathbb{E}_{t-1}[f_t(X_t)] - f_t(x) \lesssim \langle \mathbb{E}_{t-1}[g_t], x_t - x \rangle \,.$$

Furthermore, to bound $\mathbb{E}[\widehat{\mathrm{Reg}_n}]$ we need to bound $\mathbb{E}_{t-1}[\|g_t\|^2]$. Summarising, a kernel ν and gradient estimate g_t will yield a good regret bound if
(1) $\mathbb{E}_{t-1}[f_t(X_t)] - f_t(x) \lesssim \langle \mathbb{E}_{t-1}[g_t], x_t - x \rangle$ for all $x \in K$; and
(2) $\mathbb{E}_{t-1}[\|g_t\|^2]$ is small.

Remark 5.4 If the learner has access to the gradient $g_t = f_t'(x_t)$, then $f_t(x_t) - f_t(x) \leq \langle g_t, x_t - x \rangle$ for all $x \in K$ by convexity and $\|g_t\|^2 \leq 1$ since $f_t \in \mathcal{F}_{b,1}$ is Lipschitz. That is, (1) and (2) hold with $g_t = f_t'(x_t)$ and $X_t = x_t$.

5.2 Spherical Smoothing

Let $x \in K$ and $f \in \mathcal{F}_{b,1}$. Our algorithm will play some action X that is a random variable and observe $Y = f(X)$. We want a gradient estimator g that is a function of X and Y such that
(1) $\mathbb{E}[f(X)] - f(y) \lesssim \langle \mathbb{E}[g], x - y \rangle$ for all $y \in K$; and
(2) $\mathbb{E}[\|g\|^2]$ is small.
A simple and beautiful estimator is based on Stokes' theorem. Let $r \in (0,1)$ be a precision parameter and define s as the convolution between f and a uniform distribution on $\mathbb{B}_r^d$. That is,
$$s(x) = \frac{1}{\mathrm{vol}(\mathbb{B}_r^d)} \int_{\mathbb{B}_r^d} f(x+u)\, du \,.$$

Some examples are plotted in Figure 5.1. The function s is convex because it is the convolution of a convex function and a probability density. We have to be careful about the domain of s. Because f is only defined on K, the surrogate s is only defined on
$$\mathrm{dom}(s) = \{x \in K : x + \mathbb{B}_r^d \subset K\}\,.$$
By Stokes' theorem, the gradient of s at $x \in \mathrm{dom}(s)$ is
$$s'(x) = \frac{1}{\mathrm{vol}(\mathbb{B}_r^d)} \int_{\mathbb{B}_r^d} f'(x+u)\, du = \frac{d}{r} \frac{1}{\mathrm{vol}(\mathbb{S}_r^{d-1})} \int_{\mathbb{S}_r^{d-1}} f(x+u) \frac{u}{r}\, du, \quad (5.1)$$
where we also used the fact from Proposition A.1 (2) that $\mathrm{vol}(\mathbb{S}_r^{d-1})/\mathrm{vol}(\mathbb{B}_r^d) = \frac{d}{r}$. Actually in the above display we took some liberties. What if f is not differentiable?

Exercise 5.5 ★ Prove that the left-hand and right-hand sides of (5.1) holds even when f is not differentiable.

The right-hand side of (5.1) suggests a way of estimating $s'(x)$. Let U be uniformly distributed on $\mathbb{S}_r^{d-1}$ and $X = x + U$ and define the surrogate gradient estimate by

$$g = \frac{dYU}{r^2},$$

which has expectation $\mathbb{E}[g] = s'(x)$. How well does this estimator satisfy our criteria? Suppose that V has law $\mathscr{U}(\mathbb{B}_r^d)$. Then, since f is Lipschitz and using Proposition A.4 that $\mathbb{E}[\|V\|] = \frac{rd}{d+1}$, for all $y \in \text{dom}(s)$,

$$s(y) = \mathbb{E}[f(y+V)] \leq f(y) + \mathbb{E}[\|V\|] = f(y) + \frac{rd}{d+1}.$$

On the other hand, since $rV/\|V\|$ has law $\mathscr{U}(\mathbb{S}_r^{d-1})$,

$$s(x) = \mathbb{E}[f(x+V)] \geq \mathbb{E}\left[f\left(x + \frac{rV}{\|V\|}\right) - \left\|V - \frac{rV}{\|V\|}\right\|\right] = \mathbb{E}[f(X)] - \frac{r}{d+1},$$

where we used again that $\mathbb{E}[\|V\|] = \frac{rd}{d+1}$. Therefore, since s is convex,

$$\langle \mathbb{E}[g], x - y \rangle = \langle s'(x), x - y \rangle$$
$$\geq s(x) - s(y)$$
$$\geq \mathbb{E}[f(X)] - f(y) - r. \tag{5.2}$$

This seems fairly promising. When r is small, then (1) above is indeed satisfied. Moving now to (2),

$$\mathbb{E}[\|g\|^2] = \frac{d^2}{r^2}\mathbb{E}[Y^2] = \frac{d^2}{r^2}\mathbb{E}[f(X)^2] \leq \frac{d^2}{r^2}, \tag{5.3}$$

where we used the fact that $\|U\| = r$ and the assumption that $f \in \mathscr{F}_b$ is bounded on K. The situation is at a standoff. To satisfy (1) we need r to be fairly small, but then $\mathbb{E}[\|g\|^2]$ will be quite large. Nevertheless, enough has been done to make progress.

5.3 Algorithm and Regret Analysis

The surrogate and its gradient estimator can be cleanly inserted into online gradient descent to obtain the following simple algorithm for bandit convex optimisation.

5.3 Algorithm and Regret Analysis

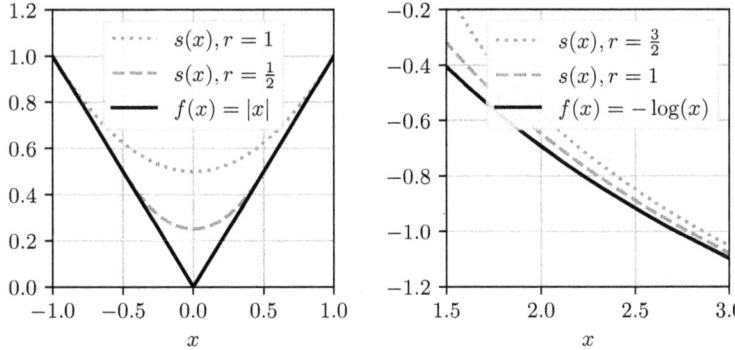

Figure 5.1 The smoothed surrogates for different functions and precisions. Because of convexity the surrogate function is always an upper bound on the original function. Notice how much better the approximation is for $-\log(x)$, which on the interval considered is much smoother than $|x|$.

```
1  args: learning rate η > 0 and precision r ∈ (0, 1)
2  initialise x₁ ∈ K_r = (1 − r)K
3  for t = 1 to n
4      sample U_t uniformly from 𝕊_r^{d−1} and play X_t = x_t + U_t
5      observe Y_t = f_t(X_t)
6      compute gradient estimate g_t = dY_t U_t / r²
7      update x_{t+1} = Π_{K_r}(x_t − ηg_t).
```

Algorithm 5.2 Bandit gradient descent

Theorem 5.6 *Suppose that*

$$\eta = \sqrt{\frac{1}{2}}\operatorname{diam}(K)^{\frac{3}{2}}d^{-\frac{1}{2}}n^{-\frac{3}{4}} \quad \text{and} \quad r = \min\left(1, \sqrt{\frac{1}{2}}\operatorname{diam}(K)^{\frac{1}{2}}d^{\frac{1}{2}}n^{-\frac{1}{4}}\right).$$

Under Assumption 5.1 the expected regret of Algorithm 5.2 is bounded by

$$\mathbb{E}[\operatorname{Reg}_n] \leq \sqrt{8}\operatorname{diam}(K)^{\frac{1}{2}}d^{\frac{1}{2}}n^{\frac{3}{4}}.$$

Proof Suppose that $r = 1$. Then $\sqrt{1/2}\operatorname{diam}(K)^{\frac{1}{2}}d^{\frac{1}{2}}n^{-\frac{1}{4}} \geq 1$, which along with the assumption that the losses are bounded in $[0, 1]$ implies that

$$\mathbb{E}[\operatorname{Reg}_n] \leq n \leq \sqrt{1/2}\operatorname{diam}(K)^{\frac{1}{2}}d^{\frac{1}{2}}n^{\frac{3}{4}}$$

and the claim is proven. For the remainder we assume that $r < 1$. The surrogate in round t is

$$s_t(x) = \frac{1}{\text{vol}(\mathbb{B}_r^d)} \int_{\mathbb{B}_r^d} f_t(x+u)\,du\,.$$

Note, by Lemma 3.4 and the assumption that $\mathbb{B}_1^d \subset K$, it follows that $K_r \subset \text{dom}(s_t)$ for all $1 \leq t \leq n$. By Proposition 3.13,

$$\min_{x \in K_r} \sum_{t=1}^{n} f_t(x) \leq rn + \min_{x \in K} \sum_{t=1}^{n} f_t(x)\,.$$

Therefore, letting $x_\star = \arg\min_{x \in K_r} \sum_{t=1}^{n} f_t(x)$,

$$\mathbb{E}[\text{Reg}_n] = \max_{x \in K} \mathbb{E}\left[\sum_{t=1}^{n}(f_t(X_t) - f_t(x))\right]$$

$$\leq rn + \mathbb{E}\left[\sum_{t=1}^{n}(f_t(X_t) - f_t(x_\star))\right]$$

$$\leq 2rn + \mathbb{E}\left[\sum_{t=1}^{n}\langle g_t, x_t - x_\star\rangle\right]\,. \qquad \text{By (5.2)}$$

By Theorem 5.6 and (5.3),

$$\mathbb{E}\left[\sum_{t=1}^{n}\langle g_t, x_t - x_\star\rangle\right] \leq \frac{\text{diam}(K)^2}{2\eta} + \frac{\eta}{2}\mathbb{E}\left[\sum_{t=1}^{n}\|g_t\|^2\right] \leq \frac{\text{diam}(K)^2}{2\eta} + \frac{\eta n d^2}{2r^2}\,.$$

Combining shows that

$$\mathbb{E}[\text{Reg}_n] \leq \frac{\text{diam}(K)^2}{2\eta} + \frac{\eta n d^2}{2r^2} + 2rn\,.$$

The claim follows by substituting the constants. □

5.4 Smoothness and Strong Convexity (🦘)

As a prelude to the next chapter, let us explore what happens when the losses $(f_t)_{t=1}^{n}$ are assumed to both smooth and strongly convex. For reasons explained after the analysis in Remark 5.12, the argument that follows only works in the improper setting (see 1.iii), which motivates the use of self-concordance that appears in the next chapter. The algorithm here is based on those by Agarwal et al. (2010) and Akhavan et al. (2020) with the differences explained in Note 5.vi. The operating assumptions in this section are as follows:

5.4 Smoothness and Strong Convexity

Assumption 5.7 The losses $(f_t)_{t=1}^n$ satisfy the following:

(1) $\text{dom}(f_t) = \mathbb{R}^d$ and the setting is improper so that the learner can play outside of K.

(2) f_t is strongly convex and smooth: $x \mapsto f_t(x) - \frac{\alpha}{2}\|x\|^2$ is convex and $x \mapsto f_t(x) - \frac{\beta}{2}\|x\|^2$ is concave for some known constants $0 < \alpha \leq \beta$.

(3) There exists a known constant $r > 0$ such that $f_t(x) \in [0, 1]$ for all $x \in K + \mathbb{B}_r^d$.

(4) There is no noise: $\varepsilon_t = 0$.

The algorithm is the same as Algorithm 5.2 but projects onto K and uses decreasing learning rates and smoothing radii.

```
1  args: learning rates (η_t)_{t=1}^n and (r_t)_{t=1}^n
2  initialise x_1 ∈ K
3  for t = 1 to n
4     sample U_t uniformly from S_{r_t}^{d-1} and play X_t = x_t + U_t
5     observe Y_t = f_t(X_t)
6     compute gradient estimate g_t = dY_t U_t / r_t^2
7     update x_{t+1} = Π_K(x_t - η_t g_t).
```

Algorithm 5.3 Bandit gradient descent with varying learning rates and smoothing radii

Note there is no guarantee that $X_t \in K$. This is why we assumed the improper setting and that the losses f_t are bounded on $K + \mathbb{B}_r^d$.

Theorem 5.8 *Suppose that*

$$\eta_t = \frac{1}{t\alpha} \quad \text{and} \quad r_t^2 = \min\left(r^2, d\sqrt{\frac{1}{2\alpha\beta t}}\right).$$

Then, under Assumption 5.7, the regret of Algorithm 5.3 is at most

$$\mathbb{E}[\text{Reg}_n] = O\left(d\sqrt{\frac{\beta n}{\alpha}} + \frac{d^2}{\alpha r^2}\log\left(1 + \frac{d^2}{\alpha\beta r^4}\right)\right).$$

Proof As a good test of your skills, we present this argument as a series of exercises. To begin, we need an analysis of gradient descent that accommodates the changing learning rates:

Exercise 5.9 Suppose that $(g_t)_{t=1}^n$ is an arbitrary sequence of vectors in $\mathbb{R}^d$ and $x_1 \in K$ and $x_{t+1} = \Pi_K(x_t - \eta_t g_t)$. Prove that for any $x \in K$,

$$\sum_{t=1}^n \langle g_t, x_t - x \rangle \leq \sum_{t=1}^n \frac{\eta_t}{2} \|g_t\|^2 + \frac{1}{2} \sum_{t=1}^n \frac{\|x_t - x\|^2}{2} \left(\frac{1}{\eta_t} - \frac{1}{\eta_{t-1}} \right),$$

where we adopt the convention that $\eta_0 \triangleq \infty$.

Moving on, let

$$s_t(x) = \frac{1}{\text{vol}(\mathbb{B}_{r_t}^d)} \int_{\mathbb{B}_{r_t}^d} f_t(x + u) \, du,$$

which is the same surrogate loss used in the proof of Theorem 5.6 but now with a smoothing radius of r_t that depends on the round. By the considerations in Section 5.2, $\mathbb{E}_{t-1}[g_t] = s_t'(x_t)$.

Exercise 5.10 Prove that s_t is smooth and strongly convex:
(1) $x \mapsto s_t(x) - \frac{\alpha}{2}\|x\|^2$ is convex; and
(2) $x \mapsto s_t(x) - \frac{\beta}{2}\|x\|^2$ is concave.

The next step is to use smoothness to refine the comparison between the surrogate loss s_t and the true loss f_t.

Exercise 5.11 Show that $\mathbb{E}_{t-1}[f_t(X_t) - f_t(x)] \leq \mathbb{E}_{t-1}[s_t(x_t) - s_t(x)] + \beta r_t^2$.

The exercise shows how smoothness improves the error between loss and surrogate to have a quadratic dependence on the smoothing radius. Let us now show how strong convexity helps. By Exercise 5.10 and Exercise 5.11,

$$\mathbb{E}[\text{Reg}_n] = \mathbb{E}\left[\sum_{t=1}^n (f_t(X_t) - f_t(x_\star))\right]$$

$$\leq \mathbb{E}\left[\sum_{t=1}^n (s_t(x_t) - s_t(x_\star))\right] + \beta \sum_{t=1}^n r_t^2$$

$$\leq \mathbb{E}\left[\sum_{t=1}^n \langle s_t'(x_t), x_t - x \rangle - \frac{\alpha}{2}\|x_t - x\|^2\right] + \beta \sum_{t=1}^n r_t^2$$

$$= \mathbb{E}\left[\sum_{t=1}^n \langle g_t, x_t - x \rangle - \frac{\alpha}{2}\|x_t - x\|^2\right] + \beta \sum_{t=1}^n r_t^2$$

$$\leq \mathbb{E}\left[\sum_{t=1}^n \frac{\eta_t}{2}\|g_t\|^2 + \frac{1}{2}\sum_{t=1}^n \|x_t - x\|^2 \left(\frac{1}{\eta_t} - \frac{1}{\eta_{t-1}} - \alpha\right)\right] + \beta \sum_{t=1}^n r_t^2.$$

Now you will see why the learning rate has the form it does. The expression with the reciprocol learning rates vanishes and one obtains

$$\mathbb{E}[\text{Reg}_n] \leq \mathbb{E}\left[\sum_{t=1}^{n} \frac{\|g_t\|^2}{2\alpha t}\right] + \beta \sum_{t=1}^{n} r_t^2$$

$$= \sum_{t=1}^{n} \frac{d^2 \mathbb{E}[Y_t^2]}{2\alpha t r_t^2} + \beta \sum_{t=1}^{n} r_t^2. \quad (5.4)$$

The result follows by substituting the definition of r_t, and using Assumption 5.7 to bound $Y_t^2 \leq 1$ and naive bounding. □

Remark 5.12 Algorithm 5.3 might play outside of the constraint set. You may wonder if we can employ the idea in Algorithm 5.2 of projecting onto a subset of K. The first problem is that we need $x_t + \mathbb{B}_{r_t}^d \subset K$ but the tuning of r_t in Theorem 5.8 has $r_1 = \Omega(1)$, which means that x_t must be really quite deep inside K. Examining, (5.4) you could instead let

$$r_t^2 = d\sqrt{\frac{\log(n)}{\alpha \beta n}} \triangleq r^2,$$

which gives the same bound as Theorem 5.8 up to a $\sqrt{\log(n)}$ factor. So now the condition is that $x_t + \mathbb{B}_r^d \subset K$. But even with smoothness and strong convexity it can happen that

$$\min_{x \in K : x + \mathbb{B}_r^d \subset K} f(x) \geq \min_{x \in K} f(x) + \Omega(r).$$

Hence the increased regret suffered by restricting K can be as large as $nr = \Omega(n^{3/4})$ and there is no improvement relative to Algorithm 5.2.

5.5 Notes

5.i Theorem 5.2 is due to Zinkevich (2003). Algorithm 5.2 essentially appears in the independent works by Flaxman et al. (2005) and Kleinberg (2005). The algorithm continues to work without Lipschitzness but the regret increases to $O(dn^{5/6})$ as explained by Flaxman et al. (2005).

5.ii By Proposition 1.7, the regret bound in Theorem 5.6 implies a bound on the sample complexity of $\tilde{O}(\text{diam}(K)^2 d^2 / \varepsilon^4)$. As far as we know, the spherical smoothing estimator was introduced by Nemirovsky and Yudin (1983) who used it to prove essentially the same sample complexity as above modulo some minor technical assumptions about the boundary. Nemirovsky and Yudin (1983) also noticed that smoothness increases the performance of the spherical estimator, which we explain in Chapter 6.

5.iii We did not say much about computation. The only complicated part is computing the projections, the hardness of which depends on how K is represented.

5.iv Garber and Kretzu (2022) show there are alternative ways to keep the iterates inside the constraint set. They assume that $\mathbb{B}_\delta^d \subset K$ for some $\delta > 0$ and design gradient-descent-based algorithms for which the regret more or less matches Theorem 5.6 and that need either $O(n)$ queries to a linear optimisation oracle or $O(n)$ queries to a separation oracle.

5.v Another way to avoid projections is to run gradient descent on the extension defined in Proposition 3.20. This is the approach we will take in Chapter 10. Yet another is to use self-concordant barriers as explained in Chapter 6, though this also comes at a computational cost.

5.vi Algorithm 5.3 is based on Agarwal et al. (2010) who study the adversarial setting and Akhavan et al. (2020) who work in the stochastic setting. Let us consider the similarities and differences.

- Because Agarwal et al. (2010) work in the adversarial setting, they used same single-point gradient estimate employed by Algorithm 5.3. On the other hand, Akhavan et al. (2020) focus on the stochastic setting and consequentially estimate the gradient by querying the loss at both x_t and X_t to reduce the second moment of the gradient estimate. An example of this idea in action is in Section 6.6.
- Agarwal et al. (2010) used a constant value for r_t rather than the decreasing value used here and by Akhavan et al. (2020). This leads to an additional logarithmic factor appearing in the main term. Moreover, Agarwal et al. (2010) assumed that K was a euclidean ball, though this assumption was not really used in the analysis.
- Agarwal et al. (2010) assumed the losses were bounded on K, possibly forgetting that the losses actually need to be bounded on the expansion $K + \mathbb{B}_r^d$ that appears in Assumption 5.7, although you can derive one from the other using smoothness at the cost of larger lower-order terms. Details of this are omitted in their article. Meanwhile, Akhavan et al. (2020) do not assume boundedness of the loss, but rather that it is Lipschitz on K.

6
Self-Concordant Regularisation

The algorithm based on gradient descent in the previous chapter is simple and computationally efficient, at least provided the projection can be computed. There are two limitations, however.

- We needed to assume the losses were Lipschitz and the regret depended polynomially on the diameter of the constraint set.
- Exploiting smoothness and/or strong convexity in the constrained setting is not straightforward due to boundary effects, as we explained in Remark 5.12.

Both limitations will be removed using 'follow-the-regularised-leader' and the beautiful machinery of self-concordant barriers. With the exception of Section 6.6, it is assumed throughout this chapter that there is no noise and the losses are bound:

Assumption 6.1 The following hold:
(1) There is no noise: $\varepsilon_t = 0$ for all t.
(2) The losses are bounded: $f_t \in \mathscr{F}_b$ for all t.

Four new regret bounds are given in this chapter, all improving on what was shown in Chapter 5 in various ways. The first removes the requirement that the loss is Lipschitz and eliminates entirely the dependence on the diameter of the constraint set. The second shows how smoothness of the losses improves the quality of the surrogate loss and leads to a dependence on the horizon of $\tilde{O}(n^{2/3})$. The highlight is showing that $\tilde{O}(\sqrt{n})$ regret is attained by a simple algorithm when the losses are assumed to be smooth and strongly convex. Without this assumption it is still possible to obtain $\tilde{O}(\sqrt{n})$ regret but with a more complicated algorithm and a much more sophisticated analysis (Chapters 10 and 11). Lastly, a little time is devoted to investigating the stochastic setting where additionally the variance of the noise is assumed to be smaller than the range of the losses (Section 6.6).

6.1 Self-Concordant Barriers

Self-concordance was introduced by Nesterov (1988) as part of the machinery of interior point methods for linear programming. A three-times-differentiable convex function $R: \text{int}(K) \to \mathbb{R}$ is a self-concordant barrier on K if

- $|D^3 R(x)[h,h,h]| \leq 2(D^2 R(x)[h,h])^{3/2}$ for all $x \in \text{int}(K)$ and $h \in \mathbb{R}^d$.
- R is a barrier: $R(x_t) \to \infty$ whenever $x_t \to \partial K$.

It is called a ϑ-self-concordant barrier if additionally

- $DR(x)[h] \leq \sqrt{\vartheta D^2 R(x)[h,h]}$ for all $x \in \text{int}(K)$ and $h \in \mathbb{R}^d$ where ϑ is a (hopefully small) positive real value.

The local norm at $x \in \text{int}(K)$ associated with R is $\|h\|_x \triangleq \|h\|_{R''(x)}$ and its dual is $\|h\|_{x\star} = \|h\|_{R''(x)^{-1}}$. The Dikin ellipsoid of radius r at x is

$$E_r^x = \{y \colon \|y - x\|_x \leq r\}.$$

We collect the following facts about ϑ-self-concordant barriers:

Lemma 6.2 *Suppose that R is a self-concordant barrier on K. The following hold:*
(1) *The Dikin ellipsoid is contained in K: $E_1^x \subset K$ for all $x \in \text{int}(K)$.*
(2) *For all $x, y \in \text{int}(K)$,*

$$R(y) \geq R(x) + \langle R'(x), y - x \rangle + \rho(-\|x - y\|_x)$$

with $\rho(s) = -\log(1-s) - s$.
(3) $\text{tr}(R''(x)^{-1}) \leq \frac{d \, \text{diam}(K)^2}{4}$ *for all $x \in \text{int}(K)$.*
Suppose additionally that R is a ϑ-self-concordant barrier and is minimised at $0 \in K$; then with π the Minkowski functional of K,
(4) $R(x) \leq R(0) - \vartheta \log(1 - \pi(x))$ *for all $x \in \text{int}(K)$.*

For some intuition, part (1) is illustrated in Figure 6.1 and (3) is a consequence of this (see proof below). Part (2) is a kind of local strong convexity with respect to the norm $\|\cdot\|_x$. Alternatively, you can view it as an explicit bound on the Taylor series expansion of R at x by noting that $\rho(s) \sim s^2/2$ for $|s| = o(1)$. Because R is a barrier it explodes near the boundary of K. Part (4) says that this explosion is quite slow, remembering from Section 3.1 that $\pi(x) < 1$ is equivalent to $x \in \text{int}(K)$. Note that in (4) we are using Assumption 6.3. Otherwise the Minkowski functional would need to be defined relative to the minimiser of R.

6.1 Self-Concordant Barriers

Proof (✿) Part (1) appears above Equation (2.2) in the notes by Nemirovski (1996). Part (2) is Equation (2.4) in the same notes. Part (3) follows from Part (1). To see why, let $\xi \in \mathbb{S}_1^{d-1}$ and notice that $x \pm R''(x)^{-1/2}\xi \in E_1^x \subset K$. Therefore

$$\|\xi\|_{R''(x)^{-1}} = \frac{1}{2}\left\|\left(x + R''(x)^{-1/2}\xi\right) - \left(x - R''(x)^{-1/2}\xi\right)\right\| \leq \frac{\operatorname{diam}(K)}{2}.$$

The result follows because

$$\operatorname{tr}(R''(x)^{-1}) = \sum_{k=1}^{d} \|e_k\|_{R''(x)^{-1}}^2 \leq \frac{d\operatorname{diam}(K)^2}{4}$$

with $(e_k)_{k=1}^d$ the standard basis vectors. Part (4) appears as Equation (3.7) in the notes by Nemirovski (1996). □

We will always assume that the coordinate system has been chosen so that $0 \in K$ and R is minimised at **0**:

Assumption 6.3 R is a ϑ-self-concordant barrier on K and the coordinates are chosen so that $\arg\min_{x \in \operatorname{int}(K)} R(x) = \mathbf{0}$.

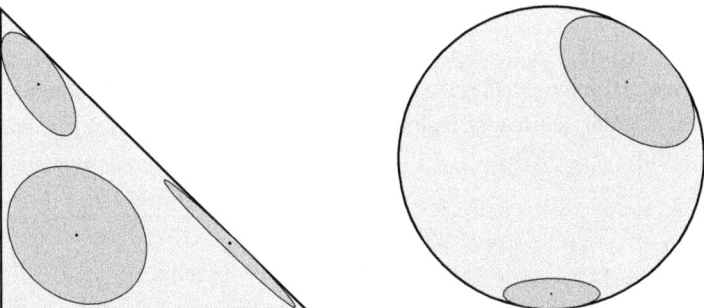

Figure 6.1 Dikin ellpsoids for a polytope and the ball using the barriers in Note 6.iv.

Lemma 6.4 *Suppose that* $\Phi : \operatorname{int}(K) \to \mathbb{R}$ *is a self-concordant barrier on* K, $x = \arg\min_{z \in \operatorname{int}(K)} \Phi(z)$ *and* $y \in \operatorname{int}(K)$ *is such that* $\|\Phi'(y)\|_{y\star} \leq \frac{1}{2}$. *Then* $\Phi(y) - \Phi(x) \leq \|\Phi'(y)\|_{y\star}^2$.

Note that $\Phi \neq R$ and we do *not* assume that Φ is minimised at **0**.

Proof (✿) Let $y \in \operatorname{int}(K)$ be such that $\|\Phi'(y)\|_{y\star} \leq \frac{1}{2}$ and abbreviate

$g = \Phi'(y)$. Then,

$$\Phi(x) \geq \Phi(y) + \langle g, x - y \rangle + \rho(-\|x - y\|_y) \qquad \text{Lemma 6.2(2)}$$
$$\geq \Phi(y) - \|g\|_{y\star} \|x - y\|_y + \rho(-\|x - y\|_y). \qquad \text{Cauchy–Schwarz}$$

Therefore,

$$\Phi(y) \leq \Phi(x) + \|g\|_{y\star} \|x - y\|_y - \rho(-\|x - y\|_y)$$
$$\leq \Phi(x) + \max_{r \geq 0} \left[r \|g\|_{y\star} - \rho(-r) \right]$$
$$= \Phi(x) - \log\left[1 - \|g\|_{y\star}\right] - \|g\|_{y\star}$$
$$\leq \Phi(x) + \|g\|_{y\star}^2$$

where the equality follows by substituting the definition of $\rho(s) = -\log(1-s) - s$ and using basic calculus and the assumption that $\|g\|_{y\star} \leq 1/2$. The final inequality follows from the elementary and naive inequality $-\log(1-t) - t \leq t^2$ for $t \leq \frac{1}{2}$. □

6.2 Follow-the-Regularised-Leader

Follow-the-regularised-leader can be viewed as a generalisation of gradient descent, which for bandits has the following abstract form. Like gradient descent, follow-the-regularised-leader maintains a sequence of iterates $(x_t)_{t=1}^n$ in K with $x_1 = \arg\min_{x \in \text{int}(K)} R(x)$.

1	**args**: $\eta > 0$
2	**for** $t = 1$ **to** n
3	compute $x_t = \arg\min_{x \in \text{int}(K)} \left[R(x) + \sum_{u=1}^{t-1} \eta \langle g_u, x \rangle \right]$
4	sample X_t based on x_t and observe Y_t
5	compute gradient estimate g_t using x_t, X_t and Y_t

Algorithm 6.1 Follow-the-regularised-leader

As with gradient descent, to make this an algorithm we need to decide on the conditional law of X_t and what to use for the gradient g_t. To get a handle on what is needed, we explain what is guaranteed on the regret relative to the linear losses defined by g_t.

6.3 Optimistic Ellipsoidal Smoothing

Theorem 6.5 *Let $x \in \text{int}(K)$ and suppose that $\eta \|g_t\|_{x_t\star} \leq 1/2$ for all t. Then for Algorithm 6.1,*

$$\widehat{\text{Reg}}_n(x) \triangleq \sum_{t=1}^{n} \langle g_t, x_t - x \rangle \leq \frac{\vartheta}{\eta} \log\left(\frac{1}{1 - \pi(x)}\right) + \eta \sum_{t=1}^{n} \|g_t\|_{x_t\star}^2.$$

The proof of Theorem 6.5 is omitted because it follows from a more general result that we prove later (Theorem 6.15).

6.3 Optimistic Ellipsoidal Smoothing

Let us momentarily drop the t indices and let $x \in \text{int}(K)$ and $f \in \mathscr{F}_b$. We will introduce a new kind of smoothing. Let Σ be positive definite and $E = \{z \in \mathbb{R}^d : \|x - z\|_{\Sigma^{-1}} \leq 1\}$, which is an ellipsoid centred at x. We will assume that $E \subset K$ and let

$$s(y) = \frac{1}{\text{vol}(E)} \int_E \left(2f\left(\tfrac{1}{2}z + \tfrac{1}{2}y\right) - f(z)\right) dz. \tag{6.1}$$

Remark 6.6 Caution! The ellipsoid E in the definition of $s(y)$ is centred at x.

The surrogate loss s behaves quite differently to the spherical smoothing used in Chapter 5. Perhaps the most notable property is that s is optimistic in the sense that $s(y) \leq f(y)$ for all $y \in K$ as we prove below. The second is that the surrogate is not a good uniform approximation of the real loss, even when $\Sigma = r\mathbb{1}$ and the precision r is very small. We want g to be an estimate of $s'(x)$, which is

$$\begin{aligned}
s'(x) &= \frac{1}{\text{vol}(E)} \int_E f'(\tfrac{1}{2}z + \tfrac{1}{2}x)\, dz \\
&= \frac{1}{\text{vol}(\mathbb{B}_1^d)} \int_{\mathbb{B}_1^d} f'(x + \tfrac{1}{2}\Sigma^{1/2}z)\, dz && \text{Change of variables} \\
&= \frac{2\Sigma^{-1/2}}{\text{vol}(\mathbb{B}_1^d)} \int_{\mathbb{S}_1^{d-1}} f(x + \tfrac{1}{2}\Sigma^{1/2}\xi)\xi\, d\xi && \text{Stokes' theorem} \\
&= \frac{2d\Sigma^{-1/2}}{\text{vol}(\mathbb{S}_1^{d-1})} \int_{\mathbb{S}_1^{d-1}} f(x + \tfrac{1}{2}\Sigma^{1/2}\xi)\xi\, d\xi. && \text{Proposition A.1(2)}
\end{aligned}$$

Please note we have cheated a little here by assuming that f is differentiable and applying Stokes' theorem. Fortunately the equality still holds even without differentiability, which is a good exercise.

Exercise 6.7 ★ Prove the equality in the above display without assuming f is differentiable.

Let ξ be uniformly distributed on $\mathbb{S}_1^{d-1}$ and $X = x + \frac{1}{2}\Sigma^{1/2}\xi$. Then, by the previous display,

$$s'(x) = 4d\Sigma^{-1}\mathbb{E}[f(X)(X-x)] \,.$$

Therefore an unbiased estimator of $s'(x)$ is

$$g = 4d\Sigma^{-1}Y(X-x) \,.$$

The above considerations yield the following lemma:

Lemma 6.8 $\mathbb{E}[g] = s'(x)$.

The next lemma explores the properties of s.

Lemma 6.9 *Suppose s is defined by (6.1) and $E = \{y: \|x - y\|_{\Sigma^{-1}} \leq 1\} \subset K$. The following hold:*

(1) *s is convex.*
(2) *$s(y) \leq f(y)$ for all $y \in K$.*
(3) *If $r \in (0, 1)$ and $\Sigma = r^2 R''(x)^{-1}$, then $\mathbb{E}[f(X) - s(x)] \leq \frac{r/2}{1-r}$.*
(4) *If f is β-smooth, then $\mathbb{E}[f(X) - s(x)] \leq \frac{3\beta \operatorname{tr}(\Sigma)}{4d}$.*
(5) *If f is α-strongly convex, then s is $\frac{\alpha}{2}$-strongly convex.*

Proof Part (1) follows immediately from convexity of f, noting that the second (negated) term in the definition of s is constant as a function of y. Part (2) follows from convexity of f as well:

$$s(y) = \frac{1}{\operatorname{vol}(E)}\int_E \left(2f\left(\tfrac{1}{2}z + \tfrac{1}{2}y\right) - f(z)\right)dz \leq \frac{1}{\operatorname{vol}(E)}\int_E f(y)\,dz = f(y) \,.$$

For part (3), let $\mathbb{R} \ni u \mapsto h_\xi(u) = f(x + u\Sigma^{1/2}\xi)$. You now have to solve the following exercise, which follows directly from the definitions.

Exercise 6.10 ★ Let v be sampled uniformly from $\mathbb{B}_1^d$ and independent of ξ, which is uniformly sampled from $\mathbb{S}_1^{d-1}$. Show that

$$\mathbb{E}[f(X)] = \mathbb{E}[h_\xi(1/2)] \quad \text{and} \quad s(x) = \mathbb{E}[2h_\xi(\|v\|/2) - h_\xi(\|v\|)] \,.$$

By definition $\Sigma = r^2 R''(x)^{-1}$ so that for $u \in [-1/r, 1/r]$, $x + u\Sigma^{1/2}\xi \in E_1^x \subset K$. Therefore h is defined on $[-1/r, 1/r]$ and $h_\xi(u) \in [0, 1]$ for all $u \in [-1/r, 1/r]$. Hence, by Corollary 3.11,

$$\operatorname{lip}_{[-1,1]}(h_\xi) \leq \frac{r}{1-r} \,. \tag{6.2}$$

Let ν be uniformly distributed on $\mathbb{B}_1^d$.

$$\mathbb{E}\left[f(X) - s(x)\right] = \mathbb{E}\left[h_\xi(1/2) + h_\xi(\|\nu\|) - 2h_\xi(\|\nu\|/2)\right]$$
$$\text{By Exercise 6.10}$$
$$= \mathbb{E}\left[(h_\xi(1/2) - h_\xi(\|\nu\|/2)) + (h_\xi(\|\nu\|) - h_\xi(\|\nu\|/2))\right]$$
$$\leq \frac{r}{1-r}\mathbb{E}\left[\left|\frac{1}{2} - \frac{\|\nu\|}{2}\right| + \left|\|\nu\| - \frac{\|\nu\|}{2}\right|\right] \quad \text{By (6.2)}$$
$$= \frac{r/2}{1-r}.$$

For part (4), by convexity $\mathbb{E}[h_\xi(u)] \geq \mathbb{E}[h_\xi(0)]$ for all $u \in \mathbb{R}$. Hence

$$\mathbb{E}\left[f(X) - s(x)\right] = \mathbb{E}\left[h_\xi(1/2) + h_\xi(\|\nu\|) - 2h_\xi(\|\nu\|/2)\right]$$
$$\text{By Exercise 6.10}$$
$$\leq \mathbb{E}\left[h_\xi(1/2) + h_\xi(\|\nu\|) - 2h_\xi(0)\right] \quad \text{convexity}$$
$$\leq \mathbb{E}\left[(1/2 + \|\nu\|)(h_\xi(1) - h_\xi(0))\right] \quad \text{convexity}$$
$$\leq \frac{3}{2}\mathbb{E}\left[f(x + \Sigma^{1/2}\xi) - f(x)\right] \quad \text{since } \mathbb{E}[\|\nu\|] \leq 1$$
$$\leq \frac{3\beta}{4}\mathbb{E}\left[\|\Sigma^{1/2}\xi\|^2\right] \quad \text{By Lemma 3.7}$$
$$= \frac{3\beta \operatorname{tr}(\Sigma)}{4d}.$$

The last equality holds because $\mathbb{E}[\|\Sigma^{1/2}\xi\|^2] = \mathbb{E}[\operatorname{tr}(\xi\xi^\top\Sigma)] = \operatorname{tr}(\mathbb{E}[\xi\xi^\top]\Sigma)$ and $\mathbb{E}[\xi\xi^\top] = \frac{1}{d}\mathbb{1}$ by a symmetry argument. Part (5) is left as a straightforward exercise. □

Exercise 6.11 ★ Prove Lemma 6.9(5).

6.4 Algorithms and Regret Analysis

We start by studying an algorithm that relies on neither smoothness nor strong convexity.

```
1  args: learning rate η > 0, r ∈ (0, 1)
2  for t = 1 to n
3     compute x_t = arg min_{x∈int(K)} Σ_{u=1}^{t-1} η ⟨g_u, x⟩ + R(x)
4     sample ξ_t uniformly from S_1^{d-1}
5     play X_t = x_t + r/2 R''(x_t)^{-1/2} ξ_t and observe Y_t
6     compute gradient g_t = 4dY_t R''(x_t)(X_t − x_t) / r^2
```

Algorithm 6.2 Follow-the-regularised-leader with ellipsoidal smoothing

Computation

Algorithm 6.2 needs to compute three non-trivial problems:

- The optimisation problem in Line 3 is a self-concordant barrier minimisation problem. Note in round $t = 1$ we have $x_t = 0$ since we assumed that R is minimised at 0. In subsequent rounds x_t can be approximated to extreme precision with $\tilde{O}(1)$ iterations of damped Newton method initialised at x_{t-1} (Exercise 6.12). Hence the computation time is dominated by the evaluation of the Hessian of R and a matrix inversion.
- You can sample from a sphere in $O(d)$ time by sampling a d-dimensional standard Gaussian and renormalising.
- The matrix inverse square root in Section 6.4 can be computed via singular value decomposition, which has complexity $O(d^3)$.

Exercise 6.12 ★★🗐 Prove that $\tilde{O}(1)$ iterations of damped Newton is sufficient to approximate x_t to extreme precision (quadratic rate). You may find Lemma 6.4 useful, along with the notes by Nemirovski (1996).

The machinery developed in Section 6.3 combined with Theorem 6.5 can be used to bound the regret of Algorithm 6.2.

Theorem 6.13 *Suppose that*

$$\eta = (\vartheta \log(n))^{\frac{3}{4}} d^{-\frac{1}{2}} n^{-\frac{3}{4}} \quad \text{and} \quad r = \min\left(1, 2d^{\frac{1}{2}} n^{-\frac{1}{4}} (\vartheta \log(n))^{\frac{1}{4}}\right).$$

Under Assumption 6.1 the expected regret of Algorithm 6.2 is upper bounded by

$$\mathbb{E}[\text{Reg}_n] \leq 1 + 4(\vartheta \log(n))^{\frac{1}{4}} d^{\frac{1}{2}} n^{\frac{3}{4}}.$$

Proof By definition, $\|X_t - x_t\|_{x_t} = \frac{r}{2} \leq \frac{1}{2}$ and therefore $X_t \in E_1^{x_t} \subset K$ where the inclusion follows from Lemma 6.2(1). Hence, the algorithm always plays inside K. Using the fact that the losses are in $\mathscr{F}_b$ it holds automatically that $\text{Reg}_n \leq n$ and when $r > \frac{1}{2}$ this already implies the bound in the theorem.

6.4 Algorithms and Regret Analysis

Suppose for the remainder that $r \leq \frac{1}{2}$. Similarly, for the same reason we may suppose for the remainder that $n \geq 4\vartheta \log(n)$. Let

$$K_{1/n} = \{x \in K : \pi(x) \leq 1 - 1/n\}$$

and $x_\star = \arg\min_{x \in K_{1/n}} \sum_{t=1}^n f_t(x)$ with ties broken arbitrarily. Such a point is guaranteed to exist by Proposition 3.13, which also shows that

$$\mathbb{E}[\text{Reg}_n] \leq 1 + \mathbb{E}[\text{Reg}_n(x_\star)].$$

Before using Theorem 6.5 we need to confirm that $\eta \|g_t\|_{x_t\star} \leq \frac{1}{2}$:

$$\eta \|g_t\|_{x_t\star} = \frac{4\eta d |Y_t|}{r^2} \|R''(x_t)(X_t - x_t)\|_{x_t\star} = \frac{2\eta d |Y_t|}{r} \leq \frac{2\eta d}{r} \leq \frac{1}{2},$$

where in the final inequality we used the assumption that $n \geq 4\vartheta \log(n)$. Let $\Sigma_t = r^2 R''(x_t)^{-1}$ and $E_t = \{y : \|x_t - y\|_{\Sigma_t^{-1}} \leq 1\} = E_r^{x_t}$. The surrogate in round t is

$$s_t(x) = \frac{1}{\text{vol}(E_t)} \int_{E_t} \left(2 f_t(\tfrac{1}{2}y + \tfrac{1}{2}x) - f_t(y)\right) dy.$$

Hence, by Theorem 6.5 and the results in Section 6.3,

$$\mathbb{E}[\text{Reg}_n] \leq 1 + \mathbb{E}\left[\sum_{t=1}^n f_t(X_t) - f_t(x_\star)\right]$$

$$\leq 1 + \frac{nr/2}{1-r} + \mathbb{E}\left[\sum_{t=1}^n s_t(x_t) - s_t(x_\star)\right] \qquad \text{Lemma 6.9(2)(3)}$$

$$\leq 1 + \frac{nr/2}{1-r} + \mathbb{E}\left[\sum_{t=1}^n \langle s_t'(x_t), x_t - x_\star \rangle\right] \qquad \text{Lemma 6.9(1)}$$

$$= 1 + \frac{nr/2}{1-r} + \mathbb{E}\left[\sum_{t=1}^n \langle g_t, x_t - x_\star \rangle\right] \qquad \text{Lemma 6.8}$$

$$\leq 1 + \frac{nr/2}{1-r} + \frac{\vartheta \log(n)}{\eta} + \mathbb{E}\left[\sum_{t=1}^n \eta \|g_t\|_{x_t\star}^2\right] \qquad \text{Theorem 6.5}$$

$$\leq 1 + nr + \frac{\vartheta \log(n)}{\eta} + \frac{4\eta n d^2}{r^2},$$

where the final inequality follows since $r \leq 1/2$ and $Y_t \in [0,1]$ and

$$\eta \|g_t\|_{x_t\star}^2 = \eta \left\| \frac{4 d Y_t R''(x_t)(X_t - x_t)}{r^2} \right\|_{x_t\star}^2 \leq \frac{16\eta d^2}{r^4} \|X_t - x_t\|_{R''(x_t)}^2 = \frac{4\eta d^2}{r^2}.$$

The result follows by substituting the values of the constants. $\square$

Notice how the dependence on the diameter that appeared in Theorem 5.6 has been replaced with a dependence on the self-concordance parameter ϑ and logarithmic dependence on the horizon. This can be a significant improvement. For example, when K is a ball, then the bound in Theorem 5.6 depends linearly on $\sqrt{\text{diam}(K)}$ while with a suitable self-concordant barrier the regret in Theorem 6.13 replaces this with $\sqrt{\log(n)}$. Essentially what is happening is that Algorithm 6.2 moves faster deep in the interior where the losses are necessarily more Lipschitz, whereas Algorithm 5.2 does not adapt the amount of regularisation to the location of x_t. For smooth functions the rate can be improved by using Lemma 6.9(4) instead of Lemma 6.9(3).

Theorem 6.14 *Suppose the losses are in $\mathscr{F}_{\mathrm{b,sm}}$, there is no noise and*

$$r^2 = \min\left(4,\ 8 \cdot 2^{1/3} \cdot 3^{-2/3} d^{\frac{2}{3}} (\vartheta \log(n))^{\frac{1}{3}} \beta^{-\frac{2}{3}} \text{diam}(K)^{-\frac{4}{3}} n^{-\frac{1}{3}}\right) \quad \text{and}$$

$$\eta = \frac{r}{2d}\sqrt{\frac{\vartheta \log(n)}{n}}.$$

Then the expected regret of Algorithm 6.2 is upper bounded by

$$\mathbb{E}[\text{Reg}_n] \leq 1 + 3d\sqrt{\vartheta n \log(n)} + \left(\frac{9}{2}\right)^{2/3} (\vartheta \beta \,\text{diam}(K)^2 \log(n))^{\frac{1}{3}} d^{\frac{2}{3}} n^{\frac{2}{3}}.$$

Proof Note the condition that $r^2 \leq 4$ is needed to ensure that $X_t \in K$. Repeat the argument in the proof of Theorem 6.13 but replace Lemma 6.9(3) with Lemma 6.9(4), which yields

$$\mathbb{E}[\text{Reg}_n] \leq 1 + \frac{\vartheta \log(n)}{\eta} + \frac{4\eta n d^2}{r^2} + \frac{3\beta r^2}{4d} \sum_{t=1}^{n} \text{tr}(R''(x_t)^{-1})$$

$$\leq 1 + \frac{\vartheta \log(n)}{\eta} + \frac{4\eta n d^2}{r^2} + \frac{3\beta n r^2 \,\text{diam}(K)^2}{16}$$

$$= 1 + \frac{4d}{r}\sqrt{n\vartheta \log(n)} + \frac{3\beta n r^2 \,\text{diam}(K)^2}{16}$$

where in the second inequality we used Lemma 6.2(3) and in the equality the definition of η. The result follows by substituting the definition of r and using the fact that if $r^2 = 4$, then

$$8 \cdot 2^{1/3} \cdot 3^{-2/3} d^{2/3} (\vartheta \log(n))^{1/3} \beta^{-2/3} \,\text{diam}(K)^{-4/3} n^{-1/3} \geq 4,$$

which implies that $\frac{3\beta n r^2 \,\text{diam}(K)^2}{16} \leq d\sqrt{\vartheta n \log(n)}$. □

The diameter now appears in the bound, as it must. Otherwise you could scale the coordinates and make the regret vanish (Section 3.3). There is no hope of removing the $\sqrt{n}$ term from Theorem 6.14, since when $\beta = 0$ the losses are linear and the lower bound for linear bandits says the regret should be at least $\Omega(d\sqrt{n})$ (Dani et al., 2008).

6.5 Smoothness and Strong Convexity

With both strong convexity and smoothness a version of follow-the-regularised-leader can achieve $O(\sqrt{n})$ regret. The main modification of the algorithm is that the linear surrogate loss functions are replaced by quadratics. For this a generalisation of Theorem 6.5 is required.

Theorem 6.15 *Suppose that $(\hat{f}_t)_{t=1}^n$ is a sequence of self-concordant functions from K to $\mathbb{R}$ and let*

$$x_t = \underbrace{\arg\min_{x \in \text{int}(K)} \left(R(x) + \eta \sum_{u=1}^{t-1} \hat{f}_u(x) \right)}_{\Phi_{t-1}(x)} \quad \text{and} \quad \|\cdot\|_{x_t \star} = \|\cdot\|_{\Phi''_t(x_t)^{-1}}.$$

Then, provided that $\eta \|\hat{f}'_t(x_t)\|_{x_t \star} \leq \frac{1}{2}$ for all t, for any $x \in \text{int}(K)$,

$$\widehat{\text{Reg}}_n(x) = \sum_{t=1}^n \left(\hat{f}_t(x_t) - \hat{f}_t(x) \right) \leq \frac{\vartheta}{\eta} \log\left(\frac{1}{1 - \pi(x)} \right) + \eta \sum_{t=1}^n \|\hat{f}'_t(x_t)\|_{x_t \star}^2,$$

Theorem 6.5 is recovered by choosing $\hat{f}_t(x) = \langle g_t, x \rangle$.

Proof By the definition of Φ_t,

$$\widehat{\text{Reg}}_n(x) = \sum_{t=1}^n \left(\hat{f}_t(x_t) - \hat{f}_t(x) \right)$$

$$= \frac{1}{\eta} \sum_{t=1}^n (\Phi_t(x_t) - \Phi_{t-1}(x_t)) - \frac{\Phi_n(x)}{\eta} + \frac{R(x)}{\eta}$$

$$= \frac{1}{\eta} \sum_{t=1}^n (\Phi_t(x_t) - \Phi_t(x_{t+1})) + \frac{\Phi_n(x_{n+1})}{\eta} - \frac{\Phi_n(x)}{\eta} + \frac{R(x) - R(x_1)}{\eta}$$

$$\leq \frac{1}{\eta} \sum_{t=1}^n (\Phi_t(x_t) - \Phi_t(x_{t+1})) + \frac{R(x) - R(x_1)}{\eta} \qquad \Phi_n(x_{n+1}) \leq \Phi_n(x)$$

$$\leq \eta \sum_{t=1}^n \|\hat{f}'_t(x_t)\|_{x_t \star}^2 + \frac{R(x) - R(x_1)}{\eta} \qquad \text{Lemma 6.4}$$

$$\leq \frac{\vartheta}{\eta} \log\left(\frac{1}{1 - \pi(x)} \right) + \eta \sum_{t=1}^n \|\hat{f}_t(x_t)\|_{t \star}^2, \qquad \text{Lemma 6.2(4)}$$

where the application of Lemma 6.4 relied on the assumption that $\eta\|\hat{f}'_t(x_t)\|_{t\star} \leq \frac{1}{2}$ and the fact that x_t minimises Φ_{t-1} on $\text{int}(K)$, which implies that $\Phi'_t(x_t) = \Phi'_{t-1}(x_t) + \hat{f}'_t(x_t) = \hat{f}'_t(x_t)$. □

The algorithm for smooth and strongly convex losses uses follow-the-regularised-leader with a self-concordant barrier and quadratic loss estimates.

---

1 **args**: learning rate $\eta > 0$
2 **for** $t = 1$ **to** n
3   let $x_t = \arg\min_{x \in \text{int}(K)}\left[R(x) + \eta \sum_{u=1}^{t-1}\left(\langle g_u, x\rangle + \frac{\alpha}{4}\|x - x_u\|^2\right)\right]$
4   let $\Sigma_t^{-1} = R''(x_t) + \frac{\eta\alpha t}{2}\mathbb{1}$
5   sample ξ_t uniformly from $\mathbb{S}_1^{d-1}$
6   play $X_t = x_t + \frac{1}{2}\Sigma_t^{1/2}\xi_t$ and observe Y_t
7   compute gradient $g_t = 4dY_t\Sigma_t^{-1}(X_t - x_t)$

Algorithm 6.3 Follow-the-regularised-leader with ellipsoidal smoothing

Let us think a little about why Algorithm 6.3 makes sense. As usual, let s_t be the surrogate as defined in Section 6.3, which by Lemma 6.9 is $\frac{\alpha}{4}$-strongly convex. The quantity g_t is an unbiased estimator of $s'_t(x_t)$. So Algorithm 6.3 is playing follow-the-regularised-leader with quadratic approximations of s_t. The inverse covariance Σ_t^{-1} is chosen to be the Hessian of the optimisation objective to find x_t. From a technical perspective this makes sense because the covariance of the gradient estimator plays well with the dual norm in the last term in Theorem 6.15. More intuitively, when the losses have high curvature, then the algorithm needs to smooth on a smaller region, which corresponds to a larger inverse covariance. This introduces additional variance in the gradient estimators, which is offset by the regularisation arising from strong convexity.

Theorem 6.16 *Suppose the losses are in $\mathscr{F}_{\text{b,sm,sc}}$, there is no noise and*

$$\eta = \frac{1}{2d}\sqrt{\frac{\vartheta\log(n) + \frac{3\beta}{2\alpha}[1 + \log(n)]}{n}}.$$

Then the expected regret of Algorithm 6.3 is upper bounded by

$$\mathbb{E}[\text{Reg}_n] \leq 1 + 4d\sqrt{n\left(\vartheta\log(n) + \frac{3\beta}{2\alpha}(1 + \log(n))\right)}.$$

Proof Assume that $n \geq 4(\vartheta\log(n) + \frac{2\beta}{\alpha}(1 + \log(n)))$, since otherwise the regret bound holds trivially using the assumption that the losses are bounded so

6.5 Smoothness and Strong Convexity

that $\mathbb{E}[\text{Reg}_n] \leq n$. The same argument as in the proof of Theorem 6.13 shows that X_t is in the Dikin ellipsoid associated with R at x_t and therefore is in K. Let $E_t = E(x_t, \Sigma_t)$ and

$$s_t = \frac{1}{\text{vol}(E_t)} \int_{E_t} \left(2 f_t(\tfrac{1}{2} x_t + \tfrac{1}{2} z) - f_t(z)\right) dz,$$

which is the optimistic surrogate from Section 6.3. Like in Theorem 6.13, let $K_{1/n} = \{x \in K : \pi(x) \leq 1 - 1/n\}$ and $x_\star = \arg\min_{x \in K_{1/n}} \sum_{t=1}^{n} f_t(x)$, which by Proposition 3.13 and Lemma 6.9(2)(4) means that

$$\mathbb{E}[\text{Reg}_n] \leq 1 + \mathbb{E}[\text{Reg}_n(x_\star)]$$

$$= 1 + \mathbb{E}\left[\sum_{t=1}^{n} (f_t(X_t) - f_t(x_\star))\right]$$

$$\leq 1 + \mathbb{E}\left[\sum_{t=1}^{n} \left(s_t(x_t) - s_t(x_\star) + \frac{3\beta}{4d} \text{tr}(\Sigma_t)\right)\right].$$

Next, let $\hat{f}_t(x) = \langle g_t, x - x_t \rangle + \frac{\alpha}{4} \|x - x_t\|^2$. By Lemma 6.9(5), s_t is $\frac{\alpha}{2}$-strongly convex and therefore

$$\mathbb{E}\left[\sum_{t=1}^{n} (s_t(x_t) - s_t(x_\star))\right] \leq \mathbb{E}\left[\sum_{t=1}^{n} \left(\langle \mathbb{E}_{t-1}[g_t], x_t - x_\star \rangle - \frac{\alpha}{4} \|x_t - x_\star\|^2\right)\right]$$

$$= \mathbb{E}\left[\sum_{t=1}^{n} (\hat{f}_t(x_t) - \hat{f}_t(x_\star))\right]$$

$$\leq \frac{\vartheta \log(n)}{\eta} + \eta \mathbb{E}\left[\sum_{t=1}^{n} \|g_t\|_{\Sigma_t}^2\right] \qquad \text{Theorem 6.15}$$

$$\leq \frac{\vartheta \log(n)}{\eta} + 4\eta n d^2.$$

The application of Theorem 6.15 relies on $\eta \|g_t\|_{\Sigma_t} \leq \frac{1}{2}$, which follows from the definition of η and our assumption that n is large enough. Using the definition of Σ_t,

$$\frac{3\beta}{4d} \sum_{t=1}^{n} \text{tr}(\Sigma_t) \leq \frac{3\beta}{2\alpha\eta} \sum_{t=1}^{n} \frac{1}{t} \leq \frac{3\beta}{2\alpha\eta} (1 + \log(n)).$$

Combining everything shows that

$$\mathbb{E}[\text{Reg}_n] \leq 1 + 4\eta n d^2 + \frac{1}{\eta}\left(\vartheta \log(n) + \frac{3\beta}{2\alpha}(1 + \log(n))\right).$$

The result follows by substituting the definition of η. □

6.6 Stochastic Setting and Variance (🦘)

In most of this book it as assumed that the losses are bounded in $[0, 1]$ and the noise is subgaussian. You may wonder what happens in the stochastic setting if the variance of the noise is much smaller than the range of the loss function. Note, there is nothing substantive to be gained in the adversarial setting since the loss functions themselves can be noisy. In this section we explain one way to handle this situation by slightly modifying Algorithm 6.2 and showing how its regret depends on the variance of the noise. The modification and analysis used here generalises to all the other results in this chapter and many beyond. The operating assumption in this section is the following:

Assumption 6.17 The setting is stochastic: $f_t = f$ for all rounds with $f \in \mathscr{F}_b$. The observed loss is $Y_t = f(X_t) + \varepsilon_t$ where the noise ε_t satisfies

(1) *(zero mean)*: $\mathbb{E}_{t-1}[\varepsilon_t | X_t] = 0$;

(2) *(boundedness)*: $|\varepsilon_t| \leq 1$ almost surely; and

(3) *(variance)*: $\mathbb{E}_{t-1}[\varepsilon_t^2 | X_t] \leq \sigma^2$ for some known $\sigma > 0$.

Remark 6.18 The boundedness assumption could be relaxed with minor modifications to the analysis if we instead assumed that ε_t was conditionally σ-subgaussian: $\mathbb{E}_{t-1}[\exp(\varepsilon_t^2/\sigma^2)|X_t] \leq 2$. Concretely, boundedness is only used in (6.3). When the noise is subgaussian you need to bound the difference between losses with high probability. The regret should be the same except possibly a logarithmic factor that vanishes as $n \to \infty$.

Let $\text{ODD}(t)$ be the set of odd natural numbers less than or equal to t. We assume for simplicity that the horizon n is even so that $\text{ODD}(n) = \{1, 3, \ldots, n-1\}$.

---

1 **args**: learning rate $\eta > 0$, $r \in (0, 1)$
2 **for** $t \in \text{ODD}(n)$:
3   compute $x_t = \arg\min_{x \in \text{int}(K)} \sum_{u \in \text{ODD}(t-1)} \eta \langle g_u, x \rangle + R(x)$
4   sample ξ_t uniformly from $\mathbb{S}_1^{d-1}$
5   play $X_t = x_t$ and observe Y_t
6   play $X_{t+1} = x_t + \frac{r}{2} R''(x_t)^{-1/2} \xi_t$ and observe Y_{t+1}
7   compute gradient $g_t = \frac{4d(Y_{t+1} - Y_t) R''(x_t)(X_{t+1} - x_t)}{r^2}$

Algorithm 6.4 Follow-the-regularised-leader with ellipsoidal smoothing

6.6 Stochastic Setting and Variance

Theorem 6.19 *Suppose that Algorithm 6.4 is run with parameters*

$$r = \max\left(d\sqrt{\frac{\vartheta \log(n)}{n}}, d^{1/2}\sigma^{1/2}n^{-1/4}(\vartheta \log(n))^{1/4}\right) \quad \text{and}$$

$$\eta = \frac{1}{12d}\sqrt{\frac{\vartheta \log(n)}{n}} \min\left(\frac{r}{\sigma}, 1\right).$$

Then, under Assumption 6.17, the regret is bounded by

$$\mathbb{E}[\mathrm{Reg}_n] = O\left(d\sqrt{n\vartheta \log(n)} + \sigma^{1/2}d^{1/2}(\vartheta \log(n))^{1/4}n^{3/4}\right).$$

When n is large, then the bound in Theorem 6.19 improves on the bound in Theorem 6.13 by a factor of $\sigma^{1/2}$. Alternatively, if the noise vanishes, the rate improves to $\tilde{O}(n^{1/2})$. The noise-free setting is quite special, since in this case there exist algorithms with much smaller sample complexity or regret (Yudin and Nemirovskii, 1976; Protasov, 1996). Nevertheless, in intermediate regimes the improvement is non-negligible.

Proof Without loss of generality assume that $r \leq 1/2$, since otherwise the claimed regret bound holds vacuously for any algorithm.

Exercise 6.20 Suppose that $t \in \mathrm{ODD}(n)$. Show that $|f(X_t) - f(X_{t+1})| \leq r/2$.

Suppose that $t \in \mathrm{ODD}(n)$. By definition,

$$\eta \|g_t\|_{x_t \star} = \frac{4\eta d |Y_{t+1} - Y_t|}{r^2} \|R''(x_t)(X_t - x_t)\|_{x_t \star}$$

$$= \frac{2\eta d |Y_{t+1} - Y_t|}{r} \overset{(a)}{\leq} \frac{6\eta d}{r} \overset{(b)}{\leq} \frac{1}{2}, \quad (6.3)$$

where (a) follows from Assumption 6.17(2) and the definitions to bound $|Y_{t+1} - Y_t| \leq 3$ and (b) from the definitions of η and r. Hence, repeating more or less exactly the proof of Theorem 6.13 shows that

$$\mathbb{E}[\mathrm{Reg}_n] \leq 1 + nr + \frac{\vartheta \log(n/2)}{\eta} + \mathbb{E}\left[\sum_{t \in \mathrm{ODD}(n)} \eta \|g_t\|_{x_t \star}^2\right]. \quad (6.4)$$

Moreover, when $t \in \mathrm{ODD}(n)$,

$$\eta \|g_t\|_{x_t \star}^2 = \eta \left\|\frac{4d(Y_{t+1} - Y_t)R''(x_t)(X_t - x_t)}{r^2}\right\|_{x_t \star}^2$$

$$\leq \frac{4\eta d^2(Y_{t+1} - Y_t)^2}{r^2}. \quad (6.5)$$

The expectation of $(Y_{t+1} - Y_t)^2$ is bounded by

$$\mathbb{E}[(Y_{t+1} - Y_t)^2] = \mathbb{E}[(f(X_{t+1}) + \varepsilon_{t+1} - f(X_t) - \varepsilon_t)^2]$$
$$\stackrel{(a)}{\leq} \mathbb{E}[(f(X_{t+1}) - f(x_t))^2] + \mathbb{E}[(\varepsilon_t - \varepsilon_{t+1})^2]$$
$$\stackrel{(b)}{\leq} \mathbb{E}[(f(X_{t+1}) - f(x_t))^2] + 2\sigma^2$$
$$\stackrel{(c)}{\leq} \frac{r^2}{4} + 2\sigma^2.$$

where (a) and (b) follow from Assumption 6.17 and (c) since $|f(X_{t+1}) - f(x_t)| \leq r/2$ by Exercise 6.20. Therefore

$$\mathbb{E}\left[\sum_{t \in \text{ODD}(n)} (Y_{t+1} - Y_t)^2\right] \leq n\sigma^2 + \frac{nr^2}{8}.$$

Combining this with (6.4) and (6.5) shows that

$$\mathbb{E}[\text{Reg}_n] \leq 1 + nr + \frac{\vartheta \log(n/2)}{\eta} + \frac{4\eta d^2}{r^2} \mathbb{E}\left[\sum_{t \in \text{ODD}(n)} (Y_{t+1} - Y_t)^2\right]$$
$$\leq 1 + nr + \frac{\vartheta \log(n/2)}{\eta} + \frac{4\eta d^2}{r^2}\left(n\sigma^2 + \frac{nr^2}{8}\right).$$

The claim now follows by substituting the constants and naive simplification. □

Exercise 6.21 ★★? Explore the possiblity of using the technique developed here for other algorithms in this book.

6.7 Notes

6.i The notion of self-concordance was introduced and refined by Nesterov (1988) and Nesterov and Nemirovsky (1989), applying it to interior point methods. The first application of self-concordance to bandits was by Abernethy et al. (2008), who studied linear bandits. Theorem 6.13 seems to be new while Theorem 6.14 is by Saha and Tewari (2011). Algorithm 6.3 and Theorem 6.16 are due to Hazan and Levy (2014). Theorem 6.19 is new but the idea is standard (Akhavan et al., 2024b, and many others). The class of smooth and strongly convex losses already appeared in the work by Polyak and Tsybakov (1990), who considered the stochastic unconstrained and improper settings. Their results show that the optimal simple regret in this case is $\Theta(n^{-1/2})$ with non-specified dependence on other quantities like the dimension. Akhavan et al. (2020, 2024a)

6.7 Notes

consider the same setting but with explicit constants and in some settings nearly matching lower bounds.

6.ii At no point in this chapter did we need Lipschitz losses. The analysis essentially exploits the fact that convex functions cannot have large gradients except very close to the boundary, where the regularisation provided by the self-concordant barrier prevents the blowup in variance from severely impacting the regret.

6.iii We have made several improvements to the statistical efficiency relative to the algorithm presented in Chapter 5. In exchange the algorithms are more complicated and computationally less efficient. Algorithms based on gradient descent run in $O(d)$ time per round except those rounds where a projection is needed. Furthermore, even when the projection is needed it is with respect to the euclidean norm and likely to be extremely fast. Meanwhile the algorithms in this chapter need a singular value decomposition to compute X_t, solve an optimisation problem to find x_t and need oracle access to a ϑ-self-concordant barrier.

6.iv The reader interested in knowing more about $(\vartheta\text{-})$self-concordant barriers is referred to the wonderful notes by Nemirovski (1996). The most obvious question is whether or not these things even exist. Here are some examples:

- When $K = \{x \colon \langle a_i, x \rangle \leq b_i, 1 \leq i \leq k\}$ is a polytope defined by k half-spaces, then $R(x) = -\sum_{i=1}^{k} \log(b_i - \langle a_i, x \rangle)$ is called the logarithmic barrier and is k-self-concordant.
- When $K = \{x \colon \|x\| \leq \rho\}$ is a ball, then $R(x) = -\log(\rho^2 - \|x\|^2)$ is a 1-self-concordant barrier on K.
- For any convex body K there exists a ϑ-self-concordant barrier with $\vartheta \leq d$. Specifically, the entropic barrier (Chewi, 2023; Bubeck and Eldan, 2015) and the universal barrier (Nesterov and Nemirovski, 1994; Lee and Yue, 2021) satisfy this.

6.v The surrogate loss only appears in the analysis. Interestingly, Hazan and Levy (2014) and Saha and Tewari (2011) analysed their algorithms using the surrogate

$$s_t(y) = \frac{1}{\text{vol}(E_r^{x_t})} \int_{E_r^{x_t} - x_t} f_t(y+u) \, du \, ,$$

which is the ellipsoidal analogue of the surrogate used in Chapter 5. Except for a constant factor this surrogate has the same gradient at x_t as the surrogate we used, which means the resulting algorithms are the same. The difficulty is that the surrogate above is not defined on all of K, which forces various contortions or assumptions in the analysis.

6.vi Even when $\beta = 0$, the regret upper bound of Algorithm 6.2 is still $\Omega(\sqrt{n})$. Since $\beta = 0$ corresponds to linear losses, the lower bounds for linear bandits (Table 2.1) show that this is not improvable. Hence, no amount of smoothness by itself can improve the regret beyond the $\sqrt{n}$ barrier. Combining higher-order smoothness (see Note 1.i) with strong convexity, however, does lead to improved regret (Polyak and Tsybakov, 1990; Akhavan et al., 2020; Novitskii and Gasnikov, 2021; Akhavan et al., 2024b). These works prove upper and lower bounds showing that the minimax simple regret is $\Theta(n^{(1-p)/p})$ in the unconstrained and improper settings and with slightly varying assumptions and dependence on the constants. This is much better than $O(1/\sqrt{n})$ when $p \gg 2$. Of these, the most refined is by Akhavan et al. (2024b), who prove an upper bound on the simple regret $O(\frac{1}{\alpha}(d^2/n)^{(p-1)/p})$ and a lower bound on the same of $\Omega(\frac{d}{\alpha}n^{-(p-1)/p})$, which match when $p = 2$. Note that the correct dependence on the smoothness parameter β has not yet been nailed down and there are some mild conditions on the magnitude of the parameters. The aforementioned works also study a variety of alternatives to strong convexity and more flexible noise models than what is assumed in this book.

6.vii Theorems 6.13 and 6.14 bound the regret for the same algorithm with different learning rates and smoothing parameters. You should wonder if it is possible to obtain the best of both bounds with a single algorithm by adaptively tuning the learning rates. At present this is not known as far as we are aware.

7
Linear and Quadratic Bandits

Function classes like $\mathscr{F}_b$ are non-parametric. In this chapter we shift gears by studying two important parametric classes: $\mathscr{F}_{b,\text{lin}}$ and $\mathscr{F}_{b,\text{quad}}$. The main purpose of this chapter is to use the machinery designed for linear bandits to prove an upper bound on the minimax regret for quadratic bandits. On the positive side the approach is both elementary and instructive. More negatively, the resulting algorithm is not computationally efficient. Before the algorithms and regret analysis we need three tools: covering numbers, optimal experimental design and the exponential weights algorithm.

7.1 Covering Numbers

Given $A, B \subset \mathbb{R}^d$, the external/internal covering numbers are defined by

$$N(A, B) = \min\left\{|\mathscr{C}| : \mathscr{C} \subset \mathbb{R}^d, A \subset \bigcup_{x \in \mathscr{C}} (x + B)\right\} \quad \text{and}$$

$$\bar{N}(A, B) = \min\left\{|\mathscr{C}| : \mathscr{C} \subset A, A \subset \bigcup_{x \in \mathscr{C}} (x + B)\right\}.$$

Both are the smallest number of translates of B needed to cover A, with the latter demanding that the 'centres' are in A. Obviously $N(A, B) \leq \bar{N}(A, B)$. The inequality can also be strict, as you will show in the following exercise.

Exercise 7.1 ★ Suppose that $A, B, C \subset \mathbb{R}^d$ and $A \subset B$. Show the following:
(1) $N(A, C) \leq \bar{N}(A, C)$ and give an example where $N(A, C) < \bar{N}(A, C)$.
(2) $N(A, C) \leq N(B, C)$ and give an example where $\bar{N}(A, C) > \bar{N}(B, C)$.
(3) $\bar{N}(A, C - C) \leq N(A, C)$.

The next proposition follows from Fact 4.1.4 and Corollary 4.1.15 in the book by Artstein-Avidan et al. (2015).

Proposition 7.2 *Suppose that $A \subset \mathbb{R}^d$ is centrally symmetric, compact and convex. Then, for any $\varepsilon \in (0, 1)$,*

$$\bar{N}(A, \varepsilon A) \leq N(A, \tfrac{\varepsilon}{2} A) \leq \left(1 + \tfrac{4}{\varepsilon}\right)^d.$$

Proposition 7.3 *Suppose that $K \subset \mathbb{R}^d$ is compact and $A = \mathrm{conv}(K - K)$. Then*

$$\bar{N}(K, \varepsilon A) \leq \left(1 + \frac{4}{\varepsilon}\right)^d.$$

Proof Since A is symmetric, $A - A = 2A$. By your solution to Exercise 7.1(3) and (2), Proposition 7.2, and letting $x \in K$ be arbitrary,

$$\bar{N}(K, \varepsilon A) \leq N(K, \tfrac{\varepsilon}{2} A) = N(K - \{x\}, \tfrac{\varepsilon}{2} A) \leq N(A, \tfrac{\varepsilon}{2} A) \leq \left(1 + \tfrac{4}{\varepsilon}\right)^d. \qquad \square$$

Proposition 7.4 *Suppose that $\varepsilon \in (0, 1)$ and $A \subset \mathbb{B}_r^d$ with $r \geq \varepsilon$. Then*

$$\bar{N}(A, \mathbb{B}_\varepsilon^d) \leq \left(1 + \frac{4r}{\varepsilon}\right)^d.$$

Proof By Exercise 7.1(3)(2) and Proposition 7.2,

$$\bar{N}(A, \mathbb{B}_\varepsilon^d) \leq N(A, \mathbb{B}_{\varepsilon/2}^d) \leq N(\mathbb{B}_r^d, \mathbb{B}_{\varepsilon/2}^d) = N(\mathbb{B}_r^d, \tfrac{\varepsilon}{2r}\mathbb{B}_r^d) \leq \left(1 + \tfrac{4r}{\varepsilon}\right)^d. \qquad \square$$

7.2 Optimal Design

Suppose that A is a nonempty compact subset of $\mathbb{R}^d$ and $\theta \in \mathbb{R}^d$ is unknown. A learner samples X from some probability measure π on A and observes $Y = \langle X, \theta \rangle$. How can this information be used to estimate θ? A simple idea is to use importance-weighted least squares. Let $G_\pi = \int_A xx^\top \, d\pi(x)$, which is called the design matrix. Assume for a moment that G_π is invertible and let

$$\hat{\theta} = G_\pi^{-1} XY.$$

A simple calculation shows that $\mathbb{E}[\hat{\theta}] = \theta$, which implies that $\mathbb{E}[\langle \hat{\theta}, x \rangle] = \langle x, \theta \rangle$ for all $x \in A$. So $\langle \hat{\theta}, x \rangle$ is an unbiased estimator of $\langle x, \theta \rangle$. Assuming that $\langle x, \theta \rangle \in [0, 1]$ for all $x \in A$, then the second moment is bounded by

$$\mathbb{E}\left[\langle \hat{\theta}, x \rangle^2\right] = \mathbb{E}\left[Y^2 x^\top G_\pi^{-1} XX^\top G_\pi^{-1} x\right] \leq \mathbb{E}\left[x^\top G_\pi^{-1} XX^\top G_\pi^{-1} x\right] = \|x\|_{G_\pi^{-1}}^2.$$

The following theorem shows there exists a π such that the right-hand side is at most d for all $x \in A$.

Theorem 7.5 (Kiefer and Wolfowitz 1960) *For any nonempty compact $A \subset \mathbb{R}^d$ with $\text{span}(A) = \mathbb{R}^d$ there exists a probability measure π supported on a subset of A such that $G_\pi = \int_A xx^\top \, d\pi(x)$ is invertible and*

$$\|x\|^2_{G_\pi^{-1}} \leq d \text{ for all } x \in A.$$

Remarkably the constant d is the best achievable for *any* compact A with $\text{span}(A) = \mathbb{R}^d$ in the sense that

$$\min_{\pi \in \Delta(A)} \max_{x \in A} \|x\|^2_{G_\pi^{-1}} = d.$$

The assumption that $\text{span}(A) = \mathbb{R}^d$ was more or less only needed to ensure that G_π is invertible. Given a matrix Q let Q^+ be the pseudoinverse (see Section A.2).

Theorem 7.6 *For any nonempty compact $A \subset \mathbb{R}^d$ there exists a probability measure π supported on a subset of A such that $A \subset \text{im}(G_\pi^\top)$ and*

$$\|x\|^2_{G_\pi^+} \leq \dim(\text{span}(A)) \text{ for all } x \in A,$$

where $G_\pi = \int_A xx^\top d\pi(x)$.

The requirement in Theorem 7.6 that $A \subset \text{im}(G_\pi^\top)$ is essential and corresponds to G_π being invertible when restricted to the subspace spanned by A.

Exercise 7.7 ★   Prove Theorem 7.6.

7.3 Exponential Weights

Let $\mathscr{C}$ be a finite set and $\ell_1, \ldots, \ell_n$ a sequence of functions from $\mathscr{C} \to \mathbb{R}$. The set $\mathscr{C}$ is sometimes referred to as the set of experts and $\ell_t(a)$ is the loss suffered by expert a in round t. A learner chooses a sequence of probability distributions $(q_t)_{t=1}^n$ in $\Delta(\mathscr{C})$ where q_t can depend on $\ell_1, \ldots, \ell_{t-1}$. Note that this is not a bandit setting. The entire loss function ℓ_t is observed after round t. The learner's aim is to be competitive with the best expert in hindsight, which is measured by the regret

$$\widehat{\text{Reg}}_n = \max_{b \in \mathscr{C}} \sum_{t=1}^n \left[\sum_{a \in \mathscr{C}} q_t(a) \ell_t(a) - \ell_t(b) \right].$$

The quantity $\sum_{a \in \mathscr{C}} q_t(a) \ell_t(a)$ is the average loss suffered by the learner if they follow the advice of expert a with probability $q_t(a)$. Given a learning rate $\eta > 0$, define a distribution q_t on $\mathscr{C}$ by

$$q_t(a) = \frac{\exp\left(-\eta \sum_{u=1}^{t-1} \ell_u(a)\right)}{\sum_{b \in \mathscr{C}} \exp\left(-\eta \sum_{u=1}^{t-1} \ell_u(b)\right)}, \tag{7.1}$$

which is called the exponential weights distribution. Staring at the definition you can see that q_t puts more mass relatively speaking on experts for which the cumulative loss is smaller. That exponential weights has small regret is perhaps the most fundamental result in online learning, as illustrated by the many applications and implications (Cesa-Bianchi and Lugosi, 2006).

Theorem 7.8 *Suppose that $\eta |\ell_t(a)| \leq 1$ for all $1 \leq t \leq n$, then the regret when q_t is given by (7.1) is upper bounded by*

$$\widehat{\text{Reg}}_n \leq \frac{\log |\mathscr{C}|}{\eta} + \eta \sum_{t=1}^{n} \sum_{a \in \mathscr{C}} q_t(a) \ell_t(a)^2.$$

Remark 7.9 There is no convexity here but the bound in Theorem 7.8 has some kind of symbolic resemblance to the bounds for gradient descent and follow-the-regularised-leader (for example, Theorem 5.2). This is no accident. Exponential weights is equivalent to follow-the-regularised-leader on the convex space of probability measures $\Delta(\mathscr{C})$ with unnormalised negentropy regularisation. The map $\Delta(\mathscr{C}) \colon q \mapsto \sum_{a \in \mathscr{C}} q(a) \ell_t(a)$ is linear and hence the tools from convex optimisation can be used.

Proof of Theorem 7.8 The following two inequalities provide crude explicit bounds on the series expansion of $\exp(\cdot)$:

$$\exp(-x) \leq 1 - x + x^2 \text{ for all } x \geq -1 \text{ ; and} \tag{7.2}$$

$$\log(1 + x) \leq x \text{ for all } x > -1. \tag{7.3}$$

Let $b \in \mathscr{C}$ and $D_t = \log(1/q_t(b))$. Note that q_{t+1} is the probability distribution with

$$q_{t+1}(b) \propto \exp\left(-\eta \sum_{u=1}^{t} \ell_u(b)\right) = \exp(-\eta \ell_t(b)) \underbrace{\exp\left(-\eta \sum_{u=1}^{t-1} \ell_u(b)\right)}_{\propto q_t}.$$

Therefore

$$q_{t+1}(b) = \frac{q_t(b) \exp(-\eta \ell_t(b))}{\sum_{a \in \mathscr{C}} q_t(a) \exp(-\eta \ell_t(a))}.$$

Then,

$$D_{t+1} = \log\left(\frac{1}{q_{t+1}(b)}\right)$$

$$= \log\left(\frac{\sum_{a \in \mathcal{C}} q_t(a) \exp(-\eta \ell_t(a))}{q_t(b) \exp(-\eta \ell_t(b))}\right)$$

$$= D_t + \log\left(\sum_{a \in \mathcal{C}} q_t(a) \exp(-\eta \ell_t(a))\right) + \eta \ell_t(b)$$

$$\leq D_t + \log\left(\sum_{a \in \mathcal{C}} q_t(a)\left[1 - \eta \ell_t(a) + \eta^2 \ell_t(a)^2\right]\right) + \eta \ell_t(b) \quad \text{by (7.2)}$$

$$= D_t + \log\left(1 + \sum_{a \in \mathcal{C}} q_t(a)\left[-\eta \ell_t(a) + \eta^2 \ell_t(a)^2\right]\right) + \eta \ell_t(b)$$

$$\leq D_t - \eta\left[\sum_{a \in \mathcal{C}} q_t(a)\ell_t(a) - \ell_t(b)\right] + \eta^2 \sum_{a \in \mathcal{C}} q_t(a)\ell_t(a)^2. \quad \text{by (7.3)}$$

Rearranging and summing over t and telescoping yields

$$\sum_{t=1}^{n}\left(\sum_{a \in \mathcal{C}} q_t(a)\ell_t(a) - \ell_t(b)\right) \leq \frac{1}{\eta}\log\left(\frac{q_{n+1}(b)}{q_1(b)}\right) + \eta \sum_{t=1}^{n}\sum_{a \in \mathcal{C}} q_t(a)\ell_t(a)^2$$

$$\leq \frac{1}{\eta}\log(|\mathcal{C}|) + \eta \sum_{t=1}^{n}\sum_{a \in \mathcal{C}} q_t(a)\ell_t(a)^2,$$

where in the final inequality we used the fact that $\log(q_{n+1}(b)) \leq 0$ and $q_1(b) = 1/|\mathcal{C}|$. Since the above calculations hold for any $b \in \mathcal{C}$ we are free to take the maximum on the left-hand side, which yields the theorem. □

Remark 7.10 When $\ell_t(a) \geq 0$ for all t and $a \in \mathcal{C}$, then the bound improves to

$$\max_{b \in \mathcal{C}} \sum_{t=1}^{n}\left(\sum_{a \in \mathcal{C}} q_t(a)\ell_t(a) - \ell_t(b)\right) \leq \frac{\log|\mathcal{C}|}{\eta} + \frac{\eta}{2}\sum_{t=1}^{n}\sum_{a \in \mathcal{C}} q_t(a)\ell_t(a)^2.$$

The proof is the same except you may now use that $\exp(-x) \leq 1 - x + x^2/2$ for $x \geq 0$.

7.4 Continuous Exponential Weights

The material in this section is not used by any algorithm in this book. It is included because it played a fundamental role in one of the most influential papers on convex bandits (Bubeck et al., 2017) and may be useful in future algorithms. The exponential weights distribution in (7.1) is defined only for finite $\mathcal{C}$. This is sometimes desirable, as we discuss in Note 7.vi. Generally though, in applications to convex bandits you need $\mathcal{C}$ to be a cover of K and for this $|\mathcal{C}|$ is exponentially large in the dimension. This is not such a problem from a sample efficiency perspective ($|\mathcal{C}|$ appears in a logarithm in Theorem 7.8) but is a disaster computationally. Continuous exponential weights is a beautiful alternative that sometimes leads to computational improvements. Suppose that $\text{vol}(K) > 0$ and let $\ell_1, \ldots, \ell_n : K \to \mathbb{R}$ be a sequence of measurable functions. The continuous exponential weights distribution is

$$q_t(x) = \frac{\exp\left(-\eta \sum_{s=1}^{t-1} \ell_s(x)\right)}{\int_K \exp\left(-\eta \sum_{s=1}^{t-1} \ell_s(y)\right) dy},$$

which, provided it exists, is a density supported on K. Given a probability density p supported on K, let

$$\widehat{\text{Reg}}_n(p) = \sum_{t=1}^{n} \int_K \ell_t(x) \left(q_t(x) - p(x)\right) dx,$$

which is the regret of continuous exponential weights relative to the density p.

Theorem 7.11 *Suppose that $\eta|\ell_t(x)| \leq 1$ for all $x \in K$ and $1 \leq t \leq n$. Then, for any density p on K,*

$$\widehat{\text{Reg}}_n(p) \leq \frac{1}{\eta} \int_K p(x) \log\left(\frac{p(x)}{q_1(x)}\right) dx + \eta \sum_{t=1}^{n} \int_K q_t(x) \ell_t(x)^2 dx.$$

The first term on the right-hand side is the relative entropy between p and q_1, which is the uniform distribution on K. Remark 7.9 applies here as well. There is no requirement that the losses (ℓ_t) or the constraint set K are convex, though the exponential weights distribution is log-concave if they are. The regret relative to a distribution is not entirely satisfactory. Ideally you want to choose p as a Dirac on the minimiser of $\sum_{t=1}^{n} \ell_t$, but this does not have a density. Unsurprisingly the idea is to choose p to be concentrated close to a minimiser. Exactly how you do this depends on the structure of the losses. When the losses are bounded and K is convex and bounded, then the situation is especially clean:

Corollary 7.12 *Suppose that K is a convex body, $\sum_{t=1}^{n} \ell_t$ is convex and $d \leq 2n$.*

Then, under the same conditions as Theorem 7.11,

$$\widehat{\text{Reg}}_n(x) = \sum_{t=1}^{n} \left(\int_K \ell_t(y) q_t(y) \, dy - \ell_t(x) \right)$$

$$\leq \frac{d}{\eta} \left[1 + \log\left(\frac{2n}{d}\right) \right] + \eta \sum_{t=1}^{n} \int_K q_t(y) \ell_t(y)^2 \, dy.$$

Exercise 7.13 ★ Prove Corollary 7.12 by taking p as the uniform distribution on $(1 - \varepsilon)x + \varepsilon K$ for suitable $\varepsilon \in [0, 1]$.

Computationally the continuous exponential weights distribution has some nice properties. Most notably, if K is convex and the cumulative loss $\sum_{s=1}^{t-1} \ell_s$ is convex, then q_t is log-concave and under mild additional assumptions can be sampled from approximately in polynomial time (Chewi, 2024).

7.5 Linear Bandits

For this section we assume there is no noise and that the losses are bounded, linear and homogeneous:

Assumption 7.14 The following hold:
(1) There is no noise: $\varepsilon_t = 0$ for all t.
(2) There exists a sequence $(\theta_t)_{t=1}^{n} \in \mathbb{R}^d$ such that $f_t = \langle \cdot, \theta_t \rangle$.
(3) The losses are bounded: $(f_t) \in \mathscr{F}_b$.

Remark 7.15 Cautious readers may notice that the above assumptions do not correspond to $\mathscr{F}_{b,\text{lin}}$ because the representation has been chosen so that the losses are homogeneous. In the notes we explain a simple way to reduce the inhomogeneous setting to the homogeneous one. Note also that the global assumption that K is convex is not actually used in this section, only that it is nonempty and compact.

The plan is to use exponential weights on a finite $\mathscr{C} \subset K$ that is sufficiently large that the optimal action in K can be approximated by something in $\mathscr{C}$. Let $A = \text{conv}(K \cup (-K))$, which is a symmetric convex body. Recall the definitions of A° and $\|\cdot\|_A$ and $\|\cdot\|_{A^\circ}$ in Section 3.1. By the assumption that the losses are bounded, for any t, $1 \geq \max_{x,y \in K} |\langle x - y, \theta_t \rangle| = \|\theta_t\|_{A^\circ}$ and therefore

$$\theta_t \in \Theta = \{\theta \in \mathbb{R}^d : \|\theta\|_{A^\circ} \leq 1\}.$$

What we need from $\mathscr{C}$ is that for all $\theta_t (\in \Theta)$ and $y \in K$ there exists an $x \in \mathscr{C}$ such that $f_t(x) - f_t(y)$ is small. Precisely, we need

$$\max_{y \in K} \min_{x \in \mathscr{C}} \langle x - y, \theta \rangle \leq \frac{1}{n} = \varepsilon.$$

Suppose that $\|x - y\|_A \leq \varepsilon$; then by Proposition 3.1 $\langle x - y, \theta \rangle \leq \|x - y\|_A \|\theta\|_{A^\circ} \leq \varepsilon$. Hence, it suffices to choose $\mathscr{C} \subset K$ such that $K \subset \bigcup_{x \in \mathscr{C}} (x + \varepsilon A)$. By Proposition 7.3, such a cover exists with

$$|\mathscr{C}| \leq \left(1 + \frac{4}{\varepsilon}\right)^d. \tag{7.4}$$

The algorithm for linear bandits plays actions in $\mathscr{C}$ and uses importance-weighted least squares (in Line 8) to estimate $\langle x, \theta_t \rangle$ for all $x \in \mathscr{C}$. The distribution proposed by exponential weights is mixed with a small amount of an optimal design on $\mathscr{C}$, which is needed so that the estimates are suitably bounded as required by Theorem 7.8.

---

1   **args**: $\eta > 0$, $\gamma \in (0, 1)$, K
2   find $\mathscr{C} \subset K$ such that $\max_{y \in K} \min_{x \in \mathscr{C}} \|x - y\|_A \leq \frac{1}{n}$
3   find optimal design π on $\mathscr{C}$ (see Theorem 7.6)
4   **for** $t = 1$ to n
5   let $q_t(x) = \dfrac{\exp\left(-\eta \sum_{u=1}^{t-1} \langle x, \hat{\theta}_u \rangle\right)}{\sum_{y \in \mathscr{C}} \exp\left(-\eta \sum_{u=1}^{t-1} \langle y, \hat{\theta}_u \rangle\right)}$
6   let $p_t = (1 - \gamma) q_t + \gamma \pi$
7   sample X_t from p_t and observe $Y_t = f_t(X_t)$
8   let $G_t = \sum_{a \in \mathscr{C}} p_t(a) a a^\top$ and $\hat{\theta}_t = G_t^+ X_t Y_t$

Algorithm 7.1   Exponential weights for linear bandits

As mentioned, Algorithm 7.1 does not need K to be a convex body. And indeed, in many applications K is a finite set (see Note 7.vi). When K is a convex body, you can use continuous exponential weights (Section 7.4) instead of the discretisation.

Exercise 7.16 ★   Replace the discrete exponential weights in Algorithm 7.1 with continuous exponential weights from Section 7.4 and adapt the proof of Theorem 7.17 below to prove that for $n \geq 2d$ the regret of this algorithm is upper-bounded by

$$\mathbb{E}[\mathrm{Reg}_n] = O\left(d \sqrt{n \log(n/d)}\right).$$

7.5 Linear Bandits

Theorem 7.17 *Suppose that*

$$\eta = \sqrt{\frac{\log |\mathcal{C}|}{2nd}} \quad \text{and} \quad \gamma = \eta d\,.$$

Under Assumption 7.14, the regret of Algorithm 7.1 is bounded by

$$\mathbb{E}[\text{Reg}_n] \leq 1 + \sqrt{8nd \log |\mathcal{C}|}\,.$$

Note that by (7.4), $\mathcal{C}$ can be chosen so that $\log |\mathcal{C}| \leq d \log(1 + 4n)$ and in this case one has $\mathbb{E}[\text{Reg}_n] = O(d\sqrt{n \log(n)})$.

Proof The algorithm is only well-defined if $\gamma \in [0, 1]$. Suppose that $\gamma \geq 1$; then

$$1 \leq \eta d = \sqrt{\frac{d \log |\mathcal{C}|}{2n}}\,.$$

In this case, no matter how the actions are chosen, boundedness of the losses implies that $\text{Reg}_n \leq n \leq \sqrt{nd \log(|\mathcal{C}|)/2}$. Suppose for the remainder that $\gamma \in (0, 1)$. Recall the definition of G_π from Section 7.2 and let

$$G_{q_t} = \sum_{x \in \mathcal{C}} q_t(x) xx^\top\,.$$

With this notation, $G_t = (1 - \gamma) G_{q_t} + \gamma G_\pi$. Of course $G_t \succeq (1 - \gamma) G_{q_t}$ and $G_t \succeq \gamma G_\pi$. Since q_t is strictly positive, $\ker(G_{q_t}) = \text{span}(\mathcal{C})^\perp$ and by assumption $\ker(G_\pi) = \text{span}(\mathcal{C})^\perp$. Hence, by Fact A.7,

$$G_t^+ \preceq \frac{1}{1 - \gamma} G_{q_t}^+ \quad \text{and} \quad G_t^+ \preceq \frac{1}{\gamma} G_\pi^+\,. \qquad (7.5)$$

Next, for any $y \in \mathcal{C}$,

$$\langle y, \mathbb{E}_{t-1}[\hat\theta_t] \rangle = \left\langle y, \sum_{x \in \mathcal{C}} p_t(x) G_t^+ x \langle x, \theta_t \rangle \right\rangle = \langle y, G_t^+ G_t \theta_t \rangle = \langle y, \theta_t \rangle\,, \quad (7.6)$$

where in the final inequality we use the assumption that G_π is an optimal design for $\mathcal{C}$ (see Theorem 7.6), so that $\mathcal{C} \subset \text{im}(G_\pi^\top) \subset \text{im}(G_t^\top)$, and Fact A.6. Furthermore,

$$\mathbb{E}_{t-1}\left[\langle x, \hat\theta_t \rangle^2\right] = \mathbb{E}_{t-1}\left[Y_t^2 x^\top G_t^+ X_t X_t^\top G_t^+ x\right] \leq \|x\|^2_{G_t^+ G_t G_t^+} = \|x\|^2_{G_t^+}\,, \quad (7.7)$$

where we used the fact that $Y_t^2 \leq 1$. Therefore,

$$\mathbb{E}_{t-1}\left[\sum_{x \in \mathscr{C}} q_t(x) \langle x, \hat{\theta}_t \rangle^2\right] \leq \sum_{x \in \mathscr{C}} q_t(x) \|x\|_{G_t^+}^2 \qquad \text{by (7.7)}$$

$$\leq \frac{1}{1-\gamma} \sum_{x \in \mathscr{C}} q_t(x) \|x\|_{G_{q_t}^+}^2 \qquad \text{by (7.5)}$$

$$= \frac{1}{1-\gamma} \operatorname{tr}(G_{q_t} G_{q_t}^+)$$

$$\leq \frac{d}{1-\gamma}, \qquad (7.8)$$

where the last inequality follows from Fact A.8. In order to apply Theorem 7.8 the loss estimates need to be suitably bounded. This is where the exploration using experimental design comes into play. For any $x \in \mathscr{C}$,

$$\eta |\langle x, \hat{\theta}_t \rangle| = \eta \left| x^\top G_t^+ X_t Y_t \right| \leq \eta \|x\|_{G_t^+} \|X_t\|_{G_t^+} \leq \frac{\eta d}{\gamma} = 1,$$

where we used (7.5) and the fact that π is an optimal design on $\mathscr{C}$ so that by Theorem 7.5, for any $x \in \mathscr{C}$, $\|x\|_{G_\pi^+} \leq \sqrt{d}$. Define $x_\star = \arg\min_{x \in \mathscr{C}} \sum_{t=1}^n \langle x, \theta_t \rangle$. Then the regret is bounded by

$$\mathbb{E}[\operatorname{Reg}_n] = \max_{x \in K} \mathbb{E}\left[\sum_{t=1}^n \langle X_t - x, \theta_t \rangle\right]$$

$$= \max_{x \in K} \sum_{t=1}^n \langle x_\star - x, \theta_t \rangle + \mathbb{E}\left[\sum_{t=1}^n \langle X_t - x_\star, \theta_t \rangle\right]. \qquad (7.9)$$

The first term in (7.9) is bounded by

$$\max_{x \in K} \sum_{t=1}^n \langle x_\star - x, \theta_t \rangle = \max_{x \in K} \min_{y \in \mathscr{C}} \sum_{t=1}^n \langle y - x, \theta_t \rangle$$

$$\leq \max_{x \in K} \min_{y \in \mathscr{C}} \sum_{t=1}^n \|y - x\|_A \|\theta_t\|_{A^\circ}$$

$$\leq \max_{x \in K} \min_{y \in \mathscr{C}} n \|y - x\|_A$$

$$\leq 1,$$

where we used Cauchy–Schwarz, the fact that $\theta_t \in \Theta = \{\theta : \|\theta\|_{A^\circ} \leq 1\}$ and the definition of the cover $\mathscr{C}$. The second term in (7.9) is bounded using

Theorem 7.8 by

$$\mathbb{E}\left[\sum_{t=1}^{n}\langle X_t - x_\star, \theta_t\rangle\right] = \mathbb{E}\left[\sum_{t=1}^{n}\sum_{x\in\mathscr{C}} p_t(x)\langle x - x_\star, \theta_t\rangle\right]$$

$$\leq n\gamma + (1-\gamma)\mathbb{E}\left[\sum_{t=1}^{n}\sum_{x\in\mathscr{C}} q_t(x)\langle x - x_\star, \theta_t\rangle\right]$$

$$= n\gamma + (1-\gamma)\mathbb{E}\left[\sum_{t=1}^{n}\sum_{x\in\mathscr{C}} q_t(x)\left\langle x - x_\star, \hat{\theta}_t\right\rangle\right] \qquad \text{by (7.6)}$$

$$\leq n\gamma + (1-\gamma)\left(\frac{\log|\mathscr{C}|}{\eta} + \mathbb{E}\left[\sum_{t=1}^{n}\sum_{x\in\mathscr{C}} q_t(x)\langle x, \hat{\theta}_t\rangle^2\right]\right) \qquad \text{by Theorem 7.8}$$

$$\leq n\gamma + \frac{\log|\mathscr{C}|}{\eta} + \eta nd, \qquad \text{by (7.8)}$$

where in the first inequality we used the fact that $p_t = (1-\gamma)q_t + \gamma\pi$ and the assumption that (f_t) are bounded so that

$$\sum_{x\in\mathscr{C}} \pi(x)\langle x - x_\star, \theta_t\rangle = \sum_{x\in\mathscr{C}} \pi(x)(f_t(x) - f_t(x_\star)) \leq 1.$$

The result follows by substituting the constants. □

7.6 Quadratic Bandits

Quadratic bandits seem much harder than linear bandits. But if you ignore the computation complexity then it turns out that quadratic bandits *are* linear bandits.

Assumption 7.18 There is no noise and the loss functions are quadratic and bounded: $(f_t) \in \mathscr{F}_{\text{b,quad}}$.

Quadratic bandits can be viewed as linear bandits by introducing a kernel feature map. Let $d_2 = \frac{d^2+3d+2}{2}$ and define a function $\phi(x)\colon \mathbb{R}^d \to \mathbb{R}^{d_2}$ by

$$\phi(x) = (1, x_1, \ldots, x_d, x_1^2, x_1x_2, \ldots, x_1x_d, x_2^2, x_2x_3, \ldots, x_{d-1}^2, x_{d-1}x_d, x_d^2).$$

So ϕ is the feature map associated with the polynomial kernel of degree 2. You should check that any $f \in \mathscr{F}_{\text{b,quad}}$ can be written as $f(x) = \langle\phi(x), \theta\rangle$ for some $\theta \in \mathbb{R}^{d_2}$.

Lemma 7.19 *Let $K \subset \mathbb{R}^d$ be a convex body. There exists a cover $\mathscr{C} \subset K$ such that*

(1) $\max_{x \in K} \min_{y \in \mathscr{C}} |f(x) - f(y)| \leq \varepsilon$ for all $f \in \mathscr{F}_{b,\text{quad}}$; and

(2) $|\mathscr{C}| \leq \left(1 + \frac{24d^{3.5}}{\varepsilon}\right)^d$.

Proof We provide the proof when $\mathbb{B}_1^d \subset K \subset d\mathbb{B}_1^d$ and leave the general case as an exercise. Let $\mathscr{C}$ be a cover of K such

$$\max_{x \in K} \min_{y \in \mathscr{C}} \|x - y\| \leq \frac{\varepsilon}{6d^{2.5}}.$$

By Proposition 7.4, $\mathscr{C}$ can be chosen so that

$$|\mathscr{C}| \leq \left(1 + \frac{24d^{3.5}}{\varepsilon}\right)^d.$$

Let $f \in \mathscr{F}_{b,\text{quad}}$ and let θ be such that $f(x) = \langle \phi(x), \theta \rangle$. Then, since $\mathbb{B}_1^d \subset K$ by assumption,

$$1 \geq \max_{x \in K} |f(x)| \geq \max_{x \in \mathbb{B}_1^d} |f(x)| \geq \frac{1}{2} \|\theta\|_\infty,$$

where the last inequality is left as an exercise:

Exercise 7.20 ★ Show that $\max_{x \in \mathbb{B}_1^d} |f(x)| \geq \frac{1}{2} \|\theta\|_\infty$.

Let $x \in K$ be arbitrary and $y \in \mathscr{C}$ be such that $\|x - y\| \leq \frac{\varepsilon}{6d^{2.5}}$. Then,

$$|f(x) - f(y)| = |\langle \phi(x) - \phi(y), \theta \rangle| \leq 2\|\phi(x) - \phi(y)\|_1 \leq 6d^{2.5} \|x - y\| \leq \varepsilon$$

where the first inequality follows from Cauchy–Schwarz and the fact that $\|\theta\|_\infty \leq 4$ by Exercise 7.20. The second follows because $x \in \mathbb{B}_d^d$ and by using Exercise 7.21 below. □

Exercise 7.21 ★ Suppose that $x, y \in \mathbb{B}_d^d$. Show that

$$\|\phi(x) - \phi(y)\|_1 \leq 3d^{2.5} \|x - y\|_\infty.$$

Exercise 7.22 ★ Prove Lemma 7.19 for arbitrary convex bodies K. You may use the fact that for any convex body K there exists an affine map T such that $\mathbb{B}_1^d \subset TK \subset d\mathbb{B}_1^d$, which follows from Theorem 3.15.

We can now simply write the kernelised version of Algorithm 7.1.

```
1  args : η > 0, γ ∈ (0, 1) and K
2  find 𝒞 ⊂ K satisfying conds. in Lemma 7.19, ε = 1/n
3  find optimal design π on {φ(a) : a ∈ 𝒞}
4  for t = 1 to n
5      let q_t(x) = exp(-η ∑_{u=1}^{t-1} ⟨φ(x), θ̂_u⟩) / ∑_{x∈𝒞} exp(-η ∑_{u=1}^{t-1} ⟨φ(x), θ̂_u⟩)
6      let p_t = (1 - γ)q_t + γπ
7      sample X_t from p_t and observe Y_t = f_t(X_t)
8      let G_t = ∑_{a∈𝒞} p_t(a)φ(a)φ(a)^⊤ and θ̂_t = G_t^+ X_t Y_t
```

Algorithm 7.2 Exponential weights for quadratic bandits

An immediate corollary of Theorem 7.17 is the following bound on the regret of Algorithm 7.2:

Theorem 7.23 *Suppose that*

$$\eta = \sqrt{\frac{\log |\mathscr{C}|}{2nd_2}} \quad \text{and} \quad \gamma = d_2 \eta.$$

Under Assumption 7.18 the expected regret of Algorithm 7.2 is bounded by

$$\mathbb{E}[\text{Reg}_n] \leq 1 + \sqrt{8nd_2 \log |\mathscr{C}|} = O\left(d^{1.5}\sqrt{n \log(nd)}\right).$$

Note that we did not use anywhere that $\mathscr{F}_{\text{b,quad}}$ only included convex quadratics. Everything works for more general quadratic losses. Even if we restrict our attention to convex quadratics, none of the algorithms we have presented so far can match this bound. Actually no efficient algorithm is known matching this bound except for special K.

7.7 Notes

7.i We promised to explain how to handle inhomogeneous linear losses. The simple solution is to let $\phi(x) = (1, x)$ and run the algorithm for linear bandits on $\phi(K)$.

7.ii Even when K is convex, (non-convex) quadratic programming is computationally hard. For example, when K is a simplex and A is the adjacency matrix of an undirected graph G, then a theorem by Motzkin and Straus (1965) says that

$$\frac{1}{2} \min_{x \in \Delta_d} (-x^\top A x) = \frac{1}{2}\left(\frac{1}{\omega(G)} - 1\right),$$

where $\omega(G)$ is the size of the largest clique in G. Since the clique decision problem is NP-complete (Karp, 1972), there (probably) does not exist an efficient algorithm for minimising non-convex quadratic functions over the simplex.

7.iii By the previous note, Algorithm 7.2 cannot be implemented efficiently, since its analysis did not make use of convexity of the losses. Sadly, even if we restrict our attention to convex quadratic loss functions and convex K, the kernel method does not seem amenable to efficient calculations. Why not? The problem is that if K is a convex body, then the set $J = \{\phi(a) : a \in K\}$ is not convex.

7.iv Algorithm 7.1 is by Bubeck et al. (2012) and Algorithm 7.2 is essentially due to Chatterji et al. (2019). Note that the latter consider kernelised bandits more generally. You could replace the quadratic kernel with a higher-degree polynomial (or even infinite-dimensional feature map) and obtain regret bounds for a larger class of losses.

7.v Note that $\mathscr{F}_{b,\text{lin}} = \mathscr{F}_{b,\text{sm}}$ when $\beta = 0$. This means that Theorem 6.14 shows that Algorithm 6.2 has regret $\mathbb{E}[\text{Reg}_n] \leq 1 + 3d\sqrt{\vartheta n \log(n)}$. The algorithm is efficient when the learner has access to a ϑ-self-concordant barrier. This special case was analysed in the first application of self-concordance to bandits by Abernethy et al. (2008).

7.vi Continuous exponential weights is generally preferable computationally when the losses and constraint set are convex, at least when the dimension is not tiny. In many applications of linear bandits K is a moderately sized finite set. For example, K might be a set of features associated with books to be recommended. In these cases Algorithm 7.1 is a good choice with $|\mathscr{C}| = K$. We will see an example of exponential weights for convex bandits in the next chapter and with $d = 1$ where either the continuous or discrete versions of exponential weights could be employed, with the latter moderately more computationally efficient.

7.vii For some time it was open whether or not $d\sqrt{n}\,\text{polylog}(n,d)$ regret is possible for linear bandits with a computationally efficient algorithm when K is a convex body represented by a membership or separation oracle. This was resolved by Hazan et al. (2016), who used continuous exponential weights but replaced the Kiefer–Wolfowitz distribution with a spanner that can be computed efficiently. The only reason not to include that algorithm here is that we are primarily focused on convex bandits and because the analysis is more sophisticated.

8
Exponential Weights

We already saw an application of exponential weights to linear and quadratic bandits in Chapter 7. The same abstract algorithm can also be used for convex bandits but the situation is more complicated. Throughout this chapter we assume the losses are bounded and there is no noise:

Assumption 8.1 The following hold:
(1) The losses are in $\mathscr{F}_b$.
(2) There is no noise, so that $Y_t = f_t(X_t)$.

Two main topics will be covered here:

○ a relatively practical algorithm for adversarial bandits when $d = 1$ with $O(\sqrt{n}\log(n))$ regret;
○ the connection via minimax duality between mirror descent and the information ratio (Russo and Van Roy, 2014) and its application to convex bandits.

The relation between the two topics is that both make use of an abstract version of exponential weights.

8.1 Exponential Weights for Convex Bandits

The version of exponential weights introduced in Chapter 7 is designed for a finite action set. As in that chapter, we will apply this algorithm to a discretisation of K, which is given in an abstract form in Algorithm 8.1 below.

```
1  args: learning rate η > 0
2  let 𝒞 ⊂ K be finite
3  for t = 1 to n
4      compute  q_t(x) = exp(-η ∑_{u=1}^{t-1} ŝ_u(x)) / ∑_{y∈𝒞} exp(-η ∑_{u=1}^{t-1} ŝ_u(y))   for all x ∈ 𝒞
5      find distribution p_t as a function of q_t
6      sample X_t from p_t and observe Y_t = f_t(X_t)
7      compute ŝ_t(x) ∀x ∈ 𝒞 using p_t, q_t, X_t and Y_t
```

Algorithm 8.1 Exponential weights for bandits

As with gradient descent, to make this concrete we need a sampling distribution p_t and a mechanism for estimating the loss function. The extra complication here is that while for gradient descent we only needed to estimate a gradient, here the algorithm needs to estimate an entire function from a single observation. From a computational perspective there is a serious problem in that $\mathscr{C}$ will need to be exponentially large in d. A potential way to mitigate this is to use continuous exponential weights (Section 7.4), which was the approach taken by Bubeck et al. (2017) and (non-obviously) by the algorithm in Chapter 10. The reason we avoid this here is twofold:

- For the one-dimensional algorithm it turns out that the discrete version is more computationally efficient and simpler.
- The minimax duality arguments are already computationally inefficient and using continuous exponential weights only serves to introduce measure-theoretic challenges.

8.2 Exponential Weights in One Dimension

For this section assume that $d = 1$ and $K = [-1, 1]$ is the interval, and let $\varepsilon = 1/\sqrt{n}$ and

$$\mathscr{C} = \{k\varepsilon : k \in \mathbb{Z}, k\varepsilon \in K\}.$$

Let $x_\star = \arg\min_{x \in \mathscr{C}} \sum_{t=1}^n f_t(x)$. The plan is to apply Theorem 7.8 to Algorithm 8.1 by carefully choosing the exploration distributions (p_t) and a mechanism for constructing the estimated surrogate losses $(\hat{s}_t)$. Provided the estimated surrogates are non-negative and letting $s_t(x) = \mathbb{E}_{t-1}[\hat{s}_t(x)]$, then

Theorem 7.8 shows that

$$\mathbb{E}\left[\sum_{t=1}^{n}\left(\sum_{x\in\mathscr{C}}q_t(x)s_t(x) - s_t(x_\star)\right)\right] = \mathbb{E}\left[\sum_{t=1}^{n}\left(\sum_{x\in\mathscr{C}}q_t(x)\hat{s}_t(x) - \hat{s}_t(x_\star)\right)\right]$$
$$\leq \frac{\log|\mathscr{C}|}{\eta} + \frac{\eta}{2}\mathbb{E}\left[\sum_{t=1}^{n}\sum_{x\in\mathscr{C}}q_t(x)\hat{s}_t(x)^2\right]. \quad (8.1)$$

Algorithm 8.1 samples X_t from distribution p_t, which means the expected regret relative to $x_\star$ is

$$\mathbb{E}[\text{Reg}_n(x_\star)] = \sum_{t=1}^{n}\mathbb{E}\left[\sum_{x\in\mathscr{C}}p_t(x)f_t(x) - f_t(x_\star)\right]. \quad (8.2)$$

The question is how to choose loss estimates $\hat{s}_t$ and exploration distribution p_t so that (8.2) can be connected to the left-hand side of (8.1) and at the same time the right-hand side of (8.1) is well controlled.

Kernel-Based Estimation

Let us focus on a single round t. Let $f: K \to [0, 1]$ be convex and $q \in \Delta(\mathscr{C})$ and assume that $q(x) > 0$ for all $x \in \mathscr{C}$. The learner samples X from $p \in \Delta(\mathscr{C})$, observes $Y = f(X)$ and uses p, q, X and Y to construct a surrogate estimate $\hat{s}: \mathscr{C} \to \mathbb{R}$ with expectation $s(x) = \mathbb{E}[\hat{s}(x)]$. Staring at (8.1) and (8.2), we will be in business if we choose p and $\hat{s}$ in such a way that all of the following hold:

(1) There exist (preferably) small constants $A, B > 0$ such that

$$\sum_{x\in\mathscr{C}}p(x)f(x) - f(x_\star) \leq A\left[\sum_{x\in\mathscr{C}}q(x)s(x) - s(x_\star)\right] + B. \quad (8.3)$$

(2) $\mathbb{E}\left[\sum_{x\in\mathscr{C}}q(x)\hat{s}(x)^2\right] = \tilde{O}(1)$.
(3) $\hat{s}(x) \geq 0$ for all $x \in \mathscr{C}$.

Remark 8.2 The requirement that $\hat{s}$ is non-negative can be relaxed to $\eta|\hat{s}(x)| \leq 1$ for all x where $\eta = O(1/\sqrt{n})$ is the learning rate. See Remark 7.10.

Because $x_\star$ is not known, the most obvious idea is to show that (8.3) holds for all points in $\mathscr{C}$, not just $x_\star$. An elegant way to construct a surrogate satisfying these properties is by using a kernel. Let $T: \mathscr{C} \times \mathscr{C} \to \mathbb{R}$ be a function with $x \mapsto T(x|y)$ a probability distribution for all y and define

$$p(x) = (Tq)(x) \triangleq \sum_{y\in\mathscr{C}}T(x|y)q(y) \quad \text{and}$$
$$s(y) = (T^*f)(y) \triangleq \sum_{x\in\mathscr{C}}T(x|y)f(x).$$

8.2 Exponential Weights in One Dimension

It may be helpful to think of T as a $|\mathscr{C}| \times |\mathscr{C}|$ matrix and T^* as its transpose (or being fancy, its adjoint). Viewing p, q, f, s as vectors in $\mathbb{R}^{|\mathscr{C}|}$ we have $p = Tq$ and $s = T^* f$. Because the map $x \mapsto T(x|y)$ is a probability distribution, the surrogate s is some kind of smoothing of f. And in fact the surrogates used in earlier chapters also have this form, though in continuous spaces. Notice that

$$\sum_{y \in \mathscr{C}} s(y) q(y) = \sum_{y \in \mathscr{C}} \left(\sum_{x \in K} T(x|y) f(x) \right) q(y)$$

$$= \sum_{x \in \mathscr{C}} f(x) \left(\sum_{y \in K} T(x|y) q(y) \right)$$

$$= \sum_{x \in \mathscr{C}} f(x) p(x). \tag{8.4}$$

This is the motivation for choosing $p = Tq$. Equivalently, using linear algebra notation: $\langle q, s \rangle = \langle q, T^* f \rangle = \langle Tq, f \rangle = \langle p, f \rangle$. Given a kernel T we now have a surrogate $s = T^* f$. Next we need a way to estimate this surrogate when the learner samples X from p and observes $Y = f(X)$. Note that $p(x) = 0$ implies that $T(x|y) = 0$ for all y, since $q(y) > 0$ for all y by assumption. Then,

$$s(y) = \sum_{x \in \mathscr{C}} T(x|y) f(x) = \sum_{x \in \mathscr{C}: p(x) > 0} \frac{T(x|y)}{p(x)} f(x) p(x),$$

which shows that when X is sampled from p and $Y = f(X)$, then the surrogate s can be be estimated by

$$\hat{s}(y) = \frac{T(X|y) Y}{p(X)}.$$

An important point is that we are allowed to choose T to depend on the exponential weights distribution q. Given $x \in \mathscr{C}$, let $\Pi_{\mathscr{C}}(x) = \arg\min_{y \in \mathscr{C}, |y| \leq |x|} |x - y|$, which is the $y \in \mathscr{C}$ closest to x in the direction of the origin. We also let $\mu = \sum_{y \in \mathscr{C}} q(y) y$ and $\mu_\pi = \Pi_{\mathscr{C}}(\mu)$. Given $x, y \in \mathscr{C}$, let $I(x, y) = \{z \in \mathscr{C} : \min(x, y) \leq z \leq \max(x, y)\}$ and

$$T(x|y) = \frac{1(x \in I(y, \mu_\pi))}{|I(y, \mu_\pi)|}. \tag{8.5}$$

That is, $x \mapsto T(x|y)$ is the uniform distribution on $I(y, \mu_\pi) \subset \mathscr{C}$. What this means is that the distribution p is obtained from q by spreading the mass q assigns to any point y uniformly between y and the projected mean μ_π. The actions of this kernel are illustrated in Figure 8.1. We can think about why this kernel might be useful.

○ By (8.4), $\langle q, s \rangle = \langle p, f \rangle$ no matter how the kernel is chosen. If we could

8 Exponential Weights

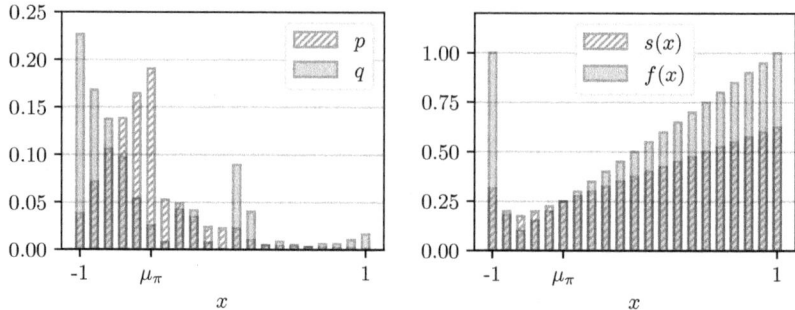

Figure 8.1 The kernel in (8.5) acting on a loss $s = T^\star f$ and distribution $p = Tq$. Notice that q is not particularly smooth while p is unimodal. The surrogate s is neither optimistic nor pessimistic, in contrast with the surrogates used in Chapters 5 and 6, which are pessimistic and optimistic respectively.

have $s(x_\star) = f(x_\star)$, then (8.3) would hold with $A = 1$ and $B = 0$. You can actually achieve this by choosing $T(x|y) = \mathbf{1}(x = y)$. But with this choice the surrogate estimate $\hat{s}$ generally has an enormous second moment, which is reduced by smoothing more broadly.

○ The reason for smoothing towards the mean is that this automatically respects the concentration properties of q. That is, if q is concentrated about its mean then the loss is also smoothed over a small region about the mean.

The following lemma establishes the two essential properties of the kernel, which is that (8.3) holds with $A = 2$ and $B = \frac{\varepsilon}{2}$ (part (1)) and that the second moment of the surrogate loss is well controlled (part (2)).

Lemma 8.3 *Let T be defined as in (8.5) and $q \in \Delta(\mathscr{C})$ be such that $q(x) > 0$ for all $x \in \mathscr{C}$, $p = Tq$ and $s = T^\star f$. Then*

(1) $\sum_{x \in \mathscr{C}} p(x)f(x) - f(y) \leq 2\left(\sum_{x \in \mathscr{C}} q(x)s(x) - s(y)\right) + \frac{\varepsilon}{2}$ *for all* $y \in \mathscr{C}$,

(2) $\sum_{x \in \mathscr{C}} \sum_{y \in \mathscr{C}} p(x)q(y)\left(\frac{T(x|y)f(x)}{p(x)}\right)^2 \leq 2 + \log(n)$.

8.2 Exponential Weights in One Dimension

Proof By definition,

$$
\begin{aligned}
s(y) &= (T^*f)(y) \\
&= \sum_{x \in \mathscr{C}} T(x|y) f(x) \\
&= \sum_{x \in \mathscr{C}} \frac{\mathbf{1}(x \in I(y, \mu_\pi))}{|I(y, \mu_\pi)|} f(x) \\
&= \sum_{x \in \mathscr{C}} \frac{\mathbf{1}(x \in I(y, \mu_\pi))}{|I(y, \mu_\pi)|} f\left(\left|\frac{x - \mu_\pi}{y - \mu_\pi}\right| y + \left|\frac{y - x}{y - \mu_\pi}\right| \mu_\pi \right) \\
&\leq \sum_{x \in \mathscr{C}} \frac{\mathbf{1}(x \in I(y, \mu_\pi))}{|I(y, \mu_\pi)|} \left[\left|\frac{x - \mu_\pi}{y - \mu_\pi}\right| f(y) + \left|\frac{y - x}{y - \mu_\pi}\right| f(\mu_\pi) \right] \quad (f \text{ convex}) \\
&= \frac{1}{2} f(y) + \frac{1}{2} f(\mu_\pi). \quad (8.6)
\end{aligned}
$$

The mean of $x \mapsto T(x|y)$ is $y/2 + \mu_\pi/2$ and therefore

$$\sum_{x \in \mathscr{C}} p(x) x = \sum_{y \in \mathscr{C}} q(y) \sum_{x \in \mathscr{C}} x T(x|y) = \frac{\mu_\pi}{2} + \frac{1}{2} \sum_{y \in \mathscr{C}} q(y) y = \frac{\mu_\pi + \mu}{2}. \quad (8.7)$$

Because f is convex and bounded in $[0, 1]$,

$$f(\mu_\pi) \leq f\left(\frac{\mu_\pi + \mu}{2}\right) + \frac{\varepsilon}{2} \stackrel{(8.7)}{=} f\left(\sum_{x \in \mathscr{C}} p(x) x\right) + \frac{\varepsilon}{2} \stackrel{f \text{ cvx}}{\leq} \sum_{x \in \mathscr{C}} p(x) f(x) + \frac{\varepsilon}{2}.$$

Combining the above display with (8.6) yields

$$s(y) \leq \frac{1}{2} f(y) + \frac{1}{2} \sum_{x \in \mathscr{C}} p(x) f(x) + \frac{\varepsilon}{4}.$$

Lastly, by (8.4), $\sum_{x \in \mathscr{C}} p(x) f(x) = \sum_{x \in \mathscr{C}} q(x) s(x)$ and hence

$$\sum_{x \in \mathscr{C}} p(x) f(x) - f(y) \leq 2 \left(\sum_{x \in \mathscr{C}} q(x) s(x) - s(y) \right) + \frac{\varepsilon}{2}.$$

This establishes (1). Part (2) follows because

$$
\begin{aligned}
\sum_{x \in \mathscr{C}} \sum_{y \in \mathscr{C}} \frac{q(y) T(x|y)^2 f(x)^2}{p(x)} &\leq \sum_{x \in \mathscr{C}} \sum_{y \in \mathscr{C}} \frac{\mathbf{1}(x \in I(y, \mu_\pi))}{|I(y, \mu_\pi)|} \frac{q(y) T(x|y)}{p(x)} \\
&\leq \sum_{x \in \mathscr{C}} \frac{1}{|I(x, \mu_\pi)|} \sum_{y \in \mathscr{C}} \frac{q(y) T(x|y)}{p(x)} \\
&= \sum_{x \in \mathscr{C}} \frac{1}{|I(x, \mu_\pi)|} \\
&\leq 2 + \log(n),
\end{aligned}
$$

where in the first inequality we used the fact that $|I(y, \mu_\pi)| \geq |I(x, \mu_\pi)|$ for $x \in I(y, \mu_\pi)$. The second inequality follows via a standard harmonic sum comparison. □

We are now in a position to use exponential weights for convex bandits using the kernel-based surrogate loss estimators analysed above. A snapshot of the loss estimators and exponential weights distribution is given in Figure 8.2.

---

1 **args**: learning rate $\eta > 0$, $\varepsilon = 1/\sqrt{n}$
2 let $\mathscr{C} = \{\varepsilon k : k \in \mathbb{Z}, k\varepsilon \in K\}$
3 **for** $t = 1$ **to** n
4   compute $q_t(x) = \frac{\exp(-\eta \sum_{u=1}^{t-1} \hat{s}_u(x))}{\sum_{y \in \mathscr{C}} \exp(-\eta \sum_{u=1}^{t-1} \hat{s}_u(y))} \quad \forall x \in \mathscr{C}$
5   let $\mu_t = \Pi_{\mathscr{C}}\left(\sum_{x \in \mathscr{C}} q_t(x) x\right)$ and
6    $T_t(x|y) = \frac{\mathbf{1}(x \in I(y, \mu_t))}{|I(y, \mu_t)|} \quad \forall x, y \in \mathscr{C}$
7   sample $X_t \sim p_t = T_t q_t$ and observe $Y_t = f_t(X_t)$
8   compute $\hat{s}_t(y) = \frac{T_t(X_t|y) Y_t}{p_t(X_t)} \quad \forall y \in \mathscr{C}$

Algorithm 8.2 Exponential weights for convex bandits: $d = 1$

Computation

Algorithm 8.2 is not written in the most efficient way. Naively computing T_t on all inputs would require $|\mathscr{C}|^2 = \Theta(n)$ time. This can be improved. Given μ_t the kernel function $T_t(x|y)$ can be computed in $O(1)$ for any $x, y \in \mathscr{C}$. Now X_t can be sampled by first sampling Z_t from q_t and then X_t from $T_t(\cdot|Z_t)$. Hence only $T_t(\cdot|Z_t)$ and $T_t(X_t|\cdot)$ need to be computed for all inputs. This way the computation per round of Algorithm 8.2 is linear in $|\mathscr{C}| = \Theta(\sqrt{n})$. Therefore in the worst case the running time over the entire interaction is at most $O(n^{3/2})$. This is worse than the gradient-based algorithms in Chapters 5 and 6 but the regret is smaller.

Theorem 8.4 *Suppose that $\eta = n^{-1/2}$. Under Assumption 8.1 and with $d = 1$ the regret of Algorithm 8.2 is upper-bounded by*

$$\mathbb{E}[\text{Reg}_n] \leq 2\sqrt{n} \log(n) + 7\sqrt{n}.$$

Proof Let $x_\star = \arg\min_{x \in \mathscr{C}} \sum_{t=1}^{n} f_t(x)$. By the definition of $\mathscr{C}$ and the fact that $(f_t) \in \mathscr{F}_b$ and $\varepsilon = \frac{1}{\sqrt{n}}$,

$$\text{Reg}_n = \sup_{x \in K} \sum_{t=1}^{n} (f_t(X_t) - f_t(x)) \leq \sqrt{n} + \sum_{t=1}^{n} (f_t(X_t) - f_t(x_\star)). \quad (8.8)$$

By Theorem 7.8 and Remark 7.10,

$$\mathbb{E}\left[\widehat{\text{Reg}}_n(x_\star)\right] \triangleq \mathbb{E}\left[\sum_{t=1}^{n}\left(\sum_{y \in \mathscr{C}} q_t(y)\hat{s}_t(y) - \hat{s}_t(x_\star)\right)\right]$$

$$\leq \frac{\log|\mathscr{C}|}{\eta} + \frac{\eta}{2}\mathbb{E}\left[\sum_{t=1}^{n}\sum_{y \in \mathscr{C}} q_t(y)\hat{s}_t(y)^2\right]$$

$$= \frac{\log|\mathscr{C}|}{\eta} + \frac{\eta}{2}\mathbb{E}\left[\sum_{t=1}^{n}\mathbb{E}_{t-1}\left[\sum_{y \in \mathscr{C}} \frac{q_t(y)T_t(X_t,y)^2 f_t(X_t)^2}{p_t(X_t)^2}\right]\right].$$

The inner conditional expectation is bounded using Lemma 8.3 by

$$\mathbb{E}_{t-1}\left[\sum_{y \in \mathscr{C}} \frac{q_t(y)T_t(X_t,y)^2 f_t(X_t)^2}{p_t(X_t)^2}\right] \leq \log(n) + 2.$$

Therefore the regret of exponential weights relative to the estimated loss function is bounded by

$$\mathbb{E}\left[\widehat{\text{Reg}}_n(x_\star)\right] \leq \frac{\log|\mathscr{C}|}{\eta} + \frac{\eta n}{2}[\log(n) + 2].$$

The next step is to compare $\mathbb{E}[\widehat{\text{Reg}}_n(x_\star)]$ and $\mathbb{E}[\text{Reg}_n(x_\star)]$. By Lemma 8.3,

$$\mathbb{E}_{t-1}[f_t(X_t)] - f_t(x_\star) = \sum_{x \in \mathscr{C}} p_t(x)f_t(x) - f_t(x_\star)$$

$$\leq 2\left[\sum_{x \in \mathscr{C}} q_t(x)s_t(x) - s_t(x_\star)\right] + \frac{1}{2\sqrt{n}}$$

$$= 2\mathbb{E}_{t-1}\left[\sum_{x \in \mathscr{C}} q_t(x)\hat{s}_t(x) - \hat{s}_t(x_\star)\right] + \frac{1}{2\sqrt{n}}.$$

Hence,

$$\mathbb{E}\left[\text{Reg}_n(x_\star)\right] \leq 2\mathbb{E}\left[\widehat{\text{Reg}}_n(x_\star)\right] + \frac{1}{2}\sqrt{n} \leq \frac{2\log|\mathscr{C}|}{\eta} + \eta n[\log(n) + 2] + \frac{1}{2}\sqrt{n}.$$

The claim follows from the choice of η, (8.8), and the fact that $\log|\mathscr{C}| \leq \log(1 + 2\sqrt{n})$ and naive simplification. □

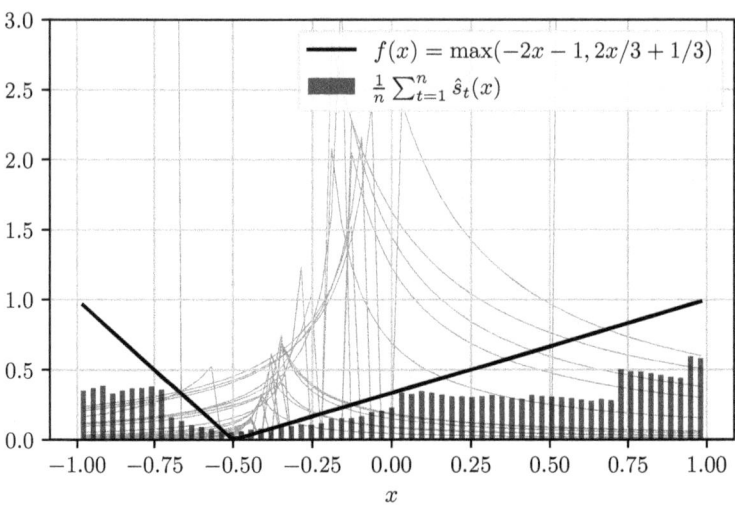

Figure 8.2 The plot shows the estimated losses during the execution of Algorithm 8.2. The thin grey lines are the individual loss estimation functions ($\hat{s}_t$) while the bar chart is the average. The individual loss estimates peak at the point played by the algorithm and decrease away from the mean. This is strange – the loss estimators are quasiconcave while their expectations are convex. Mathematically this form is easy to see by studying the kernel. You should think about why it is reasonable intuitively.

8.3 The Bregman Divergence

This section and the next introduce some tools needed in Section 8.5; specifically, the Bregman divergence, projections for Legendre functions and the modern view of exponential weights.

Bregman divergences are well-defined for any differentiable convex function but have particularly nice properties for the class of Legendre convex functions, which we now define. Our exposition here is probably too brief to really impart the right intuition. There is a beautiful article by Bauschke and Borwein (1997) that explains all the nuances. Let R be a closed proper convex function. R is called essentially smooth if it is differentiable on $\text{int}(\text{dom}(R)) \neq \emptyset$ and $\|R'(x_k)\| \to \infty$ whenever (x_k) converges to $\partial \text{dom}(R)$. R is called essentially strictly convex if it is strictly convex on all convex $C \subset \text{dom}(\partial R) = \{x \colon \partial R(x) \neq \emptyset\}$. R is called Legendre if it is both essentially smooth and essentially strictly convex. Lastly,

8.3 The Bregman Divergence

the Legendre transform of R is

$$R^\star(u) = \sup_{x \in \mathbb{R}^d} \langle u, x \rangle - R(x).$$

Legendre functions have well-behaved Legendre transforms. In particular, when R is Legendre, than R' is a bijection on suitable domains:

Proposition 8.5 (Theorem 26.5, Rockafellar 1970) *Suppose that R is Legendre and $T = R^\star$. Then $R' : \text{int}(\text{dom}(R)) \to \text{int}(\text{dom}(T))$ is a bijection and $(R')^{-1} = T'$.*

Given a convex function $R : \mathbb{R}^d \to \mathbb{R} \cup \{\infty\}$ that is differentiable on $\text{int}(\text{dom}(R))$, the Bregman divergence with respect to R is $D_R : \mathbb{R}^d \times \text{int}(\text{dom}(R)) \to \mathbb{R} \cup \{\infty\}$ defined by $D_R(x, y) = R(x) - R(y) - \langle R'(y), x - y \rangle$.

Proposition 8.6 (Generalised Pythagorean Theorem) *Suppose that $R : \mathbb{R}^d \to \mathbb{R} \cup \{\infty\}$ is Legendre and $C \subset \mathbb{R}^d$ is convex and closed with $C \cap \text{int}(\text{dom}(R)) \neq \emptyset$. For $x \in \text{int}(\text{dom}(R))$ the 'projection' $\Pi(x) = \arg\min_{y \in C} D_R(y, x)$ is unique and for any $z \in C$,*

$$D_R(z, x) \geq D_R(z, \Pi(x)) + D_R(\Pi(x), x).$$

Proof (✯) Let $y = \Pi(x)$. Under the conditions of the theorem, y exists, is unique and $y \in \text{int}(\text{dom}(R))$ (Bauschke and Borwein, 1997, Theorem 3.12). Hence R is differentiable at y and by the first-order optimality conditions for $\Pi(x)$, $\langle R'(y), z - y \rangle - \langle R'(x), z - y \rangle \geq 0$. Therefore,

$$D_R(z, y) + D_R(y, x) = R(z) - R(x) - \langle R'(y), z - y \rangle - \langle R'(x), y - x \rangle$$
$$\leq R(z) - R(x) - \langle R'(x), z - x \rangle$$
$$= D_R(z, x). \qquad \square$$

The Bregman divergence with respect to R is related to the Bregman divergence with respect to $R^\star$ as follows:

Proposition 8.7 *Suppose that R is Legendre; then for all $x, y \in \text{int}(\text{dom}(R))$,*

$$D_R(x, y) = D_{R^\star}(R'(y), R'(x)).$$

Proof (✯) Let $v = R'(y)$, $u = R'(x)$ and $T = R^\star$ and convince yourself that

$T(v) = \langle v, y \rangle - R(y)$ and $T(u) = \langle u, x \rangle - R(x)$. Then

$$\begin{aligned}
D_R(x, y) &= R(x) - R(y) - \langle R'(y), x - y \rangle \\
&= [\langle u, x \rangle - T(u)] - [\langle v, y \rangle - T(v)] - \langle v, x - y \rangle \\
&= T(v) - T(u) - \langle x, v - u \rangle \\
&\stackrel{\star}{=} T(v) - T(u) - \langle T'(u), v - u \rangle \\
&= D_{R^\star}(v, u) \\
&= D_{R^\star}(R'(y), R'(x)),
\end{aligned}$$

where ($\star$) follows from Proposition 8.5 and the rest by substituting the definitions. $\square$

8.4 Exponential Weights and Regularisation

In Chapter 7 we presented the old-school analysis of exponential weights. Later in this chapter we need the modern viewpoint that exponential weights is the same as follow-the-regularised-leader with unnormalised negative entropy (negentropy) regularisation. Unsurprisingly, the analysis is not *really* different. The modern view actually stops before the approximations made in the proof of Theorem 7.8. Most importantly, by using the language of convex analysis we are able to clarify the duality argument used later. The only reason not to introduce this approach in Chapter 7 is that it is somewhat less elementary. Let $R: \mathbb{R}^m \to \mathbb{R} \cup \{\infty\}$ be the unnormalised negative entropy function defined by

$$R(p) = \begin{cases} \sum_{k=1}^m (p_k \log(p_k) - p_k) & \text{if } p \in \mathbb{R}_+^m \\ \infty & \text{otherwise}, \end{cases}$$

where we adopt the convention that $0 \log(0) = 0$. When $p, q \in \Delta_m$, then $D_R(p, q) = \sum_{k=1}^m p_k \log(p_k/q_k)$ is the relative entropy between distributions p and q. In the next exercise you will show that R is Legendre, calculate its dual and show that follow-the-regularised-leader with R is equivalent to exponential weights:

Exercise 8.8 ★ Suppose that $x \in \mathbb{R}^m$ and $q \in (0, \infty)^m$. Show that
(1) R is Legendre and $R^\star(x) = \sum_{k=1}^m \exp(x_k)$,
(2) $\arg\min_{p \in \Delta_m} D_R(p, q) = \dfrac{q}{\|q\|_1}$ and $\arg\min_{p \in \Delta_m} \langle p, x \rangle + R(p) = \dfrac{\exp(-x)}{\|\exp(-x)\|_1}$.

Let $\mathscr{C}$ be a finite set and $m = |\mathscr{C}|$. We identify distributions and functions on $\mathscr{C}$ by vectors in $\mathbb{R}^m$. Concretely, for $p \in \Delta(\mathscr{C}) \equiv \Delta_m$ and $f: \mathscr{C} \to \mathbb{R}$

8.4 Exponential Weights and Regularisation

let $\langle p, f \rangle = \sum_{x \in \mathscr{C}} p(x) f(x)$. Given a learning rate $\eta > 0$ and a sequence of functions $(\hat{s}_t)_{t=1}^n : \mathscr{C} \to \mathbb{R}$, let

$$q_t = \arg\min_{q \in \Delta_m} \sum_{u=1}^{t-1} \eta \langle q, \hat{s}_u \rangle + R(q).$$

By Exercise 8.8, the distribution q_t can be written in its familiar form:

$$q_t(x) = \frac{\exp\left(-\eta \sum_{u=1}^{t-1} \hat{s}_u(x)\right)}{\sum_{y \in \mathscr{C}} \exp\left(-\eta \sum_{u=1}^{t-1} \hat{s}_u(y)\right)}. \tag{8.9}$$

The following refinement of Theorem 7.8 bounds the regret of exponential weights relative to the loss functions $(\hat{s}_t)$.

Theorem 8.9 *Let $(\hat{s}_t)_{t=1}^n : \mathscr{C} \to \mathbb{R}$ be a sequence of functions, q_t be defined as in (8.9) and $\eta > 0$. Then*

$$\max_{q_\star \in \Delta_m} \sum_{t=1}^n \langle q_t - q_\star, \hat{s}_t \rangle \leq \frac{\log m}{\eta} + \frac{1}{\eta} \sum_{t=1}^n \mathscr{S}_{q_t}(\eta \hat{s}_t),$$

where $\mathscr{S}_q(u) = D_{R^\star}(R'(q) - u, R'(q))$ is called the 'stability' function.

Proof (✿) Let $q_\star \in \Delta_m$, $\Phi_t(p) = \sum_{u=1}^t \eta \langle p, \hat{s}_u \rangle + R(p)$ and

$$\tilde{q}_{t+1} \triangleq \arg\min_{q \in \mathbb{R}^m} \eta \langle q, \hat{s}_t \rangle + D_R(q, q_t) = q_t \exp(-\eta \hat{s}_t), \tag{8.10}$$

where the second equality follows by solving the optimisation problem analytically. Note that $q_t \in \Delta_m^+$ holds by (8.9), which means that $\tilde{q}_{t+1} \in \Delta_m^+$ and by Exercise 8.8,

$$q_{t+1} = \arg\min_{q \in \Delta_m} D_R(q, \tilde{q}_{t+1}). \tag{8.11}$$

Repeating the proof of Theorem 6.5,

$$\sum_{t=1}^{n} \langle q_t - q_\star, \hat{s}_t \rangle \leq \frac{R(q_\star) - R(q_1)}{\eta} + \frac{1}{\eta} \sum_{t=1}^{n} (\Phi_t(q_t) - \Phi_t(q_{t+1}))$$

$$\stackrel{(a)}{=} \frac{R(q_\star) - R(q_1)}{\eta} + \frac{1}{\eta} \sum_{t=1}^{n} D_{\Phi_t}(q_t, q_{t+1})$$

$$\stackrel{(b)}{=} \frac{R(q_\star) - R(q_1)}{\eta} + \frac{1}{\eta} \sum_{t=1}^{n} D_R(q_t, q_{t+1})$$

$$\stackrel{(c)}{\leq} \frac{R(q_\star) - R(q_1)}{\eta} + \frac{1}{\eta} \sum_{t=1}^{n} D_R(q_t, \tilde{q}_{t+1})$$

$$\stackrel{(d)}{=} \frac{R(q_\star) - R(q_1)}{\eta} + \frac{1}{\eta} \sum_{t=1}^{n} D_{R^\star}(R'(\tilde{q}_{t+1}), R'(q_t))$$

$$\stackrel{(e)}{=} \frac{R(q_\star) - R(q_1)}{\eta} + \frac{1}{\eta} \sum_{t=1}^{n} D_{R^\star}(R'(q_t) - \eta \hat{s}_t, R'(q_t))$$

$$\leq \frac{\log(m)}{\eta} + \frac{1}{\eta} \sum_{t=1}^{n} \mathcal{S}_{q_t}(\eta \hat{s}_t).$$

where (a) follows from the definition of the Bregman divergence and because by the first-order optimality conditions $\langle \Phi'_t(q_{t+1}), q_t - q_{t+1} \rangle = 0$, which holds with equality because $q_t, q_{t+1} \in \Delta_m^+$. (b) is because $D_{\Phi_t} = D_R$ by virtue of the fact that the Bregman divergence of a linear function vanishes. (c) follows from (8.11) and Proposition 8.6, which yields

$$D_R(q_t, \tilde{q}_{t+1}) \geq D_R(q_t, q_{t+1}) + D_R(q_{t+1}, \tilde{q}_{t+1}) \geq D_R(q_t, q_{t+1}).$$

Finally, (d) follows from Proposition 8.7 and (e) from (8.10) and because $R'(q) = \log(q)$. □

Remark 8.10 To see why Theorem 8.9 refines Theorem 7.8 (and Remark 7.10), when $\hat{s}_t$ is nonnegative, then

$$\mathcal{S}_{q_t}(\eta \hat{s}_t) = D_{R^\star}(R'(q_t) - \eta \hat{s}_t, R'(q_t))$$

$$= \sum_{x \in \mathcal{C}} q_t(x) \exp(-\eta \hat{s}_t(x)) - 1 + \eta \langle q_t, \hat{s}_t \rangle$$

$$\leq \sum_{x \in \mathcal{C}} q_t(x) \left[1 - \eta \hat{s}_t(x) + \frac{\eta^2 \hat{s}_t(x)^2}{2} \right] - 1 + \eta \langle q_t, \hat{s}_t \rangle$$

$$= \frac{\eta^2}{2} \sum_{x \in \mathcal{C}} q_t(x) \hat{s}_t(x)^2,$$

where we used the inequality $\exp(x) \leq 1 - x + x^2/2$ for $x \geq 0$. Combining with Theorem 8.9 recovers the bound in Remark 7.10. Theorem 7.8 is recovered by assuming that $|\eta \hat{s}_t(x)| \leq 1$ for all x and using the inequality $\exp(-x) \leq 1 - x + x^2$ for $|x| \leq 1$ instead.

8.5 Exploration by Optimisation

In Section 8.2 we showed how to use exponential weights for one-dimensional bandits. While the algorithm there is efficient and straightforward to implement, much human ingenuity was needed to define the surrogate loss and exploration distribution. There is a principled way to construct both of these objects that eliminates the need for imagination at the cost of computational efficiency. Note that we are not assuming that $d = 1$ in this section. The results and concepts in this section and the next are connected in a complicated way. You may find Figure 8.3 useful to join the dots.

Assumption 8.11 Throughout this section as well as Sections 8.6 and 8.7 we assume that $\mathscr{C} \subset K$ is a finite set with $m \triangleq |\mathscr{C}|$ such that
(1) $\log m \leq d \log(1 + 16dn^2)$; and
(2) for all $f \in \mathscr{F}_b$ there exists an $x \in \mathscr{C}$ such that $f(x) \leq \inf_{y \in K} f(y) + 1/n$.

Exercise 8.12 ★ Prove a cover satisfying the conditions in Assumption 8.11 exists. You may want to combine Proposition 7.4, Proposition 3.10, Proposition 3.13 and Theorem 3.15.

Let us start by giving the regret bound for the (abstract) Algorithm 8.1.

Theorem 8.13 Let $x_\star = \arg\min_{x \in \mathscr{C}} \sum_{t=1}^n f_t(x)$ and $p_\star \in \Delta(\mathscr{C})$ be a Dirac on $x_\star$. The expected regret of Algorithm 8.1 relative to $x_\star$ is bounded by

$$\mathbb{E}[\mathrm{Reg}_n(x_\star)] \leq \frac{\log m}{\eta} + \sum_{t=1}^n \mathbb{E}\left[\langle p_t - p_\star, f_t \rangle + \langle p_\star - q_t, \hat{s}_t \rangle + \frac{1}{\eta}\mathscr{S}_{q_t}(\eta \hat{s}_t)\right].$$

Proof The proof follows immediately from Theorem 8.9:

$$\mathbb{E}[\mathrm{Reg}_n(x_\star)] = \sum_{t=1}^n \mathbb{E}\left[\langle p_t - p_\star, f_t \rangle\right]$$

$$= \sum_{t=1}^n \mathbb{E}\left[\langle p_t - p_\star, f_t \rangle + \langle p_\star - q_t, \hat{s}_t \rangle + \langle q_t - p_\star, \hat{s}_t \rangle\right]$$

$$\leq \frac{\log m}{\eta} + \sum_{t=1}^n \mathbb{E}\left[\langle p_t - p_\star, f_t \rangle + \langle p_\star - q_t, \hat{s}_t \rangle + \frac{1}{\eta}\mathscr{S}_{q_t}(\eta \hat{s}_t)\right],$$

where the second equality holds by adding and subtracting $\langle q_t - p_\star, \hat{s}_t \rangle$ and the inequality by Theorem 8.9. □

Standard methods for analysing concrete instantiations of Algorithm 8.1 essentially always bound the term inside the expectation uniformly for all t, independently of f_t and q_t and $p_\star$. Note that f_t and $p_\star$ are unknown, while q_t is the exponential weights distribution, which is known at the start of round t. In light of this, a natural idea is to choose the distribution p_t and loss estimation function $\hat{s}_t$ that minimise the upper bound. This is the idea we execute now.

Exploration by Optimisation

To simplify the notation, let us momentarily drop the time indices and let $q \in \Delta_m^+$. The learner samples X from some distribution $p \in \Delta_m^+$ and observes $Y = f(X)$. The estimated surrogate loss $\hat{s}$ is a vector in $\mathbb{R}^m$ (a function from $\mathscr{C}$ to $\mathbb{R}$) but the learner chooses it based on the observations X and Y. So let $\mathscr{E}$ be the set of all functions $e \colon \mathscr{C} \times \mathbb{R} \to \mathbb{R}^m$, with the idea that the estimated surrogate loss will be the function $\hat{s} = e(X, Y)/p(X)$. The division by $p(X)$ is a normalisation that makes a certain function defined below convex (see Exercise 8.14) and is also the reason why we insist that $p \in \Delta_m^+$ rather than Δ_m. The decision for the learner is to choose the exploration distribution $p \in \Delta_m^+$ and exploration function $e \in \mathscr{E}$. The adversary chooses $f \in \mathscr{F}_b$ and $p_\star \in \Delta_m$. Looking at Theorem 8.13, we hope you agree that the following function may be important:

$$\Lambda_{\eta,q}(p, e \| p_\star, f) = \frac{1}{\eta} \mathbb{E}\left[\langle p - p_\star, f \rangle + \left\langle p_\star - q, \frac{e(X,Y)}{p(X)} \right\rangle + \frac{1}{\eta} \mathcal{S}_q\left(\frac{\eta e(X,Y)}{p(X)} \right) \right],$$

where the expectation is over $X \sim p$ and $Y = f(X)$. You might view $\Lambda_{\eta,q}$ as a function from two pairs of tuples: (p, e) selected by the learner and $(p_\star, f)$ selected by the adversary. A fundamental quantity that appears throughout the following sections is the minimax value of this game, which is defined in stages by the following quantities:

$$\Lambda_{\eta,q}^\star(p, e) = \sup_{p_\star \in \Delta_m} \sup_{f \in \mathscr{F}_b} \Lambda_{\eta,q}(p, e \| p_\star, f) \quad \text{and}$$

$$\Lambda_{\eta,q}^\star = \inf_{p \in \Delta_m^+} \inf_{e \in \mathscr{E}} \Lambda_{\eta,q}^\star(p, e) \quad \text{and}$$

$$\Lambda^\star = \sup_{\eta > 0} \sup_{q \in \Delta_m^+} \Lambda_{\eta,q}^\star.$$

Exercise 8.14 ★ Prove that $(p, e) \mapsto \Lambda_{\eta,q}(p, e \| p_\star, f)$ is convex for any $p_\star \in \Delta_m$ and $f \in \mathscr{F}_b$. You may find it useful to expand the expectation and use the fact that $u \mapsto \mathcal{S}_q(u)$ is convex, which by the perspective construction (Boyd and Vandenberghe, 2004, §2.3.3) shows that $(u, v) \mapsto v\mathcal{S}(u/v)$ is convex on $\mathbb{R}^d \times (0, \infty)$.

8.5 Exploration by Optimisation

Since the supremum of convex functions is convex it follows from Exercise 8.14 that $(p, e) \mapsto \Lambda^\star_{\eta,q}(p, e)$ is convex. Note, however, that $\mathscr{E}$ is infinite-dimensional. So in general it may be non-trivial to efficiently minimise this function. Despite this, these functions are surprisingly easy to handle mathematically, as we shall see later. The exploration-by-optimisation algorithm is quite simple:

---
1 **args**: learning rate $\eta > 0$, precision $\varepsilon > 0$, $\mathscr{C} \subset K$
2 **for** $t = 1$ **to** n
3   compute distribution $q_t(x) = \frac{\exp(-\eta \sum_{u=1}^{t-1} \hat{s}_u(x))}{\sum_{y \in \mathscr{C}} \exp(-\eta \sum_{u=1}^{t-1} \hat{s}_u(y))}$
4   find distribution $p_t \in \Delta_m^+$ and $e_t \in \mathscr{E}$ such that $\Lambda^\star_{\eta,q_t}(p_t, e_t) \leq \Lambda^\star_{\eta,q_t} + \varepsilon$
5   sample X_t from p_t and observe $Y_t = f_t(X_t)$
6   compute $\hat{s}_t = e_t(X_t, Y_t)/p_t(X_t)$

Algorithm 8.3   Exploration by optimisation

The following theorem is almost immediate:

Theorem 8.15   *Under Assumptions 8.1 and 8.11, the expected regret of Algorithm 8.3 is bounded by*

$$\mathbb{E}[\text{Reg}_n] \leq 1 + \frac{\log m}{\eta} + n\eta\Lambda^\star + n\eta\varepsilon.$$

Proof Let $x_\star = \arg\min_{x \in \mathscr{C}} \sum_{t=1}^n f_t(x)$ and $p_\star \in \Delta(\mathscr{C})$ be a Dirac on $x_\star$. By Assumption 8.11, Theorem 8.13 and the definition of $\hat{s}_t$ in Algorithm 8.3,

$$\mathbb{E}[\text{Reg}_n] \leq 1 + \mathbb{E}[\text{Reg}_n(x_\star)]$$
$$\leq 1 + \frac{\log m}{\eta} + \sum_{t=1}^n \mathbb{E}\left[\langle p_t - p_\star, f_t\rangle + \langle p_\star - q_t, \hat{s}_t\rangle + \frac{1}{\eta}\mathscr{S}_{q_t}(\eta\hat{s}_t)\right]$$
$$\leq 1 + \frac{\log m}{\eta} + n\eta\Lambda^\star + n\eta\varepsilon. \quad \square$$

Combining the definition with Theorem 8.15 immediately yields the following corollary:

Corollary 8.16   *Under the same conditions as Theorem 8.15 and with*

$$\eta = \sqrt{\frac{\log m}{n(\varepsilon + \Lambda^\star)}},$$

the regret of Algorithm 8.3 is upper-bounded by

$$\mathbb{E}[\text{Reg}_n] \leq 1 + 2\sqrt{n\Lambda^\star \log m} + 2\sqrt{n\varepsilon \log m} \overset{\varepsilon \to 0}{\to} 1 + 2\sqrt{n\Lambda^\star \log m}\,.$$

In the next section we explain a connection between $\Lambda^\star$ and a concept used for analysing Bayesian bandit problems called the information ratio. This method will eventually show that

$$\Lambda^\star = O\left(d^4 \log(nd)\right)\,.$$

Combining this with Assumption 8.11 to bound $\log m = O(d \log(nd))$ and with Corollary 8.16 shows that the regret of Algorithm 8.3 is bounded by

$$\mathbb{E}[\text{Reg}_n] = O\left(d^{2.5}\sqrt{n} \log(dn)\right)\,.$$

Let us emphasise again that this is not much of an algorithm because there is no known computationally efficient method for solving the optimisation problem that defines p_t and e_t.

8.6 Bayesian Convex Bandits

In the Bayesian version of the convex bandit problem the learner is given a distribution ξ on $\mathscr{F}_b^n$. The loss functions $(f_t)_{t=1}^n$ are sampled from ξ and the Bayesian regret of a learning algorithm $\mathscr{A}$ is

$$\text{bReg}_n(\mathscr{A}, \xi) = \mathbb{E}\left[\sup_{x \in K} \sum_{t=1}^n (f_t(X_t) - f_t(x))\right],$$

where by 'learning algorithm' we simply mean a function that (measurably) maps history sequences to distributions over actions in $\mathscr{C}$. Note that here the expectation integrates over the randomness in the loss functions and hence the supremum over $x \in K$ appears inside the expectation. As in the rest of the book we will not say much about constructing probability spaces and measurability. The measurable space on which ξ is defined sometimes plays an important technical role. Generally speaking, in what follows it is assumed that the discrete σ-algebra is used on $\mathscr{F}_b^n$ and that ξ really is a distribution in the sense that it is supported on countably many atoms. $\text{bReg}_n(\mathscr{A}, \xi)$ is nothing more than the expectation of the standard regret, integrating over the loss functions with respect to the prior ξ. The minimax Bayesian regret is

$$\text{bReg}_n^\star = \sup_\xi \inf_\mathscr{A} \text{bReg}_n(\mathscr{A}, \xi)\,.$$

Compare this to the minimax adversarial regret, which is

$$\text{Reg}_n^\star = \inf_{\mathscr{A}} \sup_{(f_t)_{t=1}^n} \text{Reg}_n(\mathscr{A}, (f_t)_{t=1}^n) \,.$$

Whenever you see an expression like this, a minimax theorem should come to mind. Indeed, the minimax adversarial regret can be rewritten as

$$\text{Reg}_n^\star = \inf_{\mathscr{A}} \sup_{\xi} \text{bReg}_n(\mathscr{A}, \xi) \,.$$

By interpreting an algorithm as a probability measure over deterministic algorithms, both $\mathscr{A} \mapsto \text{bReg}_n(\mathscr{A}, \xi)$ and $\xi \mapsto \text{bReg}_n(\mathscr{A}, \xi)$ are linear functions and from this one should guess the following theorem as a consequence of some kind of minimax theorem.

Theorem 8.17 (Lattimore and Szepesvári 2019) $\text{Reg}_n^\star = \text{bReg}_n^\star$.

Theorem 8.17 means that one way to bound the adversarial regret is via the Bayesian regret. One positive aspect of this idea is that the existence of a prior makes the Bayesian setting more approachable. On the other hand, constructing a prior-dependent algorithm showing that the Bayesian regret is small for any prior does not give you an algorithm for the adversarial setting. The approach is non-constructive.

Remark 8.18   The above setup is the Bayesian version of the adversarial convex bandit problem. In the Bayesian version of the stochastic convex bandit problem the prior is on $\mathscr{F}_b$ rather than $\mathscr{F}_b^n$ and the observation is $f(X_t) + \varepsilon_t$ where f is sampled at the beginning of the interaction from the prior. Sometimes the noise follows some known distribution. Alternatively, the prior could be over both the loss function and the noise distribution.

8.7 Duality and the Information Ratio

We now briefly explain the main tool for bounding the Bayesian regret. Recall that in the Bayesian setting $f_1, \ldots, f_n$ are sampled from a prior ξ on $\mathscr{F}_b^n$ and let $X_\star = \arg\min_{x \in \mathscr{C}} \sum_{t=1}^n f_t(x)$ be the optimal action in $\mathscr{C}$ in hindsight, which is a random element. Let ν be a probability measure on $\Delta_m \times \mathscr{F}_b$ and $p \in \Delta_m$. Later ν will be the law of $(p_\star, f_t)$ under the posterior associated with prior ξ and data $X_1, Y_1, \ldots, X_{t-1}, Y_{t-1}$ where $p_\star$ is a Dirac on $X_\star$. Define

$$\Delta(p, \nu) = \mathbb{E}[\langle p - p_\star, f \rangle] \quad \text{and} \quad I(p, \nu) = \mathbb{E}\left[\text{KL}(\mathbb{E}[p_\star | X, f(X)], \mathbb{E}[p_\star])\right],$$

where $(X, p_\star, f)$ has law $p \otimes \nu$ and KL is the relative entropy (or Kullback–Leibler divergence). As we remarked already, $\text{KL} = D_R$ where R is the unnormalised negentropy potential. Intuitively, $\Delta(p, \nu)$ is the expected regret suffered when sampling X from p relative to $p_\star$ on loss f sampled from ν, while $I(p, \nu)$ is the information gained about the optimal action when observing X and $f(X)$. The information ratio captures the exploration/exploitation trade-off made by a learner and is defined by

$$\Psi(p, \nu) = \frac{\Delta(p, \nu)^2}{I(p, \nu)}.$$

The information ratio will be small when the regret under p is small relative to the information gained about the optimal action. The minimax information ratio is

$$\Psi^\star = \sup_{\nu \in \Delta(\Delta_m \times \mathscr{F}_b)} \min_{p \in \Delta(\mathscr{C})} \Psi(p, \nu).$$

We can now introduce the information-directed sampling algorithm, which is designed for minimising the Bayesian regret. In every round the algorithm computes the posterior based on information observed so far and then samples its action X_t from the distribution p_t minimising the information ratio.

```
1  args: prior ξ on 𝓕ᵇⁿ
2  for t = 1 to n
3      compute the posterior νₜ = ℙₜ₋₁((p⋆, fₜ) ∈ ·)
4      find pₜ = arg min_{p∈Δ(𝒞)} Ψ(p, νₜ)
5      sample Xₜ from pₜ and observe Yₜ = fₜ(Xₜ)
```

Algorithm 8.4 Information-directed sampling. The random variable $p_\star$ is a Dirac on $X^\star = \arg\min_{x \in \mathscr{C}} \sum_{t=1}^n f_t(x)$.

The next theorem bounds the regret of Algorithm 8.4 in terms of the minimax information ratio.

Theorem 8.19 *Under Assumption 8.11, the Bayesian minimax regret is bounded by*

$$\mathrm{bReg}_n^\star \leq 1 + \sqrt{n\Psi^\star \log m} \leq 1 + \sqrt{dn\Psi^\star \log\left(1 + 16dn^2\right)}.$$

Proof Let $\xi \in \Delta(\mathscr{F}_b^n)$ be any prior distribution and $\mathscr{A}$ be information-directed sampling (Algorithm 8.4). By Assumption 8.11, for all $f \in \mathscr{F}_b$ there exists an $x \in \mathscr{C}$ with

$$f(x) \leq \inf_{y \in K} f(y) + \frac{1}{n}.$$

8.7 Duality and the Information Ratio

Therefore, with $p_\star$ a Dirac on $X_\star = \arg\min_{x \in \mathscr{C}} \sum_{t=1}^n f_t$, Assumption 8.11 implies that

$$\text{bReg}_n(\xi, \mathscr{A}) = \mathbb{E}\left[\sup_{x \in K} \sum_{t=1}^n (f_t(X_t) - f_t(x))\right] \leq 1 + \mathbb{E}\left[\sum_{t=1}^n (f_t(X_t) - f_t(X_\star))\right].$$

Let $\nu_t = \mathbb{P}_{t-1}((p_\star, f_t) \in \cdot)$, which is a probability measure on $\Delta_m \times \mathscr{F}_b$. The learner samples X_t from a distribution $p_t \in \Delta(\mathscr{C})$ such that $\Psi(p_t, \nu_t) \leq \Psi^\star$, which means that

$$\Delta(p_t, \nu_t)^2 \leq I(p_t, \nu_t)\Psi^\star. \tag{8.12}$$

By the tower rule for conditional expectation and the definition of $\Delta(p_t, \nu_t)$,

$$\mathbb{E}\left[\sum_{t=1}^n (f_t(X_t) - f_t(X_\star))\right] = \mathbb{E}\left[\sum_{t=1}^n \Delta(p_t, \nu_t)\right].$$

By the definition of the information ratio,

$$\mathbb{E}\left[\sum_{t=1}^n \Delta(p_t, \nu_t)\right] \overset{(a)}{\leq} \mathbb{E}\left[\sum_{t=1}^n \sqrt{I(p_t, \nu_t)\Psi^\star}\right]$$

$$\overset{(b)}{\leq} \sqrt{n\Psi^\star \mathbb{E}\left[\sum_{t=1}^n I_t(p_t, \nu_t)\right]}$$

$$\overset{(c)}{=} \sqrt{n\Psi^\star \mathbb{E}\left[\text{KL}(\mathbb{P}_{X_\star | X_1, Y_1, \ldots, X_n, Y_n}, \mathbb{P}_{X_\star})\right]}$$

$$\overset{(d)}{\leq} \sqrt{n\Psi^\star \log(m)},$$

where (a) follows from (8.12), (b) from Cauchy–Schwarz and (c) from the chain rule for information gain (Cover and Thomas, 2012, §2.5). (d) follows because $X_\star \in \mathscr{C}$ and the information in any $\mathscr{C}$-valued random variable is at most $\log |\mathscr{C}| = \log m$. Finally, bound $\log m$ using Assumption 8.11. □

There is no obvious reason why $\Psi^\star$ should be well controlled. However, the information ratio is bounded by the following theorem:

Theorem 8.20 (Lattimore 2020) $\Psi^\star \leq Cd^4 \log(nd)$ where $C > 0$ is an absolute constant.

The proof of Theorem 8.20 is quite involved and is not included here. Even when you can sample from ν, the distribution p witnessing the upper bound on $p \mapsto \Psi(p, \nu)$ involves positioning certain convex bodies in minimal surface area position and is not practical to compute. Combining Theorem 8.20 with Theorem 8.19 and Theorem 8.17 yields the following theorem:

114   8 Exponential Weights

Theorem 8.21 $\text{Reg}_n^\star = \text{bReg}_n^\star \leq C d^{2.5} \sqrt{n} \log(dn)$.

The above theorem shows that the adversarial minimax regret and Bayesian minimax regret can be bounded in terms of the minimax information ratio. The next theorem shows that the adversarial regret of Algorithm 8.3 can also be bounded in terms of the minimax information ratio.

Theorem 8.22 (Lattimore and György 2021b) $\Lambda^\star \leq \frac{1}{4}\Psi^\star$.

Except for the one-dimensional setting (Section 8.2), the only bounds we have on $\Lambda^\star$ are via Theorem 8.22 and bounds on $\Psi^\star$. Remarkably the constant $\frac{1}{4}$ means the upper bounds obtained by the mirror descent analysis of Algorithm 8.3 and information-directed sampling exactly match:

$$\text{bReg}_n^\star \leq 1 + \sqrt{n\Psi^\star \log m} \qquad \text{by Theorem 8.19}$$

$$\text{Reg}_n^\star \leq 1 + 2\sqrt{n\Lambda^\star \log m} \qquad \text{by Corollary 8.16}$$

$$\leq 1 + \sqrt{n\Psi^\star \log m}\,. \qquad \text{by Theorem 8.22}$$

Proof sketch of Theorem 8.22   We outline the key ingredients of the argument, ignoring measure-theoretic and topological challenges associated with applying the minimax theory. Let $A = \Delta_m \times \mathcal{F}_b$ and $\Delta(A)$ be the space of probability distributions on A with the discrete σ-algebra. Given $p \in \Delta_m^+$, $e \in \mathcal{E}$ and $\nu \in \Delta(A)$, let

$$\Lambda_{\eta,q}(p, e \| \nu) = \int_A \Lambda_{\eta,q}(p, e \| p_\star, f) \, d\nu(p_\star, f)$$

$$= \frac{1}{\eta} \mathbb{E}\left[\langle p - p_\star, f \rangle + \left\langle p_\star - q, \frac{e(X,Y)}{p(X)} \right\rangle + \frac{1}{\eta} \mathcal{S}_q\left(\frac{\eta e(X,Y)}{p(X)}\right)\right], \quad (8.13)$$

where expectation integrates over $(p_\star, f, X)$ with law $\nu \otimes p$ and $Y = f(X)$. The expectation $\nu \mapsto \Lambda_{\eta,q}(p, e \| \nu)$ is linear and Exercise 8.14 shows that $(p, e) \mapsto \Lambda_{\eta,q}(p, e \| \nu)$ is convex. This hints at the possibility of applying a minimax theorem. Technically you should use Sion's theorem, which besides some kind of convex/concave structure also needs compactness. Let us just say now that the following holds:

$$\Lambda_{\eta,q}^\star = \inf_{p \in \Delta_m^+} \inf_{e \in \mathcal{E}} \sup_{\nu \in \Delta(A)} \Lambda_{\eta,q}(p, e \| \nu) = \sup_{\nu \in \Delta(A)} \inf_{p \in \Delta_m^+} \inf_{e \in \mathcal{E}} \Lambda_{\eta,q}(p, e \| \nu)\,.$$

Hence, the proof will be completed if we can show that for all $\nu \in \Delta(A)$,

$$\inf_{p \in \Delta_m^+} \inf_{e \in \mathcal{E}} \Lambda_{\eta,q}(p, e \| \nu) \leq \Psi^\star\,. \qquad (8.14)$$

When ν is given, it turns out that the estimation function e minimising (8.13)

8.7 Duality and the Information Ratio

can be computed by differentiation and is

$$e(x, y) = \frac{p(x)}{\eta} \left(R'(q) - R'(\mathbb{E}[p_\star | f(x) = y]) \right).$$

Two observations: (1) the above is not obvious – you need to confirm it yourself; (2) the conditional expectation is only well-defined if x is in the support of p and y is in the support of $f(x)$. When this is not the case you may define $e(x, y)$ in any way you please. Let $p \in \Delta_m^+$ and let $p_{\text{po}} = \mathbb{E}[p_\star | X, Y]$ and $p_{\text{pr}} = \mathbb{E}[p_\star]$, which are the posterior and prior distributions, respectively. Then

$$\Lambda_{\eta,q}(p, e\|v) = \frac{1}{\eta} \mathbb{E}\left[\langle p - p_\star, f \rangle + \left\langle p_\star - q, \frac{e(X, Y)}{p(X)} \right\rangle + \frac{1}{\eta} \mathcal{S}_q\left(\frac{\eta e(X, Y)}{p(X)}\right) \right]$$

$$\stackrel{(a)}{=} \frac{\Delta(p, v)}{\eta} + \frac{1}{\eta^2} \mathbb{E}\left[\langle p_\star, R'(q) - R'(p_{\text{po}}) \rangle - R^\star(R'(q)) + R^\star(R'(p_{\text{po}})) \right]$$

$$\stackrel{(b)}{=} \frac{\Delta(p, v)}{\eta} + \frac{1}{\eta^2} \mathbb{E}\left[\langle p_{\text{pr}}, R'(q) \rangle - \langle p_{\text{po}}, R'(p_{\text{po}}) \rangle - R^\star(R'(q)) + R^\star(R'(p_{\text{po}})) \right]$$

$$\stackrel{(c)}{=} \frac{\Delta(p, v)}{\eta} - \frac{1}{\eta^2} \mathbb{E}\left[D_{R^\star}(R'(q), R'(p_{\text{pr}})) + D_{R^\star}(R'(p_{\text{pr}}), R'(p_{\text{po}})) \right]$$

$$\stackrel{(d)}{\leq} \frac{\Delta(p, v)}{\eta} - \frac{1}{\eta^2} \mathbb{E}\left[D_{R^\star}(R'(p_{\text{pr}}), R'(p_{\text{po}})) \right]$$

$$\stackrel{(e)}{=} \frac{\Delta(p, v)}{\eta} - \frac{1}{\eta^2} \mathbb{E}\left[D_R(p_{\text{po}}, p_{\text{pr}}) \right],$$

where (a) follows from the definition of $\Lambda_{\eta,q}(p, e\|v)$ and by substituting the definition of e and using $\mathcal{S}_q(u) = D_{R^\star}(R'(q) - u, R'(q))$. (b) follows from the definitions of p_{po} and p_{pr}; (c) by the definition of the dual Bregman divergences. (d) follows since Bregman divergences are always non-negative. (e) follows from duality (Proposition 8.7). Ideally we would now choose p to be the minimiser of the information ratio $\Psi(\cdot, v)$, but this is generally only supported on two coordinates and hence not in Δ_m^+ for $m > 2$. Fortunately it is straightforward to show that when p minimises $\Psi(\cdot, v)$, then $[0, 1) \ni \delta \mapsto \Psi((1-\delta)p + \delta \mathbf{1}/m, v)$ is continuous and hence there exists a $p \in \Delta_m^+$ such that $\Psi(p, v) \leq \Psi^\star + \varepsilon$ for any $\varepsilon > 0$. Let $\varepsilon > 0$ and $p \in \Delta_m^+$ be such that $\Psi(p, v) \leq \Psi^\star + \varepsilon$. Then

$$\Lambda_{\eta,q}(p, e\|v) \leq \frac{\Delta(p, v)}{\eta} - \frac{1}{\eta^2} \mathbb{E}\left[D_R(p_{\text{po}}, p_{\text{pr}}) \right]$$

$$\leq \frac{1}{\eta}\sqrt{(\Psi^\star + \varepsilon)\mathbb{E}[D_R(p_{\text{po}}, p_{\text{pr}})]} - \frac{1}{\eta^2}\mathbb{E}[D_R(p_{\text{po}}, p_{\text{pr}})]$$

$$\leq \sup_{x \geq 0} \left(x\sqrt{\Psi^\star + \varepsilon} - x^2 \right)$$

$$= \frac{\Psi^\star + \varepsilon}{4},$$

where in the second inequality we used the definition of p and the information ratio. Since $\varepsilon > 0$ was arbitrary, (8.14) holds and the proof is complete. □

Exercise 8.23 ★★📖 Make the proof of Theorem 8.22 fully rigorous.

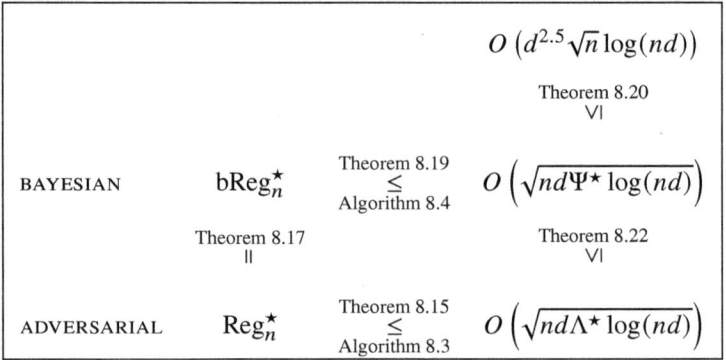

Figure 8.3 The relationship between the results in this chapter, showing two ways to bound $\operatorname{Reg}_n^\star$. The first (Bayesian) is completely non-constructive via minimax duality (Theorem 8.17). The second (adversarial) is by bounding the regret of Algorithm 8.3. The latter is only to be preferred slightly since Algorithm 8.3 has no obvious efficient implementation.

8.8 Notes

8.i Aside from inconsequential simplifications, the kernel-based method in one dimension was designed by Bubeck et al. (2017). They extended the general idea to the higher dimensions to design a polynomial time algorithm with regret $d^{10.5}\sqrt{n}$, which was the first polynomial time algorithm with $\operatorname{poly}(d)\sqrt{n}$ regret in the adversarial setting. Sadly there are many challenges to generalising Algorithm 8.2 and ultimately the higher-dimensional version is not realistically implementable.

8.ii Information-directed sampling and the core analysis was introduced by Russo and Van Roy (2014). The idea has been generalised to frequentist settings, which are explained in depth by Kirschner (2021) who also details many properties of the information ratio. The application to convex bandits to prove bounds non-constructively for adversarial bandit problems is by Bubeck et al. (2015), who were the first to show that $\tilde{O}(\sqrt{n})$ regret is possible for

8.8 Notes

adversarial convex bandits for losses in $\mathscr{F}_\flat$. The extension to higher dimensions is by Bubeck and Eldan (2018) and Lattimore (2020). The latter shows that the minimax regret for adversarial bandits is at most $\tilde{O}(d^{2.5}\sqrt{n})$. This remains the best bound known, though it is matched in all but logarithmic terms by online Newton step (Chapter 11).

8.iii The oldest and most well-known algorithm for Bayesian bandits is Thompson sampling (Thompson, 1933), which in every round samples a loss function from the posterior and plays the action that minimises the sampled loss. This algorithm has near-optimal Bayesian regret for some models, including finite-armed bandits and linear bandits (Russo and Van Roy, 2016). For convex bandits Bakhtiari et al. (2025) showed that Thompson sampling has $\tilde{O}(\sqrt{n})$ Bayesian regret in the stochastic setting when $d = 1$. They also show that for large d there exist priors for which the Bayesian regret of Thompson sampling is exponential in the dimension. In the Bayesian adversarial setting with $d = 1$ it is not known if Thompson sampling has $\tilde{O}(\sqrt{n})$ regret. Bubeck et al. (2015) showed that it does not have a bounded information ratio, which means that new proof techniques would be needed to prove $\tilde{O}(\sqrt{n})$ regret.

8.iv The duality between mirror descent and the information ratio was established by Zimmert and Lattimore (2019) and Lattimore and György (2021b) with the latter proving the more difficult direction. These connections have led to a beautiful theory on the complexity of sequential decision making in great generality (Foster et al., 2021, 2022). In brief, algorithms like exploration-by-optimisation are provably near-optimal in a minimax sense. There are many subtleties and you should read the aforementioned works.

8.v Bakhtiari et al. (2025) prove that the minimax information ratio satisfies $\Psi^\star = \tilde{\Omega}(d^2)$, which shows that the best possible bound obtainable via a naive application of the information-theoretic machinery is $\tilde{O}(d^{1.5}\sqrt{n})$.

Exercise 8.24 ★★▰/? Use the arguments by Zimmert and Lattimore (2019) and the lower bound on $\Psi^\star$ by Bakhtiari et al. (2025) to prove that $\Lambda^\star = \tilde{\Omega}(d^2)$.

The exercise shows that no matter how you explore or estimate losses, the classical analysis of exponential weights cannot yield a bound on the regret better than $\tilde{O}(d^{1.5}\sqrt{n})$. Importantly, however, lower bounds on the complexity measures do not imply lower bounds on the minimax regret. There exist other settings where the minimax regret is better than the upper bound in Theorem 8.19. For example, Lattimore and Hao (2021) show that in bandit phase retrieval the information-theoretic machinery suggests a bound of $\tilde{O}(d^{1.5}\sqrt{n})$ while the minimax regret is $\tilde{\Theta}(d\sqrt{n})$.

9
Cutting Plane Methods

Like the bisection method (Chapter 4), cutting plane methods are most naturally suited to the stochastic setting. For the remainder of the chapter we assume the setting is stochastic and the loss function is bounded:

Assumption 9.1 The following hold:

(1) The setting is stochastic, meaning that $f_t = f$ for all t; and

(2) the loss f is in $\mathscr{F}_\mathrm{b}$.

The bounds established in this chapter are worse than what we will show for online Newton step in Chapter 10, but the analysis is considerably more straightforward and the algorithms are easy to tune. To keep things simple we study the sample complexity rather than the regret, though most likely the algorithms and analysis can be adapted to the regret setting without too much difficulty as we discuss briefly in the notes. This chapter also introduces an algorithm for infinite-armed bandits that may be of independent interest. The highlight of the chapter is a mechanism for finding a suitable cutting plane with only noisy zeroth-order access to the loss function (Section 9.4). This is then applied to bound the sample complexity of the centre of gravity method (Section 9.5) and the method of the inscribed ellipsoid (Section 9.6). In both cases the sample complexity is $\tilde{O}(d^4/\varepsilon^2)$ with different computational properties. The ellipsoid method is discussed in Section 9.7 and has a moderately worse sample complexity.

Remark 9.2 This chapter is full of half-spaces and ellipsoids, so let us remind you that $E(x, A) = \{y \in \mathbb{R}^d : \|x - y\|_{A^{-1}} \leq 1\}$ is an ellipsoid centred at x and $H(x, \eta) = \{y \in \mathbb{R}^d : \langle y - x, \eta \rangle \leq 0\}$ is a half-space.

Stochastic Oracle Notation

Because of the modular nature of the algorithms in this chapter, it is not practical to keep track of the round of interaction. This necessitates a new notation for the interaction protocol. When we write $y \sim f(x)$ in an algorithm it means that $y = f(x) + \varepsilon$ where ε is 1-subgaussian conditioned on the history (all previous queries).

9.1 High-Level Idea

The basic idea is to let S be a subset of K with non-negligible volume on which the loss f is nearly minimised. Then initialise $K_1 = K$ and recursively compute a decreasing sequence (K_k) of subsets such that at least one of the following holds:

- The 'centre' x_k of K_k is a near-minimiser of f.
- $K_{k+1} \subset K_k$ contains S.

Note there are many definitions of the centre of a convex body, as we will soon see. The largest $k_{\max}$ such that $K_{k_{\max}}$ contains S can be bounded as a function of how fast $k \mapsto \text{vol}(K_k)$ decreases. Combining this with the above requirements on (K_k) and (x_k) yields a bound on how many iterations $k_{\max}$ are needed before there exists a near-minimiser among $x_1, \ldots, x_{k_{\max}}$. Generally speaking $k_{\max} = \text{poly}(d)$ and the final step is to query the loss on $x_1, \ldots, x_{k_{\max}}$ to identify a near-minimiser among them (Section 9.3). In the one-dimensional problem there is limited scope for imagination but in high dimensions there are several intersecting complexities, namely, what geometric procedure will reduce the volume sufficiently fast? Can it be computed efficiently and how does it interact with convexity? Standard methods are:

- the ellipsoid method (Shor, 1977; Yudin and Nemirovskii, 1977, 1976);
- the centre of gravity method (Newman, 1965; Levin, 1965);
- Vaidya's method (Vaidya, 1996) and its refinement by Lee et al. (2015);
- the analytic centre method (Nesterov, 1995; Atkinson and Vaidya, 1995);
- the method of the inscribed ellipsoid (Tarasov et al., 1988).

We focus on the centre of gravity method, ellipsoid method and method of the inscribed ellipsoid. Let us make the considerations above a little more concrete. By Lemma 9.4 below there exists a (usually non-regular) simplex $S \subset K$ such that the loss f is near-optimal for all $x \in S$ and $\log(\text{vol}(K)/\text{vol}(S)) = \tilde{O}(d)$. Remember a half-space is a set $H = \{y \colon \langle y - x, \eta \rangle \leq 0\} \triangleq H(x, \eta)$ for nonzero direction $\eta \in \mathbb{R}^d$ and point $x \in \mathbb{R}^d$. We will study three methods, which classically operate as follows (see also Figure 9.1):

- The centre of gravity method starts with $K_1 = K$ and iteratively updates $K_{k+1} = K_k \cap H_k$ where H_k is a half-space with boundary ∂H_k passing close to the centre of mass x_k of K_k. We additionally insist that either x_k is near-optimal or H_k contains S. A generalisation of Grünbaum's inequality shows that $\log \mathrm{vol}(K_{k+1}) \le \log \mathrm{vol}(K) - ck$ for some universal constant $c > 0$. Suppose now that $x_1, \ldots, x_k$ are not near-optimal. Then by induction $S \subset K_{k+1}$. But this implies that $\mathrm{vol}(K_{k+1}) \ge \mathrm{vol}(S)$ and this is only possible for $k = \tilde{O}(d)$. Consequentially, if $k = \tilde{\Theta}(d)$, then one of $x_1, \ldots, x_k$ is near-optimal. With deterministic zeroth-order access to the loss function the learner can simply return the $\arg\min\{f(x) : x \in x_1, \ldots, x_k\}$ while with noise it can treat the k candidates as a finite-armed bandit and use an elementary pure exploration bandit algorithm to approximate the arg min as explained in Section 9.3. In Remark 9.6 we explain why S is chosen to be a simplex.
- The method of the inscribed ellipsoid is the same as the centre of gravity method, but rather than using centre of mass it uses the centre of the largest ellipsoid contained in K_k. It can be shown that $\log \mathrm{vol}(K_{k+1}) \le \log \mathrm{vol}(K) + \tilde{O}(d) - ck$ for some universal constant $c > 0$. Hence, like the centre of gravity method, the number of iterations where $S \subset K_{k+1}$ is at most $\tilde{O}(d)$.
- The ellipsoid method starts with an ellipsoid E_1 such that $K \subset E_1$. The ellipsoid is updated by finding a half-space H_k with boundary passing close to the centre of E_k and such that $S \subset H_k$ and E_{k+1} is calculated as the smallest ellipsoid containing $E_k \cap H_k$. The classical theory of the shallow cut ellipsoid method shows that $\log \mathrm{vol}(E_{k+1}) \le \log \mathrm{vol}(E_1) - \frac{ck}{d}$ for some universal constant $c > 0$. Hence, provided that $\log \mathrm{vol}(E_1) \le \log \mathrm{vol}(K) + \tilde{O}(d)$, the number of iterations is at most $\tilde{O}(d^2)$.

The big question is how to find the half-spaces passing close to the relevant centre that contains the near-optimal simplex with high probability. Besides this there are many details to be sorted out. Most notably, how close to the centre of mass or centre of ellipsoid do we need the half-space to be?

Remark 9.3 The centre of gravity and inscribed ellipsoid methods require only $\tilde{O}(d)$ iterations while the ellipsoid method needs $\tilde{O}(d^2)$. The advantage of the latter is the remarkable fact that the smallest ellipsoid containing $E \cap H$ for ellipsoid E and half-space H has a closed-formed expression, while estimating the centre of mass or finding the maximum-volume inscribed ellipsoid is less elementary.

9.1 High-Level Idea

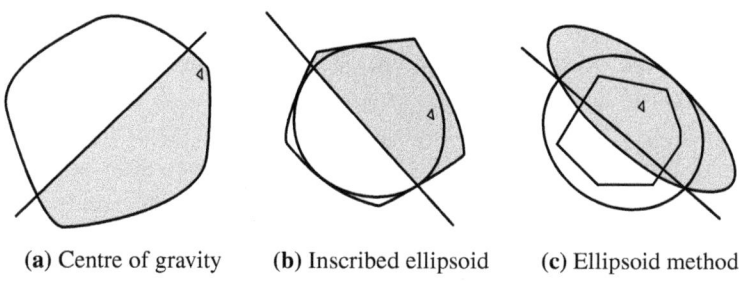

(a) Centre of gravity   (b) Inscribed ellipsoid   (c) Ellipsoid method

Figure 9.1 An illustration of one iteration of the centre of gravity, inscribed ellipsoid and ellipsoid methods.

We finish with the promised lemma establishing the existence of a near-optimal simplex S.

Lemma 9.4 *Suppose that K is a convex body and $f \in \mathcal{F}_b$. Then, for any $\varepsilon \in (0, 1)$, there exists a simplex $S = \text{conv}(x_1, \ldots, x_{d+1}) \subset K$ such that $f(x) \leq \inf_{y \in K} f(y) + \varepsilon$ for all $x \in S$ and*

$$\text{vol}(S) \geq \left(\frac{\varepsilon}{2}\right)^d \frac{\text{vol}(K)}{d!\, \text{vol}(\mathbb{B}_d^d)}.$$

In particular, by Proposition A.1(1), $\log(\text{vol}(S)) = \log(\text{vol}(K)) - O(d \log(d/\varepsilon))$.

Proof The construction is illustrated in Figure 9.2. Let $f_\star = \inf_{x \in K} f(x)$. Suppose that K is in John's position so that by Theorem 3.15, $\mathbb{B}_1^d \subset K \subset \mathbb{B}_d^d$. Letting $e_1, \ldots, e_d$ be the standard basis vectors, then obviously $T = \text{conv}(0, e_1, \ldots, e_d) \subset K$. Let x be some point such that $f(x) \leq f_\star + \frac{\varepsilon}{2}$ and $S = \{(1 - \frac{\varepsilon}{2})x + \frac{\varepsilon}{2}y : y \in T\}$. Then, for any $z \in S$ there exists a $y \in T$ such that $z = (1 - \frac{\varepsilon}{2})x + \frac{\varepsilon}{2}y$ and since $f \in \mathcal{F}_b$ is bounded and convex, $f(z) \leq (1-\frac{\varepsilon}{2})f(x) + \frac{\varepsilon}{2}f(y) \leq f(x) + \varepsilon/2 \leq f_\star + \varepsilon$. Furthermore, $\text{vol}(T) = 1/d!$ and

$$\text{vol}(S) = \left(\frac{\varepsilon}{2}\right)^d \text{vol}(T) = \left(\frac{\varepsilon}{2}\right)^d \frac{1}{d!}.$$

Meanwhile, $\text{vol}(K) \leq \text{vol}(\mathbb{B}_d^d)$, which implies that

$$\text{vol}(S) \geq \left(\frac{\varepsilon}{2}\right)^d \frac{\text{vol}(K)}{d!\, \text{vol}(\mathbb{B}_d^d)}.$$

The result for general K follows via an affine map into John's position. □

Remark 9.5 Lemma 9.4 is moderately crude. For example, you can improve the result by taking T to be the regular simplex inside $\mathbb{B}_1^d$. Alternatively one may try to avoid using John's theorem, letting T be the simplex of largest volume contained in K. For this simplex it is known that for all convex bodies K, $(\text{vol}(T)/\text{vol}(K))^{1/d} \geq c/\sqrt{d}$ for some absolute constant $c > 0$ and this is not improvable (Galicer et al., 2019). For our purpose, however, these refinements make only negligible differences to the constants in our regret bounds.

Remark 9.6 You might wonder why S is a simplex rather than just the level set $\{x \colon f(x) \leq f_\star + \varepsilon\}$, which contains S. The reason is that later we will want to prove that S is in some randomised half-space with high probability and for this it suffices to show that the vertices of S are contained in the half-space with high probability, which involves a union bound over the $d + 1$ vertices. Any convex shape with $\text{poly}(d)$ vertices would be sufficient. But there is no hope to improve the bounds in this chapter by modifying this construction except for miniscule constants.

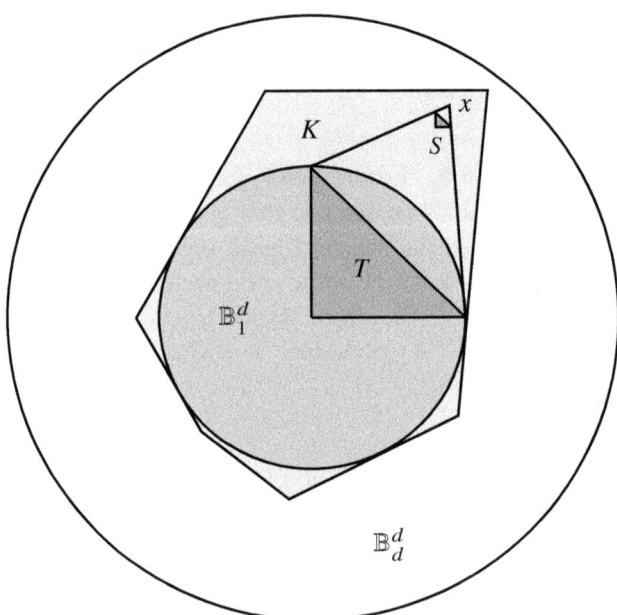

Figure 9.2 The construction used in the proof of Lemma 9.4.

9.2 Infinite-Armed Bandits

We make a brief aside to study a kind of infinite-armed bandit problem. Suppose that ρ is a probability measure on K and $h: K \to (-\infty, 1]$ is an unknown function such that $\mathbb{E}[h(X)] \geq 0$ when X has law ρ. In contrast to the rest of the book, we are looking for a procedure for (crudely) maximising h. We suppose a learner can sample from ρ and for any $x \in K$ the learner can obtain an unbiased estimate of $h(x)$ with subgaussian tails (just as in the standard convex bandit problem). We formalise this with the following assumption:

Assumption 9.7 The learner can sample from a probability measure ρ on K and $h: K \to (-\infty, 1]$ is a function such that

$$\int_K h(x) \, d\rho(x) \geq 0.$$

For any $x \in K$ the learner can sample from $\mathscr{K}(\cdot|x)$ where $\mathscr{K}$ is a probability kernel from K to $\mathbb{R}$ such that for all $x \in K$

(1) the mean of $\mathscr{K}(\cdot|x)$ is $h(x)$; and
(2) the probability measure $\mathscr{K}(\cdot|x)$ is σ-subgaussian:

$$\int_{\mathbb{R}} \exp((y/\sigma)^2) \mathscr{K}(dy|x) \leq 2.$$

There is no geometry in this problem. The function h needs to be measurable but besides this there is no requirement for continuity or any other structural properties beyond the semi-boundedness. Of course, in such circumstances there is no hope whatsoever to actually maximise h: for example, when it is the indicator function of some singleton and ρ is continuous. What can be achieved depends on the law of $h(X)$ when X has law ρ. Since we have assumed that $\mathbb{E}[h(X)] \geq 0$, it seems reasonable that we can find a point x such that $h(x)$ is close to 0. Given an $\varepsilon \in (0, 1)$ and $\delta \in (0, 1)$, we construct an algorithm that with probability at least $1 - \delta$ returns an x such that $h(x) \geq -\varepsilon$ and in expectation takes at most

$$O\left(\frac{\sigma^2 \log(1/\delta)}{\varepsilon^2}\right)$$

samples from the probability kernel $\mathscr{K}$.

Remark 9.8 The expected number of times Algorithm 9.1, presented below, samples from ρ is $O(1/\varepsilon)$. In our application, samples from $\mathscr{K}(\cdot|x)$ correspond to querying the loss function while ρ is an explicit distribution on K that is easy to sample from.

The basic idea is to sequentially sample points x from ρ and then take samples from $\mathcal{K}(\cdot|x)$ to test whether or not $h(x)$ is suitably large. The big question is how many samples to take from $\mathcal{K}(\cdot|x)$. And in fact the algorithm will vary the number of samples it takes, for reasons we now explain. Remember we assumed that $\mathbb{E}[h(X)] \geq 0$. There are multiple ways this can happen. Here are two extreme examples:

- $h(X) = 2\varepsilon$ with probability $1/2$ and $h(X) = -2\varepsilon$ otherwise
- $h(X) = 1$ with probability $2\varepsilon/(1 + 2\varepsilon)$ and $h(X) = -2\varepsilon$ otherwise

And of course there are many intermediate options and mixtures. Suppose we want to design an algorithm that finds an x with $h(x) \geq -\varepsilon$ for distributions of the first kind. Then we should repeatedly sample points x from ρ and then query $\mathcal{K}(\cdot|x)$ roughly $\tilde{O}(\sigma^2/\varepsilon^2)$ times until we can statistically prove that $h(x)$ is large enough. Since by assumption $h(X) \geq -\varepsilon$ with constant probability, in expectation this requires only $\tilde{O}(\sigma^2/\varepsilon^2)$ queries. On the other hand, for distributions of the second kind the algorithm needs in expectation $O(1/\varepsilon)$ queries to ρ to find an x with $h(x) = 1$. But to identify when this has happened only requires $\tilde{O}(\sigma^2)$ queries to $\mathcal{K}(\cdot|x)$ because the margin is large. Algorithm 9.1 essentially dovetails these two algorithms and all intermediaries on a carefully chosen grid. Concretely, the inner loop samples $O(1/\varepsilon)$ points from ρ and queries the kernel with sample sizes ranging from $\tilde{O}(\sigma^2/\varepsilon^2)$ to $\tilde{O}(\sigma^2)$. We will prove that with constant probability this inner loop succeeds in identifying an x such that $h(x) \geq -\varepsilon$. The outer loop simply repeats the inner loop to boost the probability of success. The quantity $b_{m,k}$ is chosen so that $\sum_{k=1}^{\infty} \sum_{m=1}^{\infty} b_{m,k}^{-1} = 1$ and scales the confidence level to permit a union bound over all m, k.

9.2 Infinite-Armed Bandits

```
1  def INF(ε ∈ (0, 1), δ ∈ (0, 1), ρ, 𝒦)
2    for m = 1 to ∞:
3      for k = 1 to k_max ≜ 2 + ⌊2/ε⌋:
4        b_{m,k} = [k(k + 1)][m(m + 1)]
5        n_{m,k} = ⌈64σ² log(2b_{m,k}/δ) / (ε²k²)⌉  and  C_{m,k} = 2σ√(log(2b_{m,k}/δ) / n_{m,k})
6        sample x_{m,k} from ρ
7        sample H_1,...,H_{n_{m,k}} from 𝒦(·|x_{m,k})
8        compute ĥ(x_{m,k}) = (1/n_{m,k}) Σ_{t=1}^{n_{m,k}} H_t
9        if ĥ(x_{m,k}) - C_{m,k} ≥ -ε:  return x_{m,k}
```

Algorithm 9.1 Infinite-armed bandit algorithm

Theorem 9.9 *Suppose that Algorithm 9.1 is run with inputs $\varepsilon \in (0, 1)$, $\delta \in (0, 1)$ and probability measure ρ and $\mathcal{K}$ satisfying Assumption 9.7. Then the following hold:*

(1) In expectation Algorithm 9.1 takes at most $O\left(\frac{\sigma^2 \log(1/\delta)}{\varepsilon^2}\right)$ samples from the probability kernel $\mathcal{K}$.

(2) With probability at least $1 - \delta$ Algorithm 9.1 returns an x such that $h(x) \geq -\varepsilon$.

Proof (✲) We proceed in two steps.

Step 1: Setup, concentration and correctness

Let $\mathbb{P}_m$ be the probability measure obtained by conditioning on all data obtained during the first m outer loops, let G_m be the event defined by

$$G_m = \bigcap_{k=1}^{k_{\max}} \left\{ \left| \widehat{h}(x_{m,k}) - h(x_{m,k}) \right| \leq C_{m,k} \right\}$$

and let $G = \cap_{m=1}^{\infty} G_m$, which are events that certain estimates lie close to the truth. We also define an event V_m that holds in outer iteration m when the algorithm samples a point $x_{m,k}$ with suitably large $h(x_{m,k})$, which is defined in terms of its complement by

$$V_m^c = \bigcap_{k=1}^{k_{\max}} \left\{ h(x_{m,k}) < \frac{(k-2)\varepsilon}{2} \right\}.$$

Note that $(x_{m,k})_{m,k}$ are independent and identically distributed samples from ρ. A union bound combined with Theorem B.17 shows that $\mathbb{P}(G) \geq 1 - \delta$. The same argument along with naive simplification shows that

$$\mathbb{P}_{m-1}(G_m) \geq 1/2. \tag{9.1}$$

Suppose the algorithm halts and G holds. Then

$$h(x_{k,m}) \geq \widehat{h}(x_{m,k}) - C_{m,k} \geq -\varepsilon,$$

which, since $\mathbb{P}(G) \geq 1 - \delta$, establishes correctness (part (2)).

Step 2: Bounding stopping time

Let M be the smallest m such that the algorithm halts:

$$M = \min\left\{m : \max_{1 \leq k \leq k_{\max}} \left(\widehat{h}(x_{m,k}) - C_{m,k}\right) \geq -\varepsilon\right\}.$$

Suppose that V_m and G_m both hold; then there exists a $k \in \{1, \ldots, k_{\max}\}$ such that

$$\widehat{h}(x_{m,k}) - C_{m,k} \geq h(x_{m,k}) - 2C_{m,k} \geq \frac{(k-2)\varepsilon}{2} - 2C_{m,k} \geq -\varepsilon,$$

which by construction means the algorithm halts and consequently $M \leq m$. Suppose X has law ρ. Then

$$\begin{aligned}
\mathbb{P}_{m-1}(V_m^c) &= \mathbb{P}\left(\bigcap_{k=1}^{k_{\max}} \left\{h(x_{m,k}) < \frac{(k-2)\varepsilon}{2}\right\}\right) \\
&= \prod_{k=1}^{\infty} \mathbb{P}\left(h(X) < \frac{(k-2)\varepsilon}{2}\right) \\
&= \exp\left(\sum_{k=1}^{\infty} \log\left[1 - \mathbb{P}\left(h(X) \geq \frac{(k-2)\varepsilon}{2}\right)\right]\right) \\
&\leq \exp\left(-\sum_{k=1}^{\infty} \mathbb{P}\left(h(X) \geq \frac{(k-2)\varepsilon}{2}\right)\right) \\
&\leq \exp(-1)
\end{aligned}$$

where for the second last inequality we used the fact that $\log(1 + x) \leq x$ for all x. The final inequality follows because

$$\begin{aligned}
\varepsilon &\leq \mathbb{E}[h(X) + \varepsilon] \\
&\leq \int_0^\infty \mathbb{P}(h(X) \geq t - \varepsilon)\, dt \\
&\leq \frac{\varepsilon}{2} + \frac{\varepsilon}{2} \sum_{k=1}^{\infty} \mathbb{P}\left(h(X) \geq \frac{(k-2)\varepsilon}{2}\right),
\end{aligned}$$

9.3 Best Arm Identification

where the first inequality holds because $\mathbb{E}[h(X)] \geq 0$ and the last by comparing the integral to the sum (Figure 9.3). Hence, $\mathbb{P}_{m-1}(V_m^c) \leq \exp(-1)$ and by the definitions, a union bound and (9.1),

$$\mathbb{1}(M \geq m)\mathbb{P}_{m-1}(M > m) \leq \mathbb{P}_{m-1}(V_m^c) + \mathbb{P}_{m-1}(G_m^c) \leq \exp(-1) + \frac{1}{2} \leq \frac{9}{10}.$$

Therefore $\mathbb{P}(M > m) \leq (9/10)^m$ by induction. Part (1) follows because

$$\sum_{k=1}^{k_{\max}} n_{m,k} = O\left(\frac{\sigma^2 \log(m/\delta)}{\varepsilon^2}\right)$$

and $\sum_{m=1}^{\infty} (9/10)^{m-1} \log(m/\delta) = O(\log(1/\delta))$. □

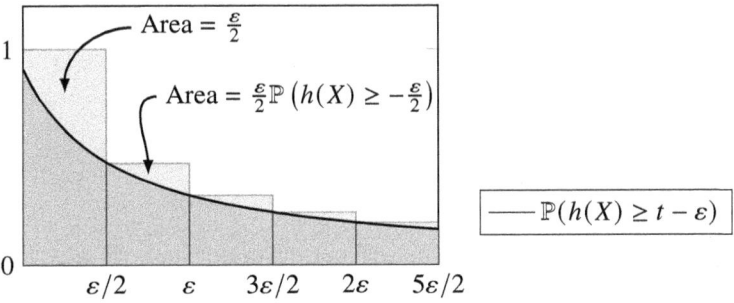

Figure 9.3 Integral approximation in the proof of Theorem 9.9.

9.3 Best Arm Identification

The methods proposed in Sections 9.5 and 9.6 effectively return a short list of candidates for near-minimisers. We need a simple subroutine to identify a near-minimiser from this list.

Theorem 9.10 *With probability at least* $1 - \delta$, *Algorithm 9.2 returns an* $x \in \{x_1, \ldots, x_m\}$ *such that*

$$f(x) \leq \min_{y \in \{x_1, \ldots, x_m\}} f(y) + \varepsilon.$$

Furthermore, it queries the loss function f *at most* $m \lceil 16 \log(2m/\delta)/\varepsilon^2 \rceil$ *times.*

Proof By Theorem B.17 and a union bound, with probability at least $1 - \delta$,

$$|\widehat{f}(x_k) - f(x_k)| \leq \frac{\varepsilon}{2} \text{ for all } 1 \leq k \leq m.$$

```
1   def BAI(ε, δ, x₁, ..., xₘ)
2       n = ⌈16 log(2m/δ) / ε²⌉
3       for k = 1 to m:
4           sample Y₁ ~ f(xₖ), ..., Yₙ ~ f(xₖ)
5           compute f̂(xₖ) = (1/n) Σₜ₌₁ⁿ Yₜ
6       return arg min{f̂(x): x ∈ x₁, ..., xₘ}
```

Algorithm 9.2 Best arm identification

Therefore, for the x returned by the algorithm and any $y \in \{x_1, \ldots, x_m\}$,

$$f(x) \leq \widehat{f}(x) + \frac{\varepsilon}{2} \leq \widehat{f}(y) + \frac{\varepsilon}{2} \leq f(y) + \varepsilon.$$ □

9.4 Finding a Cutting Plane

Let $f \in \mathscr{F}_b$ with $f_\star = \inf_{x \in K} f(x)$. All cutting plane methods abstract away the construction of the half-space. The methods assume a process that given a 'centre' x of a convex set K return a half-space H such that at least one of the following holds:

○ x is close to ∂H and H contains all near-minimisers of the loss function.
○ x is a near-minimiser of the loss function.

When the learner has gradient access to the loss function f, then the half-space $H = H(x, f'(x)) \triangleq \{y \in \mathbb{R}^d : \langle f'(x), y - x \rangle \leq 0\}$ satisfies the conditions. To see why, suppose that $f(y) \leq f(x)$. Then by convexity $f(y) \geq f(x) + \langle f'(x), y - x \rangle \geq f(y) + \langle f'(x), y - x \rangle$, which implies that $y \in H$. Hence, either $f(x) \leq f_\star + \varepsilon$ and x is a near-minimiser or $f(x) \geq f_\star + \varepsilon$ and any y with $f(y) \leq f_\star + \varepsilon$ is in H.

In the bandit setting we do not have access to the gradient, so another procedure is needed to find H. Furthermore, the condition that H contains all near-minimisers of the loss function will be relaxed to require that any specific near-minimiser is in H with high probability. We have been a bit vague about how close x needs to be to the half-space. This depends on which cutting plane method is used but fortunately can be abstracted away in the analysis of each method by using a change of coordinates. Concretely, it suffices to make the following assumption:

9.4 Finding a Cutting Plane

Assumption 9.11 K is a convex body such that $\mathbb{B}_1^d \subset K \subset \mathbb{B}_r^d$ for some $r > 1$.

The 'centre' is now taken to be $\mathbf{0}$. The mission in this section is to design a randomised algorithm that queries the loss function as few times as possible and returns a half-space H such that

- the boundary of the half-space intersects $\mathbb{B}_1^d$: $\partial H \cap \mathbb{B}_1^d \neq \emptyset$, and (9.2)
- $\mathbb{P}(y \in H) \geq 1 - \delta$ for any $y \in K$ with $f(y) \leq f(\mathbf{0}) - \varepsilon$.

Remark 9.12 The second item above implies that either $f(\mathbf{0}) \leq f_\star + 2\varepsilon$ or for any y with $f(y) \leq f_\star + \varepsilon$, $\mathbb{P}(y \in H) \geq 1 - \delta$.

Approach

A natural idea is to try and use the gradient of a smoothed surrogate. Let U have law $\mathscr{U}(\mathbb{B}_1^d)$ and

$$s(x) = \mathbb{E}[2f(U/4 + x/2) - f(U/2)], \qquad (9.3)$$

which is the same surrogate that appeared in Chapter 6. We saw there that s is differentiable, convex and optimistic: $s(x) \leq f(x)$ for all x. Generally speaking the half-space $H = \{y : \langle s'(x), y - x \rangle \leq 0\}$ need not contain the minimisers of f. But when $s(x)$ is sufficiently large, then H does contain near-minimisers of f.

Lemma 9.13 Let $H = H(x, s'(x))$. Then $y \in H$ for all y with $f(y) \leq s(x)$.

Proof Suppose that $f(y) \leq s(x)$. Then, by convexity of s,

$$f(y) \geq s(y) \geq s(x) + \langle s'(x), y - x \rangle \geq f(y) + \langle s'(x), y - x \rangle,$$

where in the first inequality we used the fact that $s \leq f$ is optimistic (Lemma 6.9). The second follows from convexity of s and the third by the assumption that $s(x) \geq f(y)$. Rearranging shows that $\langle s'(x), y - x \rangle \leq 0$ and therefore $y \in H$. □

Lemma 9.13 suggests a simple plan:

- Find an $x \in \mathbb{B}_1^d$ such that $s(x)$ is nearly as large as $f(\mathbf{0})$.
- Find an estimate $\hat{s}'(x)$ of the gradient of s at x.
- Propose the half-space $H(x, \hat{s}'(x))$.

But why should there exist a point $x \in \mathbb{B}_1^d$ where $s(x)$ is large?

Lemma 9.14 Suppose that U, V are independent random vectors with law $\mathscr{U}(\mathbb{B}_1^d)$ and $h(x) = s(x) - f(\mathbf{0})$. Then $\mathbb{E}[h(V)] \geq 0$.

Proof By convexity of f,

$$\begin{aligned}
\mathbb{E}[s(V)] &= \mathbb{E}[2f(V/2 + U/4) - f(U/2)] \\
&\geq \mathbb{E}[2f(V/2) - f(U/2)] && \text{Jensen's inequality} \\
&= \mathbb{E}[f(U/2)] && V \stackrel{d}{=} U \\
&\geq f(\mathbf{0}). && \text{Jensen's inequality}
\end{aligned}$$

Rearranging completes the proof. □

Since the maximum is larger than the expectation, Lemma 9.14 shows there exists an $x \in \mathbb{B}_1^d$ such that $s(x) \geq f(\mathbf{0})$. Moreover, a point nearly satisfying this can be found using Algorithm 9.1, as we now explain. To implement this plan we need an oracle that can provide estimates of $h(x) = s(x) - f(\mathbf{0})$ for any $x \in \mathbb{B}_1^d$. And at the same time we provide an estimator for the gradients of s, namely

$$s'(x) = \frac{4d}{\text{vol}(\mathbb{S}_1^{d-1})} \int_{\mathbb{S}_1^{d-1}} f(x/2 + u/4) u \, du. \tag{9.4}$$

---

1 **def** $\mathcal{K}(x)$
2   sample U_1, U_2 from $\mathcal{U}(\mathbb{B}_1^d)$
3   let $X_1 = U_1/4 + x/2$ and observe $Y_1 \sim f(X_1)$
4   let $X_2 = U_2/2$ and observe $Y_2 \sim f(X_2)$
5   let $X_3 = \mathbf{0}$ and observe $Y_3 \sim f(X_3)$
6   **return** $2Y_1 - Y_2 - Y_3$

Algorithm 9.3 Returns an unbiased estimate of $h(x) = s(x) - f(\mathbf{0})$

The following simple lemma shows that Algorithm 9.3 returns an unbiased estimate of $s(x) - f(\mathbf{0})$ that is also subgaussian:

Lemma 9.15 *Suppose that Algorithm 9.3 is run with input $x \in \mathbb{B}_1^d$ and has output Y. Then $\mathbb{E}[Y] = s(x) - f(\mathbf{0})$ and $\|Y - \mathbb{E}[Y]\|_{\psi_2} \leq 4$.*

Proof That $\mathbb{E}[Y] = s(x) - f(\mathbf{0})$ is immediate from the definition of the surrogate (9.3) and the construction of the algorithm. The bound on the Orlicz norm follows from the triangle inequality for Orlicz norms (Fact B.1) and because the noise is subgaussian (Assumption 1.4). □

9.4 Finding a Cutting Plane

```
1  def ESTIMATE-GRADIENT(ε, δ, x):
2     n = 484d log(2/δ) / ε²
3     for t = 1 to n:
4        sample U_t from 𝒰(𝕊₁^(d-1)) and X_t = x/2 + U_t/4
5        let Y_t ~ f(X_t)
6        ŝ'(x) ≜ (4d/n) Σ_{t=1}^n U_t Y_t
7     return ŝ'(x)
```

Algorithm 9.4 Returns an unbiased estimate of $s'(x)$

Algorithm 9.4 returns an estimate of the gradient of $s'(x)$. The following lemma provides a high-probability bound on the quality of this estimate.

Lemma 9.16 *Suppose that $\hat{s}'(x)$ is the output of Algorithm 9.4 given input $x \in \mathbb{B}_1^d$. Then, for any $\eta \in \mathbb{S}_1^{d-1}$, with probability at least $1 - \delta$,*

$$|\langle \hat{s}'(x) - s'(x), \eta \rangle| \leq \varepsilon.$$

Proof Since $Y_t = f(X_t) + \varepsilon_t$ where $\|\varepsilon_t\|_{\psi_2} \leq 1$, it follows from the assumption that $f \in \mathcal{F}_b$, the triangle inequality for the norm $\|\cdot\|_{\psi_2}$ (Fact B.1) and Lemma B.2 that

$$\|Y_t\|_{\psi_2} \leq \|\varepsilon_t\|_{\psi_2} + \|f(X_t)\|_{\psi_2} \leq 1 + \frac{1}{\sqrt{\log(2)}}.$$

Combining this with Propositions B.12 and B.14 shows that

$$\|\langle U_t, \eta \rangle Y_t\|_{\psi_1} \leq \|\langle U_t, \eta \rangle\|_{\psi_2} \|Y_t\|_{\psi_2}$$

$$\leq \|\eta\| \sqrt{\frac{4}{3(d+1)}} \left(1 + \frac{1}{\sqrt{\log(2)}}\right) \leq \frac{2.6}{\sqrt{d+1}}.$$

Let $Z_t = \langle 4dU_t Y_t - s'(x), \eta \rangle$. The random variables $Z_1, \ldots, Z_n$ are independent and $\mathbb{E}[Z_t] = 0$ for all $1 \leq t \leq n$ because by (9.4), $4dU_t Y_t$ is an unbiased estimator of $s'(x)$. By the above display and the fact that $\mathbb{E}[4dU_t Y_t] = s'_t(x)$,

$$\|Z_t\|_{\psi_1} = \|\langle 4dU_t Y_t, \eta \rangle - \mathbb{E}[\langle 4dU_t Y_t, \eta \rangle]\|_{\psi_1}$$

$$\leq \left(1 + \frac{1}{\log(2)}\right) \|4d\langle U_t, \eta \rangle Y_t\|_{\psi_1} \qquad \text{Lemma B.6}$$

$$= 4d\left(1 + \frac{1}{\log(2)}\right) \|\langle U_t, \eta \rangle Y_t\|_{\psi_1} \qquad \text{Fact B.1}$$

$$\leq 11\sqrt{d}.$$

Therefore, by Bernstein's inequality (Theorem B.18) with probability at least $1 - \delta$,

$$|\langle \hat{s}'(x) - s'(x), \eta \rangle| = \left| \frac{1}{n} \sum_{t=1}^{n} Z_t \right|$$

$$\leq 11\sqrt{d} \max\left(\sqrt{\frac{4 \log(2/\delta)}{n}}, \frac{2 \log(2/\delta)}{n} \right)$$

$$\leq \varepsilon,$$

where the last inequality follows from the definition of n. □

At last we are in a position to use Algorithm 9.1 to find a suitable point to cut and Algorithm 9.4 to estimate the gradient of the surrogate loss.

```
1  def CUT(f, ε, δ, r):
2      let ρ be the uniform measure on 𝔹₁ᵈ
3      x = INF(ε/2, δ/2, ρ, 𝒦)              # Algorithm 9.1
4      g = ESTIMATE-GRADIENT(ε/4r, δ/2, x)    # Algorithm 9.4
5      return H(x, g)
```

Algorithm 9.5 Returns a half-space satisfying (9.2) under Assumption 9.11

Theorem 9.17 *Suppose that $f(y) \leq f(0) - \varepsilon$. The following hold:*

(1) *With probability at least $1 - \delta$ Algorithm 9.5 returns a half-space H with $y \in H$ and $\partial H \cap \mathbb{B}_1^d \neq \emptyset$.*

(2) *In expectation Algorithm 9.5 makes at most $O\left(\frac{dr^2 \log(1/\delta)}{\varepsilon^2}\right)$ queries to the loss function.*

Proof Recall that $h(x) = s(x) - f(0)$. By Lemma 9.14,

$$\int_{\mathbb{B}_1^d} h(x) \, d\rho(x) \geq 0.$$

Moreover, Lemma 9.15 shows that Algorithm 9.3 supplies the kind of stochastic oracle for h needed by Algorithm 9.1. Hence, by Theorem 9.9, with probability at least $1 - \delta/2$, the call to Algorithm 9.1 returns an $x \in \mathbb{B}_1^d$ such that $h(x) \geq -\frac{\varepsilon}{2}$, which implies that $s(x) - f(0) \geq -\frac{\varepsilon}{2}$. By assumption $f(0) \geq f(y) + \varepsilon$. Combining this with a union bound and Lemma 9.16 shows that with probability at least $1 - \delta$,

$$\begin{aligned}
f(y) &\geq s(y) \\
&\geq s(x) + \langle s'(x), y - x \rangle \\
&\geq f(0) - \frac{\varepsilon}{2} + \langle s'(x), y - x \rangle \\
&\geq f(y) + \frac{\varepsilon}{2} + \langle s'(x), y - x \rangle \\
&\geq f(y) + \langle \hat{s}'(x), y - x \rangle .
\end{aligned}$$

Therefore $\langle \hat{s}(x), y - x \rangle \leq 0$, which shows that $y \in H$ as required. Since $x \in \mathbb{B}_1^d$ and $x \in \partial H(x, \hat{s}'(x))$ it follows trivially that $\partial H \cap \mathbb{B}_1^d \neq \emptyset$. The bound on the number of queries follows from Theorem 9.9 and the construction of Algorithm 9.4. □

9.5 Centre of Gravity Method

Let $K \subset \mathbb{R}^d$ be a convex body and H be a half-space. We are interested in the conditions on H and K such that $\text{vol}(K \cap H) \leq \gamma \text{vol}(K)$ for some constant γ. Grünbaum's inequality provides such a result for half-spaces H passing through the centre of mass:

Theorem 9.18 (Grünbaum 1960)   *Let K be a convex body, $y = \frac{1}{\text{vol}(K)} \int_K x \, dx$ and $H = H(y, \eta)$ for any direction $\eta \neq 0$. Then*

$$\frac{\text{vol}(K \cap H)}{\text{vol}(K)} \leq \left(\frac{d}{d+1} \right)^d \leq 1 - \frac{1}{e}.$$

The half-space need not pass through exactly the centre:

Theorem 9.19 (Bertsimas and Vempala 2004)   *Let K be a convex body in isotropic position and $H = \{x : \langle x - y, \eta \rangle\}$ for unit vector η. Then*

$$\frac{\text{vol}(K \cap H)}{\text{vol}(K)} \leq 1 + \|y\| - \frac{1}{e}.$$

By Theorem 3.16, when K is isotropic, then $\mathbb{B}_1^d \subset K \subset \mathbb{B}_{1+d}^d$ and this is more or less tight for the simplex in isotropic position. Theorem 9.19 shows that cutting K anywhere inside $\mathbb{B}_{1/(2e)}^d \subset K$ will divide the set into two nearly equal pieces. Given a convex body K, recall from the discussion prior to Theorem 3.16 that $\text{iso}_K : \mathbb{R}^d \to \mathbb{R}^d$ is the affine map such that $\text{iso}_K(K)$ is isotropic. Note that iso_K is generally non-trivial to compute exactly, but can be approximated with reasonable precision using sampling as explained in

Section 3.6. Theorem 9.19 can be combined with Algorithm 9.5 to obtain a simple algorithm for bandit convex optimisation with near-optimal sample complexity guarantees. Keeping things simple, we assume exact computation and ask you handle the approximation errors in Exercise 9.29.

---

1 **args**: $\varepsilon \in (0,1)$, $\delta \in (0,1)$
2 $k_{\max} = 1 + \left\lceil \log\left(\frac{(\varepsilon/4)^d}{d! \operatorname{vol}(\mathbb{B}_d^d)}\right) \middle/ \log(1 - 1/(2e)) \right\rceil$ and $K_1 = K$
3 **for** $k = 1$ **to** $k_{\max}$:
4     $T_k = (2e)\operatorname{ISO}_{K_k}$ and $f_k = f \circ T_k^{-1}$ and $x_k = T_k^{-1}(0)$
5     $H_k = \operatorname{CUT}(f_k, \frac{\varepsilon}{4}, \frac{\delta}{2(d+1)k_{\max}}, 4ed)$ # Algorithm 9.5
6   update $K_{k+1} = K_k \cap T_k^{-1}(H_k)$
7 **return** $\operatorname{BAI}(\frac{\varepsilon}{2}, \frac{\delta}{2}, x_1, \ldots, x_{k_{\max}})$ # Algorithm 9.2

Algorithm 9.6 Centre of gravity for convex bandits

Remark 9.20 You might wonder if the final call to BAI is necessary. Maybe the algorithm should simply return $x_{k_{\max}}$. This does not work. There is no particular reason to expect that $k \mapsto f(x_k)$ should be decreasing. Indeed, x_1 could by chance be the minimiser of f.

Theorem 9.21 *Under Assumption 9.1 the following hold:*
(1) With probability at least $1 - \delta$ Algorithm 9.6 outputs an x such that $f(x) \leq \inf_{y \in K} f(y) + \varepsilon$.
(2) The expected number of queries to the loss function made by Algorithm 9.6 is at most

$$O\left(\frac{d^4}{\varepsilon^2} \log\left(\frac{d}{\varepsilon}\right) \log\left(\frac{d \log(1/\varepsilon)}{\delta}\right)\right).$$

Proof Let $f_\star = \inf_{x \in K} f(x)$. We establish the claim in three steps, beginning with a proof that with high probability the algorithm indeed returns a point that is near-optimal. The second step proves the key lemma used in the first. The last step bounds the sample complexity.

Step 1: Correctness

Suppose that

$$\mathbb{P}\left(\min\{f(x_k): 1 \leq k \leq k_{\max}\} \leq f_\star + \frac{\varepsilon}{2}\right) \geq 1 - \frac{\delta}{2}. \tag{9.5}$$

9.5 Centre of Gravity Method

By construction the algorithm returns $\text{BAI}(\frac{\varepsilon}{2}, \frac{\delta}{2}, x_1, \ldots, x_{k_{\max}})$ and by Theorem 9.10, this subroutine returns an $x \in \{x_1, \ldots, x_k\}$ such that

$$\mathbb{P}\left(f(x) \leq \min_{1 \leq k \leq k_{\max}} f(x_k) + \frac{\varepsilon}{2}\right) \geq 1 - \frac{\delta}{2}.$$

A union bound combining the above display and (9.5) shows that with probability at least $1 - \delta$ the algorithm returns an x such that $f(x) \leq f_\star + \varepsilon$ as required. The remainder of this step is devoted to establishing (9.5). Let $S \subset K$ be a simplex such that $f(x) \leq f_\star + \varepsilon/2$ for all $x \in S$ and

$$\text{vol}(S) \geq \left(\frac{\varepsilon}{4}\right)^d \frac{\text{vol}(K)}{d! \, \text{vol}(\mathbb{B}_d^d)}, \tag{9.6}$$

which exists by Lemma 9.4. We also let $S_k = T_k(S)$, which is a simplex in $J_k = T_k(K_k)$. We prove the following lemma in the next step:

Lemma 9.22 *Suppose that $S \subset K_k$ and $f(x_k) > f_\star + \varepsilon/2$. Then*

$$\mathbb{P}_{k-1}(S \subset K_{k+1}) \geq 1 - \frac{\delta}{2k_{\max}}$$

where $\mathbb{P}_{k-1}$ is the probability measured conditioned on all information available at the end of iteration $k - 1$.

By induction, a union bound over $1 \leq k \leq k_{\max}$ and Lemma 9.22, with probability at least $1 - \frac{\delta}{2}$ at least one of the following holds:

(1) There exists a $1 \leq k \leq k_{\max}$ such that $f(x_k) \leq f_\star + \varepsilon/2$; or
(2) $S \subset K_{k_{\max}+1}$.

In a moment we show that

$$\text{vol}(K_{k_{\max}+1}) \leq \left(1 - \frac{1}{2e}\right)^{k_{\max}} \text{vol}(K) < \text{vol}(S),$$

which contradicts (2) and therefore (1) occurs with probability at least $1 - \delta$. The second inequality in the above display follows from the definition of $k_{\max}$ and (9.6). For the first, by definition $T_k = (2e) \, \text{ISO}_{K_k}$, which means that $\frac{1}{2e} J_k$ is in isotropic position. Furthermore, by the definition of the algorithm $\partial H_k \cap \mathbb{B}_1^d \neq \emptyset$ and hence $\frac{1}{2e} \partial H_k \cap \mathbb{B}_{1/2e}^d \neq \emptyset$. Then

$$\frac{\text{vol}(K_{k+1})}{\text{vol}(K_k)} = \frac{\text{vol}(\frac{1}{2e} J_{k+1})}{\text{vol}(\frac{1}{2e} J_k)} = \frac{\text{vol}(\frac{1}{2e} J_k \cap \frac{1}{2e} H_k)}{\text{vol}(\frac{1}{2e} J_k)} \leq 1 - \frac{1}{2e},$$

where the last inequality follows from Theorem 9.19.

Step 2: Proof of Lemma 9.22

Suppose that y is a vertex of $S_k = T_k(S)$. Then $f_k(y) \leq f_\star + \frac{\varepsilon}{4}$ and $f_k(0) > f_\star + \frac{\varepsilon}{2}$, which means that

$$f_k(y) < f_k(0) - \frac{\varepsilon}{4}.$$

Hence, by Theorem 9.17,

$$\mathbb{P}_{k-1}(y \in H_k) \geq 1 - \frac{\delta}{2(d+1)k_{\max}}.$$

Since H_k is convex, if all vertices of S_k are in H_k it follows that $S_k \subset H_k$. Hence, a union bound over the $d+1$ vertices of S_k combined with the above display shows that

$$\mathbb{P}_{k-1}(S_k \subset H_k) \geq 1 - \frac{\delta}{2k_{\max}}.$$

Therefore

$$\begin{aligned}
\mathbb{P}_{k-1}(S \subset K_{k+1}) &= \mathbb{P}_{k-1}\left(S \subset K_k \cap T_k^{-1}(H_k)\right) && \text{Definition of } K_{k+1} \\
&= \mathbb{P}_{k-1}\left(S \subset T_k^{-1}(H_k)\right) && \text{Since } S \subset K_k \\
&= \mathbb{P}_{k-1}(S_k \subset H_k) && \text{Since } T_k \text{ is invertible} \\
&\geq 1 - \frac{\delta}{2k_{\max}}
\end{aligned}$$

as required.

Step 3: Sample complexity

There are $k_{\max}$ iterations and

$$k_{\max} = \Theta(d \log(d/\varepsilon)).$$

The algorithm makes $k_{\max}$ calls to CUT with radius bound $r = 4ed$, precision $\frac{\varepsilon}{2}$ and confidence $\bar{\delta}$ with

$$\bar{\delta} = \frac{\delta}{2(d+1)k_{\max}}.$$

By Theorem 9.17, the expected number of queries of the loss used by each call to CUT is

$$O\left(\frac{dr^2 \log(1/\bar{\delta})}{\varepsilon^2}\right) = O\left(\frac{d^3}{\varepsilon^2} \log\left(\frac{dk_{\max}}{\delta}\right)\right).$$

Therefore the total number of queries to the loss function used by all calls to CUT is bounded in expectation by

$$O\left(\frac{d^3 k_{\max}}{\varepsilon^2} \log\left(\frac{d k_{\max}}{\delta}\right)\right) = O\left(\frac{d^4}{\varepsilon^2} \log\left(\frac{d \log(d/\varepsilon)}{\delta}\right) \log\left(\frac{d}{\varepsilon}\right)\right).$$

Finally, the call to BAI uses just

$$O\left(\frac{k_{\max}}{\varepsilon^2} \log\left(\frac{1}{\delta}\right)\right)$$

queries. The result follows by combining the previous two displays. □

The main problem with the centre of gravity method is the need to find the affine maps T_k. As we discussed in Section 3.6, when K has a reasonable representation this can be done approximately by sampling. But this is a heavy procedure that one would like to avoid.

9.6 Method of the Inscribed Ellipsoid

When K is a polytope, the method of the inscribed ellipsoid provides a more computationally efficient cutting plane mechanism than the centre of gravity method. Given a convex body $K \subset \mathbb{R}^d$, let MVIE(K) be the ellipsoid of largest volume contained in K, which is unique. Furthermore, we have the following analogue of Grünbaum's inequality:

Proposition 9.23 (Khachiyan 1990) *Let K be a convex body, E = MVIE(K) and H be a half-space with ∂H intersecting the centre of E. Then* vol(MVIE($K \cap H$)) ≤ 0.85 vol(E).

The standard method of inscribed ellipsoids initialises $K_1 = K$ and subsequently computes K_{k+1} from K_k as follows:

○ Find E_k = MVIE(K_k).
○ Let x_k be the centre of E_k and $H_k = H(x_k, g_k)$ where $g_k \in \partial f(x_k)$.
○ Update $K_{k+1} = K_k \cap H_k$.

Of course, this is only feasible with access to subgradients of the loss f. We will use Algorithm 9.5 to find H_k instead, but for this we can only guarantee that ∂H_k passes through a point close to x_k and therefore need a refinement of Proposition 9.23.

Proposition 9.24 *Let K be a convex body, E = MVIE(K) and H be a half-space such that $\partial H \cap E(\frac{1}{2}) \neq \emptyset$, where $E(\frac{1}{2})$ is the same ellipsoid with half the radius. Then* vol(MVIE($K \cap H$)) ≤ 0.97 vol(E).

138   9 Cutting Plane Methods

As far as we know this result is new, though our proof – deferred to Section 9.8 – follows that by Khachiyan (1990) in almost every detail.

```
1  args:  ε ∈ (0, 1) ,  δ ∈ (0, 1)
2  k_max = 1 + ⌈log((ε/4)^d / (d! vol(𝔹_d^d))) / log(0.97)⌉  and  K_1 = K
3  for k = 1 to k_max:
4      E_k = MVIE(K_k) = E(x_k, A_k)
5      T_k(x) = 2A_k^{-1/2}(x − x_k)  and  f_k = f ∘ T_k^{-1}
6      H_k = CUT(f_k, ε/4, δ/(2(d+1)k_max), 2d)        # Algorithm 9.5
7      update K_{k+1} = K_k ∩ T_k^{-1}(H_k)
8  return BAI(ε/2, δ/2, x_1, ..., x_{k_max})           # Algorithm 9.2
```

Algorithm 9.7 Method of the inscribed ellipsoid for convex bandits

Computation

Finding the maximum-volume enclosed ellipsoid is the most computationally heavy part of Algorithm 9.7, but this only needs to be done $\tilde{O}(d)$ cumulatively. Suppose that $P = \{x : Cx \leq b\}$ is a convex body with $C \in \mathbb{R}^{m \times d}$. Since P is a convex body, $m \geq d + 1$. Khachiyan and Todd (1993) show that $\text{MVIE}(P)$ can be computed to extreme precision in $\tilde{O}(m^{3.5})$ time. Their algorithm is based on interior point methods. More generally, the problem is a semidefinite program and is practically solvable using modern solvers (Boyd and Vandenberghe, 2004, §8.4.2). The complexity per round is dominated by evaluating the affine map in the definition of f_k, which is $O(d^2)$.

Theorem 9.25 *Under Assumption 9.1 the following hold:*
(1) With probability at least $1 - \delta$ Algorithm 9.7 outputs an x such that $f(x) \leq \inf_{y \in K} f(y) + \varepsilon$.
(2) The expected number of queries to the loss function made by Algorithm 9.7 is at most

$$O\left(\frac{d^4}{\varepsilon^2} \log\left(\frac{d}{\varepsilon}\right) \log\left(\frac{d \log(1/\varepsilon)}{\delta}\right)\right) .$$

Proof The argument is the same as the proof of Theorem 9.21. The only difference is volume calculation. Recall that $S \subset K$ is a simplex such that

$$\text{vol}(S) \geq \left(\frac{\varepsilon}{4}\right)^d \frac{\text{vol}(K)}{d! \, \text{vol}(\mathbb{B}_d^d)} ,$$

which means that $\log(\text{vol}(S)) = \Omega\,(d\log(d/\varepsilon))$. Then

$$\begin{aligned}\log(\text{vol}(K_{k+1})) &\le \log(\text{vol}(E_{k+1}(d)))\\&= d\log(d) + \log(\text{vol}(E_{k+1}))\\&\le d\log(d) + \log(\text{vol}(E_1)) + k\log(0.97)\\&\le d\log(d) + \log(\text{vol}(K)) + k\log(0.97)\,,\end{aligned}$$

where in the first inequality we used the fact that $K_{k+1} \subset E_{k+1}(d)$, which follows from John's theorem (Theorem 3.15). The second inequality follows from Proposition 9.24 and the last since $E_1 \subset K$ by definition. Hence $\text{vol}(K_{k+1}) \le \text{vol}(S)$ once $k \ge k_{\max} = \Theta(d\log(d/\varepsilon))$ iterations, just as for the centre of gravity method. □

9.7 Ellipsoid Method

The ellipsoid method is an alternative cutting plane method that is statistically less efficient than both the method of the inscribed ellipsoid and the centre of gravity method. The advantage is that it can be implemented using a separation oracle only and relatively efficiently. Given a convex body K let MVEE(K) be the ellipsoid of minimum volume containing K. The classical ellipsoid method starts with an ellipsoid E_1 containing K.

○ Let x_k be the centre of E_k.
○ If $x_k \in K$, then let $H_k = \{x: \langle x - x_k, g_k \rangle \le 0\}$ with $g_k \in \partial f(x_k)$. Otherwise let $H_k = H(x_k, \text{SEP}_K(x_k))$.
○ Let $E_{k+1} = \text{MVEE}(E_k \cap H_k)$.

We give the formula for E_{k+1} as well as references for the following claims in Note 9.vi. The beauty of the ellipsoid method is that there is a closed-form expression for MVEE($E \cap H$) when E is an ellipsoid and H is a half-space. Furthermore, $\text{vol}(E_{k+1}) = O(1 - 1/d)\,\text{vol}(E_k)$. By construction we have $K_k \subset E_k$. There is no need for x_k to be the centre of E_k. In fact, when $x_k \in E_k(\frac{1}{2d})$ it holds that $\text{vol}(E_{k+1}) \le (1 - \frac{1}{20d})\,\text{vol}(E_k)$. Based on this, one might try to implement the ellipsoid method by letting $E_k = E(x_k, A_k)$, $T_k = 2dA_k^{-1/2}(x - x_k)$ and $f_k = f \circ T_k^{-1}$, which are chosen so that

$$T_k(E_k) = \mathbb{B}_{2d}^d \quad \text{and} \quad T_k(E_k(1/(2d))) = \mathbb{B}_1^d\,.$$

We want to run Algorithm 9.5 on f_k. The problem is that there is no reason why $E_k(1/(2d)) \subset K$ should hold. Equivalently, it can happen that $\mathbb{B}_1^d \not\subset \text{dom}(f_k)$. There are two ways to remedy this.

(1) There exists a modification of the ellipsoid method that guarantees $E_k(1/r) \subset K_k \subset E_k$ with $r = O(d^{3/2})$. Then you can let $T_k = rA_k^{-1/2}(x - x_k)$ which means that

$$T_k(E_k) = \mathbb{B}_r^d \quad \text{and} \quad T_k(E_k(1/r)) = \mathbb{B}_1^d.$$

This ensures that $\mathbb{B}_1^d \subset \text{dom}(f_k)$ but the price is that $r = O(d^{3/2})$ and this leads to a final sample complexity of

$$O\left(\frac{d^6 \operatorname{polylog}(d, 1/\delta, 1/\varepsilon)}{\varepsilon^2}\right).$$

(2) Use the extension defined in Proposition 3.23 in place of f so that $\text{dom}(f_k) = \mathbb{R}^d$. The challenge is that f_k may not be bounded anymore, so the concentration analysis in the proof of Lemma 9.16 is no longer valid. To handle this, note that if the algorithm ever queries a point f_k at some y for which $T_k^{-1}(y) \notin K$, then you can use the separation oracle to define the cutting plane. On the other hand, if the probability of querying f_k at such a point is very low, then the additional variance introduced by using the surrogate loss is minimal and some version of Lemma 9.16 continues to hold. After bashing out all the details you will eventually arrive at a sample complexity bound of

$$O\left(\frac{d^5 \operatorname{polylog}(d, 1/\delta, 1/\varepsilon)}{\varepsilon^2}\right).$$

9.8 Proof of Proposition 9.24 (🦘)

We start with a lemma:

Lemma 9.26 (Lemma 1, Khachiyan 1990) *Let $E_\star = E(x_\star, A_\star) = \text{MVIE}(K)$ and $E = E(x, A) \subset K$. Then*

$$\frac{\text{vol}(E)}{\text{vol}(E_\star)} \leq \min_{\chi \in I} \chi \exp(1 - \chi), \quad I = \left[\min_{\eta \in \mathbb{S}_1^{d-1}} \frac{\|A^{-1/2}\eta\|}{\|A_\star^{-1/2}\eta\|}, \max_{\eta \in \mathbb{S}_1^{d-1}} \frac{\|A^{-1/2}\eta\|}{\|A_\star^{-1/2}\eta\|}\right].$$

Proof of Proposition 9.24 Assume by means of a coordinate change that $E_\star = \text{MVIE}(K) = E(x, D^2)$ and $G_\star = \text{MVIE}(K \cap H) = E(-x, D^{-2})$ for some diagonal matrix D with eigenvalues $\lambda_1 \geq \cdots \geq \lambda_d$ and $x \in \mathbb{R}^d$. This has been chosen so that $E_\star = x + D(\mathbb{B}_1^d)$, which means that $\text{vol}(E_\star) = \det(D) \text{vol}(\mathbb{B}_1^d)$. We claim that $E = E(0, \mathbb{1} + xx^\top) \subset K$. Recall that the support function of a

9.8 Proof of Proposition 9.24

convex set $A \subset \mathbb{R}^d$ is $h_A(u) = \sup_{x \in A} \langle u, x \rangle$. Suppose that $u \in \mathbb{R}^d$. Then

$$h_{E_\star}(u) = \langle u, x \rangle + \|Du\| \leq h_K(u)$$
$$h_{G_\star}(u) = -\langle u, x \rangle + \|D^{-1}u\| \leq h_K(u).$$

Multiplying these inequalities shows that

$$\|u\|^2 \leq \|Du\| \|D^{-1}u\| \leq (h_K(u) - \langle u, x \rangle)(h_K(u) + \langle u, x \rangle)$$
$$= h_K(u)^2 - \langle u, x \rangle^2,$$

where the first inequality follows from Cauchy–Schwarz. Rearranging shows that for any $u \in \mathbb{R}^d$,

$$h_E(u) = \left\|\sqrt{\mathbb{1} + xx^\top} u\right\| = \sqrt{\|u\|^2 + \langle u, x \rangle^2} \leq h_K(u).$$

Therefore $E \subset K$. Next, with $A^{-1/2} = \sqrt{\mathbb{1} + xx^\top}$,

$$\min_{\eta \in \mathbb{S}_1^{d-1}} \frac{\|A^{-1/2}\eta\|}{\|D\eta\|} \leq \frac{\sqrt{1 + \|x\|^2}}{\lambda_1} \leq \max_{\eta \in \mathbb{S}_1^{d-1}} \frac{\|A^{-1/2}\eta\|}{\|D\eta\|}.$$

Hence, by Lemma 9.26,

$$\frac{\sqrt{1 + \|x\|^2}}{\lambda_1 \cdots \lambda_d} = \frac{\text{vol}(E)}{\text{vol}(E_\star)} \leq \frac{\sqrt{1 + \|x\|^2}}{\lambda_1} \exp\left(1 - \frac{\sqrt{1 + \|x\|^2}}{\lambda_1}\right)$$

and therefore

$$\frac{\text{vol}(G_\star)}{\text{vol}(E_\star)} = \frac{1}{\lambda_1^2 \cdots \lambda_d^2} \leq \frac{1}{\lambda_1^2} \exp\left(2 - \frac{2\sqrt{1 + \|x\|^2}}{\lambda_1}\right).$$

By assumption there exists a point $y \in \partial H \cap E_\star(\frac{1}{2})$. By definition $y \notin \text{int}(G_\star)$. Since $y \in E_\star(\frac{1}{2})$ there exists an $\eta \in \mathbb{B}_{1/2}^d$ such that $y = x + D\eta$. Therefore

$$1 \leq \|y - (-x)\|_{D^2} = \|2x + D\eta\|_{D^2} \leq 2\lambda_1 \|x\| + \frac{\lambda_1^2}{2},$$

using in the first inequality the fact that $y \notin \text{int}(G_\star) = \{z : \|z + x\|_{D^2} < 1\}$. Rearranging shows that

$$\|x\|^2 \geq \frac{\max(0, 1 - \lambda_1^2/2)^2}{4\lambda_1^2}.$$

Therefore

$$\frac{\text{vol}(G_\star)}{\text{vol}(E_\star)} \leq \sup_{\lambda_1 > 0} \frac{1}{\lambda_1^2} \exp\left(2 - \frac{2\sqrt{1 + \frac{\max(0, 1-\lambda_1^2/2)^2}{4\lambda_1^2}}}{\lambda_1}\right) \leq 0.97. \qquad \square$$

9.9 Notes

9.i Algorithm 9.2 is due to Even-Dar et al. (2006). For our application it makes no difference, but you may be interested to know this algorithm is not quite optimal in terms of the logarithmic factors. The optimal algorithm is called median elimination and is also due to Even-Dar et al. (2006).

9.ii Infinite-armed bandits of the kind studied in Section 9.2 are still a little niche and go back to Berry et al. (1997). Generally speaking the objective is to find a near-optimal arm and various assumptions are made on h and ρ. Carpentier (2025) essentially introduced the much weaker objective of finding an action that is close to the mean of h under ρ and provided a slightly more complicated algorithm than analysed here but based on the same principles.

9.iii The algorithm for finding a suitable cutting plane is inspired by Lattimore and György (2021a) and Carpentier (2025). The former paper uses an optimistic surrogate combined with an overly complicated method for finding the cutting point. The latter uses the pessimistic surrogate from Chapter 5 along with a beautiful argument about when its gradient is nevertheless useful to define a cutting plane at certain points. She uses an infinite-armed bandit to find suitable points, but this is combined with a more complicated recursive argument. The rates we obtain here are the same up to logarithmic factors as those obtained by Carpentier (2025).

9.iv The algorithms presented in this chapter do not have well-controlled regret. What is missing is a degree of adaptivity within the mechanism for finding a cutting plane that stops early when there is a large margin. This idea was used by Lattimore and György (2021a) and can probably be adapted to the more refined algorithms in this chapter.

9.v Vaidya's method (Vaidya, 1996) and its refinement by Lee et al. (2015) provide even faster cutting plane methods for polytopes. What is needed to use these methods in combination with Algorithm 9.5 is to prove that an inexact centre suffices to drive the algorithm, just as we did for the method of inscribed ellipsoids with Proposition 9.24.

9.vi All of the assertions about the ellipsoid method in Section 9.7 are explained and proven in Chapters 3 and 4 of the wonderful book by Grötschel et al. (2012). When the half-space is not at the centre, the method is referred to as the shallow-cut ellipsoid method.

Theorem 9.27 *Suppose the dimension $d \geq 2$. Given an ellipsoid $E = E(a, A)$ and half-space $H = H(x, g)$ let $E(b, B) = \text{MVEE}(E \cap H)$. Let $\lambda = \frac{\langle g, a-x \rangle}{\|g\|_A}$. Then*

(1) *H intersects E if and only if $\lambda \in [-1, 1]$. Moreover, if $\lambda \in [-1, -1/d]$, then $E(b, B) = E(a, A)$.*

(2) *If $\lambda \in [-1/d, 1)$, then with $\eta = \frac{Ag}{\|g\|_A}$,*

$$b = a - \frac{1 + d\lambda}{d+1}\eta \quad \text{and} \quad B = \frac{d^2(1-\lambda^2)}{d^2-1}\left[A - \frac{2(1+d\lambda)}{(d+1)(1+\lambda)}\eta\eta^\top\right].$$

(3) *If $\lambda \in (-1/d, 1/d)$, then $\text{vol}(\text{MVEE}(E \cap H)) \leq \text{vol}(E)\exp\left(-\frac{(1-d\lambda)^2}{5d}\right)$.*

The proof of Theorem 9.27 is given by Grötschel et al. (2012, Chapter 3). The advantage of the ellipsoid method is that only a separation oracle is needed. The downside is that the sample complexity is a factor of d worse than what we obtained using the centre of gravity or inscribed ellipsoid methods.

Exercise 9.28 ★★★❷ Suppose K is represented by a separation oracle. Use the separation oracle to construct a polytope P such that $K \subset P$. Use the extension in Proposition 3.20 to extend the loss from a shrunk subset of K to P. Use the ideas in Section 9.7 to implement the method of the inscribed ellipsoid and obtain a polynomial time algorithm with $\tilde{O}(d^4/\varepsilon^2)$ sample complexity.

9.vii In our analysis of Algorithm 9.6 and Algorithm 9.7 we assumed exact computation of isotropic position and the maximum-volume inscribed ellipsoid. The following exercise asks you to prove these algorithms are robust to approximations:

Exercise 9.29 ★★★▤ Suppose that K is represented by a separation oracle. Show that Algorithm 9.6 is robust to approximation of isotropic position and give a complexity bound on all of the following:
- Number of queries to the loss function
- Number of calls to the separation oracle
- Number of arithmetic operations

Exercise 9.30 ★★★▤ Suppose that K is represented by an intersection of half-spaces. Show that Algorithm 9.7 is robust to approximation of the maximum-volume inscribed ellipsoid and give a complexity bound on the number of queries to the loss function and the number of arithmetic operations.

In both cases all complexities should be $\text{poly}(d, m, 1/\varepsilon, \log(R/r))$ where $m = 1$ for Exercise 9.29 and the number of constraints defining K in Exercise 9.30, and it is assumed that $\mathbb{B}_r^d \subset K \subset \mathbb{B}_R^d$ for known $0 < r \leq R$. You will need to combine results from many sources. A good place to start would be the references in Section 3.9.

10
Online Newton Step

We can now present a simple method for obtaining $\tilde{O}(d^{1.5}\sqrt{n})$ regret for losses in $\mathscr{F}_b$ with the limitation that the analysis only works in the stochastic setting where $f_t = f$ for all rounds.

Assumption 10.1 The following hold:

(1) The setting is stochastic: $f_t = f$ for all t.
(2) The loss is bounded: $f \in \mathscr{F}_b$.
(3) The constraint set is rounded: $\mathbb{B}_1^d \subset K \subset \mathbb{B}_{2d}^d$.

The assumption that K is rounded is not restrictive, since the constraint set can be repositioned as explained in Section 3.6. The bandit algorithm presented here is based on online Newton step, which is a second-order online learning algorithm. Compared to cutting plane methods in Chapter 9, the method here has an improved dimension-dependence and can be generalised to the adversarial setting (Chapter 11). On the negative side, the analysis is quite involved and the algorithm is hard to tune. We start the chapter with an intuitive argument about the role of curvature in bandit convex optimisation. There follows an introduction to online Newton step in the full information setting and a brief explanation of some concepts in convex geometry. The algorithm and its analysis are presented at the end. To ease the presentation and analysis we let $\delta \in (0, 1)$ be a small positive constant and

$$L = C \log(1/\delta),$$

where $C > 0$ is a sufficiently large universal constant. We will prove a bound on the regret that holds with probability at least $1 - \delta$ but at various points we implicitly assume that $\delta \leq \text{poly}(1/n, 1/d)$.

10.1 The Blessing and Curse of Curvature

The presence of curvature in bandit convex optimisation is both a blessing and a curse. The key to obtaining optimal regret is to make sure you exploit the positive aspects while taking care to control the negative ones. It helps to  think about the case where the loss is nearly quadratic in the sense that it has a nearly constant Hessian. The main implications of high curvature are the following:

- Smoothing should be done on a smaller radius to maintain a suitably small approximation error. This increases the variance of the gradient estimator, which makes gradient-based online learning algorithms unstable.
- The variance of the gradient estimator is modulated by the regularisation of the algorithm, which suggests that the amount of regularisation should increase with the curvature. But adding more regularisation means the algorithm moves more slowly, which normally increases its regret. The saving grace is that in the presence of curvature the regret decreases quadratically as the iterate approaches the minimiser.

We saw this behaviour already in Section 6.5 where the loss was assumed to be in $\mathscr{F}_{\text{b,sm,sc}}$. Provided that β/α is not too large, such losses are nearly quadratic. Algorithm 6.3 uses a self-concordant barrier for regularisation with an additional quadratic that depends on α and uses a gradient estimate that integrates over a region that is small for large α. That is, more curvature implies more regularisation and less smoothing. There are multiple challenges when generalising this approach to the setting where the loss is only assumed to be in $\mathscr{F}_{\text{b}}$:

- The amount of curvature is not known.
- Even if the loss is approximately quadratic, the curvature can be large in some directions and small in others.
- The loss may not even be differentiable. For example it could be piecewise linear. How should we understand the role of curvature in these situations?

The plan is to use a surrogate loss function that does so much smoothing that it is nearly quadratic on a region containing both the current iterate μ_t and the minimiser of the loss. The curvature of this surrogate can then be estimated and used in online Newton step, which we explain next.

10.2 Introducing Online Newton Step

Let $\hat{q}_1, \ldots, \hat{q}_n \colon \mathbb{R}^d \to \mathbb{R}$ be a sequence of (possibly non-convex) quadratic functions and consider the full information setting where in round t the learner proposes $\mu_t \in K$ and observes the entire function $\hat{q}_t$, and the regret relative to $x \in K$ is

$$\widetilde{\mathrm{qReg}}_n(x) = \sum_{t=1}^{n} (\hat{q}_t(\mu_t) - \hat{q}_t(x)) \,.$$

Online Newton step is a second-order method summarised in Algorithm 10.1.

---
1 **args:** $\eta > 0$, $\Sigma_1^{-1} \in \mathbb{S}_{++}^d$ and $\mu_1 \in K$
2 **for** $t = 1$ **to** n
3   let $g_t = \hat{q}_t'(\mu_t)$ and $H_t = \hat{q}_t''(\mu_t)$
4   update $\Sigma_{t+1}^{-1} = \Sigma_t^{-1} + \eta H_t$
5   update $\mu_{t+1} = \arg\min_{x \in K} \|x - [\mu_t - \eta \Sigma_{t+1} g_t]\|_{\Sigma_{t+1}^{-1}}^2$

Algorithm 10.1 Online Newton step for quadratic losses

Before the analysis, let us make some connections between online Newton method and other techniques in online learning.

Connection to Exponential Weights

A little notation is needed. Let $\Theta = \mathbb{R}^d \times \mathbb{S}_{++}^d$ and $\Theta_K = K \times \mathbb{S}_{++}^d$. Let μ_θ and Σ_θ be the obvious projections from Θ into $\mathbb{R}^d$ and $\mathbb{S}_{++}^d$ respectively and abbreviate $\mathcal{N}(\theta) = \mathcal{N}(\mu_\theta, \Sigma_\theta)$. Lastly, let $\mathrm{KL}(\theta, \vartheta)$ be the relative entropy between Gaussian distributions $\mathcal{N}(\theta)$ and $\mathcal{N}(\vartheta)$, which has an explicit form:

$$\mathrm{KL}(\theta, \vartheta) = \frac{1}{2} \left[\log \det\left(\Sigma_\vartheta \Sigma_\theta^{-1}\right) + \mathrm{tr}(\Sigma_\theta \Sigma_\vartheta^{-1}) + \|\mu_\theta - \mu_\vartheta\|_{\Sigma_\vartheta^{-1}}^2 - d \right].$$

Assume that $\frac{1}{2}\|\cdot\|_{\Sigma_1}^2 + \sum_{s=1}^t \hat{q}_s$ is convex for all t. Suppose that p_1 is the density of $\mathcal{N}(\mu_1, \Sigma_1)$ and $(p_t)_{t=1}^n$ are Gaussians with parameters $(\theta_t)_{t=1}^n \in \Theta_K$ defined inductively as follows. Given p_t, define $\tilde{\theta}_{t+1}$ as the parameters of the Gaussian with density $\tilde{p}_{t+1}$ given by

$$\tilde{p}_{t+1}(x) = \frac{p_t(x) \exp(-\eta \hat{q}_t(x))}{\int_{\mathbb{R}^d} \exp(-\eta \hat{q}_t(y)) p_t(y) \, dy} \,.$$

Then let $\theta_{t+1} = \arg\min_{\theta \in \Theta_K} \mathrm{KL}(\theta, \tilde{\theta}_{t+1})$ and $p_{t+1} = \mathcal{N}(\theta_{t+1})$. The mean μ_t and covariance Σ_t that define θ_t are exactly the iterates produced by online Newton step (van der Hoeven et al., 2018).

Classical Newton

The classical Newton method for unconstrained minimisation of a loss function $f : \mathbb{R}^d \to \mathbb{R}$ starts with $x_1 \in \mathbb{R}^d$ and uses the update rule $x_{t+1} = x_t - f''(x_t)^{-1} f'(x_t)$, which corresponds to minimising the quadratic approximation of f at x_t. Online Newton step looks superficially similar, but the preconditioning matrix is based on the accumulated curvature rather than the local curvature; and there is the learning rate, which further slows the algorithm.

High-Level Behaviour

Let us suppose for a moment that $d = 1$ and $f : [-1, 1] \to [0, 1]$ is convex and minimised at 0. In our application, the $\hat{q}_t$ will be estimates of a quadratic approximation of an extension of f. But to simplify our thinking let us suppose that f is quadratic and $\hat{q}_t = f$, which means that $g_t = f'(\mu_t)$ and $H_t = f''(\mu_t) \triangleq H$. Suppose that $\Sigma_1^{-1} = 1$. By construction, $\Sigma_t^{-1} = 1 + \eta t H$, which means that

$$\mu_{t+1} = \mu_t - \frac{\eta}{1 + \eta t H} g_t .$$

In our application $\eta = \Theta(\sqrt{1/n})$, which means that online Newton step moves very slowly as t grows unless there is very little curvature. The corresponding flow in continuous time is

$$d\mu(t) = -\frac{\eta}{1 + \eta t H} f'(\mu(t)) \, dt = -\frac{\eta H \mu(t)}{1 + \eta t H} \, dt ,$$

which has a closed-form solution $\mu(t) = \frac{\mu(0)}{1+\eta t H}$, and the regret is

$$\int_0^n (f(\mu(t)) - f(0)) \, dt = \frac{H}{2} \int_0^n \mu(t)^2 \, dt = \frac{H}{2} \int_0^n \left(\frac{\mu(0)}{1 + \eta t H}\right)^2 \, dt = O(\sqrt{n}) .$$

Of course, the regret of the gradient flow would be greatly reduced by increasing η. But in the bandit setting g_t and H_t need to be estimated and the increased regularisation is needed to control the variance. What the argument above shows is that despite the slow progress of the algorithm when $\eta = \Theta(n^{-1/2})$, a regret of $O(\sqrt{n})$ is nevertheless achievable.

Analysis

Moving now to the analysis of online Newton step, which mirrors that of other gradient-based algorithms, we have the following theorem:

Theorem 10.2 *Suppose that $\Sigma_t^{-1} \in \mathbb{S}_{++}^d$ for all $1 \le t \le n + 1$; then for any*

10.3 Regularity

$x \in K$,

$$\frac{1}{2}\|\mu_{n+1} - x\|^2_{\Sigma_{n+1}^{-1}} \leq \frac{1}{2}\|\mu_1 - x\|^2_{\Sigma_1^{-1}} + \frac{\eta^2}{2}\sum_{t=1}^n \|g_t\|^2_{\Sigma_{t+1}^{-1}} - \eta\widehat{\text{qReg}}_n(x). \quad (10.1)$$

Remark 10.3 The condition that the inverse covariance matrices are positive definite corresponds to assuming that

$$\frac{1}{2}\|\cdot\|^2_{\Sigma_1^{-1}} + \sum_{s=1}^{t-1} \hat{q}_s$$

is convex for all $1 \leq t \leq n + 1$. In most applications the first term in (10.1) is dropped and the regret is moved to the left-hand side. An interesting feature of our application of this result is that we use it to simultaneously bound the regret and $\|\mu_{n+1} - x\|_{\Sigma_{n+1}^{-1}}$.

Proof of Theorem 10.2 By definition, for any $x \in K$,

$$\frac{1}{2}\|\mu_{t+1} - x\|^2_{\Sigma_{t+1}^{-1}} \stackrel{(a)}{\leq} \frac{1}{2}\|\mu_t - x - \eta\Sigma_{t+1}g_t\|^2_{\Sigma_{t+1}^{-1}}$$

$$\stackrel{(b)}{=} \frac{1}{2}\|\mu_t - x\|^2_{\Sigma_{t+1}^{-1}} - \eta\langle g_t, \mu_t - x\rangle + \frac{\eta^2}{2}\|g_t\|^2_{\Sigma_{t+1}^{-1}}$$

$$\stackrel{(c)}{=} \frac{1}{2}\|\mu_t - x\|^2_{\Sigma_t^{-1}} - \eta(\hat{q}_t(\mu_t) - \hat{q}_t(x)) + \frac{\eta^2}{2}\|g_t\|^2_{\Sigma_{t+1}^{-1}}, \quad (10.2)$$

where in (a) we used the assumption that Σ_{t+1}^{-1} is positive definite so that $\|\cdot\|_{\Sigma_{t+1}^{-1}}$ is a norm, the fact that $x \in K$ and the definition

$$\mu_{t+1} = \arg\min_{\mu \in K} \|\mu - [\mu_t - \eta\Sigma_{t+1}g_t]\|_{\Sigma_{t+1}^{-1}}.$$

For the equalities, (b) is obtained by expanding the square, and (c) since

$$\frac{1}{2}\|\mu_t - x\|^2_{\Sigma_{t+1}^{-1}} = \frac{1}{2}\|\mu_t - x\|^2_{\Sigma_t^{-1}} + \frac{\eta}{2}(\mu_t - x)^\top H_t(\mu_t - x)$$

$$= \frac{1}{2}\|\mu_t - x\|^2_{\Sigma_t^{-1}} - \eta(\hat{q}_t(\mu_t) - \hat{q}_t(x)) + \eta\langle g_t, \mu_t - x\rangle.$$

The proof is completed by summing the inequality in (10.2) over t from 1 to n. □

10.3 Regularity

In our application of online Newton step to bandits it will be important that the constraint set K is suitably rounded. We explained the basics already in

Section 3.6 but here we introduce a more subtle concept based on the mean width of the polar body. Under Assumption 10.1,

$$\mathbb{B}_1^d \subset K \subset \mathbb{B}_{2d}^d. \tag{10.3}$$

Note, any improvements in the constant 2 would only lead to minor constant-factor improvements in the regret. Let π be the Minkowski functional of K (Section 3.1) and

$$K_\varepsilon = \{x \in K : \pi(x) \leq 1 - \varepsilon\} = (1 - \varepsilon)K.$$

Let X be uniformly distributed on $\mathbb{S}_1^{d-1}$ and define $M(K) = \mathbb{E}[\pi(X)]$. The Minkowski functional is the support function of the polar of K (Lemma 3.3(5)), which means that for $x \in \mathbb{S}_1^{d-1}$, $\pi(x) + \pi(-x)$ is the width of the polar K° in direction x. Hence $M(K)$ is half the mean width of K° as illustrated in Figure 10.1. For our application it is best if K is positioned so that $M(K)$ is small. Thanks to our assumption that $\mathbb{B}_1^d \subset K \subset \mathbb{B}_{2d}^d$, $\frac{1}{2d}\|x\| \leq \pi(x) \leq \|x\|$ and hence $M(K) \in [\frac{1}{2d}, 1]$. This estimate is often loose, however. Table 10.1 gives bounds on the inner and outer radii and $M(K)$ for K in various classical positions. While Löwner's position yields the strongest bound, all rows are relevant when computation is important, with the best position depending on how K is represented and what computational resources are available.

Remark 10.4 It is not obvious that there exists an affine transformation T such that $(TK)^\circ$ is in isotropic position, much less that T can be approximately computed efficiently. More details can be found in Note 10.iii.

	CONDITIONS	BOUNDS	$M(K)$
10.1.a	$\frac{1}{d}K$ in Löwner's position	$\mathbb{B}_1^d \subset K \subset \mathbb{B}_d^d$	$\tilde{O}(d^{-1/2})$
10.1.b	K isotropic	$\mathbb{B}_1^d \subset K \subset \mathbb{B}_{d+1}^d$	≤ 1
10.1.c	K symmetric, isotropic	$\mathbb{B}_1^d \subset K \subset \mathbb{B}_{d+1}^d$	$\tilde{O}(d^{-1/10})$
10.1.d	K in John's position	$\mathbb{B}_1^d \subset K \subset \mathbb{B}_d^d$	≤ 1
10.1.e	$(d+1)K^\circ$ isotropic	$\mathbb{B}_1^d \subset K \subset \mathbb{B}_{d+1}^d$	$\tilde{O}(d^{-1/4})$
10.1.f	K symmetric, $\frac{1}{\sqrt{d}}K$ in John's position	$\mathbb{B}_{\sqrt{d}}^d \subset K \subset \mathbb{B}_d^d$	$\leq 1/\sqrt{d}$
10.1.g	K symmetric, $(d+1)K^\circ$ isotropic	$\mathbb{B}_1^d \subset K \subset \mathbb{B}_{d+1}^d$	$\tilde{O}(d^{-1/2})$

Table 10.1 Classical positions and bounds on the inner and outer radii and $M(K)$. More discussion and references appear in the notes of this chapter.

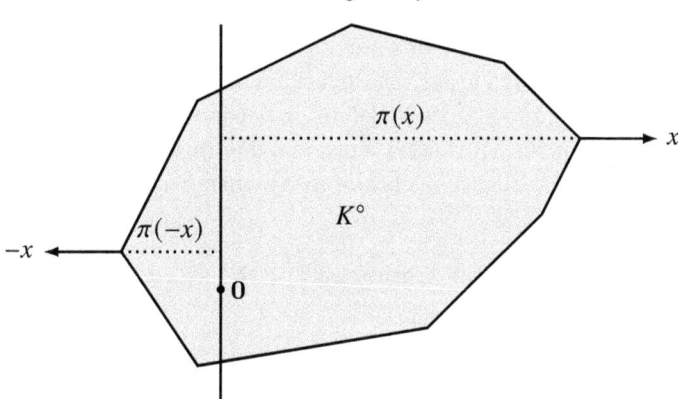

Figure 10.1 The width of K° in direction x is $\pi(x) + \pi(-x)$. The quantity $M(K)$ is obtained by integrating the width uniformly over all directions in $x \in \mathbb{S}_1^{d-1}$ and dividing by two.

Proof of claims in Table 10.1 (10.1.a) Let $w(K)$ be the half mean width of a convex body K, which is defined by $w(K) = \mathbb{E}[h_K(\theta)]$ where θ has law $\mathscr{U}(\mathbb{S}_1^{d-1})$ and h_K is the support function of K. Suppose that $\frac{1}{d}K$ is in Löwner's position. By definition $(K/d)^\circ = dK^\circ$ is in John's position. Combining John's theorem and the fact that polarity reverses inclusion again shows that $\mathbb{B}_1^d \subset K \subset \mathbb{B}_d^d$. Let S be a regular simplex in John's position. Barthe (1998) proved that the mean width of a convex body in John's position is maximised by S and a result of Finch (2011) shows that $w(S) = O(\sqrt{d \log(d)})$. Therefore $M(K) = w(K^\circ) = \frac{1}{d} w(dK^\circ) \leq \frac{1}{d} w(S) = O(\sqrt{\log(d)/d})$.

(10.1.b, 10.1.d) Well-roundedness follows from Theorem 3.16 and Theorem 3.15, respectively. Since in both positions $\mathbb{B}_1^d \subset K$, it follows that $K^\circ \subset \mathbb{B}_1^d$ and hence $M(K) \leq 1$. Note, this claim is not improvable for John's position as explained in Note 10.ii.

(10.1.c) Well-roundedness follows as in 10.1.b. The bound on $M(K)$ is supplied by Giannopoulos and Milman (2014) and is most likely conservative.

(10.1.e) That $\mathbb{B}_1^d \subset K \subset \mathbb{B}_{d+1}^d$ follows because polarity reverses inclusion and by Theorem 3.16. The bound on $M(K)$ is due to Pivovarov (2010).

(10.1.f) Suppose that K is symmetric and in John's position. Then by John's theorem (Artstein-Avidan et al., 2015, Theorem 2.1.3), $\mathbb{B}_1^d \subset K \subset \mathbb{B}_{\sqrt{d}}^d$. Then use the scaling and repeat the argument for 10.1.d.

(10.1.g) As for (10.1.e) but use the result of Milman (2015) to bound $M(K)$.

□

An essential ingredient in many previous regret analyses is a bound on the magnitude of the observed losses. The algorithm in this chapter replaces the real loss with the extended loss function defined in Section 3.7 and the magnitude of this loss depends on the Minkowski functional. For this reason it is essential to have a good understanding of the law of $\pi(X)$ when X is Gaussian, which the next two lemmas provide.

Lemma 10.5 *Suppose that X has law $\mathcal{N}(\mu, \Sigma)$ with $\mu \in K$ and $\Sigma \preceq \sigma^2 \mathbb{1}$. Then*

(1) $\mathbb{E}[\pi(X)] \leq 1 + \sigma M(K)\sqrt{d}$; and

(2) $\mathbb{P}\left(|\pi(X) - \mathbb{E}[\pi(X)]| \geq \sqrt{2\sigma^2 \log(2/\delta)}\right) \leq \delta$ for all $\delta \in (0, 1)$.

Proof Since π is sub-additive (Lemma 3.3),

$$\begin{aligned}\mathbb{E}[\pi(X)] &= \mathbb{E}[\pi(X - \mu + \mu)] \\ &\leq \mathbb{E}[\pi(X - \mu)] + \pi(\mu) \\ &\leq 1 + \mathbb{E}[\pi(X - \mu)].\end{aligned} \quad (10.4)$$

By assumption $\sigma^2 \mathbb{1} - \Sigma$ is positive semidefinite. Let W and U be independent of X and have laws $\mathcal{N}(0, \sigma^2 \mathbb{1})$ and $\mathcal{N}(0, \sigma^2 \mathbb{1} - \Sigma)$ respectively. Note that $U + X - \mu$ has the same law as W and by Jensen's inequality $\mathbb{E}[\pi(X - \mu)] \leq \mathbb{E}[\pi(X - \mu + U)] = \mathbb{E}[\pi(W)]$. Furthermore, since $W/\|W\|$ and $\|W\|$ are independent,

$$\mathbb{E}[\pi(X - \mu)] \leq \mathbb{E}[\pi(W)] = \mathbb{E}\left[\pi\left(\frac{W}{\|W\|}\right)\right] \mathbb{E}[\|W\|] \leq \sigma M(K)\sqrt{d},$$

where we used the facts that $\mathbb{E}[\|W\|] \leq \mathbb{E}[\|W\|^2]^{1/2} = \sigma \sqrt{d}$ and $W/\|W\|$ is uniformly distributed on $\mathbb{S}_1^{d-1}$. Combining this with (10.4) completes the proof of part (1). For part (2), by Lemma 3.3(7) and the assumption that $\mathbb{B}_1^d \subset K$ we have $\text{lip}(\pi) \leq 1$. The result follows from Theorem B.16. □

As mentioned, we are planning to use the extension introduced in Section 3.7 where the functions $\pi_\wedge(x) = \max(1, \pi(x)/(1-\varepsilon))$ and $v(x) = \pi_\wedge(x) - 1$ appear with $\varepsilon \in (0, 1/2)$. The following bound will be useful:

Lemma 10.6 *Let $\varepsilon \in (0, 1/2)$, $\pi_\wedge(x) = \max(1, \pi(x)/(1-\varepsilon))$ and $v(x) = \pi_\wedge(x) - 1$. Suppose that X has law $\mathcal{N}(\mu, \Sigma)$ with $\mu \in K_\varepsilon$ and $\|\Sigma\| \leq \frac{1}{\delta}$. Then*

$$\mathbb{E}[v(X)^2] \leq L\left(1 + \max\left(1, M(K)\sqrt{d}\right)\sqrt{\|\Sigma\|}\right)\left[\text{tr}\left(\Sigma \lim_{\varrho \to 0} \mathbb{E}[v''_\varrho(X)]\right) + \delta\right],$$

where $v_\varrho = v * \phi_\varrho$ with ϕ_ϱ the smoothing kernel defined in Section 3.8.

Proof (🦘) By Lemma B.8,

$$\mathbb{E}[v(X)^2] \leq \|v(X)\|_{\psi_1} \left(\mathbb{E}[v(X)] \left(1 + \log\left(\frac{\mathbb{E}[v(X)^2]}{\delta^2}\right) \right) + \delta \right). \quad (10.5)$$

By convexity and the fact that lip$(v) < \infty$,

$$\begin{aligned}
\mathbb{E}[v(X)] &= \lim_{\varrho \to 0} \mathbb{E}[v_\varrho(X)] \\
&\leq \lim_{\varrho \to 0} \left[v_\varrho(\mu) + \mathbb{E}\left[\langle v'_\varrho(X), X - \mu \rangle \right] \right] &&\text{Convexity} \\
&= \lim_{\varrho \to 0} \mathbb{E}\left[\langle v'_\varrho(X), X - \mu \rangle \right] \\
&= \lim_{\varrho \to 0} \mathbb{E}\left[\langle \Sigma v'_\varrho(X), \Sigma^{-1}(X - \mu) \rangle \right] \\
&= \operatorname{tr}\left(\Sigma \lim_{\varrho \to 0} \mathbb{E}[v''_\varrho(X)] \right). &&\text{Integration by parts}
\end{aligned}$$

By the assumption that $\varepsilon < 1/2$ and because lip$(\pi) \leq 1$, it follows that lip$(v) \leq 2$. Hence, using Theorem B.16 and Lemma 10.5(1),

$$\begin{aligned}
\|v(X)\|_{\psi_1} &\leq \|v(X) - \mathbb{E}[v(X)]\|_{\psi_1} + \|\mathbb{E}[v(X)]\|_{\psi_1} \\
&\leq 2\sqrt{6}\,\|\Sigma\| + \frac{\mathbb{E}[v(X)]}{\log(2)} \\
&\leq 2\sqrt{6}\,\|\Sigma\| + \frac{2(1 + M(K)\sqrt{d\,\|\Sigma\|})}{\log(2)}.
\end{aligned}$$

The second moment $\mathbb{E}[v(X)^2]$ that appears in (10.5) can now be bounded using Lemma B.4 and the result follows by naive simplification. □

10.4 Extension and Surrogate Losses

As in Chapter 6 we use a quadratic surrogate. Unlike that chapter, however, the curvature of the surrogate now depends on the loss function and needs to be estimated. The other distinction is that in Chapter 6 the actions were sampled from a scaled Dikin ellipsoid, which is guaranteed to be contained in K. By contrast, the algorithm presented in this chapter will sample from a Gaussian, which means its actions may lie outside of K, possibly with high probability. This problem is handled by making use of the extension in Section 3.7. Let π be the Minkowski functional of K and for $\varepsilon \in (0, 1/2)$ let $K_\varepsilon = (1 - \varepsilon)K$, $\pi_\wedge(x) = \max(1, \pi(x)/(1 - \varepsilon))$ and

$$e(x) = \pi_\wedge(x) f\left(\frac{x}{\pi_\wedge(x)}\right) + \frac{2(\pi_\wedge(x) - 1)}{\varepsilon}. \quad (10.6)$$

Note that $\pi_\wedge(x) - 1 = 0$ and $e(x) = f(x)$ for $x \in K_\varepsilon$ and Proposition 3.23 ensures that $x \mapsto \pi_\wedge(x) f(x/\pi_\wedge(x)) + \frac{1-\varepsilon}{\varepsilon}(\pi_\wedge(x) - 1)$ is convex. The additional factor in the second term of the above display ensures that e has slightly more curvature, which gives the algorithm an additional nudge to play inside K_ε. The extension in (10.6) is defined on all of $\mathbb{R}^d$ and can be queried at any $x \in \mathbb{R}^d$ by evaluating the real loss f at $x/\pi_\wedge(x)$. To simplify the notation it is convenient to abstract away this reduction by redefining the meaning of the actions X_t and observed losses Y_t. In round t the algorithm samples X_t from a Gaussian $\mathcal{N}(\mu_t, \Sigma_t)$ but actually plays $X_t/\pi_\wedge(X_t) \in K_\varepsilon$, observes $f(X_t/\pi_\wedge(X_t)) + \varepsilon_t$ and computes the (noisy) loss relative to the extension as

$$Y_t = e(X_t) + \pi_\wedge(X_t)\varepsilon_t = \pi_\wedge(X_t)\left[f\left(\frac{X_t}{\pi_\wedge(X_t)}\right) + \varepsilon_t\right] + \frac{2(\pi_\wedge(X_t) - 1)}{\varepsilon}.$$

Note that the noise term is now effectively $\pi_\wedge(X_t)\varepsilon_t$, which conditioned on X_t can have variance as large as $\pi_\wedge(X_t)^2$. With the new meaning of X_t, the regret is

$$\text{Reg}_n = \sup_{x \in K} \sum_{t=1}^n \left(f\left(\frac{X_t}{\pi_\wedge(X_t)}\right) - f(x)\right).$$

By Proposition 3.23, $f(x) = e(x/\pi_\wedge(x)) \le e(x)$ for all $x \in \mathbb{R}^d$ and $e(x) = f(x)$ for all $x \in K_\varepsilon$, which when combined with Proposition 3.13 shows that

$$\text{Reg}_n \le n\varepsilon + \max_{x \in K_\varepsilon} \sum_{t=1}^n \left(f\left(\frac{X_t}{\pi_\wedge(X_t)}\right) - f(x)\right)$$

$$\le n\varepsilon + \max_{x \in K_\varepsilon} \sum_{t=1}^n (e(X_t) - e(x)).$$

Therefore the true regret is upper bounded in terms of the regret relative to the extension.

Surrogate Losses

The algorithm makes use of a quadratic surrogate loss

$$q_t(x) = \langle s_t'(\mu), x - \mu_t \rangle + \frac{1}{4}\|x - \mu_t\|_{s''(\mu_t)}^2, \tag{10.7}$$

where $s_t : \mathbb{R}^d \to \mathbb{R}$ is the convex surrogate defined by

$$s_t(x) = \mathbb{E}_{t-1}\left[\left(1 - \frac{1}{\lambda}\right)e(X_t) + \frac{1}{\lambda}e((1-\lambda)X_t + \lambda x)\right]$$

with $\lambda \in (0, \frac{1}{d+1})$ a tuning parameter that determines the amount of smoothing. We spend all of Chapter 12 on the intuitions and analysis of this surrogate loss.

10.4 Extension and Surrogate Losses

You can skip ahead to that chapter now or accept the following properties as gospel.

Proposition 10.7 *Let q_t be the function defined in (10.7) and suppose that $x \in \mathbb{R}^d$ satisfies $\lambda \|x - \mu_t\|_{\Sigma_t^{-1}} \leq \frac{1}{\sqrt{L}}$ and $\lambda \leq \frac{1}{dL^2}$. Then*

$$\mathbb{E}_{t-1}[e(X_t)] - e(x) \leq q_t(\mu_t) - q_t(x) + \frac{4}{\lambda}\operatorname{tr}\left(q_t''(\mu_t)\Sigma_t\right) + \frac{1}{n}.$$

Proof (🦘) By Corollary 12.11,

$$\mathbb{E}_{t-1}[e(X_t)] - e(x) \leq q_t(\mu_t) - q_t(x) + \frac{2}{\lambda}\operatorname{tr}(s_t''(\mu_t)\Sigma_t) + \delta\left[\frac{2d}{\lambda} + \frac{1}{\lambda^2}\right]$$

$$\leq q_t(\mu_t) - q_t(x) + \frac{4}{\lambda}\operatorname{tr}(q_t''(\mu_t)\Sigma_t) + \frac{1}{n},$$

where the second inequality follows because $q_t''(\mu_t) = s_t''(\mu_t)/2$ and by naively bounding the constants. □

Estimation

The function q_t cannot be reconstructed from X_t and Y_t alone. But it can be estimated by

$$\hat{q}_t(x) = \langle g_t, x - \mu_t \rangle + \frac{1}{2}(x - \mu_t)^\top H_t (x - \mu_t),$$

where g_t and H_t are defined by

$$g_t = \frac{R_t Y_t \Sigma_t^{-1}(X_t - \mu_t)}{(1-\lambda)^2} \quad \text{and}$$

$$H_t = \frac{\lambda R_t Y_t}{2(1-\lambda)^2}\left[\frac{\Sigma_t^{-1}(X_t - \mu_t)(X_t - \mu_t)^\top \Sigma_t^{-1}}{(1-\lambda)^2} - \Sigma_t^{-1}\right],$$

with p_t the density of $\mathcal{N}(\mu_t, \Sigma_t)$ and

$$R_t = \frac{p_t\left(\frac{X_t - \lambda\mu}{1-\lambda}\right)}{(1-\lambda)^d p_t(X_t)}.$$

By Proposition 12.14, which follows from a change of measure and Stein's lemma,

$$\mathbb{E}_{t-1}[g_t] = s_t'(\mu_t) = q_t'(\mu_t) \quad \text{and} \quad \mathbb{E}_{t-1}[H_t] = \frac{1}{2}s_t''(\mu_t) = q_t''(\mu_t).$$

10.5 Algorithm and Analysis

The algorithm combines online Newton step with the quadratic surrogate estimates from Section 10.4.

```
1  args : η, λ, σ², ε
2  μ₁ = 0, Σ₁ = σ²𝟙
3  for t = 1 to n
4      sample Xₜ from 𝒩(μₜ, Σₜ) with density pₜ
5      observe Yₜ = π∧(Xₜ) (f(Xₜ/π∧(Xₜ)) + εₜ) + 2(π∧(Xₜ)−1)/ε
6      let Rₜ = pₜ((Xₜ−λμₜ)/(1−λ)) / ((1−λ)ᵈ pₜ(Xₜ))
7      compute gₜ = RₜYₜΣₜ⁻¹(Xₜ−μₜ) / (1−λ)²
8      compute Hₜ = λRₜYₜ/(2(1−λ)²) [Σₜ⁻¹(Xₜ−μₜ)(Xₜ−μₜ)ᵀΣₜ⁻¹/(1−λ)² − Σₜ⁻¹]
9      compute Σₜ₊₁⁻¹ = Σₜ⁻¹ + ηHₜ
10     compute μₜ₊₁ = arg min_{μ∈K_ε} ‖μ − [μₜ − ηΣₜ₊₁gₜ]‖_{Σₜ₊₁⁻¹}
```

Algorithm 10.2 Online Newton step for convex bandits

Computation

Algorithm 10.2 is straightforward to implement and relatively efficient. The main computational bottlenecks are as follows:

○ *Gaussian sampling*: The algorithm samples from a Gaussian with mean μ_t and covariance Σ_t. Given access to standard Gaussian noise, this more or less corresponds to computing an eigenvalue decomposition of the covariance matrix Σ_t, which at least naively requires $O(d^3)$ operations per round. Probably this can be improved with a careful incremental implementation. See Note 10.vii.

○ *Minkowski functional*: Remember that

$$\pi_\wedge(X_t) = \max(1, \pi(X_t)/(1-\varepsilon)).$$

This can be approximated to accuracy $1/n^2$ using bisection search and only logarithmically many queries to a membership oracle for K. The increase in regret due to the approximation is negligible.

○ *Projections*: The projection in Line 10 is a convex optimisation problem and the hardness depends on how K is represented (Table 3.1). Note that the projection is only needed in rounds t where $\mu_t - \eta\Sigma_{t+1}g_t \notin K_\varepsilon$.

10.5 Algorithm and Analysis

The algorithm needs $\tilde{O}(d^2)$ memory to store the covariance matrix. There is also the initial rounding procedure to put K into a good position, which only needs to be done once and is discussed in Section 3.6 and in the notes for this chapter.

Theorem 10.8 *Let $M = \max(d^{-1/2}, M(K))$ and*

$$\sigma = \frac{1}{M\sqrt{2d}} \qquad \lambda = \frac{1}{4d^{1.5}ML^2} \qquad \eta = \frac{dM}{3}\sqrt{\frac{1}{n}} \qquad \varepsilon = \frac{240d^2ML^4}{\sqrt{n}}.$$

Under Assumption 10.1, with probability at least $1-\delta$ the regret of Algorithm 10.2 is bounded by

$$\text{Reg}_n \leq 480d^2ML^4\sqrt{n}.$$

According to Table 10.1, if K/d is in Löwner's position, then $M = \tilde{O}(d^{-1/2})$ and the regret is $\tilde{O}(d^{1.5}\sqrt{n})$. The detailed proof of Theorem 10.8 is deferred to Section 10.6, but we give an outline below.

Proof outline The rigorous proof depends on a relatively intricate concentration analysis, which we brush over for now.

Step 1: Regret comparison

To begin, let $x_\star = \arg\min_{x \in K_\varepsilon} f(x)$ and

$$\text{eReg}_n(x_\star) = \sum_{t=1}^{n} (\mathbb{E}_{t-1}[e(X_t)] - e(x_\star)).$$

The regret with respect to the quadratic surrogates and its estimates are

$$\text{qReg}_n(x_\star) = \sum_{t=1}^{n}(q_t(\mu_t) - q_t(x_\star)) \quad \text{and}$$

$$\widehat{\text{qReg}}_n(x_\star) = \sum_{t=1}^{n}(\hat{q}_t(\mu_t) - \hat{q}_t(x_\star)).$$

We start by comparing the true regret to the regret relative to the extended losses:

$$\operatorname{Reg}_n \leq n\varepsilon + \sum_{t=1}^{n} (f(X_t/\pi_\wedge(X_t)) - f(x_\star)) \qquad \text{Proposition 3.13}$$

$$\overset{\text{whp}}{\lesssim} n\varepsilon + \sum_{t=1}^{n} (\mathbb{E}_{t-1}[f(X_t/\pi_\wedge(X_t))] - f(x_\star)) \qquad \text{Concentration}$$

$$\leq n\varepsilon + \sum_{t=1}^{n} (\mathbb{E}_{t-1}[e(X_t)] - f(x_\star)) \qquad \text{Proposition 3.23(4)}$$

$$= n\varepsilon + \sum_{t=1}^{n} (\mathbb{E}_{t-1}[e(X_t)] - e(x_\star)) \qquad \text{Proposition 3.23(1)}$$

$$= \tilde{O}\left(Md^2 \sqrt{n}\right) + \operatorname{eReg}_n(x_\star), \qquad (10.8)$$

where the final line follows from the definition of ε. Therefore it suffices to bound $\operatorname{eReg}_n(x_\star)$. The plan is to use Proposition 10.7 to compare the regrets relative to the extension and the quadratic surrogates. A serious issue is that the quadratic surrogate is only well-behaved on an ellipsoid about μ_t. Concretely, we will need to show that with high probability

$$F_t \triangleq \frac{1}{2}\|\mu_t - x_\star\|^2_{\Sigma_t^{-1}} = \tilde{O}(1/\lambda^2) \text{ for all } 1 \leq t \leq n.$$

Let τ be the first round where $F_{\tau+1}$ is not $\tilde{O}(1/\lambda^2)$, with τ defined to be n if no such round exists. By Proposition 10.7, for any $t \leq \tau$

$$\mathbb{E}_{t-1}[e(X_t)] - e(x_\star) \lesssim q_t(\mu_t) - q_t(x_\star) + \frac{4}{\lambda} \operatorname{tr}(q_t''(\mu_t)\Sigma_t),$$

where we ignored the final miniscule term in Proposition 10.7. Hence,

$$\operatorname{eReg}_\tau(x_\star) \lesssim \operatorname{qReg}_\tau(x_\star) + \frac{4}{\lambda} \sum_{t=1}^{n} \operatorname{tr}(q_t''(\mu_t)\Sigma_t)$$

$$\overset{\text{whp}}{\lesssim} \widetilde{\operatorname{qReg}}_\tau(x_\star) + \frac{4}{\lambda} \sum_{t=1}^{n} \operatorname{tr}(q_t''(\mu_t)\Sigma_t), \qquad (10.9)$$

where in the second inequality we used the fact that with high probability the estimated quadratic losses are close cumulatively to the unobserved quadratic losses. By Theorem 10.2,

$$F_{\tau+1} \leq F_1 + \frac{\eta^2}{2}\sum_{t=1}^{\tau}\|g_t\|_{\Sigma_t}^2 - \eta\widehat{\text{qReg}}_\tau(x_\star)$$

$$\leq \frac{2d^2}{\sigma^2} + \frac{\eta^2}{2}\sum_{t=1}^{\tau}\|g_t\|_{\Sigma_t}^2 - \eta\widehat{\text{qReg}}_\tau(x_\star)$$

$$\stackrel{\text{whp}}{\leq} \frac{2d^2}{\sigma^2} + \frac{\eta^2}{2}\sum_{t=1}^{\tau}\|g_t\|_{\Sigma_t}^2 + \frac{4\eta}{\lambda}\sum_{t=1}^{\tau}\text{tr}(q_t''(\mu_t)\Sigma_t) - \eta\text{eReg}_\tau(x_\star), \quad (10.10)$$

where in the second inequality we used the assumption that $K \subset \mathbb{B}_{2d}^d$ and $\mu_1 = \mathbf{0}$ to bound $F_1 = \frac{1}{2\sigma^2}\|x - \mu_1\|^2 \leq 2d^2/\sigma^2$. The third inequality follows from (10.9). There are two terms in the right-hand side that need a little more manipulation, which we break out into two additional steps.

Step 2: Bounding gradient norms

By definition

$$\|g_t\|_{\Sigma_t}^2 = \frac{R_t^2 Y_t^2}{(1-\lambda)^4}\|X_t - \mu_t\|_{\Sigma_t^{-1}}^2 \stackrel{\text{whp}}{=} \tilde{O}\left(dY_t^2\right),$$

where we used the facts that $0 \leq R_t \leq 3$ (Lemma 12.16) and $\lambda \in (0, 1/2)$ and that $\Sigma_t^{-1/2}(X_t - \mu_t)$ is a standard Gaussian. Summing shows that

$$\frac{\eta^2}{2}\sum_{t=1}^{\tau}\|g_t\|_{\Sigma_t}^2 \stackrel{\text{whp}}{=} \tilde{O}\left(d\eta^2 \sum_{t=1}^{\tau} Y_t^2\right).$$

We saw expressions like this in many other analyses and simply bounded $Y_t^2 \leq 1$. But because we have used the extended loss this is not possible anymore. Fortunately, one can prove that the algorithm mostly plays close to K_ε where the extended loss and true losses are equal. A complex argument eventually shows that with high probability $\sum_{t=1}^{\tau} Y_t^2 = \tilde{O}(n)$.

Step 3: Bounding the trace term

We claim the sum of traces in (10.10) is bounded by

$$\frac{4}{\lambda}\sum_{t=1}^{\tau}\text{tr}(q_t''(\mu_t)\Sigma_t) = \tilde{O}\left(\frac{d}{\lambda\eta}\right). \quad (10.11)$$

By definition $\mathbb{E}_{s-1}[H_s] = q_s''(\mu_s)$ and therefore it is plausible (and true) that with high probability

$$\Sigma_t^{-1} = \Sigma_1^{-1} + \eta\sum_{s=1}^{t-1} H_s \approx \Sigma_1^{-1} + \eta\sum_{s=1}^{t-1} q_s''(\mu_s).$$

Let us make a continuous-time approximation, which often provides a good ansatz for such problems. Let $\bar{\Sigma}(t)^{-1} = \Sigma_1^{-1} + \eta \int_1^t \bar{H}_{\lfloor s \rfloor} \, ds$ where $\bar{H}_s = q_s''(\mu_s)$. Then

$$\sum_{t=1}^{\tau} \text{tr}(\bar{H}_t \Sigma_t) \approx \frac{1}{\eta} \int_1^{\tau} \text{tr}\left(\frac{d}{dt}(\bar{\Sigma}(t)^{-1}) \bar{\Sigma}(t)\right) dt$$

$$= \frac{1}{\eta} \int_1^{\tau} \frac{d}{dt}[-\log \det(\bar{\Sigma}(t))] \, dt$$

$$= \frac{1}{\eta} \log \det(\bar{\Sigma}(1)\bar{\Sigma}(\tau)^{-1})$$

$$\overset{(\star)}{\leq} \frac{d}{\eta} \log\left(\frac{\text{tr}(\bar{\Sigma}(1)\bar{\Sigma}(\tau)^{-1})}{d}\right)$$

$$\overset{\text{whp}}{=} \tilde{O}\left(\frac{d}{\eta}\right),$$

where $(\star)$ follows from the arithmetic–geometric mean inequality and the final inequality follows by proving that $\|\bar{\Sigma}(\tau)^{-1}\| \leq \text{poly}(n, d)$ with high probability. This justifies (10.11).

Step 4: Combining

By the previous two steps and (10.10),

$$F_{\tau+1} \overset{\text{whp}}{\lesssim} \frac{2d^2}{\sigma^2} + \tilde{O}(\eta^2 nd) + \tilde{O}\left(\frac{d}{\lambda}\right) - \eta \text{eReg}_\tau(x_\star)$$

$$= \tilde{O}(1/\lambda^2) - \eta \text{eReg}_\tau(x_\star). \tag{10.12}$$

Since $\text{eReg}_\tau(x_\star) \geq 0$, this shows that $F_{\tau+1} = \tilde{O}(1/\lambda^2)$ and by the definition of τ this means that $\tau = n$. (10.12) also shows that

$$\text{eReg}_n(x_\star) = \tilde{O}(1/(\eta\lambda^2)) = \tilde{O}(Md^2 \sqrt{n}),$$

which when combined with (10.8) completes the argument. $\square$

Remark 10.9 Looking at (10.12), you may wonder: why not choose σ to be very large? The reason is hidden in the calculations needed in the second step. Consider the case that $d = 1$ and $K = [-1, 1]$. In the very first round the algorithm samples $X_t \sim \mathcal{N}(0, \sigma^2 \mathbb{1})$ and therefore $\mathbb{E}[|X_1|] \approx \sigma$. Hence, if $\sigma \gg 1$, then by the definition of the extended loss

$$\mathbb{E}[e(X_1)] = \Omega\left(\frac{\sigma}{\varepsilon}\right) \approx \sigma \sqrt{n}.$$

So the regret in even a single round is $\Omega(\sigma \sqrt{n})$.

10.6 Proof of Theorem 10.8

At various points we need that $\varepsilon \in (0, 1/2)$, which only holds for sufficiently large n. Note, however, that if $\varepsilon \geq 1/2$, then the regret bound in the theorem is implied by the assumption that $f \in \mathscr{F}_b$ so that $\text{Reg}_n \leq n$. Hence, for the remainder we assume that $\varepsilon \in (0, 1/2)$. The main complication is that the conclusion of Proposition 10.7 only holds for some x and the losses of the extension of f are very much not bounded in $[0, 1]$. At various points in the analysis we refer to various relations between the constants. These are collected in Section 10.8. Let

$$F_t = \frac{1}{2} \|\mu_t - x_\star\|_{\Sigma_t^{-1}}^2.$$

In order to make our analysis go through we need to argue that $F_t \leq \frac{1}{2L\lambda^2}$ for all t with high probability. There are a few other complications. Most notably, the algorithm is not properly defined if Σ_t fails to be positive definite. Hence we need to prove that this occurs with low probability. Note that $\mathbb{E}_{t-1}[H_t]$ is the Hessian of a convex function and hence positive semidefinite. Thus we will use concentration-of-measure to show that Σ_t indeed stays positive definite with high probability. Define the following quantities:

$$S_t = \sum_{u=1}^{t} H_u \quad \text{and} \quad \bar{S}_t = \sum_{u=1}^{t} \mathbb{E}_{u-1}[H_u] \quad \text{and} \quad \bar{\Sigma}_t^{-1} = \Sigma_1^{-1} + \eta \bar{S}_{t-1}.$$

We also let

$$\text{qReg}_\tau(x) = \sum_{t=1}^{\tau}(q_t(\mu_t) - q_t(x)) \quad \text{and} \quad \widetilde{\text{qReg}}_\tau(x) = \sum_{t=1}^{\tau}(\hat{q}_t(\mu_t) - \hat{q}_t(x)).$$

Definition 10.10 Let τ be the first round when one of the following does *not* hold:
(1) $F_{\tau+1} \leq \frac{1}{2L\lambda^2}$.
(2) $\Sigma_{\tau+1}$ is positive definite.
(3) $\delta\mathbb{1} \preceq \frac{1}{2}\bar{\Sigma}_{\tau+1}^{-1} \preceq \Sigma_{\tau+1}^{-1} \preceq \frac{3}{2}\bar{\Sigma}_{\tau+1}^{-1} \preceq \delta^{-1}\mathbb{1}$.

In case no such round exists, then τ is defined to be n.

Note that F_{t+1} and Σ_{t+1} are measurable with respect to $\mathscr{F}_t$, which means that τ is a stopping time with respect to the filtration $(\mathscr{F}_t)_{t=1}^n$. A simple consequence of the definition of τ is that for any $t \leq \tau$,

$$\|\Sigma_t\| \leq 2\|\bar{\Sigma}_t\| = 2\left\|\left(\frac{1}{\sigma^2}\mathbb{1} + \eta \bar{S}_t\right)^{-1}\right\| \leq 2\sigma^2, \qquad (10.13)$$

where the last step follows because $\bar{S}_t \in \mathbb{S}_+^d$.

Step 1: Regret relative to the extension

Most of our analysis bounds the regret with respect to the extension of f, which is only meaningful because the regret relative to the extension is nearly an upper bound on the regret relative to the real loss. Let $x_\star = \arg\min_{x \in K_\varepsilon} e(x)$ and

$$\mathrm{e\overline{Reg}}_n(x_\star) = \sum_{t=1}^n \mathbb{E}_{t-1}[e(X_t) - e(x_\star)].$$

Let E0 be the event that

$$\sum_{t=1}^n f(X_t/\pi_\wedge(X_t)) \leq \sum_{t=1}^n \mathbb{E}_{t-1}[f(X_t/\pi_\wedge(X_t))] + \sqrt{2n\log(7/\delta)}.$$

Since $X_t/\pi_\wedge(X_t) \in K_\varepsilon \subset K$ and $f \in \mathscr{F}_\mathrm{b}$, by Azuma's inequality (Theorem B.19) $\mathbb{P}(\mathrm{E}0) \geq 1 - \delta/7$. Suppose the above high-probability event occurs; then by Proposition 3.13 and Proposition 3.23,

$$\mathrm{Reg}_n \leq n\varepsilon + \max_{x \in K_\varepsilon} \mathrm{Reg}_n(x)$$

$$\leq n\varepsilon + \sqrt{2n\log(1/\delta)} + \max_{x \in K_\varepsilon} \sum_{t=1}^n \mathbb{E}_{t-1}[f(X_t/\pi_\wedge(X_t)) - f(x)]$$

$$\leq n\varepsilon + \sqrt{2n\log(1/\delta)} + \max_{x \in K_\varepsilon} \sum_{t=1}^n \mathbb{E}_{t-1}[e(X_t) - e(x)]$$

$$= n\varepsilon + \sqrt{2n\log(1/\delta)} + \mathrm{e\overline{Reg}}_n(x_\star). \qquad (10.14)$$

Therefore it suffices to bound $\mathrm{e\overline{Reg}}_n(x_\star)$.

Step 2: Concentration

We need to show that the behaviour of the various estimators used by Algorithm 10.2 is suitably regular with high probability. Define an event E1 by

$$\mathrm{E}1 = \left\{\max_{1 \leq t \leq \tau} |\varepsilon_t| \leq \sqrt{\log(14n/\delta)}\right\}. \qquad (\mathrm{E}1)$$

By Lemma B.3 and a union bound, $\mathbb{P}(\mathrm{E}1) \geq 1 - \delta/7$. The magnitude of the observed losses depends heavily on $\pi(X_t)$. Define an event E2 by

$$\mathrm{E}2 = \left\{\max_{1 \leq t \leq \tau} \pi(X_t) \leq \sqrt{L}\right\}. \qquad (\mathrm{E}2)$$

Lemma 10.11 $\mathbb{P}(\mathrm{E}2) \geq 1 - \delta/7$.

10.6 Proof of Theorem 10.8

Proof By Lemma 10.5 and a union bound, with probability at least $1 - \delta/7$ for all $t \leq \tau$,

$$\begin{aligned}
\pi(X_t) &\leq \mathbb{E}_{t-1}[\pi(X_t)] + \sqrt{2\,\|\Sigma_t\|\log(14n/\delta)} & \text{by Lemma 10.5(2)} \\
&\leq 1 + M\sqrt{d\,\|\Sigma_t\|} + \sqrt{2\,\|\Sigma_t\|\log(14n/\delta)} & \text{by Lemma 10.5(1)} \\
&\leq 1 + \sigma M\sqrt{2d} + 2\sigma\sqrt{\log(14n/\delta)} & \text{by (10.13)} \\
&\leq \sqrt{L}\,.
\end{aligned}$$

where the final inequality holds by the definition of the constants, which satisfy $\sigma \leq \sigma M\sqrt{2d} \leq 1$ (Table 10.2.f in Section 10.8). □

We also need to control the magnitude of $\|X_t - \mu_t\|_{\Sigma_t^{-1}}$. Define an event E3 by

$$\text{E3} = \left\{ \max_{1 \leq t \leq \tau} \|X_t - \mu_t\|_{\Sigma_t^{-1}} \leq \sqrt{\frac{8d}{3}\log(14n/\delta)} \right\}. \quad (\text{E3})$$

By Lemma B.3 and Proposition B.13, $\mathbb{P}(\text{E3}) \geq 1 - \delta/7$. The next lemma bounds the sum $\sum_{t=1}^{\tau} \mathbb{E}_{t-1}[Y_t^2]$. Because the extended loss matches the true loss on K_ε and the latter is bounded in $[0, 1]$, we should expect that when $X_t \in K_\varepsilon$, then $Y_t = \tilde{O}(1)$ with high probability. In other words, provided the algorithm is playing mostly in K_ε, then we should hope that $\sum_{t=1}^{\tau} \mathbb{E}_{t-1}[Y_t^2] = \tilde{O}(n)$. This is exactly what the following lemma says. The proof is deferred to Section 10.7 but should not be skipped.

Lemma 10.12 *Let $Y_{\max} = \max_{1 \leq t \leq \tau}(|Y_t| + \mathbb{E}_{t-1}[|Y_t|])$. On $\text{E1} \cap \text{E2} \cap \text{E3}$ the following hold:*

(1) $Y_{\max} \leq \frac{L}{\varepsilon}$.

(2) $\sum_{t=1}^{\tau} \mathbb{E}_{t-1}[Y_t^2] \leq 10n$.

We also need to control $\sum_{t=1}^{\tau} Y_t^2$. Let E4 be the event defined by

$$\text{E4} = \left\{ \sum_{t=1}^{\tau} Y_t^2 \leq 21n \right\}. \quad (\text{E4})$$

Lemma 10.13 $\mathbb{P}(\text{E4} \cup (\text{E1} \cap \text{E2} \cap \text{E3})^c) \geq 1 - \delta/7$.

Proof Let $E_t = \{|Y_t| \leq L/\varepsilon\}$. By Theorem B.22, with probability at least

$1 - \delta/7$,

$$\sum_{t=1}^{\tau} \mathbf{1}_{E_t} Y_t^2 \overset{(a)}{\leq} 2 \sum_{t=1}^{\tau} \mathbb{E}_{t-1}[\mathbf{1}_{E_t} Y_t^2] + \frac{L^2 \log(7/\delta)}{\varepsilon^2}$$

$$\overset{(b)}{\leq} 2 \sum_{t=1}^{\tau} \mathbb{E}_{t-1}[Y_t^2] + \frac{L^3}{\varepsilon^2}$$

$$\overset{(c)}{\leq} n + 2 \sum_{t=1}^{\tau} \mathbb{E}_{t-1}[Y_t^2].$$

where (a) follows from Theorem B.22, (b) by the definition of L and (c) by Table 10.2.a. By Lemma 10.12, on E1 ∩ E2 ∩ E3, E_t holds for all $t \leq \tau$ and in this case $\sum_{t=1}^{\tau} \mathbf{1}_{E_t} Y_t^2 = \sum_{t=1}^{\tau} Y_t^2$ and $\sum_{t=1}^{\tau} \mathbb{E}_{t-1}[Y_t^2] \leq 10n$. Hence, $\mathbb{P}(\text{E4} \cup (\text{E1} \cap \text{E2} \cap \text{E3})^c) \geq 1 - \delta/7$. □

The last two events control the concentration of the estimated quadratic surrogate about its mean at the optimal point and the concentration of the Hessian estimates. Let E5 be the event that

$$\text{E5} = \left\{ \text{qReg}_\tau(x_\star) \leq \widetilde{\text{qReg}}_\tau(x_\star) + \frac{4\sqrt{n}L}{\lambda} \right\}. \tag{E5}$$

Lemma 10.14 $\mathbb{P}(\text{E5} \cup (\text{E1} \cap \text{E2} \cap \text{E3} \cap \text{E4})^c) \geq 1 - \delta/7$.

Proof By the definition of τ, for all $t \leq \tau$,

$$\lambda \|\mu_t - x_\star\|_{\Sigma_t^{-1}} \leq \frac{1}{\sqrt{L}}.$$

Hence, by Proposition 12.24(1), with probability at least $1 - \delta/7$,

$$\sum_{t=1}^{\tau} (\hat{q}_t(x_\star) - q_t(x_\star)) \leq 1 + \frac{1}{\lambda} \left[\sqrt{\sum_{t=1}^{\tau} \mathbb{E}_{t-1}[Y_t^2] L} + Y_{\max} L \right]. \tag{10.15}$$

10.6 Proof of Theorem 10.8

On this event and E1 ∩ E2 ∩ E3,

$$\text{qReg}_\tau(x_\star) - \widetilde{\text{qReg}}_\tau(x_\star) = \sum_{t=1}^\tau (q_t(\mu_t) - q_t(x_\star)) - \sum_{t=1}^\tau (\hat{q}_t(\mu_t) - \hat{q}_t(x_\star))$$

$$\stackrel{(a)}{=} \sum_{t=1}^\tau (\hat{q}_t(x_\star) - q_t(x_\star))$$

$$\stackrel{(b)}{\leq} 1 + \frac{1}{\lambda}\left[\sqrt{\sum_{t=1}^\tau \mathbb{E}_{t-1}[Y_t^2]L} + Y_{\max}L\right]$$

$$\stackrel{(c)}{\leq} 1 + \frac{1}{\lambda}\left[\sqrt{10nL} + \frac{L^2}{\varepsilon}\right]$$

$$\stackrel{(d)}{\leq} \frac{4}{\lambda}\sqrt{nL},$$

where (a) holds because $q_t(\mu_t) = \hat{q}_t(\mu_t) = 0$, (b) from (10.15), (c) from Lemma 10.12(1)(2) and (d) by naive simplification. □

Finally, let E6 be the event that

$$\text{E6} = \left\{-6\lambda L^2 \sqrt{dn}\bar{\Sigma}_\tau^{-1} \preceq S_\tau - \bar{S}_\tau \preceq 6\lambda L^2\sqrt{dn}\bar{\Sigma}_\tau^{-1}\right\}. \tag{E6}$$

Lemma 10.15 $\mathbb{P}(\text{E6} \cup (\text{E1} \cap \text{E2} \cap \text{E3} \cap \text{E4})^c) \geq 1 - \delta/7$.

Proof By Proposition 12.27 with $\Sigma^{-1} = \frac{3}{2}\bar{\Sigma}_\tau^{-1}$, with probability at least $1 - \delta/7$,

$$\bar{S}_\tau - S_\tau \preceq \lambda L^2\left[1 + \sqrt{d\sum_{t=1}^\tau \mathbb{E}_{t-1}[Y_t^2] + d^2 Y_{\max}}\right]\frac{3}{2}\bar{\Sigma}_\tau^{-1} \quad \text{and}$$

$$S_\tau - \bar{S}_\tau \preceq \lambda L^2\left[1 + \sqrt{d\sum_{t=1}^\tau \mathbb{E}_{t-1}[Y_t^2] + d^2 Y_{\max}}\right]\frac{3}{2}\bar{\Sigma}_\tau^{-1}.$$

As before, the claim follows from Lemma 10.12(1)(2) and Table 10.2.b, which says that $\frac{d^2 L}{\varepsilon} \leq \frac{1}{L}\sqrt{dn}$. □

Let $E = \text{E0} \cap \text{E1} \cap \text{E2} \cap \text{E3} \cap \text{E4} \cap \text{E5} \cap \text{E6}$ be the intersection of all these high-probability events. A union bound over all the calculations above shows that $\mathbb{P}(E) \geq 1 - \delta$. For the remainder of the proof we bound the regret on E.

Step 3: Simple bounds

We can now make some elementary conclusions that hold on the intersection of all the high probability events outlined in the previous step. To begin, by

Lemma 10.12(2),

$$\sum_{t=1}^{\tau} \|g_t\|_{\Sigma_t}^2 = \sum_{t=1}^{\tau} \left\| \frac{R_t Y_t \Sigma_t^{-1}(X_t - \mu_t)}{(1-\lambda)^2} \right\|_{\Sigma_t}^2$$

$$\leq \left(\sum_{t=1}^{\tau} Y_t^2\right) \max_{1 \leq t \leq \tau} \left(\frac{R_t}{(1-\lambda)^2}\right)^2 \|X_t - \mu_t\|_{\Sigma_t^{-1}}^2$$

$$\leq dnL, \qquad (10.16)$$

where in the last inequality we combined E3 to bound the norm and E4 to bound the sum of squared losses with Lemma 12.16 to bound $0 \leq R_t \leq 3$ and used the fact that $\lambda \leq \frac{1}{2}$. By the definition of E6,

$$\Sigma_{\tau+1}^{-1} = \Sigma_1^{-1} + \eta S_\tau \preceq \Sigma_1^{-1} + \eta \bar{S}_\tau + 6\eta \lambda L^2 \sqrt{dn} \bar{\Sigma}_\tau^{-1} \preceq \frac{3}{2} \bar{\Sigma}_{\tau+1}^{-1},$$

where the final inequality follows from the definitions of η and λ (Table 10.2.c) and because $\bar{\Sigma}_\tau^{-1} \preceq \bar{\Sigma}_{\tau+1}^{-1}$. Similarly,

$$\Sigma_{\tau+1}^{-1} \succeq \Sigma_1^{-1} + \eta \bar{S}_\tau - \frac{1}{2}\bar{\Sigma}_\tau^{-1} = \bar{\Sigma}_{\tau+1}^{-1} - \frac{1}{2}\bar{\Sigma}_\tau^{-1} \succeq \frac{1}{2}\bar{\Sigma}_{\tau+1}^{-1}.$$

Combining shows that

$$\frac{1}{2}\bar{\Sigma}_{\tau+1}^{-1} \preceq \Sigma_{\tau+1}^{-1} \preceq \frac{3}{2}\bar{\Sigma}_{\tau+1}^{-1}. \qquad (10.17)$$

We also want to show that $2\delta \mathbb{1} \preceq \bar{\Sigma}_{\tau+1}^{-1} \preceq \frac{2}{3\delta}\mathbb{1}$. The left-hand inequality is immediate because $\bar{\Sigma}_{\tau+1} \preceq \bar{\Sigma}_1 = \sigma^2 \mathbb{1} \preceq \frac{1}{2\delta}\mathbb{1}$. By Proposition 12.6, for any $t \leq \tau$,

$$\|\mathbb{E}_{t-1}[H_t]\| = \frac{1}{2}\|s_t''(\mu_t)\|$$

$$\leq \frac{\lambda \operatorname{lip}(e)}{2(1-\lambda)} \sqrt{d \|\Sigma_t^{-1}\|}$$

$$\leq \frac{\lambda \operatorname{lip}(e)}{2(1-\lambda)} \sqrt{\frac{3d}{2} \|\bar{\Sigma}_t^{-1}\|}$$

$$\leq \frac{\lambda \operatorname{lip}(e)}{2(1-\lambda)} \sqrt{\frac{d}{\delta}},$$

where the final inequality follows from Definition 10.10 and because $t \leq \tau$. Therefore, by ensuring that $\delta = O(1/\operatorname{poly}(n,d))$ is small enough and bounding $\operatorname{lip}(e) = O(1/\varepsilon)$ using Proposition 3.23,

$$\|\bar{\Sigma}_{\tau+1}^{-1}\| = \left\|\bar{\Sigma}_1^{-1} + \eta \sum_{u=1}^{\tau} \bar{H}_u\right\| \leq \|\bar{\Sigma}_1^{-1}\| + \frac{\eta n \lambda \operatorname{lip}(e)}{2(1-\lambda)} \sqrt{\frac{d}{\delta}} \leq \frac{1}{\delta}. \qquad (10.18)$$

10.6 Proof of Theorem 10.8

Therefore both Definition 10.10(2) and Definition 10.10(3) hold and so the only way that $\tau \neq n$ is if $F_{\tau+1} > \frac{1}{2L\lambda^2}$.

Step 4: Trace/Logdet inequalities

Online Newton step bounds the regret relative to the estimated quadratic surrogate losses, which are close to the true quadratic losses. The regret relative to the extension can be bounded in terms of the regret relative to quadratic surrogates:

Lemma 10.16 *On event E,* $\mathrm{e\overline{Reg}}_\tau(x_\star) \leq \mathrm{qReg}_\tau(x_\star) + \dfrac{dL}{\lambda\eta}$.

Proof By the definition of τ, for $t \leq \tau$ it holds that $\lambda \|\mu_t - x_\star\|_{\Sigma_t^{-1}} \leq \frac{1}{\sqrt{L}}$. Hence, by Proposition 10.7,

$$\mathrm{e\overline{Reg}}_\tau(x_\star) \leq \mathrm{qReg}_\tau(x_\star) + \frac{4}{\lambda}\sum_{t=1}^{\tau} \mathrm{tr}(q_t''(\mu_t)\Sigma_t) + 1. \qquad (10.19)$$

By Proposition 12.6 and Proposition 3.23, for any $t \leq \tau$,

$$\eta \left\| \Sigma_t^{1/2} q_t''(\mu_t) \Sigma_t^{1/2} \right\| \leq \frac{\eta\lambda \operatorname{lip}(e)}{2(1-\lambda)} \sqrt{d \|\Sigma_t\|} \leq \frac{2\eta\lambda\sigma\sqrt{2d}}{\varepsilon(1-\lambda)} \leq 1, \qquad (10.20)$$

where in the second last inequality we used (10.13) to bound $\|\Sigma_t\| \leq 2\sigma^2$ and Proposition 3.23 and the assumption that $\mathbb{B}_1^d \subset K$ to bound $\operatorname{lip}(e) \leq \frac{2}{\varepsilon(1-\varepsilon)} \leq \frac{4}{\varepsilon}$. The final inequality holds because of the choice of λ, η and ε (Table 10.2.d). Hence, by Lemma A.9,

$$\frac{4}{\lambda}\sum_{t=1}^{\tau} \mathrm{tr}(q_t''(\mu_t)\Sigma_t) \overset{(a)}{\leq} \frac{16}{\lambda\eta} \sum_{t=1}^{\tau} \log\det\left(\mathbb{1} + \frac{\eta q_t''(\mu_t)\Sigma_t}{2}\right)$$

$$\overset{(b)}{\leq} \frac{16}{\lambda\eta} \sum_{t=1}^{\tau} \log\det\left(\mathbb{1} + \eta q_t''(\mu_t)\bar{\Sigma}_t\right)$$

$$= \frac{16}{\lambda\eta} \sum_{t=1}^{\tau} \log\det\left(\bar{\Sigma}_t \bar{\Sigma}_{t+1}^{-1}\right)$$

$$= \frac{16}{\lambda\eta} \log\det\left(\bar{\Sigma}_1 \bar{\Sigma}_{\tau+1}^{-1}\right)$$

$$\overset{(c)}{\leq} \frac{16}{\lambda\eta} \log\det\left(\frac{\sigma^2}{\delta}\mathbb{1}\right)$$

$$\overset{(d)}{\leq} \frac{dL}{\lambda\eta} - 1, \qquad (10.21)$$

where (a) follows from Lemma A.9 and (10.20), (b) because for $t \leq \tau$,

$\Sigma_t \preceq 2\bar{\Sigma}_t$, and (c) follows from (10.18). Lastly, (d) holds by the definition of L. The claim of the lemma now follows from (10.19). □

Step 5: Regret

By (10.17), for any $t \leq \tau$,

$$\|g_t\|_{\Sigma_{t+1}}^2 \leq 2\|g_t\|_{\bar{\Sigma}_{t+1}}^2 \leq 2\|g_t\|_{\bar{\Sigma}_t}^2 \leq 3\|g_t\|_{\Sigma_t}^2 . \qquad (10.22)$$

By Theorem 10.2 and the bounds in (10.16) and (E5),

$$\begin{aligned}
F_{\tau+1} &= \frac{1}{2}\|x_\star - \mu_{\tau+1}\|_{\Sigma_{\tau+1}^{-1}}^2 \\
&\stackrel{(a)}{\leq} \frac{\|x_\star\|^2}{2\sigma^2} + \frac{\eta^2}{2}\sum_{t=1}^{\tau}\|g_t\|_{\Sigma_{t+1}}^2 - \eta q\widehat{\mathrm{Reg}}_\tau(x_\star) \\
&\stackrel{(b)}{\leq} \frac{\|x_\star\|^2}{2\sigma^2} + \frac{3\eta^2 n d L}{2} - \eta q\widehat{\mathrm{Reg}}_\tau(x_\star) \\
&\stackrel{(c)}{\leq} \frac{\|x_\star\|^2}{2\sigma^2} + \frac{3\eta^2 n d L}{2} + \frac{4\eta\sqrt{n}L}{\lambda} - \eta q\mathrm{Reg}_\tau(x_\star) \\
&\stackrel{(d)}{\leq} \frac{\|x_\star\|^2}{2\sigma^2} + \frac{3\eta^2 n d L}{2} + \frac{dL}{\lambda} + \frac{4\eta\sqrt{n}L}{\lambda} - \eta \mathrm{e}\overline{\mathrm{Reg}}_\tau(x_\star) \\
&\stackrel{(e)}{\leq} \frac{2d^2}{\sigma^2} + \frac{3\eta^2 n d L}{2} + \frac{dL}{\lambda} + \frac{4\eta\sqrt{n}L}{\lambda} - \eta \mathrm{e}\overline{\mathrm{Reg}}_\tau(x_\star) \\
&\stackrel{(f)}{\leq} \frac{1}{2L\lambda^2} - \eta \mathrm{e}\overline{\mathrm{Reg}}_\tau(x_\star),
\end{aligned}$$

where (a) follows from Theorem 10.2, (b) from (10.16) and (10.22), (c) holds on event E5, and (d) follows from Lemma 10.16. (e) follows because we assumed that $K \subset \mathbb{B}_{2d}^d$. Lastly, (f) follows by substituting the definition of the constants Table 10.2.e. Therefore all of the following hold:

(1) $F_{\tau+1} \leq \frac{1}{2L\lambda^2}$.

(2) $\mathrm{e}\overline{\mathrm{Reg}}_\tau(x_\star) \leq \frac{1}{2L\eta\lambda^2}$.

(3) $\Sigma_{\tau+1}$ is positive definite and $\delta \mathbb{1} \preceq \frac{1}{2}\bar{\Sigma}_{\tau+1}^{-1} \preceq \Sigma_{\tau+1}^{-1} \preceq \frac{3}{2}\bar{\Sigma}_{\tau+1}^{-1} \preceq \delta^{-1}\mathbb{1}$.
By Definition 10.10, on this event we have $\tau = n$ and hence $\mathrm{e}\overline{\mathrm{Reg}}_n(x_\star) \leq \frac{1}{2L\eta\lambda^2}$. At long last, Theorem 10.8 now follows from the definitions of η and λ and (10.14).

10.7 Proof of Lemma 10.12

Staring with part (1), let $t \leq \tau$. Then, on E1 and E2,

$$\begin{aligned} |Y_t| &= |e(X_t) + \pi_\wedge(X_t)\varepsilon_t| \\ &= \left|\pi_\wedge(X_t)f\left(\frac{X_t}{\pi_\wedge(X_t)}\right) + \frac{2(\pi_\wedge(X_t) - 1)}{\varepsilon} + \pi_\wedge(X_t)\varepsilon_t\right| \\ &\leq \frac{L}{2\varepsilon}, \end{aligned} \qquad (10.23)$$

where in the final inequality we used the definitions of E1 and E2 and the definition $\pi_\wedge(X_t) = \max(1, \pi(X_t)/(1+\varepsilon))$. The expectation is bounded by

$$\begin{aligned} \mathbb{E}_{t-1}[|Y_t|] &= \mathbb{E}_{t-1}\left[\left|\pi_\wedge(X_t)f\left(\frac{X_t}{\pi_\wedge(X_t)}\right) + \frac{2(\pi_\wedge(X_t)-1)}{\varepsilon} + \pi_\wedge(X_t)\varepsilon_t\right|\right] \\ &\overset{(a)}{\leq} \frac{2}{\varepsilon}\mathbb{E}_{t-1}\left[\pi_\wedge(X_t)\right] + \mathbb{E}_{t-1}[|\pi_\wedge(X_t)\varepsilon_t|] \\ &\overset{(b)}{\leq} \frac{3}{\varepsilon}\mathbb{E}_{t-1}\left[\pi_\wedge(X_t)\right] \\ &\overset{(c)}{\leq} \frac{3}{\varepsilon}\left(1 + \sigma M\sqrt{2d}\right) \\ &\overset{(d)}{\leq} \frac{L}{2\varepsilon}, \end{aligned} \qquad (10.24)$$

where (a) follows because $f \in \mathscr{F}_b$ is bounded; (b) holds because $\mathbb{E}_{t-1}[|\varepsilon_t||X_t] \leq 1$ and by naively bounding $1 \leq 1/\varepsilon$; and (c) follows from Lemma 10.5 and because $\|\Sigma_t\| \leq 2\sigma^2$ by (10.13). Lastly, (d) is true because $\sigma M\sqrt{2d} \leq 1$ (Table 10.2.f). Combining (10.23) and (10.24) completes the proof of part (1). Part (2) is more interesting. The main point is that under E1, E2, E3 the only way that Y_t can be large is if X_t is far outside of K_ε. By the definition of the algorithm $\mu_t \in K_\varepsilon$, which means that for X_t to be large the covariance Σ_t must also be relatively large. But because Σ_t^{-1} increases with curvature and the extended loss function has considerable curvature near ∂K_ε, we should expect that as the algorithm plays outside K_ε the covariance Σ_t will decrease and hence X_t gets closer to K_ε and $Y_t = \tilde{O}(1)$. Recall that $v(x) = \pi_\wedge(x) - 1$ and $v_\varrho = v * \phi_\varrho$ where ϕ_ϱ is the smoothing kernel from

Section 3.8. Then

$$\sum_{t=1}^{\tau} \mathbb{E}_{t-1}[Y_t^2] = \sum_{t=1}^{\tau} \mathbb{E}_{t-1}\left[\left(\pi_\wedge(X_t)\left(f(X_t/\pi_\wedge(X_t)) + \varepsilon_t\right) + \frac{2v(X_t)}{\varepsilon}\right)^2\right]$$

$$\stackrel{(a)}{\leq} \sum_{t=1}^{\tau} \mathbb{E}_{t-1}\left[4\pi_\wedge(X_t)^2 + \frac{8v(X_t)^2}{\varepsilon^2}\right]$$

$$\stackrel{(b)}{\leq} \sum_{t=1}^{\tau} \mathbb{E}_{t-1}\left[8 + \frac{10v(X_t)^2}{\varepsilon^2}\right]$$

$$\stackrel{(c)}{\leq} 8n + \frac{10}{\varepsilon^2}\sum_{t=1}^{\tau} L\left(1 + M\sqrt{d\|\Sigma_t\|}\right)\left[\mathrm{tr}\left(\Sigma_t \lim_{\varrho \to 0} \mathbb{E}_{t-1}[v_\varrho''(X_t)]\right) + \delta\right]$$

$$\stackrel{(d)}{\leq} 8n + \frac{20L}{\varepsilon^2}\sum_{t=1}^{\tau}\left[\mathrm{tr}\left(\Sigma_t \lim_{\varrho \to 0} \mathbb{E}_{t-1}[v_\varrho''(X_t)]\right) + \delta\right]$$

$$\stackrel{(e)}{\leq} 9n + \frac{80L}{\lambda\varepsilon}\sum_{t=1}^{\tau} \mathrm{tr}\left(\Sigma_t q_t''(\mu_t)\right) \stackrel{(f)}{\leq} 9n + \frac{20dL^2}{\lambda\eta\varepsilon} \stackrel{(g)}{\leq} 10n$$

where (a) uses that $(a+b)^2 \leq 2a^2 + 2b^2$ and the assumption that ε_t subgaussian under $\mathbb{P}_{t-1}(\cdot|X_t)$ so that $\mathbb{E}_{t-1}[(f(X_t/\pi_\wedge(X_t)) + \varepsilon_t)^2|X_t] \leq 2$. (b) uses that $\varepsilon \leq 1/2$ and again that $(a+b)^2 \leq 2a^2 + 2b^2$; (c) follows from Lemma 10.6 and because $M = \max(M(K), 1/\sqrt{d})$; (d) follows from (10.13) to bound $\|\Sigma_t\| \leq 2\sigma^2$ and the definition of the constraints (Table 10.2.f); (f) follows from (10.21); and (g) uses the definition of the constants again (Table 10.2.g). It remains to justify (e). Recall that

$$e(x) = \left[\pi_\wedge(x) f\left(\frac{x}{\pi_\wedge(x)}\right) + \frac{v(x)}{\varepsilon}\right] + \frac{v(x)}{\varepsilon} \triangleq h(x) + \frac{v(x)}{\varepsilon}.$$

Now h is convex by Proposition 3.23 and $\mathrm{lip}(h) < \infty$, and hence by Proposition 3.24, Proposition 12.8 and Table 10.2.h,

$$\mathrm{tr}(\Sigma_t q_t''(\mu_t)) = \frac{1}{2}\mathrm{tr}(\Sigma_t s_t''(\mu_t))$$

$$\geq \frac{\lambda}{4}\mathrm{tr}\left(\Sigma_t \lim_{\varrho \to 0} \mathbb{E}_{t-1}\left[e_\varrho''(X_t)\right]\right) - \frac{\delta d}{2}$$

$$\geq \frac{\lambda}{4\varepsilon}\mathrm{tr}\left(\Sigma_t \lim_{\varrho \to 0} \mathbb{E}_{t-1}\left[v_\varrho''(X_t)\right]\right) - \frac{\delta d}{2},$$

where the last inequality holds because $e_\varrho''(x) = h_\varrho''(x) + \frac{1}{\varepsilon}v_\varrho''(x) \succeq \frac{1}{\varepsilon}v_\varrho''(x)$. Rearranging shows that

$$\mathrm{tr}\left(\Sigma_t \lim_{\varrho \to 0} \mathbb{E}_{t-1}\left[v_\varrho''(X_t)\right]\right) + \delta \leq \frac{4\varepsilon}{\lambda}\mathrm{tr}\left(\Sigma_t q_t''(\mu_t)\right) + \delta\left[1 + \frac{2\varepsilon d}{\lambda}\right],$$

which by naively bounding the terms involving δ suffices to establish (e).

10.8 Constraints

Most bandit algorithms are fairly straightforward to tune as we saw in Chapters 5 to 8. Regrettably the parameters of Algorithm 10.2 interact in a more complicated way. The constraints needed for the analysis are listed in Table 10.2.

	CONSTRAINT
10.2.a	$\frac{L^3}{\varepsilon^2} \leq n$
10.2.b	$\frac{d^2 L}{\varepsilon} \leq \frac{1}{L}\sqrt{dn}$
10.2.c	$6\eta\lambda L^2\sqrt{dn} \leq \frac{1}{2}$
10.2.d	$\frac{2\sigma\eta\lambda}{\varepsilon(1-\lambda)}\sqrt{2d} \leq 1$
10.2.e	$\frac{2d^2}{\sigma^2} + \frac{3\eta^2 ndL}{2} + \frac{dL}{\lambda} + \frac{4\eta\sqrt{nL}}{\lambda} \leq \frac{1}{2L\lambda^2}$
10.2.f	$\sigma M\sqrt{2d} \leq 1$
10.2.g	$\frac{20dL^2}{\lambda\eta\varepsilon} \leq n$
10.2.h	$\lambda \leq \frac{1}{dL^2}$

Table 10.2 Constraints on the constants needed in the analysis of Algorithm 10.2.

You can check (laboriously) that the constants defined by

$$\sigma = \frac{1}{M\sqrt{2d}} \qquad \lambda = \frac{1}{4d^{1.5}ML^2} \qquad \eta = \frac{dM}{3}\sqrt{\frac{1}{n}} \qquad \varepsilon = \frac{240d^2ML^4}{\sqrt{n}}$$

satisfy all of the above constraints.

10.9 Notes

10.i Let us collect some notes on the trade-offs between the various positions.
- Löwner's position yields a regret of $\tilde{O}(d^{1.5}\sqrt{n})$ for any K. But in general

it can only be computed efficiently when K is the convex hull of a small number of vertices.
- Isotropic position yields $\tilde{O}(d^2\sqrt{n})$ regret for any K and can be computed relatively efficiently when K is given by a separation or membership oracle. The bound improves to $\tilde{O}(d^{1.9}\sqrt{n})$ when K is symmetric.
- John's position yields $\tilde{O}(d^2\sqrt{n})$ regret for any K and can be computed efficiently when K is a polytope represented by the intersection of half-spaces. When K is symmetric, the regret improves to $\tilde{O}(d^{1.5}\sqrt{n})$.
- When the polar of K is isotropic, then the regret is $\tilde{O}(d^{1.75}\sqrt{n})$ in general and $\tilde{O}(d^{1.5}\sqrt{n})$ when K is symmetric. Positioning K such that the polar is isotropic is quite delicate and is discussed in detail in 10.iii below.

10.ii No scaling of John's position yields the same uniform bound on $M(K)$ as Löwner's position. Let K be such that $K^\circ = \mathbb{B}_1^d \cap \{u \colon u_1 \geq -1/d\}$, which is the convex body formed as the intersection of the unit ball and a half-space. Theorem 9.27 shows that K° is in Löwner's position and therefore K is in John's position. But $M(K) \geq \frac{1}{2}$ is obvious and yet $-de_1 \in K$ holds since $\sup_{u \in K^\circ} \langle -de_1, u \rangle = 1$. Therefore $\max_{x \in K} \|x\| \geq d$. Since for $\gamma > 0$, $M(\gamma K) = \frac{1}{\gamma} M(K)$,

$$M(\gamma K) \max_{x \in \gamma K} \|x\| \geq \frac{d}{2} \text{ for all } \gamma \in (0, \infty).$$

Therefore every scaling of K such that $\text{diam}(K) = O(d)$ has $M(K) = \Omega(1)$. This suggests the following problem:

Exercise 10.17 ★★★📄? Does there exist a polynomial-time algorithm for positioning the constraint set such that $\mathbb{B}_1^d \subset K \subset \mathbb{B}_{2d}^d$ and $M(K) = \tilde{O}(d^{-1/2})$ when
- $K = \{x \colon Ax \leq b\}$ is a polytope?
- K is given by a separation or membership oracle?

10.iii The existence and computation of an affine map T such that $(TK)^\circ$ is isotropic is quite interesting. Let

$$\text{cen}(K) = \frac{1}{\text{vol}(K)} \int_K x \, dx \quad \text{and}$$

$$\text{cov}(K) = \frac{1}{\text{vol}(K)} \int_K (x - \text{cen}(K))(x - \text{cen}(K))^\top \, dx.$$

We want to find an affine map T such that $\text{cen}((TK)^\circ) = \mathbf{0}$ and $\text{cov}((TK)^\circ) = \mathbb{1}$. An elementary calculation shows that $(AK)^\circ = A^{-1}K^\circ$ for positive definite A. The behaviour of $x \mapsto (K - x)^\circ$, however, is more complicated. Nevertheless, there exists an $s \in \text{int}(K)$ called the Santáló point such that $\text{cen}((K - s)^\circ) = \mathbf{0}$,

10.9 Notes

as explained by Schneider (2013). Meyer and Werner (1998) show that $x \mapsto \text{vol}((K - x)^\circ)$ is strictly convex on the interior of K and the minimiser of this function is the Santaló point (Santaló, 1949). Hence, letting s be the Santaló point of K, $A = \text{cov}((K - s)^\circ)^{1/2}$ and $Tx = Ax - As$, it follows that $(TK)^\circ$ is isotropic. Regarding computation, given $x \in \text{int}(K)$ it is possible in principle to estimate $\text{vol}((K - x)^\circ)$ by sampling and hence use zeroth-order convex optimisation to find the Santaló point. Once s has been found, the matrix A can be estimated by sampling from $(K - s)^\circ$. A reasonable guess is that a suitable approximation of T can be found in polynomial time using this procedure, but the devil is in the details of the approximation errors:

Exercise 10.18 ★★★▨? Suppose that K is a polytope or represented by a separation oracle. Does there exist a polynomial time algorithm to position K so that K° is approximately isotropic with errors small enough that the relevant results in Table 10.1 hold (approximately)? The problem is studied when $d = 2$ by Kaiser (1993).

10.iv Online Newton step was originally designed for full-information online convex optimisation (Hazan et al., 2007). Its use as an algorithm for driving bandit convex optimisation methods has been developed by a number of authors. Suggala et al. (2021, 2024) studied the quadratic and near-quadratic settings, while Lattimore and György (2023) considered Lipschitz convex functions in the unconstrained setting. The algorithm and analysis in this chapter follows the work by Fokkema et al. (2024).

10.v You should be a little unhappy about the non-specific constants in Theorem 10.8. How can you run the algorithm if the constants depend on universal constants and unspecified logarithmic factors? The problem is that the theory is overly conservative. In practice both η and λ should be much larger than the theory would suggest, even if you tracked the constants through the analysis quite carefully. This is quite a standard phenomenon, and usually not a problem. Here there is a little twist, however. If you choose η or λ too large, then the algorithm can explode with non-negligible probability. For example, the covariance matrix might stop being positive definite at some point, or F_t could grow too large and the algorithm may move slowly relative to the regret suffered. Hopefully this issue can be resolved in the future but for now you should be cautious.

10.vi An interesting question is whether or not Algorithm 10.2 can be adapted to exploit low-variance noise, possibly using the idea in Section 6.6. The principal challenge is the huge range of the extension, which you could mitigate by assuming the loss is Lipschitz and using Proposition 3.20. Or, even better, by developing some new techniques:

Exercise 10.19 ★★★? Analyse the regret of Algorithm 10.2 or some modification thereof under Assumption 6.17.

10.vii There are several ways to improve the computational complexity of Algorithm 10.2. At the moment the complexity when K is a polytope is $O(d^3 + md^2)$ with the former term due to computing the eigenvalue decomposition of the covariance matrix and the latter from the projection (Table 3.1). Note that $m \geq d + 1$ is needed for K to be a convex body, so the second term always dominates.

Exercise 10.20 ★★▣? Suppose that $\Sigma^{1/2}$ is stored in memory and $u \in \mathbb{R}^d$.
(1)   Find a high-quality approximation of $(\Sigma^{-1} + uu^\top)^{-1/2}$ that can be computed using $\tilde{O}(d^2)$ arithmetic operations.
(2)   Show how to use (1) to reduce the complexity of the Gaussian sampling in Algorithm 10.2 to $\tilde{O}(d^2)$ arithmetic operations per round.

For (1) you may find the results by Hale et al. (2008) useful. The next exercise is more speculative:

Exercise 10.21 ★★★? Modify Algorithm 10.2 by removing the projection onto K_ε and prove whether or not the regret bound in Theorem 10.8 still holds. We only used that $\mu_t \in K_\varepsilon$ in the proof of Lemma 10.12, which uses Lemma 10.5. Intuitively, even without the projection the algorithm should keep μ_t close to K_ε since the extended loss grows rapidly outside K_ε. Alternatively, you may argue that the projections happen rarely, possibly after modifying the algorithm in some way.

11
Online Newton Step for Adversarial Losses

Because the optimistic Gaussian surrogate is only well-behaved on a shrinking ellipsoidal focus region, algorithms that use it are most naturally analysed in the stochastic setting, where it is already a challenge to prove that the optimal action remains in the focus region. In the adversarial setting there is limited hope to ensure the optimal action in hindsight remains in the focus region. The plan is to use a mechanism that detects when the minimiser leaves the focus region and restarts the algorithm. This is combined with an argument that the regret is negative whenever a restart occurs. The formal setting studied in this chapter is characterised by the following assumption:

Assumption 11.1 The following hold:
(1) The losses are bounded: $f_t \in \mathscr{F}_\flat$ for all t.
(2) The constraint set is rounded: $\mathbb{B}_1^d \subset K \subset \mathbb{B}_{2d}^d$.

This is the same assumption as in Chapter 10 except that the setting is now adversarial. The highlight is a computationally efficient algorithm and regret bound of $\tilde{O}(d^{2.5}\sqrt{n})$ under Assumption 11.1. As in Chapter 10 we assume that $\delta \in (0, 1)$ is a small user-defined constant that satisfies $\delta \leq \text{poly}(1/d, 1/n)$ and

$$L = C \log(1/\delta)$$

where $C > 0$ is a universal constant. The analysis in this chapter builds on and refers to the arguments in Chapter 10, which should be read first.

11.1 Approximate Convex Minimisation (🦘)

The version of online Newton step for adversarial convex bandits makes use of a subroutine for approximately minimising a nearly convex function.

Assumption 11.2 $K \subset \mathbb{R}^d$ is a convex body and $h\colon K \to \mathbb{R}$, $\hat{h}\colon K \to \mathbb{R}$ and $\hat{h}'\colon K \to \mathbb{R}^d$ are functions such that
(1) h is convex and differentiable;
(2) $|h(x) - \hat{h}(x)| \leq \varepsilon_0$ for all $x \in K$; and
(3) $\langle h'(x) - \hat{h}'(x), x - y \rangle \leq \varepsilon_1$ for all $x, y \in K$.

Note, in spite of the notation, there is no need for $\hat{h}'$ to be the gradient of $\hat{h}$. The objective is to find a procedure that finds a near-minimiser of $\hat{h}$, which is an approximately convex function. This can be accomplished in many ways, but the most straightforward idea is to use gradient descent with the 'gradients' provided by $\hat{h}'$.

```
1  args: η > 0, A ∈ 𝕊^d_{++}
2  let x_1 ∈ K
3  for t = 1 to n
4      x_{t+1} = arg min_{x ∈ K} ||x_t − ηAĥ'(x_t) − x||_{A^{-1}}
5  return (1/n) Σ_{t=1}^n x_t
```

Algorithm 11.1 Approximate gradient descent

Remark 11.3 The matrix A accepted as input by Algorithm 11.1 corresponds to a change of coordinates, which you will discover is needed in our application because gradient descent is not equivariant under coordinate changes.

Theorem 11.4 *Suppose that $\|x - y\|_{A^{-1}}^2 \leq 1$ for all $x, y \in K$ and that $\|\hat{h}'(x)\|_A \leq G$ for all $x \in K$. Then, under Assumption 11.2, the output y of Algorithm 11.1 with $\eta = G/\sqrt{n}$ satisfies*

$$\hat{h}(y) \leq \inf_{x \in K} \hat{h}(x) + \varepsilon_1 + 2\varepsilon_0 + \frac{G}{\sqrt{n}}.$$

Proof We follow the standard analysis of gradient descent. Let $x \in K$ be arbitrary. Then

$$\frac{1}{2}\|x_{t+1} - x\|_{A^{-1}}^2 \leq \frac{1}{2}\|x_t - \eta A \hat{h}'(x_t) - x\|_{A^{-1}}^2$$

$$= \frac{1}{2}\|x_t - x\|_{A^{-1}}^2 - \eta \langle \hat{h}'(x_t), x_t - x \rangle + \frac{\eta^2}{2}\|\hat{h}'(x_t)\|_A^2$$

$$\leq \frac{1}{2}\|x_t - x\|_{A^{-1}}^2 - \eta \langle h'(x_t), x_t - x \rangle + \eta \varepsilon_1 + \frac{\eta^2}{2}\|\hat{h}'(x_t)\|_A^2$$

$$\leq \frac{1}{2}\|x_t - x\|_{A^{-1}}^2 - \eta \langle h'(x_t), x_t - x \rangle + \eta \varepsilon_1 + \frac{G^2 \eta^2}{2}.$$

11.2 Decaying Online Newton Step

Summing and telescoping shows that

$$\sum_{t=1}^{n}(h(x_t) - h(x)) \le \sum_{t=1}^{n}\langle h'(x_t), x_t - x\rangle \qquad h \text{ convex}$$

$$\le n\varepsilon_1 + \frac{n\eta G^2}{2} + \frac{1}{2\eta}$$

$$= n\varepsilon_1 + G\sqrt{n}. \qquad (11.1)$$

By the definition of the algorithm $y = \frac{1}{n}\sum_{t=1}^{n} x_t$ is the average of the iterates. Then, by convexity,

$$\hat{h}(y) - \hat{h}(x) \le 2\varepsilon_0 + h(y) - h(x) \qquad \text{By assumption}$$

$$\le 2\varepsilon_0 + \frac{1}{n}\sum_{t=1}^{n}(h(x_t) - h(x)) \qquad h \text{ convex}$$

$$\le 2\varepsilon_0 + \varepsilon_1 + \frac{G}{\sqrt{n}}. \qquad \text{By (11.1)}$$

The result follows since $x \in K$ was arbitrary. □

Corollary 11.5 *Under the same conditions as Theorem 11.4, running Algorithm 11.1 for* $n = \left\lceil \frac{G^2}{(2\varepsilon_0+\varepsilon_1)^2} \right\rceil$ *iterations yields a point y such that*

$$\hat{h}(y) \le \inf_{x\in K} \hat{h}(x) + 4\varepsilon_0 + 2\varepsilon_1.$$

A theoretically faster but less practical solution is to use the ellipsoid method, as we explain in Note 11.ii.

11.2 Decaying Online Newton Step

We introduce a modification of online Newton step that decays the covariance matrix. As in Section 10.2, let $(\hat{q}_t)_{t=1}^{n}$ be a sequence of quadratic functions and $(K_t)_{t=0}^{n}$ be a sequence of nonempty compact convex sets such that $K_{t+1} \subset K_t$ for all t. Decaying online Newton step produces a sequence of iterates (μ_t) and covariances (Σ_t) such that $\mu_{t+1} \in K_t$.

```
1  args: η > 0, μ₁ ∈ K₀ and Σ₁ ∈ 𝕊₊ᵈ
2  for t = 1 to n
3     compute γₜ ∈ (0, 1] and Kₜ ⊂ Kₜ₋₁ in some way
4     let gₜ = q̂ₜ(μₜ) and Hₜ = q̂ₜ″(μₜ)
5     update Σₜ₊₁⁻¹ = γₜΣₜ⁻¹ + ηHₜ
6     update μₜ₊₁ = arg min_{μ∈Kₜ} ‖μ − (μₜ − ηΣₜ₊₁gₜ)‖²_{Σₜ₊₁⁻¹}
```

Algorithm 11.2 Decaying online Newton step

Theorem 11.6 *Suppose that Algorithm 11.2 is run on a sequence of quadratics $(\hat{q}_t)_{t=1}^n$ and produces iterates $(\mu_t)_{t=1}^{n+1}$ and covariances $(\Sigma_t)_{t=1}^{n+1}$. Then, provided that $\Sigma_1^{-1}, \ldots, \Sigma_{n+1}^{-1} \in \mathbb{S}_{++}^d$, for any $x \in K_n$*

$$\frac{1}{2\eta} \|\mu_{n+1} - x\|_{\Sigma_{n+1}^{-1}}^2 \leq \frac{1}{2\eta} \|\mu_1 - x\|_{\Sigma_1^{-1}}^2 + \frac{\eta}{2} \sum_{t=1}^n \|g_t\|_{\Sigma_{t+1}}^2 - \frac{\Gamma_n(x)}{\eta} - \widetilde{qReg}_n(x),$$

where $\widetilde{qReg}_n(x) = \sum_{t=1}^n (\hat{q}_t(\mu_t) - \hat{q}_t(x))$ and $\Gamma_n(x) = \frac{1}{2} \sum_{t=1}^n (1 - \gamma_t) \|x - \mu_t\|_{\Sigma_t^{-1}}^2$.

Remark 11.7 The sets $(K_t)_{t=0}^n$ and decay factors $(\gamma_t)_{t=1}^n$ can be data-dependent. In our application (K_t) will be defined as the intersection of ellipsoidal focus regions on which the surrogate loss is well-behaved.

Before the proof, let us say something about why the regret bound is useful. What is new compared to the standard version of online Newton step (Theorem 10.2) is the negative terms appearing on the right-hand side. These can be considerable when x is far from the centre of the ellipsoid $E(\mu_t, \Sigma_t)$. This is precisely the focus region where our surrogate is well-behaved, which means that once a comparator leaves the focus region the regret with respect to the estimated quadratic surrogates will be negative, at least when the parameters are tuned correctly.

Proof of Theorem 11.6 Let $x \in K_n$. By definition,

$$\frac{1}{2}\|\mu_{t+1} - x\|^2_{\Sigma^{-1}_{t+1}} \leq \frac{1}{2}\|\mu_t - \eta\Sigma_{t+1}g_t - x\|^2_{\Sigma^{-1}_{t+1}}$$

$$= \frac{1}{2}\|\mu_t - x\|^2_{\Sigma^{-1}_{t+1}} + \frac{\eta^2}{2}\|g_t\|^2_{\Sigma_{t+1}} - \eta\langle g_t, \mu_t - x\rangle$$

$$= \frac{1}{2}\|\mu_t - x\|^2_{\gamma_t\Sigma^{-1}_t} + \frac{\eta^2}{2}\|g_t\|^2_{\Sigma_{t+1}} - \eta(\hat{q}_t(\mu_t) - \hat{q}_t(x))$$

$$= \frac{1}{2}\|\mu_t - x\|^2_{\Sigma^{-1}_t} + \frac{\eta^2}{2}\|g_t\|^2_{\Sigma_{t+1}} - \eta(\hat{q}_t(\mu_t) - \hat{q}_t(x)) - \frac{1 - \gamma_t}{2}\|\mu_t - x\|^2_{\Sigma^{-1}_t},$$

where in the inequality we used the fact that $x \in K_n \subset K_t$ and the assumption that Σ^{-1}_{t+1} is positive definite. Summing, telescoping and rearranging completes the claim. □

11.3 Regularity and Extensions

Remember that $M(K) = \mathbb{E}[\pi(X)]$, where π is the Minkowski functional associated with K and X is uniformly distributed on $\mathbb{S}^{d-1}_1$. Under Assumption 11.1, $\mathbb{B}^d_1 \subset K$ and therefore $M(K) \leq 1$. In contrast to Chapter 10, there is nothing to be gained here by improving $M(K)$ from $O(1)$ to $\tilde{O}(d^{-1/2})$. Given an $\varepsilon \in (0, 1)$ to be tuned later, the extension of the loss function f_t is

$$e_t(x) = \pi_\wedge(x) f_t\left(\frac{x}{\pi_\wedge(x)}\right) + \frac{2(\pi_\wedge(x) - 1)}{\varepsilon},$$

where $\pi_\wedge(x) = \max(1, \pi(x)/(1 - \varepsilon))$. Remember that $K_\varepsilon = (1 - \varepsilon)K$. As in Chapter 10 we abuse notation by saying that the algorithm samples X_t from $\mathcal{N}(\mu_t, \Sigma_t)$, plays $X_t/\pi_\wedge(X_t)$ and observes

$$Y_t = \pi_\wedge(X_t)\left(f_t\left(\frac{X_t}{\pi_\wedge(X_t)}\right) + \varepsilon_t\right) + \frac{2(\pi_\wedge(X_t) - 1)}{\varepsilon}.$$

The surrogate loss in round t is defined by

$$s_t(x) = \mathbb{E}_{t-1}\left[\left(1 - \frac{1}{\lambda}\right)e_t(X_t) + \frac{1}{\lambda}e_t((1 - \lambda)X_t + \lambda x)\right]$$

and its quadratic approximation is $q_t(x) = \langle s'_t(\mu_t), x - \mu_t\rangle + \frac{1}{4}\|x - \mu_t\|^2_{s''_t(\mu_t)}$. Let p_t be the density of $\mathcal{N}(\mu_t, \Sigma_t)$. The surrogate and its gradient and Hessian are estimated by

$$\hat{s}_t(x) = \left(1 - \frac{1}{\lambda} + \frac{\bar{r}_t(x)}{\lambda}\right) Y_t \quad \text{and}$$

$$\hat{s}'_t(x) = \frac{\bar{r}_t(x) Y_t}{1 - \lambda} \Sigma_t^{-1} \left(\frac{X_t - \lambda x}{1 - \lambda} - \mu_t\right) \quad \text{and} \qquad (11.2)$$

$$\hat{s}''_t(x) = \frac{\lambda \bar{r}_t(x) Y_t}{(1-\lambda)^2} \left[\Sigma_t^{-1} \left(\frac{X_t - \lambda x}{1-\lambda} - \mu_t\right)\left(\frac{X_t - \lambda x}{1-\lambda} - \mu_t\right)^\top \Sigma_t^{-1} - \Sigma_t^{-1}\right] \quad (11.3)$$

with

$$\bar{r}_t(x) = \min\left(\frac{p_t\left(\frac{X_t - \lambda x}{1-\lambda}\right)}{(1-\lambda)^d p_t(X_t)},\ \exp(2)\right).$$

Finally, $\hat{q}_t(x) = \langle \hat{s}'_t(\mu_t), x - \mu_t \rangle + \frac{1}{4} \|x - \mu_t\|^2_{\hat{s}''_t(\mu_t)}$ is the estimate of the quadratic surrogate. These are the same estimators that appear in Chapters 10 and 12.

11.4 Algorithm

The algorithm is a modification of Algorithm 10.2 for the stochastic setting. The main differences are that decaying online Newton step replaces the classical version and a gadget is introduced to restart the algorithm if negative regret is detected. The estimated regret with respect to the estimated cumulative surrogate losses is $\widehat{\mathrm{sReg}}_t(x) = \sum_{u=1}^{t} (\hat{s}_u(\mu_u) - \hat{s}_u(x))$.

11.4 Algorithm

---
1 **args**: $\eta, \lambda, \sigma^2, \varepsilon, \gamma, \rho$
2 $\mu_1 = 0$, $\Sigma_1 = \sigma^2 \mathbb{1}$ and $K_0 = K_\varepsilon$
3 **for** $t = 1$ **to** n
4   compute $K_t = \left\{ x \in K_{t-1} : \lambda \|x - \mu_t\|_{\Sigma_t^{-1}} \leq \frac{1}{\sqrt{2L}} \right\}$
5   sample X_t from $\mathcal{N}(\mu_t, \Sigma_t)$
6   observe $Y_t = \pi_\wedge(X_t)\left(f_t\left(\frac{X_t}{\pi_\wedge(X_t)}\right) + \varepsilon_t \right) + \frac{2(\pi_\wedge(X_t) - 1)}{\varepsilon}$
7   compute $g_t = \hat{s}_t'(\mu_t)$ and $H_t = \frac{1}{2}\hat{s}_t''(\mu_t)$ using (11.2), (11.3)
8   compute $z_{t-1} = \arg\min_{z \in \mathbb{R}^d} \left[\Gamma_{t-1}(z) \triangleq \sum_{s=1}^{t-1}(1-\gamma_s)\|z - \mu_s\|^2_{\Sigma_s^{-1}} \right]$
9    $\gamma_t = \begin{cases} 1 & \text{if } \Gamma_{t-1}(z_{t-1}) \geq 3\rho \\ \gamma & \text{if } \Sigma_t^{-1} \not\preceq \sum_{s=1}^{t-1} \mathbb{1}(\gamma_s \neq 1)\Sigma_s^{-1} \\ \gamma & \text{if } \|\mu_t - z_{t-1}\|^2_{\Sigma_t^{-1}} \geq \frac{1}{8L\lambda^2} \\ 1 & \text{otherwise} \end{cases}$
10   compute $\Sigma_{t+1}^{-1} = \gamma_t \Sigma_t^{-1} + \eta H_t$
11   compute $\mu_{t+1} = \arg\min_{\mu \in K_t} \|\mu - [\mu_t - \eta \Sigma_{t+1} g_t]\|_{\Sigma_{t+1}^{-1}}$
12   find $y_t \in K_t$ such that $\eta \widetilde{\text{sReg}}_t(y_t) \geq \max_{y \in K_t} \eta \widetilde{\text{sReg}}_t(y) - \rho$
13   **if** $\widetilde{\text{sReg}}_t(y_t) \leq -2\rho$ **then**: restart
---

Algorithm 11.3 Online Newton step for adversarial convex bandits

Computation

Algorithm 11.3 can be implemented in polynomial time provided that K is suitably represented. The difficult steps are:

o Sampling from the Gaussian, which naively requires an eigenvalue decomposition of the covariance matrix.

o The computation of z_{t-1} in Line 8, which is an unconstrained convex quadratic minimisation problem and therefore has a closed-form solution:

$$z_{t-1} = \left(\sum_{s=1}^{t-1}(1-\gamma_s)\Sigma_s^{-1} \right)^{-1} \sum_{s=1}^{t-1}(1-\gamma_s)\Sigma_s^{-1}\mu_s,$$

with the convention that $z_{t-1} = 0$ when $t = 1$.

o The projection in Line 11 depends on the representation of K. Note that the projection is onto K_t, which is the intersection of K and the ellipsoidal focus regions. When K is a polytope, then this is a quadratic program and can be

solved efficiently using interior point methods. Note, however, there are $O(t)$ quadratic constraints due to the intersecting ellipsoidal focus regions.
- The most challenging problem is the non-convex problem in Line 12, for which you can use Algorithm 11.1 or the ellipsoid method as explained in Section 11.7.

Explanation of the Parameters

Algorithm 11.3 has many tuning parameters, including two new ones compared to the stochastic setting. The role of the parameters and their values up to logarithmic factors are given in Table 11.1.

PARAMETER		APPROX. VALUE
η	learning rate	$\sqrt{d/n}$
λ	smoothing parameter for surrogate	$\frac{1}{d^2}$
σ^2	defines the initial covariance	$\frac{1}{d}$
ε	defines the set on which the extension is defined	$\sqrt{d^5/n}$
γ	determines the decay of the covariance	$1 - \frac{1}{d}$
ρ	margin that triggers restart condition	d^3

Table 11.1 Table of tuning constants. Constants and logarithmic factors are omitted, but are given in Theorem 11.8.

11.5 Analysis

Theorem 11.8 *Suppose Algorithm 11.3 is run with parameters*

$$\lambda = \frac{1}{Cd^2L^3} \qquad \eta = \frac{\sqrt{d/n}}{CL} \qquad \gamma = 2^{-\frac{1}{1+dL}}$$

$$\sigma^2 = \frac{1}{dL^4} \qquad \rho = 2Cd^3L^4 \qquad \varepsilon = \frac{d^{2.5}L^5}{\sqrt{n}}.$$

Then, under Assumption 11.1, with probability at least $1 - \delta$, the regret of Algorithm 11.3 is bounded by

$$\mathrm{Reg}_n = O\left(d^{2.5}L^5\sqrt{n}\right).$$

11.5 Analysis

Proof The argument largely follows the analysis in Section 10.5, but with several additional steps. Most importantly, we need to show the following hold with high probability:

(1) If the algorithm restarts, then the regret is negative.
(2) If the minimiser of the surrogate moves outside the focus region, then the algorithm restarts.

Let $\bar{H}_t = \mathbb{E}_{t-1}[H_t]$ and define $\bar{\Sigma}_t^{-1}$ inductively by $\bar{\Sigma}_1^{-1} = \Sigma_1^{-1}$ and

$$\bar{\Sigma}_{t+1}^{-1} = \gamma_t \bar{\Sigma}_t^{-1} + \eta \bar{H}_t .$$

Define

$$x_\tau^e = \arg\min_{x \in K_\varepsilon} \sum_{t=1}^\tau e_t(x) \qquad x_\tau^s = \arg\min_{x \in K_\varepsilon} \sum_{t=1}^\tau s_t(x)$$

$$y_\tau^s = \arg\min_{y \in K_\tau} \sum_{t=1}^\tau s_t(y) \qquad y_\tau^{\hat{s}} = \arg\min_{y \in K_\tau} \sum_{t=1}^\tau \hat{s}_t(x) .$$

The superscript indicates which functions are being minimised. Note also the different domains, with x_τ^e and x_τ^s in K_ε and y_τ^s and $y_\tau^{\hat{s}}$ in K_τ. As in Section 10.5, we define a stopping time.

Definition 11.9 Let τ be the first round when one of the following does *not* hold:
(1) $x_\tau^s \in K_{\tau+1}$.
(2) $\Sigma_{\tau+1}$ is positive definite.
(3) $\delta \mathbb{1} \preceq \frac{1}{2}\bar{\Sigma}_{\tau+1}^{-1} \preceq \Sigma_{\tau+1}^{-1} \preceq 2\bar{\Sigma}_{\tau+1}^{-1} \preceq \frac{1}{\delta}\mathbb{1}$.
(4) The algorithm does not restart at the end of round τ.

If the conditions hold for all rounds, then τ is defined to be n.

Note that τ is a stopping time with respect to $(\mathcal{F}_t)_{t=1}^n$ because x_t^s, K_{t+1} and Σ_{t+1} are $\mathcal{F}_t$-measurable.

Step 1: Regret relative to extension

Let

$$\mathrm{eReg}_n(x_n^e) = \sum_{t=1}^n \left(\mathbb{E}_{t-1}[e_t(X_t)] - e_t(x_n^e) \right) .$$

Repeating the analysis in the proof of Theorem 10.8 shows that with probability at least $1 - \delta/7$,

$$\mathrm{Reg}_n \leq n\varepsilon + \sqrt{2n \log(7/\delta)} + \mathrm{eReg}_n(x_n^e) . \qquad (\mathrm{E0})$$

Hence for the remainder we focus on bounding $\mathrm{eReg}_n(x_n^e)$ with high probability.

Step 2: Concentration

Define events

$$\text{E1} = \left\{ \max_{1 \leq t \leq \tau} |\varepsilon_t| \leq \sqrt{\log(14n/\delta)} \right\} \tag{E1}$$

$$\text{E2} = \left\{ \max_{1 \leq t \leq \tau} \pi(X_t) \leq \sqrt{L} \right\} \tag{E2}$$

$$\text{E3} = \left\{ \max_{1 \leq t \leq \tau} \|X_t - \mu_t\|_{\Sigma_t^{-1}} \leq \sqrt{\frac{8d}{3} \log(14n/\delta)} \right\}. \tag{E3}$$

Repeating the arguments in the proof of Theorem 10.8 and using Table 11.2.a (Section 11.8) shows that $\mathbb{P}(\text{E1} \cap \text{E2} \cap \text{E3}) \geq 1 - 3\delta/7$. The next lemma bounds the sum $\sum_{t=1}^{\tau} \mathbb{E}_{t-1}[Y_t^2]$.

Lemma 11.10 *Let* $Y_{\max} = \max_{1 \leq t \leq \tau} (|Y_t| + \mathbb{E}_{t-1}[|Y_t|])$. *On* E1 $\cap$ E2 $\cap$ E3 *the following hold:*
(1) $Y_{\max} \leq \frac{L}{\varepsilon}$.
(2) $\sum_{t=1}^{\tau} \mathbb{E}_{t-1}[Y_t^2] \leq 10n$.

Proof See the proof of Lemma 10.12 except that (10.13) is replaced by (11.6) and use Table 11.2.b. □

We also need to bound $\sum_{t=1}^{\tau} Y_t^2$ with high probability. Let E4 be the event defined by

$$\text{E4} = \left\{ \sum_{t=1}^{\tau} Y_t^2 \leq 21n \right\}. \tag{E4}$$

Lemma 11.11 $\mathbb{P}(\text{E4} \cup (\text{E1} \cap \text{E2} \cap \text{E3})^c) \geq 1 - \delta/7$.

Proof See the proof of Lemma 10.13. □

The last two events control the concentration of the estimated quadratic surrogate about its mean at the optimal point and the concentration of the Hessian estimates. Let $\text{cnf} = \frac{3L^2 \sqrt{dn}}{\lambda}$ and E5 be the event that all of the following hold for all $t \leq \tau$:
(1) $\left| \sum_{u=1}^{t} (\hat{q}_u(x) - q_u(x)) \right| \leq \text{cnf}$ for all $x \in K_t$.
(2) $\left| \sum_{u=1}^{t} (\hat{s}_u(x) - s_u(x)) \right| \leq \text{cnf}$ for all $x \in K_t$.
(3) $\left| \sum_{u=1}^{t} \langle \hat{s}_u'(x) - s_u'(x), x - y \rangle \right| \leq \text{cnf}$ for all $x, y \in K_t$.

Lemma 11.12 $\mathbb{P}(\text{E5} \cup (\text{E1} \cap \text{E2} \cap \text{E3} \cap \text{E4})^c) \geq 1 - \delta/7$.

Note, the dimension-dependence in cnf appears because the concentration bound needs to hold uniformly for all $x \in K_\tau$, which is accomplished by a

11.5 Analysis

covering argument and union bound. By contrast, in the stochastic setting bounds of this kind were only needed at the minimiser of the loss.

Proof Use Proposition 12.24(2), Proposition 12.23(2) and Proposition 12.30(2) in combination with Lemma 11.10. □

Comparing $\bar{\Sigma}_t$ and Σ_t is slightly more delicate thanks to the decay. Let $w_0 = 1$ and $w_t = \prod_{s=1}^{t} \gamma_s$. A simple induction shows that

$$\Sigma_{t+1}^{-1} = w_t \left[\frac{1}{\sigma^2} \mathbb{1} + \eta \sum_{s=1}^{t} \frac{H_s}{w_s} \right] \triangleq w_t \left[\frac{1}{\sigma^2} \mathbb{1} + \eta S_t \right] \quad \text{and}$$

$$\bar{\Sigma}_{t+1}^{-1} = w_t \left[\frac{1}{\sigma^2} \mathbb{1} + \eta \sum_{s=1}^{t} \frac{\bar{H}_s}{w_s} \right] \triangleq w_t \left[\frac{1}{\sigma^2} \mathbb{1} + \eta \bar{S}_t \right].$$

The next lemma characterises the important properties of the weights $(w_t)_{t=1}^{\tau}$. The proof is deferred to Section 11.6.

Lemma 11.13 *The following hold:*
(1) $\sum_{t=1}^{\tau} \mathbb{1}(\gamma_t \neq 1) \leq 1 + dL$.
(2) $w_t \in [1/2, 1]$ *for all* $t \leq \tau$.
(3) w_t *is* $\mathscr{F}_{t-1}$-*measurable for all* t.

Finally, let E6 be the event that

$$\text{E6} = \left\{ -3\lambda L^2 \sqrt{dn} \bar{\Sigma}_\tau^{-1} \preceq \bar{S}_\tau - S_\tau \preceq 3\lambda L^2 \sqrt{dn} \bar{\Sigma}_\tau^{-1} \right\}. \tag{E6}$$

Lemma 11.14 $\mathbb{P}(\text{E6} \cup (\text{E1} \cap \text{E2} \cap \text{E3} \cap \text{E4})^c) \geq 1 - \delta/7$.

Proof By Proposition 12.27 (and Remark 12.29 and Lemma 11.13) with $\Sigma^{-1} = \frac{3}{2}\bar{\Sigma}_\tau^{-1}$, with probability at least $1 - \delta$,

$$-\lambda L^2 \left[1 + \sqrt{d \sum_{t=1}^{\tau} \mathbb{E}_{t-1}[Y_t^2] + d^2 Y_{\max}} \right] \frac{3}{2} \bar{\Sigma}_\tau^{-1} \preceq \bar{S}_\tau - S_\tau$$

$$\preceq \lambda L^2 \left[1 + \sqrt{d \sum_{t=1}^{\tau} \mathbb{E}_{t-1}[Y_t^2] + d^2 Y_{\max}} \right] \frac{3}{2} \bar{\Sigma}_\tau^{-1}.$$

The claim now follows from Lemma 11.10. □

Let $E = \text{E0} \cap \text{E1} \cap \text{E2} \cap \text{E3} \cap \text{E4} \cap \text{E5} \cap \text{E6}$ be the intersection of all these high-probability events. A union bound over the preceding lemmas shows that $\mathbb{P}(E) \geq 1 - \delta$. For the remainder of the proof we bound the regret on E.

Step 3: Simple bounds

We can now make some elementary conclusions that hold on the intersection of all the high-probability events outlined in the previous step. Repeating the calculation used to derive (10.16) but using Lemma 11.10(2),

$$\sum_{t=1}^{\tau} \|g_t\|_{\Sigma_t}^2 \leq dnL. \tag{11.4}$$

By the definition of E6,

$$\Sigma_{\tau+1}^{-1} = w_\tau \left[\Sigma_1^{-1} + \eta S_\tau\right]$$
$$\preceq w_\tau \left[\Sigma_1^{-1} + \eta \bar{S}_\tau + 3\eta\lambda L^2\sqrt{dn}\bar{\Sigma}_\tau^{-1}\right]$$
$$\preceq w_\tau \left[\Sigma_1^{-1} + \eta \bar{S}_\tau + \frac{1}{2}\bar{\Sigma}_\tau^{-1}\right] \qquad \text{by Table 11.2.d}$$
$$= \bar{\Sigma}_{\tau+1}^{-1} + \frac{w_\tau}{2}\bar{\Sigma}_\tau^{-1}$$
$$\preceq \frac{3}{2}\bar{\Sigma}_{\tau+1}^{-1},$$

where the final inequality holds because $\bar{\Sigma}_{\tau+1}^{-1} = \gamma_t\bar{\Sigma}_\tau^{-1} + \eta\bar{H}_\tau \succeq \gamma_\tau\bar{\Sigma}_\tau^{-1} \succeq w_\tau\bar{\Sigma}_\tau^{-1}$. Similarly,

$$\Sigma_{\tau+1}^{-1} \succeq w_\tau[\Sigma_1^{-1} + \eta\bar{S}_\tau] - \frac{w_\tau}{2}\bar{\Sigma}_\tau^{-1} = \bar{\Sigma}_{\tau+1}^{-1} - \frac{w_\tau}{2}\bar{\Sigma}_\tau^{-1} \succeq \frac{1}{2}\bar{\Sigma}_{\tau+1}^{-1}.$$

Combining shows that

$$\frac{1}{2}\bar{\Sigma}_{\tau+1}^{-1} \preceq \Sigma_{\tau+1}^{-1} \preceq \frac{3}{2}\bar{\Sigma}_{\tau+1}^{-1}.$$

We also need to show that

$$2\delta \mathbb{1} \preceq \bar{\Sigma}_{\tau+1}^{-1} \preceq \frac{1}{2\delta}\mathbb{1}, \tag{11.5}$$

which follows from exactly the same argument as in the proof of Theorem 10.8. Therefore both Definition 11.9(2) and Definition 11.9(3) hold and so the only way that $\tau \neq n$ is if $x_\tau^s \notin K_{\tau+1}$ or the algorithm restarts at the end of round τ. The map $t \mapsto \Sigma_t$ is nearly non-increasing in the following sense. Given $s \leq t \leq \tau$,

$$\Sigma_t \preceq 2\bar{\Sigma}_t = \frac{2}{w_{t-1}}\left(\Sigma_1^{-1} + \eta\bar{S}_t\right)^{-1}$$
$$\preceq \frac{2}{w_{t-1}}\left(\Sigma_1^{-1} + \eta\bar{S}_s\right)^{-1}$$
$$= \frac{2w_{s-1}}{w_{t-1}}\bar{\Sigma}_s$$
$$\preceq 4\bar{\Sigma}_s \preceq 8\Sigma_s. \tag{11.6}$$

11.5 Analysis

The decay of the inverse covariance matrix has an important implication. Recall the definition of (Γ_t) in Line 8 of Algorithm 11.3.

Lemma 11.15 *Suppose that $x \in \partial K_\tau$. Then $\Gamma_\tau(x) \geq 3\rho$.*

The proof is deferred to Section 11.6. We also need an elementary bound on the magnitude of the surrogate losses.

Lemma 11.16 *Suppose that $x \in K_\varepsilon$. Then $-\frac{10}{\lambda \varepsilon} \leq s_t(x) \leq 1$.*

Exercise 11.17 ★ Prove Lemma 11.16 using the following steps:
(1) For the upper bound, combine the properties of the extension (Proposition 3.23) and Lemma 12.3(2).
(2) For the lower bound, use the definition of s_t, non-negativity of e_t and its definition, Lemma 10.5(1) and the fact that $M(K)\sqrt{d\sigma^2} \leq 1$.

Step 4: Trace/logdet inequalities

Again, we repeat the corresponding argument in the proof of Theorem 10.8. The argument is made slightly more complicated by the decaying covariance matrices.

Lemma 11.18 *The following holds:*

$$\frac{4}{\lambda} \sum_{t=1}^{\tau} \operatorname{tr}(\bar{H}_t \Sigma_t) \leq \frac{dL}{\lambda \eta}.$$

Proof By Proposition 12.6 and Proposition 3.23, for any $t \leq \tau$,

$$\eta \left\| \Sigma_t^{1/2} q_t''(\mu_t) \Sigma_t^{1/2} \right\| \leq \frac{\eta \lambda \operatorname{lip}(e_t)}{4(1-\lambda)} \sqrt{d \|\Sigma_t\|} \leq \frac{\eta \lambda \sigma \sqrt{d}}{\varepsilon(1-\lambda)} \leq 1, \quad (11.7)$$

where we used (11.6) to bound $\|\Sigma_t\| \leq 4\sigma^2$. The final inequality follows from Table 11.2.f. Note that

$$\bar{\Sigma}_{t+1}^{-1} = \gamma_t \bar{\Sigma}_t^{-1} + \eta \bar{H}_t \succeq \gamma_t \bar{\Sigma}_t^{-1}.$$

By Lemma A.10,

$$\log \det(\mathbb{1} + \eta \bar{H}_t \bar{\Sigma}_t) = \log \det(\gamma_t \mathbb{1} + \eta \bar{H}_t \bar{\Sigma}_t + (1-\gamma_t)\mathbb{1})$$

$$\leq \log \det(\gamma_t \mathbb{1} + \eta \bar{H}_t \bar{\Sigma}_t) + \frac{d(1-\gamma_t)}{\gamma_t}$$

$$= \log \det(\bar{\Sigma}_t \bar{\Sigma}_{t+1}^{-1}) + \frac{d(1-\gamma_t)}{\gamma_t}$$

$$\leq \log \det(\bar{\Sigma}_t \bar{\Sigma}_{t+1}^{-1}) + \frac{\mathbb{1}(\gamma_t \neq 1)}{\sqrt{L}}, \quad (11.8)$$

where the final inequality follows because either $\gamma_t = 1$ or $\gamma = 2^{-\frac{1}{1+dL}} \approx 1 - \frac{\log(2)}{1+dL}$. Combining (11.7), (11.8) and Lemma A.9,

$$\frac{4}{\lambda} \sum_{t=1}^{\tau} \text{tr}(\bar{H}_t \Sigma_t) \stackrel{(a)}{\leq} \frac{16}{\lambda \eta} \sum_{t=1}^{\tau} \log \det \left(\mathbb{1} + \frac{\eta \bar{H}_t \Sigma_t}{2} \right)$$

$$\stackrel{(b)}{\leq} \frac{16}{\lambda \eta} \sum_{t=1}^{\tau} \log \det \left(\mathbb{1} + \eta \bar{H}_t \bar{\Sigma}_t \right)$$

$$\stackrel{(c)}{\leq} \frac{16}{\lambda \eta \sqrt{L}} \sum_{t=1}^{\tau} \mathbb{1}(\gamma_t \neq 1) + \frac{16}{\lambda \eta} \sum_{t=1}^{\tau} \log \det \left(\bar{\Sigma}_t \bar{\Sigma}_{t+1}^{-1} \right)$$

$$\stackrel{(d)}{\leq} \frac{dL}{2\lambda \eta} + \frac{16}{\lambda \eta} \log \det \left(\mathbb{1} + \eta \sigma^2 \bar{S}_\tau \right)$$

$$\stackrel{(e)}{\leq} \frac{dL}{2\lambda \eta} + \frac{16}{\lambda \eta} \log \det \left(\mathbb{1} + \frac{\sigma^2 \mathbb{1}}{\delta} \right)$$

$$\stackrel{(f)}{\leq} \frac{dL}{\lambda \eta},$$

where (a) follows from Lemma A.9, (b) since $\Sigma_t \preceq 2\bar{\Sigma}_t$, (c) by (11.8), (d) from Lemma 11.13(1) and by telescoping the sum of log-determinants, and (e) by bounding $\eta \bar{S}_\tau \preceq \frac{1}{w_\tau} \bar{\Sigma}_{\tau+1}^{-1} \preceq \frac{1}{\delta} \mathbb{1}$ using (11.5) and Lemma 11.13 to bound $w_\tau \geq 1/2$. (f) follows by naive simplification. □

A simple consequence is a bound on the regret relative to the extension in terms of the regret relative to the quadratic surrogates.

Lemma 11.19 *The following hold:*
(1) $\text{eReg}(x_\tau^e) \leq \text{sReg}(x_\tau^s) + 1 + \frac{dL}{\eta \lambda}$.
(2) $\text{eReg}(x_\tau^e) \leq \text{qReg}(x_\tau^s) + 2 + \frac{dL}{\eta \lambda}$ whenever $x_\tau^s \in K_\tau$.

Proof We have

$$\text{eReg}(x_\tau^e) \leq \text{sReg}(x_\tau^e) + \frac{2}{\lambda} \sum_{t=1}^{\tau} \text{tr}(s_t''(\mu_t) \Sigma_t) + 1 \qquad \text{by Proposition 12.10}$$

$$\leq \text{sReg}(x_\tau^s) + \frac{2}{\lambda} \sum_{t=1}^{\tau} \text{tr}(s_t''(\mu_t) \Sigma_t) + 1 \qquad \text{by def. } x_\tau^s$$

$$= \text{sReg}(x_\tau^s) + \frac{4}{\lambda} \sum_{t=1}^{\tau} \text{tr}(\bar{H}_t \Sigma_t) + 1 \qquad \text{by def. } \bar{H}_t$$

$$\leq \text{sReg}(x_\tau^s) + \frac{dL}{\eta \lambda} + 1. \qquad \text{by Lemma 11.18}$$

11.5 Analysis

The second part follows from Proposition 12.9, the definition of K_τ and naively bounding constants. □

Next steps

So far the analysis has largely followed that in the stochastic setting, but now there is a serious deviation. Based on the arguments so far, it has been established that with high probability the only way $\tau \neq n$ is if $x_\tau^s \notin K_{\tau+1}$. While in the stochastic setting it was possible to prove that the minimiser of the loss stays in the focus region, this is no longer the case. Instead, it is necessary to consider a case-by-case analysis and handle the restarts:

○ When $x_\tau^s \in K_\tau$ it can be shown that $\mathrm{eReg}_\tau(x_\tau^e)$ is small and simultaneously that $x_\tau^s \in K_{\tau+1}$ with the latter showing that $\tau = n$.
○ When $x_\tau^s \notin K_\tau$, then the algorithm restarts at the end of round τ.
○ Whenever the algorithm restarts, then the regret relative to the extension is negative.

Step 5: Regret

Suppose that $x_\tau^s \in K_\tau$ and the algorithm has not restarted at the end of round τ; then by Theorem 11.6

$$\frac{1}{2}\|x_\tau^s - \mu_{\tau+1}\|_{\Sigma_{\tau+1}^{-1}}^2 \overset{(a)}{\leq} \frac{\|x_\tau^s\|^2}{2\sigma^2} + \frac{\eta^2}{2}\sum_{t=1}^{\tau}\|g_t\|_{\Sigma_{t+1}}^2 - \eta\widetilde{\mathrm{qReg}}(x_\tau^s) - \Gamma_\tau(x_\tau^s)$$

$$\overset{(b)}{\leq} \frac{2d^2}{\sigma^2} + 4\eta^2 dnL - \eta\widetilde{\mathrm{qReg}}(x_\tau^s) - \Gamma_\tau(x_\tau^s)$$

$$\overset{(c)}{\leq} \frac{2d^2}{\sigma^2} + 4\eta^2 dnL + \eta\,\mathrm{cnf} - \eta\mathrm{qReg}(x_\tau^s) - \Gamma_\tau(x_\tau^s)$$

$$\overset{(d)}{\leq} \frac{2d^2}{\sigma^2} + 4\eta^2 dnL + \eta\,\mathrm{cnf} + 2\eta + \frac{dL}{\lambda} - \eta\mathrm{eReg}(x_\tau^e)$$

$$\overset{(e)}{\leq} \rho - \eta\mathrm{eReg}(x_\tau^e),$$

where (a) follows from Theorem 11.6 and the assumption that $x_\tau^s \in K_\tau$, and (b) by the assumption that $K \subset \mathbb{B}_{2d}^d$ and by (11.4) and (11.6) to bound $\Sigma_{t+1} \preceq 8\Sigma_t$. (c) holds on E5. (d) follows from Lemma 11.19 and because $x_\tau^s \in K_\tau$; and also because $\Gamma_\tau(x_\tau^s) \geq 0$. (e) follows from the definition of the constants (Table 11.2.c). Rearranging shows that

$$\mathrm{eReg}(x_\tau^e) \leq \frac{\rho}{\eta}.$$

Furthermore, since the algorithm has not restarted in round τ it holds that

$$\frac{1}{2}\|x_\tau^s - \mu_{\tau+1}\|^2_{\Sigma_{\tau+1}^{-1}} \leq \frac{2d^2}{\sigma^2} + 4\eta^2 dnL + \eta \operatorname{cnf} - \eta q\operatorname{Reg}_\tau(x_\tau^s)$$

$$\leq \frac{2d^2}{\sigma^2} + 4\eta^2 dnL + \eta \operatorname{cnf} + 1 - \eta\operatorname{sReg}_\tau(x_\tau^s) \qquad \text{by Proposition 12.9}$$

$$\leq \frac{2d^2}{\sigma^2} + 4\eta^2 dnL + \eta \operatorname{cnf} + 1 - \eta\operatorname{sReg}_\tau(y_\tau)$$

$$\leq \frac{2d^2}{\sigma^2} + 4\eta^2 dnL + 2\eta \operatorname{cnf} + 1 - \eta\widetilde{\operatorname{sReg}}_\tau(y_\tau) \qquad \text{on } \text{E5}$$

$$\leq 3\rho \leq \frac{1}{4L\lambda^2},$$

where the second-last inequality follows because the algorithm did not restart, so that $\eta\widetilde{\operatorname{sReg}}_\tau(y_\tau) \geq -2\rho$. The last inequality follows from Table 11.2.h. Rearranging shows that $\lambda\|x_\tau^s - \mu_{\tau+1}\|_{\Sigma_{\tau+1}^{-1}} \leq 1/\sqrt{2L}$, which when combined with the assumption that $x_\tau^s \in K_\tau$ shows that $x_\tau^s \in K_{\tau+1}$. Hence by Definition 11.9, $\tau = n$ and we have successfully bounded $\operatorname{eReg}(x_n^e) \leq \frac{\rho}{\eta}$.

Step 6: Restart analysis

Suppose at the end of round τ that the algorithm restarts, which means that

$$\eta\widetilde{\operatorname{sReg}}_\tau(y_\tau^s) = \max_{y \in K_\tau} \eta\widetilde{\operatorname{sReg}}_\tau(y) \leq \eta\widetilde{\operatorname{sReg}}_\tau(y_\tau) + \rho \leq -\rho, \qquad (11.9)$$

where in the first inequality we used the definition of y_τ in Line 12 of Algorithm 11.3 and in the second we used the fact that a restart is triggered when $\eta\widetilde{\operatorname{sReg}}_\tau(y_\tau) \leq -2\rho$. Then

$$\eta\operatorname{eReg}_\tau(x_\tau^e) \overset{(a)}{\leq} 1 + \frac{dL}{\lambda} + \eta\operatorname{sReg}_\tau(x_\tau^e)$$

$$\overset{(b)}{\leq} 1 + \frac{dL}{\lambda} + \eta\operatorname{sReg}_\tau(x_\tau^s)$$

$$\overset{(c)}{\leq} 1 + \frac{dL}{\lambda} + \eta\operatorname{sReg}_\tau(x_{\tau-1}^s) + \eta\left(s_\tau(x_{\tau-1}^s) - s_\tau(x_\tau^s)\right)$$

$$\overset{(d)}{\leq} 1 + \frac{dL}{\lambda} + \eta\operatorname{cnf} + \eta\left(1 + \frac{10}{\varepsilon\lambda}\right) + \eta\widetilde{\operatorname{sReg}}_\tau(x_{\tau-1}^s)$$

$$\overset{(e)}{\leq} 1 + \frac{dL}{\lambda} + \eta\operatorname{cnf} + \eta\left(1 + \frac{10}{\varepsilon\lambda}\right) + \eta\widetilde{\operatorname{sReg}}_\tau(y_\tau^s)$$

$$\overset{(f)}{\leq} \rho + \eta\widetilde{\operatorname{sReg}}_\tau(y_\tau^s)$$

$$\overset{(g)}{\leq} 0,$$

where (a) follows from Lemma 11.19, (b) by the definition of x_τ^s; and (c) by the definition of $x_{\tau-1}^s$. (d) holds on E5 and by Lemma 11.16. (e) follows from the definition of τ so that $x_{\tau-1}^s \in K_\tau$ and the definition of y_τ^s as the maximiser of $\widetilde{\text{sReg}}_\tau$ over K_τ. (f) follows from the definition of the constants (Table 11.2.e) and (g) from (11.9). Hence, whenever the algorithm restarts the regret with respect to the extension is negative. On the other hand, if x_τ^s leaves K_τ, then $y_\tau^s \in \partial K_\tau$ and

$$\begin{aligned}
\|y_\tau^s - \mu_{\tau+1}\|_{\Sigma_{\tau+1}^{-1}}^2 &\overset{(a)}{\leq} \frac{2d^2}{\sigma^2} + 4\eta^2 dnL + \eta \operatorname{cnf} - \eta q \operatorname{Reg}_\tau(y_\tau^s) - \Gamma_\tau(y_\tau^s) \\
&\overset{(b)}{\leq} 1 + \frac{2d^2}{\sigma^2} + 4\eta^2 dnL + \eta \operatorname{cnf} - \eta \operatorname{sReg}_\tau(y_\tau^s) - \Gamma_\tau(y_\tau^s) \\
&\overset{(c)}{\leq} 1 + \frac{2d^2}{\sigma^2} + 4\eta^2 dnL + \eta \operatorname{cnf} - \eta \operatorname{sReg}_\tau(y_\tau^{\hat{s}}) - \Gamma_\tau(y_\tau^s) \\
&\overset{(d)}{\leq} 1 + \frac{2d^2}{\sigma^2} + 4\eta^2 dnL + 2\eta \operatorname{cnf} - \eta \widetilde{\operatorname{sReg}}_\tau(y_\tau^{\hat{s}}) - \Gamma_\tau(y_\tau^s) \\
&\overset{(e)}{\leq} 1 + \frac{2d^2}{\sigma^2} + 4\eta^2 dnL + 2\eta \operatorname{cnf} - \eta \widetilde{\operatorname{sReg}}_\tau(y_\tau^{\hat{s}}) - 3\rho \\
&\overset{(f)}{\leq} -2\rho - \eta \widetilde{\operatorname{sReg}}_\tau(y_\tau^{\hat{s}}),
\end{aligned}$$

where (a) follows from the same calculations as in step 4, (b) from Proposition 12.9, and (c) by the definition of y_τ^s and $y_\tau^{\hat{s}}$. (d) holds on E5, (e) from Lemma 11.15 and (f) by the definition of the constants (Table 11.2.g). Therefore $\eta \widetilde{\operatorname{sReg}}_\tau(y_\tau^{\hat{s}}) \leq -2\rho$. Hence, by Line 12 of Algorithm 11.3,

$$\eta \widetilde{\operatorname{sReg}}_\tau(y_\tau) \leq \eta \widetilde{\operatorname{sReg}}_\tau(y_\tau^{\hat{s}}) \leq -2\rho$$

and a restart is triggered. □

11.6 Decay Analysis

The purpose of this section is to prove Lemmas 11.13 and 11.15, both of which are related to the decaying covariance matrix. Recall that

$$z_{t-1} = \underset{z \in \mathbb{R}^d}{\arg\min} \left(\Gamma_{t-1}(z) \triangleq \sum_{s=1}^{t-1} (1 - \gamma_s) \|z - \mu_s\|_{\Sigma_s^{-1}}^2 \right)$$

and with $D_t = \sum_{s=1}^{t} \mathbf{1}(\gamma_s \neq 1)\Sigma_s^{-1}$,

$$\gamma_t = \begin{cases} 1 & \text{if } \Gamma_{t-1}(z_{t-1}) \geq 3\rho \\ \gamma & \text{if } \Sigma_t^{-1} \npreceq D_{t-1} \\ \gamma & \text{if } \|\mu_t - z_{t-1}\|_{\Sigma_t^{-1}}^2 \geq \frac{1}{8L\lambda^2} \\ 1 & \text{otherwise}. \end{cases}$$

Remember also that $w_t = \prod_{s=1}^{t} \gamma_s$.

Proof of Lemma 11.13 We start with part (1), which is the only difficult part. By definition, $\mathbf{1}(\gamma_t \neq 1) = A_t + B_t$ where

$$A_t = \mathbf{1}\left(\Sigma_t^{-1} \npreceq D_{t-1} \text{ and } \Gamma_{t-1}(z_{t-1}) < 3\rho\right) \quad \text{and}$$

$$B_t = \mathbf{1}\left(A_t = 0 \text{ and } \|\mu_t - z_{t-1}\|_{\Sigma_t^{-1}}^2 \geq \frac{1}{8L\lambda^2} \text{ and } \Gamma_{t-1}(z_{t-1}) < 3\rho\right).$$

By Definition 11.9, for $s \leq \tau$, Σ_s^{-1} is positive definite and therefore $D_{t-1} \preceq D_t$ for all $t \leq \tau$. Furthermore, in rounds t where $A_t = 1$ it holds that $D_t = D_{t-1} + \Sigma_t^{-1}$ and $\Sigma_t^{-1} \npreceq D_{t-1}$, which means that $\mathbb{1} \preceq D_{t-1}^{-1/2} D_t D_{t-1}^{-1/2} = \mathbb{1} + D_{t-1}^{-1/2} \Sigma_t^{-1} D_{t-1}^{-1/2} \npreceq 2\mathbb{1}$ and therefore

$$\log \det D_{t-1}^{-1} D_t = \log \det D_{t-1}^{-1/2} D_t D_{t-1}^{-1/2} \geq \log(2).$$

Hence,

$$\sum_{t=1}^{\tau} A_t \log(2) \leq \sum_{t=1}^{\tau} \log \det D_{t-1}^{-1} D_t$$
$$= \log \det D_1^{-1} D_\tau$$
$$= \log \det \left(\Sigma_1 \sum_{t=1}^{\tau} \mathbf{1}(\gamma_t \neq 1)\Sigma_t^{-1}\right)$$
$$\leq d \log\left(\frac{n\sigma^2}{\delta}\right) \leq dL \log(2),$$

where the last inequality follows from Definition 11.9. Rearranging shows that

$$\sum_{t=1}^{\tau} A_t \leq dL.$$

Moving now to bound $\sum_{t=1}^{\tau} B_t$, recall that Γ_t is a convex quadratic minimised at $z_t \in \mathbb{R}^d$. Let $\Gamma_t^\star = \Gamma_t(z_t)$. Note that $t \mapsto \Gamma_t^\star$ is non-decreasing by the definition

11.6 Decay Analysis

of Γ_t. A simple calculation shows that when $\gamma_t \neq 1$, then in rounds t where $B_t = 1$,

$$\Gamma_t^\star \stackrel{(a)}{=} \Gamma_{t-1}^\star + (1-\gamma)\|z_{t-1} - \mu_t\|_{\Sigma_t^{-1} - \Sigma_t^{-1} D_t^{-1} \Sigma_t^{-1}}^2$$

$$\stackrel{(b)}{\geq} \Gamma_{t-1}^\star + \frac{1-\gamma}{2}\|z_{t-1} - \mu_t\|_{\Sigma_t^{-1}}^2$$

$$\stackrel{(c)}{\geq} \Gamma_{t-1}^\star + \frac{1-\gamma}{16L\lambda^2}$$

$$\stackrel{(d)}{\geq} \Gamma_{t-1}^\star + 3\rho,$$

where in (a) we used Lemma A.11 with $A = \Sigma_t^{-1}$ and $B = D_{t-1}$. (b) follows because $B_t = 1$ implies that $D_t = D_{t-1} + \Sigma_t^{-1} \succeq 2\Sigma_t^{-1}$, which shows that $\Sigma_t^{-1} D_t^{-1} \Sigma_t^{-1} \preceq \frac{1}{2}\Sigma_t^{-1}$. (c) follows from the definition of B_t and (d) from the definition of the constants (Table 11.2.h). Since $B_t = 1$ can only happen if $\Gamma_{t-1}^\star < 3\rho$, it follows that $\sum_{t=1}^T B_t \leq 1$. Combining the two parts shows that $\sum_{t=1}^T \mathbb{1}(\gamma_t \neq 1) = \sum_{t=1}^T A_t + \sum_{t=1}^T B_t \leq 1 + dL$, which establishes part (1). Part (2) follows from part (1) since

$$w_t = \prod_{s=1}^t \gamma_s \geq \gamma^{1+dL} = \frac{1}{2}.$$

Measurability of the weights (part (3)) follows from the construction of the algorithm. □

Proof of Lemma 11.15 Let $x \notin K_\tau$. By the definition of K_τ there exists a $t \leq \tau$ such that

$$\|x - \mu_t\|_{\Sigma_t^{-1}}^2 \geq \frac{1}{2L\lambda^2}. \tag{11.10}$$

Since $\Gamma_\tau(x) \geq \Gamma_t(x)$ it suffices to show that $\Gamma_t(x) \geq 3\rho$. Suppose that $\gamma_t = \gamma$; then

$$\Gamma_t(x) = \sum_{s=1}^t (1-\gamma_s)\|x - \mu_s\|_{\Sigma_s^{-1}}^2 \geq (1-\gamma)\|x - \mu_t\|_{\Sigma_t^{-1}}^2 \stackrel{(a)}{\geq} \frac{1-\gamma}{2L\lambda^2} \stackrel{(b)}{\geq} 3\rho,$$

where (a) follows from (11.10) and (b) from the definition of the constants (Table 11.2.h). For the remainder assume that $\gamma_t = 1$. According to the definition of γ_t there are two ways this can happen. On the one hand, if $\Gamma_{t-1}(z_{t-1}) \geq 3\rho$, then trivially $\Gamma_t(x) = \Gamma_{t-1}(x) \geq \Gamma_{t-1}(z_{t-1}) \geq 3\rho$. On the other hand, if

$\Gamma_{t-1}(z_{t-1}) < 3\rho$ and $\gamma_t = 1$, then

$$\Sigma_t^{-1} \preceq \sum_{s=1}^{t-1} \mathbf{1}(\gamma_s \neq 1)\Sigma_s^{-1} \quad \text{and} \tag{11.11}$$

$$\|\mu_t - z_{t-1}\|_{\Sigma_t^{-1}}^2 \leq \frac{1}{8L\lambda^2}. \tag{11.12}$$

Therefore,

$$\Gamma_t(x) = \Gamma_{t-1}(x)$$

$$= \sum_{s=1}^{t-1}(1-\gamma_s)\|x - \mu_s\|_{\Sigma_s^{-1}}^2$$

$$= (1-\gamma)\sum_{s=1}^{t-1}\mathbf{1}(\gamma_s \neq 1)\|x - \mu_s\|_{\Sigma_s^{-1}}^2$$

$$\overset{(a)}{\geq} (1-\gamma)\sum_{s=1}^{t-1}\mathbf{1}(\gamma_s \neq 1)\left[\frac{1}{2}\|x - z_{t-1}\|_{\Sigma_s^{-1}}^2 - \|z_{t-1} - \mu_s\|_{\Sigma_s^{-1}}^2\right]$$

$$= \frac{1-\gamma}{2}\sum_{s=1}^{t-1}\mathbf{1}(\gamma_s \neq 1)\|x - z_{t-1}\|_{\Sigma_s^{-1}}^2 - \Gamma_{t-1}(z_{t-1})$$

$$\overset{(b)}{\geq} \frac{1-\gamma}{2}\|x - z_{t-1}\|_{\Sigma_t^{-1}}^2 - 3\rho$$

$$\overset{(c)}{\geq} \frac{1-\gamma}{2}\left[\frac{1}{2}\|x - \mu_t\|_{\Sigma_t^{-1}}^2 - \|\mu_t - z_{t-1}\|_{\Sigma_t^{-1}}^2\right] - 3\rho$$

$$\overset{(d)}{\geq} \frac{1-\gamma}{16\lambda^2 L} - 3\rho$$

$$\overset{(e)}{\geq} 3\rho,$$

where (a) follows from the inequality $\|a+b\|^2 \leq 2\|a\|^2 + 2\|b\|^2$, (b) by the assumption that $\Gamma_{t-1}(z_{t_1}) \leq 3\rho$ and (11.11), (c) by the same inequality as (a). (d) by (11.10) and (11.12) and (e) by the definition of the constants (Table 11.2.h). □

11.7 Approximate Optimisation

We need to explain how Algorithm 11.3 might implement the optimisation problem in Line 12 to find a point $x \in K_t$ such that

$$\eta\widetilde{\text{sReg}}_t(x) \geq \max_{x \in K_t} \eta\widetilde{\text{sReg}}_t(x) - \rho, \tag{11.13}$$

11.8 Constraints

which is equivalent to finding an $x \in K_t$ such that

$$\eta \sum_{u=1}^{t} \hat{s}_u(x) \leq \min_{y \in K_t} \eta \sum_{u=1}^{t} \hat{s}_u(y) + \rho.$$

The plan is to use gradient descent (Algorithm 11.1). To this end, let $t \leq \tau$ be fixed for the remainder of the section and

$$\hat{h}(x) = \eta \sum_{u=1}^{t} \hat{s}_u(x) \quad \text{and} \quad h(x) = \eta \sum_{u=1}^{t} s_u(x) \quad \text{and} \quad \hat{h}'(x) = \eta \sum_{u=1}^{t} \hat{s}'_u(x).$$

The following is needed in order to apply Corollary 11.5:

Lemma 11.20 *Given any $t \leq \tau$, the following hold:*
(1) *Bounded gradients:* $\max_{x \in K_t} \|\hat{h}'(x)\|_{\Sigma_t^{-1}} = O(\text{poly}(d, n))$.
(2) *Approximate values:* $\max_{x \in K_t} |h(x) - \hat{h}(x)| \leq \frac{\rho}{6}$.
(3) *Approximate gradients:* $\max_{x, y \in K_t} \langle h'(x) - \hat{h}'(x), x - y \rangle \leq \frac{\rho}{6}$.

Lemma 11.20 when combined with Corollary 11.5 shows that Algorithm 11.1 when run with $A = \Sigma_t^{-1}$, $K = K_t$, gradient function $\hat{h}'(x) = \eta \sum_{u=1}^{t} \hat{s}_u(x)$ and $n = O(\text{poly}(n, d))$ returns a point x satisfying (11.13).

Exercise 11.21 ★★ Prove Lemma 11.20. You may find the entries in Table 11.2.i and 11.2.j useful.

11.8 Constraints

As in Chapter 10, the analysis in this chapter depends on a complicated set of constraints on the parameters, which are given in Table 11.2.

You can check that the constraints are satisfied when

$$\lambda = \frac{2}{Cd^2L^3} \qquad \eta = \frac{\sqrt{d/n}}{CL} \qquad \gamma = 2^{-\frac{1}{1+dL}}$$

$$\sigma^2 = \frac{1}{dL^4} \qquad \rho = Cd^3L^4 \qquad \varepsilon = \frac{d^{2.5}C^3L^6}{\sqrt{n}},$$

where $C > 0$ is a suitably large absolute constant.

Remark 11.22 Let us comment on where there might be room for improvement and on the tightness of the choices of the parameters. First, it seems nearly essential that $1 - \gamma = \tilde{O}(1/d)$. But satisfying Table 11.2.c ensures that $\frac{d}{\lambda} = \tilde{O}(\rho)$ and satisfying Table 11.2.h ensures that $(1 - \gamma)/\lambda^2 = \tilde{\Omega}(\rho)$, which means that $\lambda = \tilde{O}(\frac{1-\gamma}{d}) = \tilde{O}(1/d^2)$. But $cnf = \tilde{\Omega}(\frac{1}{\lambda}\sqrt{dn})$, so the regret with this choice

11 Online Newton Step for Adversarial Losses

	CONSTRAINT
11.2.a	$\sigma\sqrt{d} \leq 1$
11.2.b	$\frac{40dL^2}{\varepsilon\eta\lambda} \leq 2n$
11.2.c	$\frac{2d^2}{\sigma^2} + 4\eta^2 dnL + \eta\,\text{cnf} + 2\eta + \frac{dL}{\lambda} \leq \rho$
11.2.d	$3\eta\lambda L^2 \sqrt{dn} \leq \frac{1}{2}$
11.2.e	$\frac{dL}{\lambda} + \eta\,\text{cnf} + \eta\left(1 + \frac{10}{\varepsilon\lambda}\right) \leq \rho$
11.2.f	$\frac{\eta\lambda\sigma\sqrt{d}}{\varepsilon(1-\lambda)} \leq 1$
11.2.g	$1 + \frac{2d^2}{\sigma^2} + 4\eta^2 dnL + 2\eta\,\text{cnf} \leq \rho$
11.2.h	$\rho \leq \frac{1-\gamma}{96L\lambda^2}$
11.2.i	$\eta\,\text{cnf} \leq \frac{\rho}{6}$
11.2.j	$\text{cnf} = \frac{3L^2\sqrt{dn}}{\lambda}$

Table 11.2 Constraints on the parameters used in the analysis of Algorithm 11.3

of λ is at least $\tilde{\Omega}(\text{cnf}) = \tilde{\Omega}(d^{2.5}\sqrt{n})$, which is the rate achieved. The $\sqrt{d}$ in cnf arises from a union bound that may be loose. If this could be improved to $\text{cnf} = \frac{1}{\lambda}\sqrt{n}$, then the regret would become $d^2\sqrt{n}$.

11.9 Notes

11.i The algorithm and analysis here are refined versions of those proposed by Fokkema et al. (2024). The restarting has been used to handle adversarial losses by a number of authors (Hazan and Li, 2016; Bubeck et al., 2017; Suggala et al., 2021). The gadget used here most closely resembles that by Suggala et al. (2021). The main difference is the mechanisms for deciding when to decay the inverse covariance. At a high level both decay the inverse covariance when the focus region changes too much. They use an argument based on reduction of volume, which is less computationally efficient than the more algebraic calculations used in Algorithm 11.3.

11.ii We mentioned that the ellipsoid method can replace gradient descent for approximately minimising a near-convex function. We adopt the notation and assumptions in Theorem 11.4. Let us additionally assume access to a separation oracle for K and extend $\hat{h}' \colon K \to \mathbb{R}^d$ to $\hat{h}' \colon \mathbb{R}^d \to \mathbb{R}^d$ by defining $\hat{h}'(x)$ to be the output of the separation oracle for $x \notin K$. Let E_1 be an ellipsoid such that $K \subset E_1$ and define (E_k) centred at (x_k) inductively by $E_{k+1} = \text{MVEE}(E_k \cap \{x \colon \langle \hat{h}'(x_k), x - x_k \rangle \leq 0\})$. Let $x \in K$ be arbitrary and suppose that $\hat{h}(x) \leq \hat{h}(x_k) - 2\varepsilon_0 - \varepsilon_1$. Then

$$\begin{aligned}\langle \hat{h}'(x_k), x - x_k \rangle &\leq \langle h'(x_k), x - x_k \rangle + \varepsilon_1 \\ &\leq h(x) - h(x_k) + \varepsilon_1 \\ &\leq \hat{h}(x) - \hat{h}(x_k) + 2\varepsilon_0 + \varepsilon_1 \\ &\leq 0,\end{aligned}$$

which means that $x \in K_{k+1}$. Following the standard argument of the ellipsoid method shows that with $m = O(d^2 \log(G/\max(\varepsilon_0, \varepsilon_1)))$ it holds that

$$\min_{k \leq m} \hat{h}(x_k) \leq \inf_{x \in K} \hat{h}(x) + 4\varepsilon_0 + 2\varepsilon_1.$$

11.iii The running time per round of Algorithm 11.3 depends polynomially on t. The reason is two-fold: (1) the focus region K_t has at least t quadratic constraints, which means the projection in Line 11 involves a large number of constraints; (2) approximately maximising the empirical regret in Line 12 requires storing and accumulating all previous data during the approximate convex optimisation procedure. The following exercise is quite speculative:

Exercise 11.23 ★★★? Suppose that K is represented as a polytope or via a separation oracle. Modify Algorithm 11.3 to have $O(\text{poly}(d, \log(n)))$ running time per round. The following is a suggestion only:
(1) Show that the focus region can be updated only $\tilde{O}(d)$ times when the ellipsoid $E(\mu_t, \Sigma_t)$ changes dramatically.
(2) Show that the optimisation procedure in Line 12 can be warm-started or implemented in a streaming fashion to reduce the complexity per round.

11.iv As with Algorithm 10.2 from the previous chapter, the analysis of Algorithm 11.3 relies on complex and moderately non-explicit parameters. In principle you can calculate the constants explicitly, but in practice the resulting choices will be overly conservative. And the problem that poor approximations of the optimal constants may lead to linear regret is even worse here than in Chapter 10, thanks to the additional constants that define the decay of the inverse covariance and the restart condition.

12
Gaussian Optimistic Smoothing

The purpose of this chapter is to introduce and analyse the surrogate loss functions used in Chapters 10 and 11. The results are stated in as much generality as possible to facilitate their use in future applications. In case you want a quick summary of the results, read this introductory section for the basic definitions and then head directly to Section 12.9.

Suppose that $f: \mathbb{R}^d \to \mathbb{R}$ is convex and X is a random vector in $\mathbb{R}^d$. We are interested in the problem of estimating the entire function f from a single observation $Y = f(X) + \varepsilon$ where $\mathbb{E}[\varepsilon|X] = 0$ and $\mathbb{E}[\exp(\varepsilon^2)|X] \leq 2$. Given a parameter $\lambda \in (0, 1)$, define the surrogate by

$$s(x) = \mathbb{E}\left[\left(1 - \frac{1}{\lambda}\right) f(X) + \frac{1}{\lambda} f((1-\lambda)X + \lambda x)\right]. \qquad (12.1)$$

A geometric intuition for this surrogate is shown in Figure 12.1 while the surrogate loss itself is plotted in Figures 12.2 and 12.3. We saw this surrogate in Chapters 6 and 9 with $\lambda = 1/2$ and where X was supported on an ellipsoid. For the remainder we assume that the law of X is Gaussian with mean μ and covariance Σ. The density of X with respect to the Lebesgue measure is

$$p(x) = \left(\frac{1}{2\pi}\right)^{d/2} \sqrt{\det \Sigma^{-1}} \exp\left(-\frac{1}{2}\|x - \mu\|_{\Sigma^{-1}}^2\right).$$

We also make use of a quadratic approximation of the surrogate defined by

$$q(x) = \langle s'(\mu), x - \mu \rangle + \frac{1}{4}\|x - \mu\|_{s''(\mu)}^2,$$

which is related to the second-order expansion of s at μ except that the zeroth-order term is dropped and the leading constant of the quadratic term is $\frac{1}{4}$ rather than $\frac{1}{2}$. Since we dropped the zeroth-order term you should not expect that $q(x) \approx s(x)$. Rather we will see that $q(x) - q(\mu)$ is comparable to $s(x) - s(\mu)$ for suitable x.

12 Gaussian Optimistic Smoothing

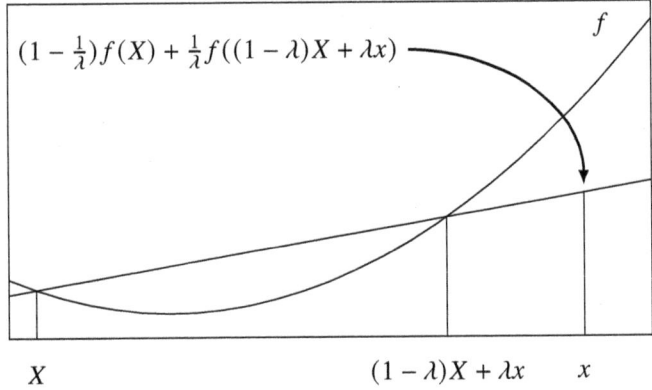

Figure 12.1 The plot shows a lower bound on $f(x)$ obtained by the linear approximation of f using points X and $(1 - \lambda)X + \lambda x$. The optimistic surrogate is obtained by averaging over all such approximations according to the law of X.

Assumptions and Logarithmic Factors

Because the analysis is quite intricate and we are not so concerned about constants and logarithmic factors, we make the following assumption:

Assumption 12.1 The following hold:
(1) *Convexity:* $f : \mathbb{R}^d \to \mathbb{R}$ is convex and K is a convex body.
(2) *Gaussian iterates:* X has law $\mathcal{N}(\mu, \Sigma)$ and $\mu \in K$.
(3) *Subgaussian responses:* $Y = f(X) + \varepsilon$ with
$$\mathbb{E}[\varepsilon|X] = 0 \quad \text{and} \quad \mathbb{E}[\exp(\varepsilon^2)|X] \leq 2\,.$$
(4) *Boundedness:* $\delta \in (0, 1)$ is a constant such that
$$\max\left(d, \mathrm{lip}(f), \sup_{x \in K} |f(x)|, \|\Sigma\|, \|\Sigma^{-1}\|, 1/\lambda\right) \leq \frac{1}{\delta}\,;$$
moreover, $\lambda \leq \frac{1}{d+1}$.

We let L be a logarithmic constant:
$$L = C \log(1/\delta)$$
where $C > 0$ is a large non-specified universal positive constant. We also let (C_k) be a collection of k-dependent universal positive constants.

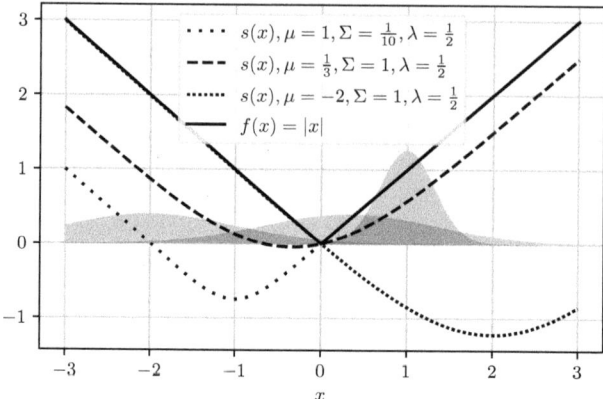

Figure 12.2 The surrogate for different choices of μ and Σ with $\lambda = \frac{1}{2}$ in all cases. Notice that the surrogate is always optimistic in the sense that $s(x) \leq f(x)$ for all x. Moreover, the quality of the approximation depends on whether or not x is in the region where the relevant Gaussian is well-concentrated and the amount of curvature of f in that region.

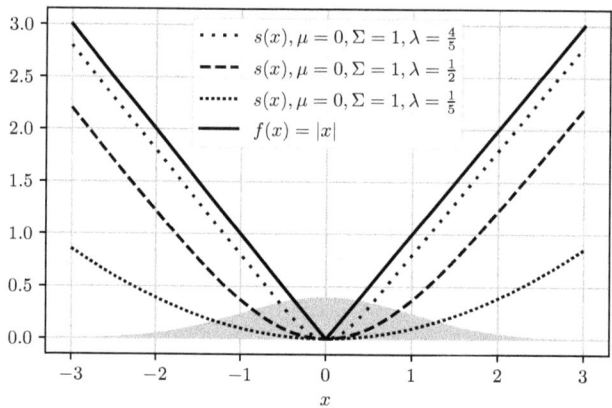

Figure 12.3 The surrogate for μ and Σ constant and different choices of λ. You can see that smaller λ yields a smoother surrogate, but also one that has more approximation error.

12.1 Smoothing

Our analysis would often be made considerably easier if $f \in \mathscr{F}_{sm}$. Let $\varrho = \exp(-L/200)$, which is a miniscule constant, and let

$$f_\varrho = f \star \phi_\varrho$$

where ϕ_ϱ is the smoothing kernel defined in Section 3.8. The following lemma is nothing but a rewriting of Proposition 3.24.

Lemma 12.2 *The following hold:*
(1) f_ϱ *is twice differentiable and β-smooth with $\beta = (d+1)(d+6)\mathrm{lip}(f)/\varrho$.*
(2) $\|f_\varrho - f\|_\infty \leq \varrho \, \mathrm{lip}(f)$.

The surrogate loss associated with the smoothed loss f_ϱ is

$$s_\varrho(x) = \mathbb{E}\left[\left(1 - \frac{1}{\lambda}\right) f_\varrho(X) + \frac{1}{\lambda} f_\varrho((1-\lambda)X + \lambda x)\right].$$

By definition, ϱ is tiny, which means that s_ϱ may not be *that* smooth, but it is just enough for our purposes.

12.2 Elementary Properties

An immediate consequence of the definitions is that s is convex, Lipschitz and a lower bound on f.

Lemma 12.3 *The function s in (12.1) is well-defined, infinitely differentiable and*
(1) *s is convex;*
(2) *$s(x) \leq f(x)$ for all $x \in \mathbb{R}^d$; and*
(3) *$\mathrm{lip}(s) \leq \mathrm{lip}(f)$.*

Proof That s is well-defined, infinitely differentiable and Lipschitz is left as an exercise. Part (1) is immediate from the convexity of f. Part (2) also uses convexity of f and Jensen's inequality:

$$s(x) = \mathbb{E}\left[\left(1 - \frac{1}{\lambda}\right) f(X) + \frac{1}{\lambda} f((1-\lambda)X + \lambda x)\right]$$
$$\leq \mathbb{E}\left[\left(1 - \frac{1}{\lambda}\right) f(X) + \frac{1}{\lambda}[(1-\lambda)f(X) + \lambda f(x)]\right]$$
$$= f(x). \qquad \square$$

Exercise 12.4 ★ Prove the omitted parts of Lemma 12.3.

Perhaps the most important property of s is that it is not too far below f on an ellipsoidal region about μ. Establishing this is quite involved, however, and relies on a better understanding of the Hessian of s.

12.3 Properties of the Hessian

The next important property is a kind of continuity of the Hessian.

Proposition 12.5 *If $\lambda \|x - y\|_{\Sigma^{-1}} \le L^{-1/2}$, then $s''(x) \preceq 2s''(y) + \delta \Sigma^{-1}$.*

Proof The interesting part is to establish a version of the claim for the smoothed surrogate loss, which is followed by a mundane comparison.

Step 1: Smoothed analysis

Let $\varepsilon = \frac{\lambda(y-x)}{1-\lambda}$ and assume by changing coordinates that $\mu = 0$. By definition,

$$s''_\varrho(x) = \lambda \mathbb{E}\left[f''_\varrho((1-\lambda)X + \lambda x)\right]$$
$$= \lambda \int_{\mathbb{R}^d} f''_\varrho((1-\lambda)z + \lambda x) p(z)\,dz$$
$$= \lambda \int_{\mathbb{R}^d} f''_\varrho((1-\lambda)w + \lambda y) p(w + \varepsilon)\,dw,$$

where the exchange of integral and derivatives is justified by the assumption that $\mathrm{lip}(f) < \infty$. The last equality holds by a change of coordinates. Given a set $B \subset \mathbb{R}^d$ let

$$I(B) = \lambda \int_B f''_\varrho((1-\lambda)w + \lambda y) p(w + \varepsilon)\,dw.$$

The plan is to construct a set A for which $\mathbb{P}(X \notin A)$ is negligible and $I(A) \preceq 2s''_\varrho(y)$ and then argue that $I(A^c)$ is negligible. Consider the density ratio

$$\frac{p(w + \varepsilon)}{p(w)} = \exp\left(-\frac{1}{2}\|w + \varepsilon\|^2_{\Sigma^{-1}} + \frac{1}{2}\|w\|^2_{\Sigma^{-1}}\right)$$
$$= \exp\left(-\frac{1}{2}\|\varepsilon\|^2_{\Sigma^{-1}} - \langle w, \varepsilon\rangle_{\Sigma^{-1}}\right).$$

12.3 Properties of the Hessian

Next, let $A = \{w: -\frac{1}{2}\|\varepsilon\|_{\Sigma^{-1}}^2 - \langle w, \varepsilon\rangle_{\Sigma^{-1}} \leq \log(2)\}$, which is chosen so that

$$I(A) = \lambda \int_A f_\varrho''((1-\lambda)w + \lambda y) p(w + \varepsilon) \, dw$$

$$\preceq 2\lambda \int_A f_\varrho''((1-\lambda)w + \lambda y) p(w) \, dw$$

$$\preceq 2\lambda \int_{\mathbb{R}^d} f_\varrho''((1-\lambda)w + \lambda y) p(w) \, dw$$

$$= 2s_\varrho''(y),$$

where the first inequality uses the fact that f_ϱ is convex so that $f_\varrho'' \succeq 0$ and the definition of A. The second follows from convexity of f_ϱ. Moving now to bound the integral over A^c, recall the definition of β in Lemma 12.2. By convexity of the spectral norm,

$$\|I(A^c)\| = \left\|\lambda \int_{A^c} f_\varrho''((1-\lambda)w + \lambda y) p(w + \varepsilon) \, dw\right\|$$

$$\leq \lambda\beta \int_{A^c} p(w + \varepsilon) \, dw$$

$$= \lambda\beta \mathbb{P}(X - \varepsilon \in A^c)$$

$$= \lambda\beta \mathbb{P}\left(-\frac{1}{2}\|\varepsilon\|_{\Sigma^{-1}}^2 - \langle X - \varepsilon, \Sigma^{-1}\varepsilon\rangle > \log(2)\right)$$

$$\leq \lambda\beta \exp\left(-\frac{\left(\log(2) - \frac{1}{2}\|\varepsilon\|_{\Sigma^{-1}}^2\right)^2}{2\|\varepsilon\|_{\Sigma^{-1}}^2}\right),$$

where in the final inequality we used Theorem B.15 and the fact that $\langle X, \Sigma^{-1}\varepsilon\rangle$ has law $\mathcal{N}(0, \|\varepsilon\|_{\Sigma^{-1}}^2)$, as well as the fact that $\frac{1}{2}\|\varepsilon\|_{\Sigma^{-1}}^2 \leq \log(2)$, which holds for suitably large L by the assumptions in the proposition statement. Therefore,

$$s_\varrho''(x) \preceq 2s_\varrho''(y) + \lambda\beta \exp\left(-\frac{\left(\log(2) - \frac{1}{2}\|\varepsilon\|_{\Sigma^{-1}}^2\right)^2}{2\|\varepsilon\|_{\Sigma^{-1}}^2}\right)\mathbb{1}$$

$$\preceq 2s_\varrho''(y) + \lambda\beta \exp\left(-\frac{L}{100}\right)\mathbb{1}, \qquad (12.2)$$

where the last inequality follows because $\lambda \leq 1/2$ by Assumption 12.1 and the conditions in the statement that $\lambda\|x - y\|_{\Sigma^{-1}} \leq 1/\sqrt{L}$, so that

$$\|\varepsilon\|_{\Sigma^{-1}}^2 = \left(\frac{\lambda}{1-\lambda}\right)^2 \|x - y\|_{\Sigma^{-1}}^2 \leq \frac{1}{L(1-\lambda)^2} \leq \frac{4}{L} \leq \log(2).$$

Step 2: Comparison

We now compare s'' and s''_ϱ. Let

$$M(z) = \Sigma^{-1/2} z z^\top \Sigma^{-1/2} - \mathbb{1}.$$

Then, using convexity of the spectral norm and Lemma 12.2,

$$\left\|\Sigma^{1/2}(s''(x) - s''_\varrho(x))\Sigma^{1/2}\right\| \stackrel{(a)}{=} \frac{\lambda}{(1-\lambda)^2} \left\|\int_{\mathbb{R}^d}(f - f_\varrho)((1-\lambda)z + \lambda x) M(z) p(z)\, dz\right\|$$

$$\stackrel{(b)}{\leq} \frac{\lambda \varrho \operatorname{lip}(f)}{(1-\lambda)^2} \int_{\mathbb{R}^d} \|M(z)\| p(z)\, dz$$

$$\stackrel{(c)}{=} \frac{\lambda \varrho \operatorname{lip}(f)}{(1-\lambda)^2} \int_{\mathbb{R}^d} \left\|\Sigma^{-1/2} z z^\top \Sigma^{-1/2} - \mathbb{1}\right\| p(z)\, dz$$

$$\stackrel{(d)}{\leq} \frac{(d+1)\lambda \varrho \operatorname{lip}(f)}{(1-\lambda)^2}, \tag{12.3}$$

where (a) follows by (twice) integrating by parts, (b) by Lemma 12.2, (c) by substituting the definition of M and (d) since $\Sigma^{-1/2} z$ under $p(z)$ is a standard Gaussian and for $W \sim \mathcal{N}(\mathbf{0}, \mathbb{1})$, $\mathbb{E}[\|WW^\top - \mathbb{1}\|] \leq \mathbb{E}[\|WW^\top\|] + 1 = \mathbb{E}[\|W\|^2] + 1 = d + 1$. Therefore,

$$s''(x) \stackrel{(a)}{\preceq} s''_\varrho(x) + \frac{(d+1)\lambda \varrho \operatorname{lip}(f)}{(1-\lambda)^2}\Sigma^{-1}$$

$$\stackrel{(b)}{\preceq} 2 s''_\varrho(y) + \lambda \beta \exp\left(-\frac{L}{100}\right)\mathbb{1} + \frac{(d+1)\lambda \varrho \operatorname{lip}(f)}{(1-\lambda)^2}\Sigma^{-1}$$

$$\stackrel{(c)}{\preceq} 2 s''(y) + \lambda \beta \exp\left(-\frac{L}{100}\right)\mathbb{1} + \frac{2(d+1)\lambda \varrho \operatorname{lip}(f)}{(1-\lambda)^2}\Sigma^{-1}$$

$$\stackrel{(d)}{\preceq} 2 s''(y) + \delta \Sigma^{-1},$$

where (a) follows from (12.3), (b) from (12.2) and (c) from (12.3) again. Lastly, (d) follows from the definitions of $\varrho = \exp(-L/200)$ and $\beta = (d+1)(d+6)\operatorname{lip}(f)/\varrho$ in Section 12.1 and Assumption 12.1 that $\delta \mathbb{1} \preceq \Sigma^{-1}$. □

Since f is Lipschitz and s is a smoothing of f, the Hessian of s cannot be too large relative to $\|\Sigma^{-1}\|$, as the next proposition shows.

Proposition 12.6 *For any $z \in \mathbb{R}^d$:*
(1) $\|s''(z)\| \leq \frac{\lambda \operatorname{lip}(f)}{1-\lambda}\sqrt{d\|\Sigma^{-1}\|}$;
(2) $\|\Sigma^{1/2} s''(z) \Sigma^{1/2}\| \leq \frac{\lambda \operatorname{lip}(f)}{1-\lambda}\sqrt{d\|\Sigma\|}$.

Proof Assume for a moment that f is twice differentiable. Then, exchanging derivatives and the expectation and integrating by parts shows that for any

$\eta \in \mathbb{S}_1^{d-1}$,

$$\begin{aligned}
\eta^\top s''(z)\eta &= \lambda \mathbb{E}[\eta^\top f''((1-\lambda)X + \lambda z)\eta] \\
&= \frac{\lambda}{1-\lambda} \mathbb{E}\left[\langle \eta, f'((1-\lambda)X + \lambda z)\rangle \langle \eta, \Sigma^{-1}(X-\mu)\rangle\right] \\
&\leq \frac{\lambda \operatorname{lip}(f)}{1-\lambda} \mathbb{E}\left[\|\Sigma^{-1}(X-\mu)\|\right] \\
&\leq \frac{\lambda \operatorname{lip}(f)}{1-\lambda} \|\Sigma^{-1}\|^{1/2} \mathbb{E}\left[\|X-\mu\|_{\Sigma^{-1}}\right] \\
&\leq \frac{\lambda \operatorname{lip}(f)}{1-\lambda} \sqrt{d\|\Sigma^{-1}\|}\,.
\end{aligned}$$

Then use the fact that $\|s''(z)\| = \max_{\eta \in \mathbb{S}_1^{d-1}} \eta^\top s''(z)\eta$. The second part follows from the same argument. In case f is not twice-differentiable, apply the above argument to s_ϱ and f_ϱ and pass to the limit as $\varrho \to 0$. Alternatively, use direct means to justify the second equality above with $\langle \cdot, f'(\cdot)\rangle$ replaced with the directional derivative $Df(\cdot)[\cdot]$. The second part follows from the same argument and is left as an exercise. □

Exercise 12.7 ★ Prove the second part of Proposition 12.6.

Lastly, we compare the Hessian of the surrogate to the mean Hessian of the loss f.

Proposition 12.8 *Suppose that* $\lambda \leq \frac{1}{dL^2}$. *Then*

$$\lim_{\varrho \to 0} \mathbb{E}[f''_\varrho(X)] \preceq \frac{1}{\lambda}\left[2s''(\mu) + 2\delta\Sigma^{-1}\right]\,.$$

Note, the limit of the smoothing is used because f may not be twice differentiable. This corresponds to viewing the Hessian of f as an operator on suitable distributions.

Proof Let Z have law $\mathcal{N}(\mu, \frac{2-\lambda}{\lambda}\Sigma)$, which is chosen so that $(1-\lambda)X + \lambda Z$ has the same law as X. Therefore,

$$\mathbb{E}[s''_\varrho(Z)] = \lambda \mathbb{E}[f''_\varrho((1-\lambda)X + \lambda Z)] = \lambda \mathbb{E}[f''_\varrho(X)]\,.$$

Passing to the limit shows that

$$\mathbb{E}[s''(Z)] = \lambda \lim_{\varrho \to 0} \mathbb{E}[f''_\varrho(X)]\,.$$

Define event $A = \{\lambda \|Z-\mu\|_{\Sigma^{-1}} \leq L^{-1/2}\}$. By Proposition 12.5,

$$\mathbf{1}_A s''(Z) \preceq 2s''(\mu) + \delta \Sigma^{-1}\,. \qquad (12.4)$$

By the definition of Z, $\sqrt{\frac{\lambda}{2-\lambda}}\Sigma^{-1/2}(Z-\mu)$ has law $\mathcal{N}(\mathbf{0},\mathbb{1})$. Therefore, by Proposition B.13 and Lemma B.3,

$$\mathbb{P}(A^c) = \mathbb{P}\left(\lambda\|Z-\mu\|_{\Sigma^{-1}} > L^{-1/2}\right)$$

$$= \mathbb{P}\left(\left\|\sqrt{\frac{\lambda}{2-\lambda}}\Sigma^{-1/2}(Z-\mu)\right\|^2 > \frac{1}{\lambda(2-\lambda)L}\right)$$

$$\leq 2\exp\left(-\frac{3}{8d\lambda(2-\lambda)L}\right)$$

$$\leq 2\exp\left(-\frac{3L}{16}\right). \qquad \text{since } \lambda \leq \frac{1}{dL^2}$$

Combining the above display with (12.4) and Proposition 12.6 shows that

$$\mathbb{E}[s''(Z)] = \mathbb{E}[\mathbf{1}_A s''(Z) + \mathbf{1}_{A^c} s''(Z)]$$

$$\preceq 2s''(\mu) + \delta\Sigma^{-1} + \mathbb{P}(A^c)\frac{\lambda\,\mathrm{lip}(f)}{1-\lambda}\sqrt{d\|\Sigma^{-1}\|}\mathbb{1}$$

$$\preceq 2s''(\mu) + \delta\Sigma^{-1} + 2\exp\left(-\frac{3L}{16}\right)\frac{\lambda\,\mathrm{lip}(f)}{1-\lambda}\sqrt{d\|\Sigma^{-1}\|}\mathbb{1}$$

$$\preceq 2s''(\mu) + 2\delta\Sigma^{-1},$$

where the final inequality follows from the definition of L and by Assumption 12.1. $\qquad\square$

12.4 Properties of the Quadratic Surrogate

Recall that the quadratic surrogate is

$$q(x) = \langle s'(\mu), x-\mu\rangle + \frac{1}{4}\|x-\mu\|^2_{s''(\mu)}.$$

Obviously q inherits convexity from s. By Proposition 12.5, s has a nearly constant Hessian in a region about μ from which it follows that $q(x) - q(\mu) \lesssim s(x) - s(\mu)$ on a region about μ, as the following proposition shows:

Proposition 12.9 *Suppose that* $\lambda\|x-\mu\|_{\Sigma^{-1}} \leq \frac{1}{\sqrt{L}}$; *then*

$$s(\mu) - s(x) \leq q(\mu) - q(x) + \frac{\delta}{\lambda^2}.$$

Proof By Proposition 12.5, for any $y \in [\mu, x]$,

$$s''(y) \succeq \frac{1}{2}\left[s''(\mu) - \delta\Sigma^{-1}\right].$$

By Taylor's theorem there exists a $y \in [\mu, x]$ such that

$$s(x) = s(\mu) + \langle s'(\mu), x - \mu \rangle + \frac{1}{2} \|x - \mu\|^2_{s''(y)}$$

$$\geq s(\mu) + \langle s'(\mu), x - \mu \rangle + \frac{1}{4} \|x - \mu\|^2_{s''(\mu)} - \frac{\delta}{4} \|x - \mu\|^2_{\Sigma^{-1}}$$

$$\geq s(\mu) + \langle s'(\mu), x - \mu \rangle + \frac{1}{4} \|x - \mu\|^2_{s''(\mu)} - \frac{\delta}{4\lambda^2 L}$$

$$\geq s(\mu) + q(x) - \frac{\delta}{\lambda^2} .$$

The result follows by rearranging and because $q(\mu) = 0$. □

12.5 Lower Bound on the Surrogate

We have shown that $s \leq f$ holds everywhere. In general there is no uniform upper bound on the entire function $f - s$, but $f(\mu) - s(\mu)$ can be upper-bounded in terms of the curvature of s as μ.

Proposition 12.10 *Provided that* $\lambda \leq \frac{1}{dL^2}$,

$$f(\mu) \leq \mathbb{E}[f(X)] \leq s(\mu) + \frac{2}{\lambda} \operatorname{tr}(s''(\mu)\Sigma) + \frac{2\delta d}{\lambda} .$$

Proof The first inequality is immediate from Jensen's inequality and because $\mathbb{E}[X] = \mu$. Let Z be a random variable that is independent of X and has law $\mathcal{N}(\mu, \rho^2 \Sigma)$ where $\rho^2 = \frac{2-\lambda}{\lambda}$ is chosen so that $(1 - \lambda)^2 + \lambda^2 \rho^2 = 1$. Then

$$\mathbb{E}[s(Z)] = \mathbb{E}\left[\left(1 - \frac{1}{\lambda}\right) f(X) + \frac{1}{\lambda} f((1 - \lambda)X + \lambda Z)\right]$$

$$= \mathbb{E}\left[\left(1 - \frac{1}{\lambda}\right) f(X) + \frac{1}{\lambda} f(X)\right]$$

$$= \mathbb{E}[f(X)] ,$$

where we used the fact that $(1 - \lambda)X + \lambda Z$ has the same law as X. Let us now compare $\mathbb{E}[s(Z)]$ to $s(\mu)$. By Taylor's theorem, for every $z \in \mathbb{R}^d$ there exists a $\xi_z \in [\mu, z]$ such that $s(z) = s(\mu) + s'(\mu)^\top (z - \mu) + \frac{1}{2}\|z - \mu\|^2_{s''(\xi_z)}$. By Proposition 12.5, if z is close enough to μ, then $s''(z)$ is close to $s''(\mu)$. Define

$$A = \{z \in \mathbb{R}^d : \lambda \|z - \mu\|_{\Sigma^{-1}} \leq L^{-1/2}\} .$$

Note that $\mu \in A$ and that A is convex. Hence, if $z \in A$, then $\xi_z \in A$ and by

Proposition 12.5, $s''(\xi_z) \preceq 2s''(\mu) + \delta\Sigma^{-1}$. Then

$$\mathbb{E}[s(Z)] = \mathbb{E}\left[s(\mu) + s'(\mu)^\top(Z-\mu) + \frac{1}{2}\|Z-\mu\|^2_{s''(\xi_z)}\right]$$

$$= s(\mu) + \underbrace{\mathbb{E}\left[\frac{\mathbf{1}_A(Z)}{2}\|Z-\mu\|^2_{s''(\xi_z)}\right]}_{D} + \underbrace{\mathbb{E}\left[\frac{\mathbf{1}_{A^c}(Z)}{2}\|Z-\mu\|^2_{s''(\xi_z)}\right]}_{E}.$$

The dominant term D is bounded using Proposition 12.5 and the definition of A:

$$D = \mathbb{E}\left[\frac{\mathbf{1}_A(Z)}{2}\|Z-\mu\|^2_{s''(\xi_z)}\right]$$

$$\leq \mathbb{E}\left[\|Z-\mu\|^2_{s''(\mu)} + \frac{\delta}{2}\|Z-\mu\|^2_{\Sigma^{-1}}\right] \qquad \text{by Proposition 12.5}$$

$$= \mathrm{tr}\left(s''(\mu)\mathbb{E}\left[(Z-\mu)(Z-\mu)^\top\right]\right) + \frac{\delta}{2}\mathbb{E}\left[\|Z-\mu\|^2_{\Sigma^{-1}}\right]$$

$$= \rho^2 \mathrm{tr}(s''(\mu)\Sigma) + \frac{\delta d\rho^2}{2}$$

$$\leq \frac{2}{\lambda}\mathrm{tr}(s''(\mu)\Sigma) + \frac{\delta d}{\lambda}. \qquad \text{since } \rho^2 \leq \frac{2}{\lambda}$$

Collecting the results shows that

$$\mathbb{E}[f(X)] = \mathbb{E}[s(Z)] \leq s(\mu) + \frac{2}{\lambda}\mathrm{tr}(s''(\mu)\Sigma) + \frac{\delta d}{\lambda} + E.$$

All that remains is to bound the error term, which follows by showing that $Z \in A^c$ holds with vanishingly small probability.

Bounding the error term

Let

$$M = \sup_{z \in \mathbb{R}^d}\left\|\Sigma^{1/2}s''(z)\Sigma^{1/2}\right\| \leq \frac{\lambda\,\mathrm{lip}(f)}{1-\lambda}\sqrt{\frac{d}{\delta}}, \qquad (12.5)$$

where the inequality follows from Proposition 12.6 and the assumption that $\|\Sigma\| \leq \frac{1}{\delta}$. Let W have law $\mathcal{N}(\mathbf{0}, \mathbf{1})$ and note that $\frac{1}{\rho}\Sigma^{-1/2}(Z-\mu)$ also has law

$\mathcal{N}(\mathbf{0}, \mathbb{1})$. Then,

$$\begin{aligned}
E &= \frac{1}{2}\mathbb{E}\left[\|Z-\mu\|^2_{s''(\xi_Z)} \mathbf{1}_{A^c}(Z)\right] \\
&\leq \frac{M}{2}\mathbb{E}\left[\|Z-\mu\|^2_{\Sigma^{-1}} \mathbf{1}_{A^c}(Z)\right] \\
&= \frac{M\rho^2}{2}\mathbb{E}\left[\|W\|^2 \mathbf{1}_{A^c}(Z)\right] \\
&\leq \frac{M\rho^2}{2}\sqrt{\mathbb{E}\left[\|W\|^4_{\Sigma^{-1}}\right]\mathbb{P}(Z \notin A)} \\
&= \frac{M\rho^2}{2}\sqrt{(d^2+2d)\mathbb{P}\left(\|W\|^2 \geq \frac{1}{\lambda^2\rho^2 L}\right)} \\
&\leq Md\rho^2\sqrt{\mathbb{P}\left(\|W\|^2 \geq \frac{1}{\lambda^2\rho^2 L}\right)},
\end{aligned} \qquad (12.6)$$

where we used the definition of M, Cauchy–Schwarz and Proposition A.3. By Proposition B.13, $\left\|\|W\|^2\right\|_{\psi_1} \leq 3d$ and by Lemma B.3 and the assumption that $\lambda \leq \frac{1}{dL^2}$,

$$\mathbb{P}\left(\|W\|^2 \geq \frac{1}{\lambda^2\rho^2 L}\right) \leq 2\exp\left(-\frac{1}{3d\lambda^2\rho^2 L}\right) \leq 2\exp\left(-\frac{1}{6d\lambda L}\right) \leq 2\exp\left(-\frac{L}{6}\right).$$

Combining the above with (12.6) and (12.5) and naively simplifying the constants by ensuring L is large enough shows that $E \leq \frac{\delta d}{\lambda}$. □

Corollary 12.11 *Suppose that $\lambda \leq \frac{1}{dL^2}$ and $\lambda \|x-\mu\|_{\Sigma^{-1}} \leq \frac{1}{\sqrt{L}}$. Then*

$$\mathbb{E}[f(X)] - f(x) \leq q(\mu) - q(x) + \frac{2}{\lambda}\mathrm{tr}(s''(\mu)\Sigma) + \delta\left[\frac{2d}{\lambda} + \frac{1}{\lambda^2}\right].$$

Proof By Lemma 12.3(2) and Proposition 12.10 and Proposition 12.9,

$$\begin{aligned}
\mathbb{E}[f(X)] - f(x) &\leq s(\mu) - s(x) + \frac{2}{\lambda}\mathrm{tr}(s''(\mu)\Sigma) + \frac{2\delta d}{\lambda} \\
&\leq q(\mu) - q(x) + \frac{2}{\lambda}\mathrm{tr}(s''(\mu)\Sigma) + \delta\left[\frac{2d}{\lambda} + \frac{1}{\lambda^2}\right]. \quad \square
\end{aligned}$$

12.6 Estimation

The surrogate loss function can be estimated from X and Y using a change of measure. Precisely,

$$s(z) = \int_{\mathbb{R}^d} \left(\left(1 - \frac{1}{\lambda}\right) f(x) + \frac{1}{\lambda} f((1-\lambda)x + \lambda z)\right) p(x) \, dx$$

$$= \int_{\mathbb{R}^d} \left(1 - \frac{1}{\lambda} + \frac{p\left(\frac{x - \lambda z}{1-\lambda}\right)}{\lambda(1-\lambda)^d p(x)}\right) f(x) p(x) \, dx$$

$$= \int_{\mathbb{R}^d} \left(1 - \frac{1}{\lambda} + \frac{r(x, z)}{\lambda}\right) f(x) p(x) \, dx, \quad (12.7)$$

where $r(x, z)$ is the change of measure defined by

$$r(x, z) = \left(\frac{1}{1-\lambda}\right)^d \frac{p\left(\frac{x - \lambda z}{1-\lambda}\right)}{p(x)}, \quad (12.8)$$

which satisfies

$$\frac{\partial r(x, z)}{\partial z} = \frac{\lambda r(x, z)}{1-\lambda} \Sigma^{-1} \left(\frac{x - \lambda z}{1-\lambda} - \mu\right)$$

$$\frac{\partial^2 r(x, z)}{\partial z^2} = \frac{\lambda^2 r(x, z)}{(1-\lambda)^2} \left[\Sigma^{-1} \left(\frac{X - \lambda z}{1-\lambda} - \mu\right)\left(\frac{X - \lambda z}{1-\lambda} - \mu\right)^\top \Sigma^{-1} - \Sigma^{-1}\right].$$

Looking at (12.7) and exchanging derivatives and expectations, we might estimate s and its derivatives by

$$\tilde{s}(z) = \left(1 - \frac{1}{\lambda} + \frac{r(X, z)}{\lambda}\right) Y$$

$$\tilde{s}'(z) = \frac{r(X, z) Y}{1-\lambda} \Sigma^{-1} \left(\frac{X - \lambda z}{1-\lambda} - \mu\right)$$

$$\tilde{s}''(z) = \frac{\lambda r(X, z) Y}{(1-\lambda)^2} \left[\Sigma^{-1} \left(\frac{X - \lambda z}{1-\lambda} - \mu\right)\left(\frac{X - \lambda z}{1-\lambda} - \mu\right)^\top \Sigma^{-1} - \Sigma^{-1}\right].$$

And indeed, these are unbiased estimators of $s(z)$, $s'(z)$ and $s''(z)$, respectively.

Exercise 12.12 ★ Show that $\mathbb{E}[\tilde{s}(z)] = s(z)$, $\mathbb{E}[\tilde{s}'(z)] = s'(z)$ and $\mathbb{E}[\tilde{s}''(z)] = s''(z)$ for all $z \in \mathbb{R}^d$.

The quantity $r(X, z)$, however, is not especially well behaved and for this

12.6 Estimation

reason we let $\bar{r}(x, z) = \min(\exp(2), r(x, z))$ and define estimators

$$\hat{s}(z) = \left(1 - \frac{1}{\lambda} + \frac{\bar{r}(X, z)}{\lambda}\right) Y$$

$$\hat{s}'(z) = \frac{\bar{r}(X, z)Y}{1 - \lambda} \Sigma^{-1} \left(\frac{X - \lambda z}{1 - \lambda} - \mu\right)$$

$$\hat{s}''(z) = \frac{\lambda \bar{r}(X, z)Y}{(1 - \lambda)^2} \left[\Sigma^{-1} \left(\frac{X - \lambda z}{1 - \lambda} - \mu\right)\left(\frac{X - \lambda z}{1 - \lambda} - \mu\right)^\top \Sigma^{-1} - \Sigma^{-1}\right].$$

Remark 12.13 Our notation for these estimators is a little clumsy because $\hat{s}'(z)$ and $\hat{s}''(z)$ are not the derivatives of $\hat{s}(z)$.

Note that while s is convex, in general neither $x \mapsto \hat{s}(x)$ nor $x \mapsto \tilde{s}(x)$ are (see Figure 12.4 in Section 12.8). Mostly we are interested in estimating gradients and Hessians of the surrogate at μ, which satisfy

$$\hat{s}'(\mu) = \frac{r(X, \mu) Y \Sigma^{-1}(X - \mu)}{(1 - \lambda)^2}.$$

$$\hat{s}''(\mu) = \frac{\lambda r(X, \mu) Y}{(1 - \lambda)^2} \left[\frac{\Sigma^{-1}(X - \mu)(X - \mu)^\top \Sigma^{-1}}{(1 - \lambda)^2} - \Sigma^{-1}\right].$$

Note that $r(x, \mu) = \bar{r}(x, \mu)$ for all x thanks to Lemma 12.16 in the next section.

Proposition 12.14 Provided that $\lambda \|z - \mu\|_{\Sigma^{-1}} \leq \sqrt{\frac{1}{L}}$, the following hold:
(1) $|\mathbb{E}[\hat{s}(z)] - s(z)| \leq \delta$;
(2) $\|\mathbb{E}[\hat{s}'(z)] - s'(z)\| \leq \delta$;
(3) $\|\mathbb{E}[\hat{s}''(z)] - s''(z)\| \leq \delta$.
Moreover, $\mathbb{E}[\hat{s}(\mu)] = s(\mu)$, $\mathbb{E}[\hat{s}'(\mu)] = s'(\mu)$ and $\mathbb{E}[\hat{s}''(\mu)] = s''(\mu)$.

Proof Let E be the event that $r(X, z) > \exp(2)$. Then

$$|r(X, z) - \bar{r}(X, z)| \leq 1_E r(X, z).$$

By Lemma 12.16,

$$r(X, z) \leq \exp\left(1 + \frac{\lambda}{(1 - \lambda)^2} \langle X - \mu, z - \mu \rangle_{\Sigma^{-1}}\right).$$

Therefore, using the definition of E and the fact that $\lambda \langle X - \mu, z - \mu \rangle_{\Sigma^{-1}}$ has law $\mathcal{N}(0, \lambda^2 \|z - \mu\|_{\Sigma^{-1}}^2)$,

$$\mathbb{P}(E) = \mathbb{P}(r(X, z) > \exp(2))$$
$$\leq \mathbb{P}\left(\lambda \langle X - \mu, z - \mu \rangle_{\Sigma^{-1}} > (1 - \lambda)^2\right)$$
$$\leq \exp\left(-\frac{(1 - \lambda)^4}{2\lambda^2 \|z - \mu\|_{\Sigma^{-1}}^2}\right) \qquad \text{by Theorem B.15}$$
$$\leq \exp\left(-\frac{(1 - \lambda)^4 L}{2}\right).$$

You showed in Exercise 12.12 that $\tilde{s}(z)$ is an unbiased estimator of $s(z)$ and therefore

$$|\mathbb{E}[\hat{s}(z)] - s(z)| = |\mathbb{E}[\hat{s}(z) - \tilde{s}(z)]|$$
$$= \left|\mathbb{E}\left[\frac{Y(\bar{r}(X, z) - r(X, z))}{\lambda}\right]\right|$$
$$\leq \mathbb{E}\left[\frac{\mathbf{1}_E |Y| r(X, z)}{\lambda}\right]$$
$$\leq \frac{1}{\lambda} \mathbb{E}[Y^4]^{\frac{1}{4}} \mathbb{E}[r(X, z)^4]^{\frac{1}{4}} \sqrt{\mathbb{P}(E)}$$
$$\leq \delta,$$

where we used Lemma 12.19 and Lemma 12.20 below. The proofs of parts (2) and (3) follow the same argument. That the estimators are unbiased when $z = \mu$ follows from the observation that $\bar{r}(x, \mu) = r(x, \mu)$ for all x and Exercise 12.12. □

Exercise 12.15 ★ Prove Proposition 12.14(2) and (3).

12.7 Concentration (⋆)

In this section we explore the tail behaviour of the estimators in the previous section. Almost all of the results here are only used as technical lemmas in the previous and next sections. Recall that r is the change of measure function defined by

$$r(x, z) = \frac{p\left(\frac{x - \lambda z}{1 - \lambda}\right)}{(1 - \lambda)^d p(x)} \quad \text{and} \quad \bar{r}(x, z) = \min(\exp(2), r(x, z)),$$

where p is the density of the $\mathcal{N}(\mu, \Sigma)$. The next few lemmas bound the magnitude, gradients and moments of r.

12.7 Concentration

Lemma 12.16 *For all $x, z \in \mathbb{R}^d$,*
$$r(x, z) \leq \exp\left(1 + \frac{\lambda}{(1-\lambda)^2} \langle x - \mu, z - \mu\rangle_{\Sigma^{-1}}\right).$$

Proof Let us assume without loss of generality that $\mu = 0$. By definition,
$$\begin{aligned}
r(x, z) &= \frac{p\left(\frac{x-\lambda z}{1-\lambda}\right)}{(1-\lambda)^d p(x)} \\
&= \frac{1}{(1-\lambda)^d} \exp\left(-\frac{1}{2}\left\|\frac{x - \lambda z}{1-\lambda}\right\|_{\Sigma^{-1}}^2 + \frac{1}{2}\|x\|_{\Sigma^{-1}}^2\right) \\
&\leq \frac{1}{(1-\lambda)^d} \exp\left(\frac{\lambda \langle x, z\rangle_{\Sigma^{-1}}}{(1-\lambda)^2}\right) \\
&\leq \exp\left(1 + \frac{\lambda \langle x, z\rangle_{\Sigma^{-1}}}{(1-\lambda)^2}\right),
\end{aligned}$$
where in the final inequality we used Assumption 12.1 that $\lambda \leq \frac{1}{d+1}$ so that $(1-\lambda)^{-d} \leq (1 + \frac{1}{d})^d \leq \exp(1)$. □

The next lemma loosely bounds the Lipschitz constant of $z \mapsto \bar{r}(x, z)$.

Lemma 12.17 *Suppose that $A = \{z: \lambda \|z - \mu\|_{\Sigma^{-1}} \leq 1\}$ and $x \in \mathbb{R}^d$. Then*
$$\mathrm{lip}_A(\bar{r}(x, \cdot)) \leq \frac{1}{\delta}.$$

Exercise 12.18 ★ Prove Lemma 12.17.

Later we need some conservative upper bounds on the moments of the various estimators. The easiest way to obtain these is to bound the moments of the constituent parts and combine them using Hölder's inequality. Remember in what follows that X has law $\mathcal{N}(\mu, \Sigma)$.

Lemma 12.19 *For any $k \geq 1$, $\mathbb{E}[r(X, x)^k] \leq C_k \exp\left(C_k \lambda^2 \|x - \mu\|_{\Sigma^{-1}}^2\right)$.*

Proof By Lemma 12.16 and Proposition A.3,
$$\begin{aligned}
\mathbb{E}[r(X, x)^k] &\leq \exp(k)\mathbb{E}\left[\exp\left(\frac{\lambda k}{(1-\lambda)^2}\langle X - \mu, x - \mu\rangle_{\Sigma^{-1}}\right)\right] \\
&= \exp(k) \exp\left(\frac{\lambda^2 k^2}{2(1-\lambda)^4}\|x - \mu\|_{\Sigma^{-1}}^2\right) \\
&\leq C_k \exp\left(C_k \lambda^2 \|x - \mu\|_{\Sigma^{-1}}^2\right). \quad \square
\end{aligned}$$

Lemma 12.20 *Suppose that $\mu \in K$. Then, for any $k \geq 1$,*
$$\mathbb{E}[|f(X)|^k] \leq C_k \delta^{-2k} \quad \text{and} \quad \mathbb{E}[|Y|^k] \leq C_k \delta^{-2k}.$$

Proof Since $\mu \in K$, by Assumption 12.1, $|f(\mu)| \leq 1/\delta$, so

$$\begin{aligned}\mathbb{E}[|f(X)|^k] &= \mathbb{E}\left[|f(X) - f(\mu) + f(\mu)|^k\right] \\ &\leq 2^{k-1}\delta^{-k} + 2^{k-1}\mathrm{lip}(f)^k \mathbb{E}\left[\|X - \mu\|^k\right] \\ &\leq 2^{k-1}\delta^{-k} + 2^{k-1}\mathrm{lip}(f)^k \|\Sigma\|^{\frac{k}{2}} \mathbb{E}\left[\|X - \mu\|_{\Sigma^{-1}}^k\right] \\ &\leq C_k \delta^{-2k},\end{aligned}$$

where we used the fact that $(a + b)^k \leq 2^{k-1}[a^k + b^k]$, Proposition B.13 and Lemma B.4 to bound the moments of $\|X - \mu\|_{\Sigma^{-1}}$ and Assumption 12.1. And of course we made sure to choose C_k as a suitably large k-dependent constant. The second part follows from the first using the fact that $Y = f(X) + \varepsilon$ where ε is conditionally subgaussian (Assumption 12.1). □

12.8 Sequential Concentration

We now focus on the sequential aspects of concentration. Let $f_1, \ldots, f_n : \mathbb{R}^d \to \mathbb{R}$ be a sequence of convex functions. Assume that $X_1, Y_1, \ldots, X_n, Y_n$ is the sequence of actions and losses generated by an algorithm interacting with a convex bandit, which is adapted as usual to the filtration $(\mathscr{F}_t)_{t=1}^n$. Let τ be a stopping time with respect to the filtration $(\mathscr{F}_t)$. As usual, we let $\mathbb{P}_t = \mathbb{P}(\cdot|\mathscr{F}_t)$ and $\mathbb{E}_t$ be the corresponding expectation operator. We let $\|\cdot\|_{t,\psi_k}$ be the kth Orlicz norm with respect to $\mathbb{P}_t$. The next assumption generalises Assumption 12.1 to the sequential setting:

Assumption 12.21 The following hold almost surely for all $1 \leq t \leq \tau$:
(1) *Convexity:* K is a convex body and f_t is convex.
(2) *Gaussian iterates:* X_t has law $\mathcal{N}(\mu_t, \Sigma_t)$ under $\mathbb{P}_{t-1}$ and $\mu_t \in K$.
(3) *Subgaussian responses:* $Y_t = f_t(X_t) + \varepsilon_t$ where

$$\mathbb{E}_{t-1}[\varepsilon_t | X_t] = 0 \quad \text{and} \quad \mathbb{E}_{t-1}[\exp(\varepsilon_t^2)|X_t] \leq 2.$$

(4) *Boundedness:* $\lambda \leq \frac{1}{d+1}$ and

$$\max\left(n, d, \mathrm{lip}(f_t), \sup_{x \in K} |f_t(x)|, 1/\lambda, \|\Sigma_t\|, \|\Sigma_t^{-1}\|\right) \leq \frac{1}{\delta}.$$

As before, we let L be a logarithmic factor:

$$L = C \log(1/\delta),$$

12.8 Sequential Concentration

where $C > 0$ is a universal constant. The surrogate function and its quadratic approximation now change from round to round and are given by

$$s_t(z) = \mathbb{E}_{t-1}\left[\left(1 - \frac{1}{\lambda}\right) f_t(X_t) + \frac{1}{\lambda} f_t((1-\lambda)X_t + \lambda z)\right] \quad \text{and}$$

$$q_t(z) = \langle s'_t(\mu_t), z - \mu_t \rangle + \frac{1}{4}\|z - \mu_t\|^2_{s''_t(\mu_t)}.$$

Note that even when $f_t = f$ is unchanging, the surrogate depends on μ_t and Σ_t and may still change from round to round. Let p_t be the density of $\mathcal{N}(\mu_t, \Sigma_t)$ and

$$\bar{r}_t(x, z) = \min\left(\exp(2), \frac{p_t\left(\frac{x-\lambda z}{1-\lambda}\right)}{(1-\lambda)^d p_t(x)}\right).$$

We abbreviate $\bar{r}_t(z) = \bar{r}_t(X_t, z)$. The estimators of s_t and its derivatives are

$$\hat{s}_t(z) = \left(1 - \frac{1}{\lambda} + \frac{\bar{r}_t(z)}{\lambda}\right) Y_t$$

$$\hat{s}'_t(z) = \frac{\bar{r}_t(z) Y_t}{1-\lambda} \Sigma_t^{-1}\left(\frac{X_t - \lambda z}{1-\lambda} - \mu_t\right)$$

$$\hat{s}''_t(z) = \frac{\lambda \bar{r}_t(z) Y_t}{(1-\lambda)^2}\left[\Sigma_t^{-1}\left(\frac{X_t - \lambda z}{1-\lambda} - \mu_t\right)\left(\frac{X_t - \lambda z}{1-\lambda} - \mu_t\right)^\top \Sigma_t^{-1} - \Sigma_t^{-1}\right].$$

Throughout we let $g_t = \hat{s}'_t(\mu_t)$, $H_t = \frac{1}{2}\hat{s}''_t(\mu_t)$, $\bar{g}_t = s'_t(\mu_t)$ and $\bar{H}_t = \frac{1}{2}s''_t(\mu_t)$, which means an estimator of the quadratic surrogate is

$$\hat{q}_t(x) = \langle g_t, x - \mu_t \rangle + \frac{1}{2}(x - \mu_t)^\top H_t (x - \mu_t)$$

and the actual quadratic surrogate is

$$q_t(x) = \langle \bar{g}_t, x - \mu_t \rangle + \frac{1}{2}(x - \mu_t)^\top \bar{H}_t (x - \mu_t).$$

Objectives and Plan

The questions in this section concern concentration of quantities like $\sum_{t=1}^{\tau}(\hat{s}_t - s_t)$. This is an entire function, so we need to be precise about what is meant by concentration. Typical results show that functions like this are small at a specific x or for all x in some set. The magnitude of the errors generally depends on some kind of cumulative predictable variation and our bounds reflect that. The change of measure $\bar{r}_t(x)$ that appears in the definition of the estimators is well-behaved when x is close enough to μ. Because of this most of the concentration bounds

12 Gaussian Optimistic Smoothing

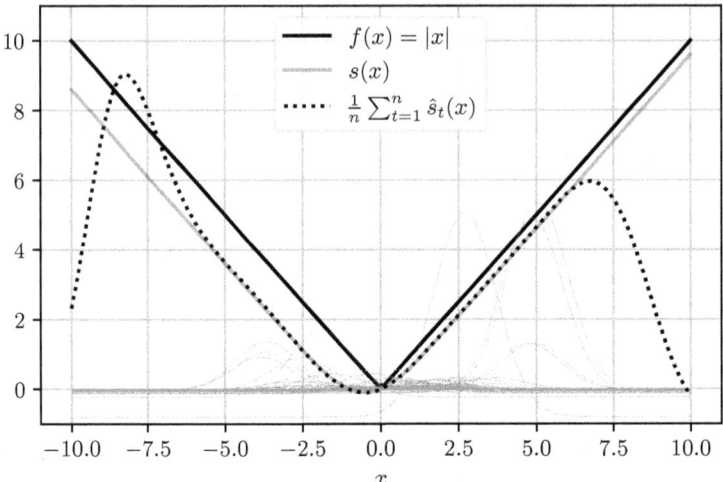

Figure 12.4 The concentration of $\sum_{t=1}^{n} \hat{s}_t(x)/n$ with $f_t = f = |\cdot|$, $n = 10^5$, $\mu = 1/2$, $\Sigma = 1$ and $\lambda = 1/2$. The thin lines correspond to the first one hundred estimated surrogates. The estimate is very close to the real surrogate on an interval around μ but can be extremely poorly behaved far away, even with n so large. Note also that the estimated surrogate is convex near μ but not everywhere.

that follow only hold on a subset of $\mathbb{R}^d$. An illustrative experiment is given in Figure 12.4. Given $r > 0$, let

$$K_\tau(r) = \left\{ x \in \mathbb{R}^d : \max_{1 \leq t \leq \tau} \lambda \|x - \mu_t\|_{\Sigma_t^{-1}} \leq r \right\},$$

which is an intersection of ellipsoids and hence convex. The set $K_\tau(r)$ is often referred to as the focus region. The general flavour of the results is as follows:

- Given a deterministic x, $\sum_{t=1}^{\tau} (\hat{s}_t(x) - s_t(x))$ is well-concentrated about zero provided that $x \in K_\tau(1/\sqrt{2L})$ almost surely.
- The function $\sum_{t=1}^{\tau} (\hat{s}_t(x) - s_t(x))$ is well-concentrated about zero for all $x \in K_\tau(1/\sqrt{2L})$, with a slightly wider confidence interval than the case above.

The predictable variation of the estimators is mostly caused by the variance in the losses. Let $V_\tau = \sum_{t=1}^{\tau} \mathbb{E}_{t-1}[Y_t^2]$ and $Y_{\max} = \max_{1 \leq t \leq \tau} |Y_t| + \mathbb{E}_{t-1}[|Y_t|]$. Generally speaking, in applications the losses (Y_t) will be bounded in $O(1)$ with high probability and in this case $V_\tau = O(n)$. Our concentration bounds will be

12.8 Sequential Concentration

established using a martingale version of Bernstein's inequality (Theorem B.20), which is a variance-aware concentration inequality.

Concentration Bounds

We start with a naive bound on V_τ and $Y_{\max}$, which is only used to bound these quantities when they appear in logarithmic terms.

Proposition 12.22 *With probability at least $1 - \delta/2$,*
$$\max(Y_{\max}, V_\tau) \leq \mathrm{poly}(1/\delta).$$

Proof Combine Markov's inequality, a union bound and Lemma 12.20. □

The first significant result is a Bernstein-like concentration bound for the sum of the surrogate loss estimators:

Proposition 12.23 *Under Assumption 12.21, the following hold:*
(1) Let $x \in \mathbb{R}^d$ be a non-random vector such that $x \in K_\tau(1/\sqrt{L})$ almost surely. Then, with probability at least $1 - \delta$,
$$\left|\sum_{t=1}^\tau (\hat{s}_t(x) - s_t(x))\right| \leq 1 + \frac{1}{\lambda}\left[\sqrt{LV_\tau} + LY_{\max}\right].$$

(2) With probability at least $1 - \delta$,
$$\max_{x \in K_\tau(1/\sqrt{2L})} \left|\sum_{t=1}^\tau (\hat{s}_t(x) - s_t(x))\right| \leq 2 + \frac{1}{\lambda}\sqrt{dLV_\tau} + \frac{dLY_{\max}}{\lambda}.$$

You should view these bounds as a kind of Bernstein inequality with the term involving $Y_{\max}$ the lower-order term and $V_\tau = O(n)$ with high probability.

Proof Starting with part (1), let $x \in \mathbb{R}^d$ be such that $x \in K_\tau(1/\sqrt{L})$ almost surely and recall that
$$\hat{s}_t(x) = \left(1 + \frac{\bar{r}_t(x) - 1}{\lambda}\right) Y_t.$$

Let $\Delta_t = \hat{s}_t(x) - \mathbb{E}_{t-1}[\hat{s}_t(x)]$. A martingale version of Bernstein's inequality (Theorem B.20) applied to the sequence $(\Delta_t)_{t=1}^\tau$ says that with probability at least $1 - \delta/2$,
$$\left|\sum_{t=1}^\tau \Delta_t\right| \leq 3\sqrt{M \log\left(\frac{4\max(B, \sqrt{M})}{\delta}\right)} + 2B \log\left(\frac{4\max(B, \sqrt{M})}{\delta}\right), \quad (12.9)$$

where $M = \sum_{t=1}^{\tau} \mathbb{E}_{t-1}[\Delta_t^2]$ and $B = \max(1, \max_{1 \leq t \leq \tau} |\Delta_t|)$. We now bound the random variables M and B. By definition,

$$M \leq \sum_{t=1}^{\tau} \mathbb{E}_{t-1}[\hat{s}_t(x)^2] \leq \frac{\exp(4)}{\lambda^2} \sum_{t=1}^{\tau} \mathbb{E}_{t-1}[Y_t^2] = \frac{\exp(4)}{\lambda^2} V_\tau,$$

where we used the fact that $\bar{r}_t(x) \leq \exp(2)$. Additionally,

$$\begin{aligned}
B &= \max\left(1, \max_{1 \leq t \leq \tau} |\Delta_t|\right) \\
&\leq 1 + \max_{1 \leq t \leq \tau} |\hat{s}_t(x) - \mathbb{E}_{t-1}[\hat{s}_t(x)]| \\
&\leq 1 + \max_{1 \leq t \leq \tau} (|\hat{s}_t(x)| + |\mathbb{E}_{t-1}[\hat{s}_t(x)]|) \\
&\leq 1 + \frac{\exp(2)}{\lambda} \max_{1 \leq t \leq \tau} (|Y_t| + \mathbb{E}_{t-1}[|Y_t|]) \\
&= 1 + \frac{\exp(2) Y_{\max}}{\lambda}.
\end{aligned}$$

By Proposition 12.22, with probability at least $1 - \delta/2$,

$$\max(B, \sqrt{M}) \leq \text{poly}(1/\delta).$$

Combining with (12.9) shows that with probability at least $1 - \delta$,

$$\left|\sum_{t=1}^{\tau} \Delta_t\right| \leq \frac{1}{\lambda}\left[\sqrt{V_\tau L} + L Y_{\max}\right].$$

Note that so far we have not used the fact that $x \in K_\tau(1/\sqrt{L})$. The argument above shows that $\sum_{t=1}^{\tau} (\hat{s}_t(x) - \mathbb{E}_{t-1}[\hat{s}_t(x)])$ concentrates well for any $x \in \mathbb{R}^d$. All that remains is to argue that $\mathbb{E}_{t-1}[\hat{s}_t(x)]$ is close to $s_t(x)$. Since $x \in K_\tau(1/\sqrt{L})$, by Proposition 12.14,

$$\begin{aligned}
\left|\sum_{t=1}^{\tau} (\hat{s}_t(x) - s_t(x))\right| &\leq n\delta + \left|\sum_{t=1}^{\tau} (\hat{s}_t(x) - \mathbb{E}_{t-1}[\hat{s}_t(x)])\right| \\
&\leq 1 + \left|\sum_{t=1}^{\tau} \Delta_t\right| \\
&\leq 1 + \frac{1}{\lambda}\left[\sqrt{V_\tau L} + L Y_{\max}\right].
\end{aligned}$$

This completes the proof of Part (1). Moving now to part (2), abbreviate $K_\tau = K_\tau(1/\sqrt{2L})$. By Assumption 12.21, $\Sigma \preceq \frac{1}{\delta}\mathbb{1}$ and $\lambda \geq \delta$, and by the definition of K_τ,

$$K_\tau \subset \left\{x : \lambda \|x - \mu_1\|_{\Sigma_1^{-1}} \leq 1/\sqrt{2L}\right\} \subset \left\{x : \|x - \mu_1\| \leq \delta^{-3/2}\right\} \triangleq J. \quad (12.10)$$

12.8 Sequential Concentration

The argument follows along the same lines as part (1) but now we need an additional covering and Lipschitz argument. Let $\mathscr{C}$ be a finite cover of J such that for all $y \in J$ there exists an $x \in \mathscr{C}$ such that $\|x - y\| \leq \varepsilon$ with

$$\varepsilon = \text{poly}(\delta). \tag{12.11}$$

Vershynin (2018, Corollary 4.2.13) shows that $\mathscr{C}$ can be chosen so that

$$|\mathscr{C}| \leq \left(\frac{2\,\text{diam}(J)}{\varepsilon} + 1\right)^d.$$

By (12.10), $\text{diam}(J) \leq 2\delta^{-3/2}$. Hence, by the definition of $L = C\log(1/\delta)$ for suitably large universal constant C, it follows that $\log|\mathscr{C}| \leq dL$. Repeating the argument in Part (1) along with a union bound over $\mathscr{C}$ shows that with probability at least $1 - \delta$ the following both hold:

(i) $\max_{x \in \mathscr{C}} \left|\sum_{t=1}^{\tau} (\hat{s}_t(x) - \mathbb{E}_{t-1}[\hat{s}_t(x)])\right| \leq \frac{1}{\lambda}\left[\sqrt{dV_\tau L} + dLY_{\max}\right]$;

(ii) $\max(Y_{\max}, V_\tau) \leq \text{poly}(1/\delta)$.

For the remainder we assume these events occur. Let $y \in K_\tau$. By the construction of $\mathscr{C}$ there exists an $x \in \mathscr{C}$ such that $\|x - y\| \leq \varepsilon$. Since $y \in K_\tau$ for any $t \leq \tau$,

$$\lambda \|x - \mu_t\|_{\Sigma_t^{-1}} \leq \lambda \|x - y\|_{\Sigma_t^{-1}} + \lambda \|y - \mu_t\|_{\Sigma_t^{-1}} \leq \frac{\lambda\varepsilon}{\sqrt{\delta}} + \frac{1}{\sqrt{2L}} \leq \frac{1}{\sqrt{L}},$$

where we used the definition of K_τ, the triangle inequality, the definition of ε in (12.11) and naive bounding. Therefore $x \in K_\tau(1/\sqrt{L})$ and for any $t \leq \tau$,

$$|\hat{s}_t(x) - \hat{s}_t(y)| = \frac{|\bar{r}_t(x) - \bar{r}_t(y)|\,|Y_t|}{\lambda} \leq \frac{|Y_t|}{\lambda\delta}\|x - y\| \leq \frac{\varepsilon Y_{\max}}{\lambda\delta} \leq \frac{1}{2n}.$$

where we used Lemma 12.17 and the assumption that $\|x - y\| \leq \varepsilon$. By Lemma 12.3(3),

$$\text{lip}(s_t) \leq \text{lip}(f_t) \leq \frac{1}{\delta}.$$

Hence $|s_t(x) - s_t(y)| \leq \frac{\varepsilon}{\delta} \leq \frac{1}{2n}$. Therefore

$$\left|\sum_{t=1}^{\tau}(\hat{s}_t(y) - s_t(y))\right| \leq 1 + \left|\sum_{t=1}^{\tau}(\hat{s}_t(x) - s_t(x))\right|$$

$$\leq 2 + \left|\sum_{t=1}^{\tau}(\hat{s}_t(x) - \mathbb{E}_{t-1}[\hat{s}_t(x)])\right| \quad \text{by Proposition 12.14}$$

$$\leq 2 + \frac{1}{\lambda}\left[\sqrt{dV_\tau L} + dLY_{\max}\right],$$

which completes the proof. □

More or less the same result holds for the quadratic surrogates estimates.

Proposition 12.24 *Under Assumption 12.21, the following hold:*
(1) *Let $x \in \mathbb{R}^d$ be a non-random vector such that $x \in K_\tau(1/\sqrt{L})$ almost surely. Then, with probability at least $1 - \delta$,*

$$\left|\sum_{t=1}^{\tau}(q_t(x) - \hat{q}_t(x))\right| \leq 1 + \frac{1}{\lambda}\left[\sqrt{V_\tau L} + Y_{\max}L\right].$$

(2) *With probability at least $1 - \delta$,*

$$\max_{x \in K_\tau(1/\sqrt{2L})}\left|\sum_{t=1}^{\tau}(q_t(x) - \hat{q}_t(x))\right| \leq 1 + \frac{1}{\lambda}\left[\sqrt{dV_\tau L} + dY_{\max}L\right].$$

Proof Let $x \in \mathbb{R}^d$ be a non-random vector such that $x \in K_\tau(1/\sqrt{L})$ almost surely and $\Delta_t = \hat{q}_t(x) - q_t(x)$, which satisfies $\mathbb{E}_{t-1}[\Delta_t] = 0$ by Proposition 12.14 and the definition of $\hat{q}_t$. By Theorem B.20, with probability at least $1 - \delta/4$,

$$\left|\sum_{t=1}^{\tau}\Delta_t\right| \leq 3\sqrt{M\log\left(\frac{8\max(B, \sqrt{M})}{\delta}\right)} + 2B\log\left(\frac{8\max(B, \sqrt{M})}{\delta}\right), \quad (12.12)$$

where $M = \sum_{t=1}^{\tau}\mathbb{E}_{t-1}[\Delta_t^2]$ and $B = \max_{1 \leq t \leq \tau}|\Delta_t|$. Moreover, by Proposition 12.22, with probability at least $1 - \delta/2$,

$$\max(Y_{\max}, V_\tau) \leq \text{poly}(1/\delta). \quad (12.13)$$

Since $\mathbb{E}_{t-1}[\hat{q}_t(x)] = q_t(x)$ we have

$$\mathbb{E}_{t-1}[\Delta_t^2] \leq \mathbb{E}_{t-1}[\hat{q}_t(x)^2] \quad \text{and} \quad |\Delta_t| \leq |\hat{q}_t(x)| + \mathbb{E}_{t-1}[|\hat{q}_t(x)|].$$

Let $U_t = \langle x - \mu_t, X_t - \mu_t \rangle_{\Sigma_t^{-1}}$. Substituting the definitions of g_t and H_t yields

$$\hat{q}_t(x) = \langle g_t, x - \mu_t\rangle + \frac{1}{2}(x - \mu_t)^\top H_t(x - \mu_t)$$

$$= \bar{r}_t(\mu_t)Y_t\left[\frac{U_t}{1-\lambda} + \frac{\lambda U_t^2}{4(1-\lambda)^4} - \frac{\lambda\|x-\mu_t\|_{\Sigma_t^{-1}}^2}{4(1-\lambda)^2}\right].$$

Using the fact from Lemma 12.16 that $\bar{r}_t(\mu_t) \in [0, \exp(1)]$, $\lambda \leq 1/2$ and the condition that $x \in K_\tau(1/\sqrt{L})$, it follows that

$$|\hat{q}_t(x)| \leq |Y_t|\exp(1)\left[2|U_t| + 4\lambda|U_t|^2 + \frac{1}{\lambda L}\right]. \quad (12.14)$$

The law of U_t under $\mathbb{P}_{t-1}$ is $\mathcal{N}(0, \|x - \mu_t\|_{\Sigma_t^{-1}})$.

Exercise 12.25 ★ Complete the following steps:

12.8 Sequential Concentration

(i) Show that $\|U_t^2\|_{t-1,\psi_1} \leq \frac{8}{3L\lambda^2}$.

(ii) Use (12.14), part (i), Assumption 12.21 and Lemma B.8 to show that

$$\mathbb{E}_{t-1}[\hat{q}_t(x)^2] \leq \delta + \frac{C\mathbb{E}_{t-1}[Y_t^2]}{\lambda^2} \qquad \mathbb{E}_{t-1}[|\hat{q}_t(x)|] \leq \delta + \frac{C\mathbb{E}_{t-1}[|Y_t|]}{\lambda}.$$

(iii) Use Lemma B.3 to show that with probability at least $1 - \delta/4$

$$|\hat{q}_t(x)| \leq \frac{C|Y_t|}{\lambda} \text{ for all } 1 \leq t \leq \tau. \tag{12.15}$$

By a union bound, with probability at least $1 - \delta$ the high-probability events in (12.12), (12.13) and (12.15) all hold. For the remainder assume these events hold. Your solution to Exercise 12.25 shows that

$$M = \sum_{t=1}^{\tau} \mathbb{E}_{t-1}[\Delta_t^2] \leq n\delta + \frac{CV_{\tau}}{\lambda^2}.$$

Moreover,

$$B = \max_{1 \leq t \leq \tau} |\Delta_t| \leq \max_{1 \leq t \leq \tau} (|\hat{q}_t(x)| + \mathbb{E}_{t-1}[|\hat{q}_t(x)|]) \leq \delta + \frac{CY_{\max}}{\lambda}.$$

Combining these with (12.12) shows that

$$\left|\sum_{t=1}^{\tau}(q_t(x) - \hat{q}_t(x))\right| \leq 1 + \frac{1}{\lambda}\left[\sqrt{V_{\tau}L} + LY_{\max}\right].$$

Part (2) follows by repeating more or less the same argument as the covering argument in Proposition 12.23. □

Exercise 12.26 ★ Prove Proposition 12.24(2).

The next proposition shows that the accumulation of second derivatives along the sequence $\mu_1, \ldots, \mu_{\tau}$ is well-concentrated.

Proposition 12.27 *Let $\mathcal{S} \subset \mathbb{S}_+^d$ be the (random) set of positive definite matrices such that $\Sigma_t^{-1} \preceq \Sigma^{-1}$ for all $t \leq \tau$ and $S_{\tau} = \sum_{t=1}^{\tau} \hat{s}_t''(\mu_t)$ and $\bar{S}_{\tau} = \sum_{t=1}^{\tau} s_t''(\mu_t)$. With probability at least $1 - \delta$, for all $\Sigma^{-1} \in \mathcal{S}$,*

$$-\lambda L^2 \left[1 + \sqrt{dV_{\tau}} + d^2 Y_{\max}\right] \Sigma^{-1} \preceq S_{\tau} - \bar{S}_{\tau} \preceq \lambda L^2 \left[1 + \sqrt{dV_{\tau}} + d^2 Y_{\max}\right] \Sigma^{-1}.$$

Proof By definition of the Löwner order, the claim is equivalent to showing that with probability at least $1 - \delta$ for all $u \in \mathbb{S}_1^{d-1}$ and $\Sigma \in \mathcal{S}$,

$$|u^{\top}(S_{\tau} - \bar{S}_{\tau})u| \leq \lambda L^2 \left[1 + \sqrt{dV_{\tau}} + d^2 Y_{\max}\right] \|u\|_{\Sigma^{-1}}^2. \tag{12.16}$$

The approach followed will be the usual one:

- Prove that (12.16) holds for all u in a finite cover of $\mathbb{S}_1^{d-1}$ with slightly smaller constants.
- Extend to all $u \in \mathbb{S}_1^{d-1}$ by a Lipschitz argument.

Let $\mathscr{C}_{\mathbb{S}}$ be a cover of $\mathbb{S}_1^{d-1}$ such that for all $u \in \mathbb{S}_1^{d-1}$ there exists a $v \in \mathscr{C}_{\mathbb{S}}$ such that $\|u - v\| \leq \varepsilon$ where $\varepsilon = \text{poly}(\delta)$ is a small constant. Vershynin (2018, Corollary 4.2.13) shows that $\mathscr{C}_{\mathbb{S}}$ can be chosen so that

$$\log |\mathscr{C}_{\mathbb{S}}| \leq d \log\left(\frac{2}{\varepsilon} + 1\right) \leq dL.$$

Let $W_t = \Sigma_t^{-1/2}(X_t - \mu_t)$, which is a standard Gaussian under $\mathbb{P}_{t-1}$. By definition,

$$\hat{s}_t''(\mu_t) = \frac{\lambda \bar{r}_t(\mu_t) Y_t}{(1-\lambda)^2} \left[\frac{\Sigma_t^{-1}(X_t - \mu_t)(X_t - \mu_t)^\top \Sigma_t^{-1}}{(1-\lambda)^2} - \Sigma_t^{-1}\right]$$

$$= \frac{\lambda \bar{r}_t(\mu_t) Y_t}{(1-\lambda)^2} \left[\frac{\Sigma_t^{-1/2} W_t W_t^\top \Sigma_t^{-1/2}}{(1-\lambda)^2} - \Sigma_t^{-1}\right].$$

Let $u \in \mathscr{C}_{\mathbb{S}}$ and define

$$Q_{t,u} = \frac{\lambda \bar{r}_t(\mu_t)}{(1-\lambda)^2} \left[\frac{\langle \Sigma_t^{-1/2} u, W_t \rangle^2}{(1-\lambda)^2} - \|u\|_{\Sigma_t^{-1}}^2\right],$$

which is chosen so that $u^\top \hat{s}_t''(\mu_t) u = Y_t Q_{t,u}$. By Proposition 12.14 $\mathbb{E}_{t-1}[\hat{s}_t''(\mu_t)] = s_t''(\mu_t)$. Hence

$$\Delta_{t,u} = Y_t Q_{t,u} - \mathbb{E}_{t-1}[Y_t Q_{t,u}] = u^\top \hat{s}_t''(\mu_t) u - u^\top s_t''(\mu_t) u.$$

By Lemma 12.16, $\bar{r}_t(\mu_t) \leq \exp(1)$ and hence by (B.1) and Propositions B.12 and B.13 and naively simplifying constants,

$$\|Q_{t,u}\|_{t-1,\psi_1} \leq 150\lambda \|u\|_{\Sigma_t^{-1}}^2. \tag{12.17}$$

Therefore, since the variance of a random variable is upper-bounded by its second moment and by Lemma B.8 with $k = 2$,

$$\mathbb{E}_{t-1}[\Delta_{t,u}^2] \leq \mathbb{E}_{t-1}[Y_t^2 Q_{t,u}^2]$$

$$\leq \lambda^2 \left(\delta + L^2 \mathbb{E}_{t-1}[Y_t^2]\right) \|u\|_{\Sigma_t^{-1}}^4$$

$$\leq \text{poly}(1/\delta) \left(1 + \mathbb{E}_{t-1}[Y_t^2]\right),$$

where the final inequality crudely uses the fact that $u \in \mathbb{S}_1^{d-1}$ and the assumption that $\|\Sigma_t^{-1}\| \leq 1/\delta$. A union bound combined with (12.17) and Lemma B.3 and

12.8 Sequential Concentration

Lemma B.8 with $k = 1$ shows that with probability at least $1 - \delta/4$ for all $u \in \mathcal{C}_\mathbb{S}$ and $1 \leq t \leq \tau$,

$$|\Delta_{t,u}| \leq \lambda d(Y_{\max} + \delta) L \|u\|_{\Sigma_t^{-1}}^2 \leq \text{poly}(1/\delta)(1 + Y_{\max}).$$

By Proposition 12.22, with probability at least $1 - \delta/2$, $\max(Y_{\max}, V_\tau) \leq \text{poly}(1/\delta)$. Combining these high-probability bounds and another union bound over $\mathcal{C}_\mathbb{S}$ with Theorem B.20 shows that with probability at least $1 - \delta$ for all $u \in \mathcal{C}_\mathbb{S}$ and any $\Sigma \in \mathcal{S}$,

$$\left|\sum_{t=1}^\tau \Delta_{t,u}\right| \leq \sqrt{dL \sum_{t=1}^\tau \mathbb{E}_{t-1}[\Delta_{t,u}^2]} + dL \max_{1 \leq t \leq \tau} |\Delta_{t,u}|$$

$$\leq \lambda \|u\|_{\Sigma^{-1}}^2 L^2 \left[1 + \sqrt{d \sum_{t=1}^\tau \mathbb{E}_{t-1}[Y_t^2]} + d^2 Y_{\max}\right],$$

where we used the assumption that $\Sigma_t^{-1} \preceq \Sigma^{-1}$ for all $t \leq \tau$. The claim is finished by a Lipschitz argument:

Exercise 12.28 ★ Complete the proof by showing that with high-probability $u \mapsto \Delta_{t,u}$ is suitably Lipschitz and using the properties of the cover $\mathcal{C}$.

□

Remark 12.29 Suppose that $(a_t)_{t=1}^n$ is a sequence such that $a_t \in [0, C]$ almost surely and a_t is $\mathcal{F}_{t-1}$-measurable for all t. Redefine

$$S_\tau = \sum_{t=1}^\tau a_t \hat{s}_t''(\mu_t) \quad \text{and} \quad \bar{S}_\tau = \sum_{t=1}^\tau a_t s_t''(\mu_t).$$

Then Proposition 12.27 continues to hold with essentially the same proof.

Finally, the gradient estimates of the surrogate loss also concentrate.

Proposition 12.30 *Let $\mathcal{S} \subset \mathbb{S}_+^d$ be the (random) set of positive definite matrices such that $\Sigma_t^{-1} \preceq \Sigma^{-1}$ for all $t \leq \tau$. The following hold:*
(1) *Suppose that $x \in K_\tau(1/\sqrt{2L})$ almost surely. Then, for any $u \in \mathbb{R}^d$, with probability at least $1 - \delta$, for any $\Sigma \in \mathcal{S}$,*

$$\left|\sum_{t=1}^\tau \langle \hat{s}_t'(x) - s_t'(x), u\rangle\right| \leq \|u\|_{\Sigma^{-1}} L \left[1 + \sqrt{V_\tau} + Y_{\max}\right].$$

(2) *With probability at least $1 - \delta$ for all $x \in K_\tau(1/\sqrt{2L})$, $u \in \mathbb{R}^d$ and $\Sigma \in \mathcal{S}$,*

$$\left|\sum_{t=1}^\tau \langle \hat{s}_t'(x) - s_t'(x), u\rangle\right| \leq \|u\|_{\Sigma^{-1}} L \left[1 + \sqrt{dV_\tau} + d^2 Y_{\max}\right].$$

Proof Let $u \in \mathbb{R}^d$ and x be such that $x \in K_\tau(1/\sqrt{2L})$ almost surely. By definition,

$$\langle \hat{s}_t(x), u \rangle = \frac{\bar{r}_t(x) Y_t}{1-\lambda} \left\langle u, \Sigma_t^{-1} \left(\frac{X_t - \lambda x}{1-\lambda} - \mu_t \right) \right\rangle.$$

Let $\Delta_t = \langle \hat{s}_t(x), u \rangle - \mathbb{E}_{t-1}[\langle \hat{s}_t(x), u \rangle]$. As usual, we need to bound $\mathbb{E}_{t-1}[\Delta_t^2]$ and $\max_{1 \leq t \leq \tau} |\Delta_t|$. Let

$$Q_t = \frac{\bar{r}_t(x)}{1-\lambda} \left\langle u, \Sigma_t^{-1} \left(\frac{X_t - \lambda x}{1-\lambda} - \mu_t \right) \right\rangle,$$

which is chosen so that $\Delta_t = Y_t Q_t$. By definition $\bar{r}_t(x) \leq \exp(2)$ and therefore

$$\|Q_t\|_{t-1,\psi_2} \leq C \|u\|_{\Sigma_t^{-1}} \left[1 + \lambda \|x - \mu_t\|_{\Sigma_t^{-1}} \right] \leq 2C \|u\|_{\Sigma_t^{-1}}.$$

Hence, by Lemma B.8,

$$\mathbb{E}_{t-1}[\Delta_t^2] \leq \|u\|_{\Sigma_t^{-1}}^2 \left(\delta + \mathbb{E}_{t-1}[Y_t^2] \right) L.$$

Also by Lemma B.8 in combination with Lemma B.3 and a union bound, with probability at least $1 - \delta/2$, for all $t \leq \tau$

$$|\Delta_t| \leq \|u\|_{\Sigma_t^{-1}} (\delta + Y_{\max}) \sqrt{L}.$$

Part (1) now follows from Theorem B.20 and Proposition 12.14. For part (2), combine the above with the covering argument in Proposition 12.23, covering both $K_1(1/\sqrt{2L})$ and $\mathbb{S}_1^{d-1}$. □

Exercise 12.31 ★ Prove Proposition 12.30(2).

12.9 Summary

Let us summarise what has been shown. The surrogate loss function is convex (Lemma 12.3(1)) and optimistic:

$$s(x) \leq f(x) \text{ for all } x \in \mathbb{R}^d. \qquad \text{Lemma 12.3(2)}$$

On the other hand, the surrogate evaluated at μ is relatively close to $f(\mu)$:

$$\mathbb{E}[f(X)] \leq s(\mu) + \frac{2}{\lambda} \operatorname{tr}(s''(\mu)\Sigma) + \frac{2\delta d}{\lambda}. \qquad \text{Proposition 12.10}$$

Furthermore, the quadratic surrogate offers the same benefits on the focus region. Specifically, Corollary 12.11 shows that for any x such that $\lambda \|x - \mu\|_{\Sigma^{-1}} \leq \frac{1}{L}$,

$$\mathbb{E}[f(X)] - f(x) \leq q(\mu) - q(x) + \frac{2}{\lambda} \operatorname{tr}(s''(\mu)\Sigma) + \delta \left[\frac{2d}{\lambda} + \frac{1}{\lambda^2} \right].$$

The effectiveness of the quadratic surrogate arises from the fact that s is nearly quadratic on the focus region. Proposition 12.5 shows that provided $\lambda \|x - y\|_{\Sigma^{-1}} \leq L^{-1/2}$, then $s''(x) \preceq 2s''(y) + \delta\Sigma^{-1}$.

Sequential Concentration

Recall the notation of the sequential setting explained in Section 12.8; particularly, that

$$K_\tau(r) = \left\{x \in K: \max_{t \leq \tau} \lambda \|x - \mu_t\|_{\Sigma_t^{-1}} \leq r\right\}.$$

Remember also that $V_\tau = \sum_{t=1}^\tau \mathbb{E}_{t-1}[Y_t^2]$ and $Y_{\max} = \max_{1 \leq t \leq \tau}(|Y_t| + \mathbb{E}_{t-1}[|Y_t|])$. The following results hold under Assumption 12.21. The surrogate is well-concentrated in the sense that by Proposition 12.23,

(1) for $x \in \mathbb{R}^d$ such that $x \in K_\tau(1/\sqrt{L})$ almost surely, with probability at least $1 - \delta$,

$$\left|\sum_{t=1}^\tau (\hat{s}_t(x) - s_t(x))\right| \geq 1 + \frac{1}{\lambda}\left[\sqrt{LV_\tau} + LY_{\max}\right];$$

(2) with probability at least $1 - \delta$,

$$\sup_{x \in K_\tau(1/\sqrt{2L})} \left|\sum_{t=1}^\tau (\hat{s}_t(x) - s_t(x))\right| \leq 1 + \frac{1}{\lambda}\left[\sqrt{dLV_\tau} + dLY_{\max}\right].$$

Similar results hold for the quadratic surrogate. Precisely, by Proposition 12.24,

(1) given any $x \in \mathbb{R}^d$ such that $x \in K_\tau(1/\sqrt{L})$ almost surely, with probability at least $1 - \delta$,

$$\left|\sum_{t=1}^\tau \hat{q}_t(x) - q_t(x)\right| \leq 1 + \frac{1}{\lambda}\left[\sqrt{V_\tau L} + Y_{\max} L\right];$$

(2) with probability at least $1 - \delta$,

$$\sup_{x \in K_\tau(1/\sqrt{2L})} \left|\sum_{t=1}^\tau \hat{q}_t(x) - q_t(x)\right| \leq 1 + \frac{1}{\lambda}\left[\sqrt{dV_\tau L} + dY_{\max} L\right].$$

The Hessian estimates are also reasonably well-behaved. Recall that $\mathcal{S}$ is the random set of matrices Σ^{-1} such that $\Sigma_t^{-1} \preceq \Sigma^{-1}$ for all $t \leq \tau$. Then, with probability at least $1 - \delta$, for all $\Sigma \in \mathcal{S}$,

$$-\lambda L^2\left[1 + \sqrt{dV_\tau} + d^2 Y_{\max}\right]\Sigma^{-1} \preceq S_\tau - \bar{S}_\tau \preceq \lambda L^2\left[1 + \sqrt{dV_\tau} + d^2 Y_{\max}\right]\Sigma^{-1},$$

where $S_\tau = \sum_{t=1}^\tau \hat{s}_t''(\mu_t)$ and $\bar{S}_\tau = \sum_{t=1}^\tau s_t''(\mu_t)$. Lastly, the gradient estimates concentrate. Let $\mathcal{S}$ be as above. The following hold:

(1) For $x \in \mathbb{R}^d$ with $x \in K_\tau(1/\sqrt{2L})$ almost surely and $u \in \mathbb{R}^d$, with probability at least $1 - \delta$, for any $\Sigma \in \mathcal{S}$,

$$\left| \sum_{t=1}^{\tau} \langle \hat{s}'_t(x) - s'_t(x), u \rangle \right| \le \|u\|_{\Sigma^{-1}} L \left[1 + \sqrt{V_\tau} + Y_{\max} \right].$$

(2) With probability at least $1 - \delta$ for all $x \in K_\tau(1/\sqrt{2L})$ and all $u \in \mathbb{R}^d$ and any $\Sigma \in \mathcal{S}$,

$$\left| \sum_{t=1}^{\tau} \langle \hat{s}'_t(x) - s'_t(x), u \rangle \right| \le \|u\|_{\Sigma^{-1}} L \left[1 + \sqrt{dV_\tau} + d^2 Y_{\max} \right].$$

12.10 Notes

12.i The optimistic surrogate was introduced in a slightly different form by Bubeck et al. (2017) and in the present form by Lattimore and György (2021a). The quadratic approximation was first used by Lattimore and György (2023), who proved most of the results in this chapter or variants thereof.

12.ii The parameter λ determines the amount of smoothing. The change of measure in (12.8) blows up as $\lambda \ge 1/d$. Meanwhile, for $\lambda \in (0, 1/d)$ there are trade-offs:
- A large value of λ increases the power of the lower bound of Proposition 12.10, showing that s is not too far below f.
- A large value of λ decreases the focus region on which the quadratic surrogate is close to the non-quadratic surrogate and where the concentration properties of the estimators are well-behaved.

13
Submodular Minimisation

Let $[d] = \{1, \ldots, d\}$ for some integer d and $\mathscr{P}$ its powerset. A function $f: \mathscr{P} \to [0, 1]$ is submodular if for all $X \subset Y \subset [d]$ and $x \in [d] \setminus Y$,

$$f(X \cup \{x\}) - f(X) \geq f(Y \cup \{x\}) - f(Y).$$

Submodular functions are sometimes viewed as a combinatorial analogue of convexity via a gadget called the Lovász extension that we explain in a moment. In bandit submodular minimisation the adversary secretly chooses a sequence $(f_t)_{t=1}^n: \mathscr{P} \to [0, 1]$ of submodular functions. Then, in each round t, the learner chooses a set $X_t \in \mathscr{P}$ and observes $Y_t = f_t(X_t) + \varepsilon_t$. The optimal set is

$$X_\star = \arg\min_{X \in \mathscr{P}} \sum_{t=1}^n f_t(X)$$

and the regret definition is unchanged. As usual, one can consider the stochastic version of the problem, where $f_t = f$ for some unknown f and all t. The raison d'être of this chapter is to explain how convex bandit algorithms can be used for bandit submodular minimisation. In particular, $\tilde{O}(d^{1.5}\sqrt{n})$ regret is possible in the stochastic setting by combining Algorithm 10.2 with the Lovász extension; and in the adversarial setting Algorithm 11.3 yields a regret bound of $\tilde{O}(d^{2.5}\sqrt{n})$. Besides this we explain how the special structure of bandit submodular minimisation means that the algorithm in Chapter 5 can be improved to have regret $O(dn^{2/3})$ and $O(d^3/\varepsilon^2)$ sample complexity.

Remark 13.1 The classical optimisation problem of finding the minimum of a submodular function $f: \mathscr{P} \to [0, 1]$ is quite interesting and we give some pointers in Note 13.v.

Many problems in economics and operations research have some kind of submodularity based on the principles of diminishing returns or economies of scale. Consider the following toy example. A specialty chocolate manufacturer is considering offering a subset of $[d]$ items on their website. The expected earnings when offering item k is some unknown $p(k)$ and for $X \subset [d]$ let $c(X)$ be the cost of offering subset X. The expected loss (costs minus earnings) when offering X is

$$f(X) = c(X) - \sum_{k \in X} p(k).$$

Thanks to economies of scale one might expect that when $k \notin Y \supset X$ the cost of adding k to Y may be less than adding it to X:

$$c(X \cup \{k\}) - c(X) \geq c(Y \cup \{k\}) - c(Y),$$

which implies that f is submodular. You can find many applications of submodular function minimisation in the survey by McCormick (2005).

13.1 Lovász Extension

Let $f \colon \mathscr{P} \to [0, 1]$ be a submodular function. We can and will identify $\mathscr{P}$ with $\{0, 1\}^d$ in terms of the indicator function, so that $(1, 1, \ldots, 1) \equiv [d]$, $(0, 0, \ldots, 0) \equiv \varnothing$, $(1, 0, 1, 0, 0, \ldots, 0) = \{1, 3\}$ and so on. The Lovász extension is a function $g \colon [0, 1]^d \to [0, 1]$ defined by

$$g(x) = \int_0^1 f(\{i \colon x_i \geq u\}) \, du. \tag{13.1}$$

An illustration of the Lovász extension is shown in Figure 13.1 and its integral representation above is shown in Figure 13.2. There are many ways to represent the Lovász extension. A simple one is given in the following exercise:

Exercise 13.2 ★ Suppose that U is uniformly distributed on $[0, 1]$ and $S = \{i \colon x_i \geq U\}$. Show that $\mathbb{E}[f(S)] = g(x)$.

You should be able to see that if $x \in \{0, 1\}^d$, then $g(x) = f(x)$, where we have abused notation by using the identification between $\{0, 1\}^d$ and $\mathscr{P}$. The following classical theorem is what makes this chapter possible:

Theorem 13.3 *Let g be the Lovász extension of f. The following hold:*
(1) *g is convex;*
(2) *g is piecewise linear; and*
(3) *g is minimised on a vertex of the hypercube.*

Proof A sequence $S_1, \ldots, S_m \in \mathscr{P}$ is a chain if $S_1 \subsetneq S_2 \subsetneq \cdots \subsetneq S_m$.

13.1 Lovász Extension

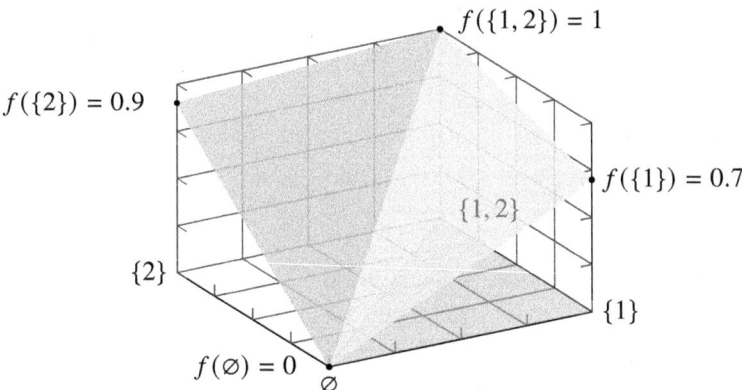

Figure 13.1 The Lovász extension for the submodular function defined by $f(\emptyset) = 0, f(\{1\}) = 0.7, f(\{2\}) = 0.9, f(\{1,2\}) = 1$. The Lovász extension is piecewise linear with each piece corresponding to a permutation σ of $[d]$. The piece associated with permutation σ is the simplex spanned by the sets $\emptyset, \{\sigma(1)\}, \{\sigma(1), \sigma(2)\}, \cdots, \{\sigma(1), \cdots, \sigma(d)\}$ where a set is associated with a corner of the binary hypercube by its indicator function. In the figure $d = 2$ so there are only $d! = 2$ pieces.

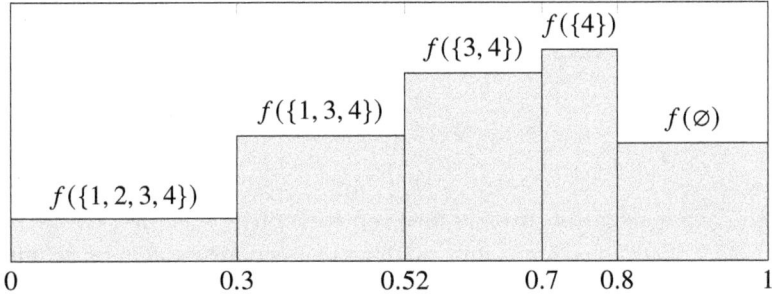

Figure 13.2 An example of the integral computation in (13.1) with $d = 4$, unspecified f and $x = [0.52, 0.3, 0.7, 0.8]$; $g(x)$ is the area in grey.

Remember that we identify $U \in \mathscr{P}$ with an element in $\{0,1\}^d \subset [0,1]^d$. The convex closure of f is the function

$$h(x) = \min\left(\sum_{U \in \mathscr{P}} p(U)f(U) : \sum_{U \in \mathscr{P}} p(U)U = x, p \in \Delta(\mathscr{P})\right),$$

which is convex by the theory of linear programming (Bertsimas and Tsitsiklis,

1997, §5.2). Suppose that f is submodular. We will show that $g = h$. Define $\phi(p) = \sum_{U \in \mathscr{P}} p(U)|U|^2$ and let $x \in [0,1]^d$ be fixed. By compactness, there exists a $p \in \Delta(\mathscr{P})$ such that

$$h(x) = \sum_{U \in \mathscr{P}} p(U)f(U) \quad \text{and} \quad x = \sum_{U \in \mathscr{P}} p(U)U.$$

In case of ties, let p maximise ϕ. Suppose that $\{S: p(S) > 0\}$ is not a chain; that is, there exist $S, T \in \mathscr{P}$ with $p(S) \geq p(T) > 0$ and $S \not\subset T$ and $T \not\subset S$. Consider $q = p - p(T)\mathbf{1}_T - p(T)\mathbf{1}_S + p(T)\mathbf{1}_{S \cap T} + p(T)\mathbf{1}_{S \cup T}$. Without any assumptions, $\sum_{U \in \mathscr{P}} q(U)U = x$ and by submodularity, $f(S \cup T) + f(S \cap T) \leq f(S) + f(T)$, which implies that $\sum_{U \in \mathscr{P}} q(U)f(U) \leq \sum_{U \in \mathscr{P}} p(U)f(U)$. Furthermore,

$$|S \cup T|^2 + |S \cap T|^2 = |S|^2 + |T|^2 + 2|T \setminus S||S \setminus T| > |S|^2 + |T|^2.$$

But from this it follows that $\phi(q) > \phi(p)$, contradicting our assumption that p maximises ϕ. Therefore $\{S: p(S) > 0\}$ is a chain and $\sum_{S \in \mathscr{P}} p(S)S = x$. We leave you to prove that there is a unique chain satisfying these properties and to conclude from (13.1) that $h(x) = g(x)$. Part (2) follows since h is piecewise linear (Bertsimas and Tsitsiklis, 1997, §5.2). Part (3) is immediate since g is an average of f-values and the minimum is never larger than the average. □

Exercise 13.4 ★ Finish the proof of Theorem 13.3(1) as instructed above.

The Lovász extension also has nice computational properties. Given exact access to f you can compute it by noticing that the integrand in its definition is piecewise linear with at most $d + 1$ pieces. You only need to evaluate f at $d + 1$ different sets, all of which are easily found by sorting the coordinates of x. Given $x \in [0,1]^d$ let $\sigma(\cdot|x): [d] \to [d]$ be a permutation such that $k \mapsto x_{\sigma(k|x)}$ is non-increasing with ties broken arbitrarily. We adopt the convention that $\sigma(0|x) = 0$, $\sigma(d+1|x) = d+1$, $x_0 = 1$ and $x_{d+1} = 0$. Let $S(k|x) = \{\sigma(i|x): i \in [k]\}$, which means that

$$\varnothing = S(0|x) \subset S(1|x) \subset \cdots \subset S(d|x) = [d].$$

When all coordinates of x are distinct, then $S(k|x)$ contains exactly the coordinates associated with the k largest entries of x. Then, with g the Lovász

13.1 Lovász Extension

extension of submodular function f,

$$g(x) = \int_0^1 f(\{i : x_i \geq u\}) \, du$$

$$= \sum_{k=0}^{d} f(S(k|x)) \left(x_{\sigma(k|x)} - x_{\sigma(k+1|x)}\right)$$

$$= f(S(0|x)) + \sum_{k=1}^{d} x_{\sigma(k|x)} \left(f(S(k|x)) - f(S(k-1|x))\right).$$

There is also a nice expression for the subgradients of the Lovász extension. Staring at the above equality yields the following standard proposition:

Proposition 13.5 *Let g be the Lovász extension of a submodular function f, $x \in [0, 1]^d$ and $\sigma^{-1}(\cdot|x)$ be the inverse of the permutation $\sigma(\cdot|x)$. Then the vector $u \in \mathbb{R}^d$ with*

$$u_k = f(S(\sigma^{-1}(k|x)|x)) - f(S(\sigma^{-1}(k|x) - 1|x))$$

is a subgradient of g at x.

Exercise 13.6 ★ Prove Proposition 13.5.

You may wonder what properties the Lovász extension has. For example, is it smooth, strongly convex or Lipschitz? A look at the definition reveals that it is piecewise linear and hence it cannot be strongly convex and is only smooth in the special case that it is linear. It is 2-Lipschitz, however:

Proposition 13.7 (Lemma 1, Jegelka and Bilmes 2011) *The Lovász extension g of a submodular function $f : \mathscr{P} \to [0, 1]$ satisfies $\mathrm{lip}(g) \leq 2$.*

Proof By Theorem 13.3, g is convex and piecewise linear so that $\mathrm{lip}(g) \leq \sup_x \|g'(x)\|$ where the supremum is over all x where g is differentiable. Let $x \in (0, 1)^d$ be any point where g is differentiable and abbreviate $S(k) = S(k|x)$ and $\sigma(k) = \sigma(k|x)$. By Proposition 13.5,

$$g'_k(x) = f(S(\sigma^{-1}(k))) - f(S(\sigma^{-1}(k) - 1)).$$

Let $P = \{k : g'_k(x) > 0\}$; then

$$\|g'(x)\| \leq \|g'(x)\|_1 = \sum_{k \in P} g'_k(x) - \sum_{k \in [d] \setminus P} g'_k(x)$$

$$= 2 \sum_{k \in P} g'_k(x) - \sum_{k \in [d]} g'_k(x). \quad (13.2)$$

The last term telescopes:

$$-\sum_{k\in[d]} g'_k(x) = f(\varnothing) - f([d]). \tag{13.3}$$

For the other term in (13.2), reorder the terms in the sum so that

$$2\sum_{k\in P} g'_k(x) = 2\sum_{m=1}^{|P|}(f(S(\pi(m))) - f(S(\pi(m)-1))),$$

where $m \mapsto |S(\pi(m))|$ is increasing. This sum does not obviously telescope. Let us now make use of submodularity. Let $a_m = S(\pi(m)) \setminus S(\pi(m)-1)$ and $A_m = \{a_1, \ldots, a_m\}$. Since $\varnothing \subset S(1) \subset \cdots \subset S(d) = [d]$ is a chain, we have $A_m \subset S(\pi(m))$ and therefore by submodularity,

$$f(A_m) - f(A_{m-1}) \geq f(S(\pi(m))) - f(S(\pi(m)-1)).$$

Therefore

$$2\sum_{m=1}^{|P|}(f(S(\pi(m))) - f(S(\pi(m)-1))) \leq 2\sum_{m=1}^{|P|}(f(A_m) - f(A_{m-1})) \tag{13.4}$$

$$= 2f(A_{|P|}) - 2f(\varnothing). \tag{13.5}$$

Combining (13.3) and (13.5) with (13.2) shows that

$$\|g'(x)\| \leq 2f(A_{|P|}) - f(\varnothing) - f([d]) \leq 2. \qquad \square$$

13.2 Bandit Submodular Minimisation

We now explain how to use the Lovász extension as a bridge between bandit convex optimisation on the hypercube and bandit submodular minimisation. Let g_t be the Lovász extension of f_t and $K = [0,1]^d$ the hypercube.

Exercise 13.8 ★ Show that $f = \sum_{t=1}^n f_t$ is submodular and the Lovász extension f is $\sum_{t=1}^n g_t$.

Your solution to Exercise 13.8 combined with Theorem 13.3(3) shows that $\sum_{t=1}^n g_t$ is minimised at some $x_\star \in \{0,1\}^d$. Consider a bandit convex optimisation algorithm playing on K and let $(X_t^K)_{t=1}^n$ be actions in K proposed by the bandit algorithms. We need a way to select the real actions $X_t \subset [d]$ and return losses to the algorithm. This is done by sampling λ_t uniformly from $[0,1]$ and letting $X_t = \{i : (X_t^K)_i \geq \lambda_t\}$. Then the loss is $Y_t = f_t(X_t) + \varepsilon_t$. By Exercise 13.2, $\mathbb{E}_{t-1}[Y_t] = g_t(X_t^K)$ so this procedure is equivalent to the learner interacting with the Lovász extension sequence. The following proposition shows that the regret of iterates (X_t^K) with respect to the Lovász extension implies a regret bound for the original bandit submodular optimisation problem.

Proposition 13.9 *Let* $(X_t^K)_{t=1}^n \in K$ *and let* $(X_t)_{t=1}^n$ *and* $(Y_t)_{t=1}^n$ *be defined as above. Then, with probability at least* $1 - \delta$,

$$\text{Reg}_n \triangleq \sum_{t=1}^n (f_t(X_t) - f_t(X_\star)) \leq \text{gReg}_n + \sqrt{2n \log(1/\delta)},$$

where $\text{gReg}_n = \sum_{t=1}^n \left(g_t(X_t^K) - g_t(x_\star)\right)$.

Proof As we argued above, $\sum_{t=1}^n g_t(x_\star) = \sum_{t=1}^n f_t(X_\star)$. Then

$$\text{gReg}_n = \sum_{t=1}^n \left(g_t(X_t^K) - g_t(x_\star)\right)$$

$$= \sum_{t=1}^n \left(g_t(X_t^K) - f_t(X_\star)\right)$$

$$= \sum_{t=1}^n (f_t(X_t) - f_t(X_\star)) + \sum_{t=1}^n \left(g_t(X_t^K) - f_t(X_t)\right)$$

$$= \text{Reg}_n + \sum_{t=1}^n \left(g_t(X_t^K) - f_t(X_t)\right).$$

By definition,

$$g_t(X_t^K) = \mathbb{E}_{t-1}[f_t(X_t)|X_t^K].$$

Therefore the sum is a martingale with increments bounded in $[-1, 1]$ and by Azuma's inequality (Theorem B.19), with probability at least $1 - \delta$,

$$\text{Reg}_n \leq \text{gReg}_n + \sqrt{2n \log(1/\delta)}. \qquad \square$$

Consequently, any algorithm for bandit convex optimisation can be used for submodular minimisation with very little overhead. When looking at the complete list of algorithms in Section 2.5, remember that for the hypercube we have $\text{diam}(K) = \sqrt{d}$ and the self-concordance parameter is $\vartheta = \Theta(d)$. Moreover, except for scaling K is already in Löwner's position. The special structure of the Lovász extension allows for at least one new idea, which we explain in Section 13.3. Table 13.1 more or less summarises the state of the art in bandit submodular optimisation.

AUTHOR	REGRET/COMP	COMPUTE	NOTES
Hazan and Kale (2012)	$dn^{2/3}$	$O(d \log d)$	–
Fokkema et al. (2024)	$d^{1.5}\sqrt{n}$	$O(d^2) + \Pi + $ SVD	stochastic only
Fokkema et al. (2024)	$d^{2.5}\sqrt{n}$	$\text{poly}(d, n)$	–
This book	$\frac{d^3}{\varepsilon^2}$	$O(d \log(d))$	stochastic only

Table 13.1 Regret bounds for various algorithms for bandit submodular minimisation

13.3 Gradient Descent for Submodular Minimisation

By applying the algorithm in Chapter 5 you can immediately obtain a regret of $\mathbb{E}[\text{Reg}_n] = O(d^{3/4}n^{3/4})$. It is instructive to revisit gradient descent for submodular minimisation via the Lovász extension because the special structure of the problem leads to a significant improvement with almost no additional work. At the same time, in Chapter 2 we promised to explain the phenomenon noted by Shamir (2013) that for quadratic bandits the simple regret is $\Theta(d^2/n)$ while the cumulative regret is $\Omega(d\sqrt{n})$. This curious situation is a consequence of two factors:

○ in the simple regret setting the learner can afford to play actions far from the minimiser $x_\star$; and
○ in many parametric settings these actions can be far more informative than playing actions close to $x_\star$ because they allow the learner to reduce variance.

This situation arises in submodular bandits, for which a very simple algorithm has $\text{sReg}_n = O(d^{1.5}/\sqrt{n})$ simple regret, while the algorithms with $\text{Reg}_n = O(d^{1.5}\sqrt{n})$ are all sophisticated second-order methods. The idea is to play gradient descent on the Lovász extension and estimate the gradient by sampling from a subset of corners of the hypercube. The cumulative regret incurred with this approach is linear but the variance of the gradient estimate is small, which leads to small simple regret.

Gradient Descent

Algorithm 13.1 plays gradient descent on the Lovász extension to produce a sequence of iterates $(x_t)_{t=1}^n$ but replaces the spherical smoothing using in Algorithm 5.2 with another mechanism for estimating the gradient. With probability $\gamma \in (0, 1)$ the algorithm explores and otherwise it exploits:

13.3 Gradient Descent for Submodular Minimisation

- When exploring, the algorithm samples k_t uniformly on $\{0, 1, \ldots, d\}$ and plays $S_t = S(k_t|x_t)$. The result can be used to estimate an element of $\partial g_t(x_t)$ using importance-weighting and Proposition 13.5.
- When exploiting, the algorithm samples λ_t uniformly from $[0, 1]$ and plays $\{k : (x_t)_k \geq \lambda_t\}$, which in expectation leads to a loss of $g_t(x_t)$.

When minimising the simple regret we choose $\gamma = 1$ so that the algorithm always explores. Otherwise γ is tuned to balance exploration and exploitation.

---

1 **args**: $\eta > 0$, $\gamma \in (0, 1)$
2 let $x_1 \in [0, 1]^d$
3 **for** $t = 1$ **to** n
4 sample λ_t from $\mathscr{U}([0, 1])$ and let $S_t = \{k : (x_t)_k \geq \lambda_t\}$
5 sample k_t uniformly from $\{0, 1, \ldots, d\}$
6 let $E_t = \begin{cases} 1 & \text{with prob. } \gamma \\ 0 & \text{with prob. } 1 - \gamma \end{cases}$ and $X_t = \begin{cases} S(k_t|x_t) & \text{if } E_t = 1 \\ S_t & \text{if } E_t = 0 \end{cases}$
7 observe $Y_t = f(X_t) + \varepsilon_t$
8 let $\hat{v}_t = \frac{(d+1)Y_t E_t}{\gamma} \left[\mathbf{1}(k_t \neq 0) e_{\sigma(k_t|x_t)} - \mathbf{1}(k_t \neq d) e_{\sigma(k_t+1|x_t)} \right]$
9 update $x_{t+1} = \arg\min_{x \in [0,1]^d} \|x - [x_t - \eta \hat{v}_t]\|$
10 let $\widehat{X}_n = \frac{1}{n} \sum_{t=1}^n x_t$
11 sample U from $\mathscr{U}([0, 1])$
12 **return** $\widehat{S}_n = \{k : (\widehat{X}_n)_k \geq U\}$

Algorithm 13.1 Gradient descent for bandit submodular simple regret minimisation

Theorem 13.10 *The following hold for Algorithm 13.1:*
(1) *Suppose that* $\gamma = (1 + d)n^{-1/3}$ *and* $\eta = \frac{1}{2}n^{-2/3}$. *Then the cumulative regret in the adversarial setting is bounded by*

$$\mathbb{E}[\mathrm{Reg}_n] \leq 3(d + 1)n^{2/3} = O(dn^{2/3}).$$

(2) *Suppose that* $\gamma = 1$ *and* $\eta = \frac{1}{2+2d}\sqrt{\frac{d}{n}}$. *Then in the stochastic setting the simple regret of Algorithm 13.1 is bounded by*

$$\mathbb{E}\left[\mathrm{sReg}_n\right] \leq 2(1 + d)\sqrt{\frac{d}{n}} = O\left(\frac{d^{1.5}}{\sqrt{n}}\right).$$

Proof Since $\mathrm{Reg}_n \leq n$ for any algorithm, we assume for the remainder that

$\gamma \in (0, 1]$ since otherwise the claimed regret bound in Part (1) holds for any algorithm. Let g_t be the Lovász extension of f_t and $v_t \in \partial g_t(x_t)$ be the subgradient defined in Proposition 13.5.

Exercise 13.11 ★ Show that $\mathbb{E}_{t-1}[\hat{v}_t] = v_t$.

We are now in a position to bound the regret of the iterates:

$$\mathbb{E}\left[\sum_{t=1}^{n}(g_t(x_t) - g_t(x_\star))\right] \stackrel{(a)}{\leq} \mathbb{E}\left[\sum_{t=1}^{n} \langle v_t, x_t - x_\star \rangle\right]$$

$$\stackrel{(b)}{\leq} \frac{\operatorname{diam}(K)^2}{2\eta} + \frac{\eta}{2}\sum_{t=1}^{n}\mathbb{E}\left[\|\hat{v}_t\|^2\right]$$

$$\stackrel{(c)}{=} \frac{d}{2\eta} + \frac{\eta}{2}\sum_{t=1}^{n}\mathbb{E}\left[\|\hat{v}_t\|^2\right]$$

$$\stackrel{(d)}{\leq} \frac{d}{2\eta} + \frac{2\eta n(d+1)^2}{\gamma}, \tag{13.6}$$

where (a) follows from convexity of g_t, (b) by Exercise 13.11 and Theorem 5.2 and (c) since $\operatorname{diam}(K) = \sqrt{d}$. (d) follows because

$$\mathbb{E}\left[\|\hat{v}_t\|^2\right] \leq 2\mathbb{E}\left[E_t\left(\frac{(d+1)Y_t}{\gamma}\right)^2\right] \leq 4\mathbb{E}\left[E_t\left(\frac{d+1}{\gamma}\right)^2\right] \leq \frac{4(d+1)^2}{\gamma},$$

where we used (1.3) and the assumption that f_t is bounded in $[0, 1]$ to bound $\mathbb{E}_{t-1}[Y_t^2|E_t] = \mathbb{E}_{t-1}[(f_t(X_t) + \varepsilon_t)^2|E_t] \leq 2$. By definition the regret satisfies

$$\mathbb{E}[\operatorname{Reg}_n] = \mathbb{E}\left[\sum_{t=1}^{n} f_t(X_t) - f_t(x_\star)\right]$$

$$= \mathbb{E}\left[\sum_{t=1}^{n} f_t(X_t) - g_t(x_t)\right] + \mathbb{E}\left[\sum_{t=1}^{n} g_t(x_t) - g_t(x_\star)\right]$$

$$\leq n\gamma + \frac{d}{2\eta} + \frac{2\eta n(d+1)^2}{\gamma},$$

where in the final inequality we used the fact that

$$\mathbb{E}_{t-1}[f_t(X_t)] = \mathbb{E}_{t-1}[E_t f_t(X_t)] + \mathbb{E}_{t-1}[(1 - E_t)f_t(X_t)]$$
$$= \mathbb{E}_{t-1}[E_t f_t(X_t)] + \mathbb{E}_{t-1}[(1 - E_t)f_t(S_t)]$$
$$= \mathbb{E}_{t-1}[E_t f_t(X_t)] + (1 - \gamma)g_t(x_t)$$
$$\leq \gamma + g_t(x_t).$$

The bound on the adversarial regret now follows by substituting the definition

13.4 Notes

of the parameters. To bound the simple regret in the stochastic setting where $f_t = f$ and $g = g_t$ is the Lovász extension of f, by substituting the parameters into (13.6),

$$\mathbb{E}\left[\sum_{t=1}^n (g(x_t) - g(x_\star))\right] \leq 2(d+1)\sqrt{dn}. \tag{13.7}$$

Then, using the definitions at the end of the algorithm and convexity of the Lovász extension,

$$\mathbb{E}\left[f(\widehat{S}_n)\right] \stackrel{\text{Ex. 13.2}}{=} \mathbb{E}\left[g(\widehat{X}_n)\right] \stackrel{g \text{ cvx}}{\leq} \mathbb{E}\left[\frac{1}{n}\sum_{t=1}^n g(x_t)\right] \stackrel{\text{by (13.7)}}{\leq} g(x_\star) + 2(d+1)\sqrt{\frac{d}{n}}.$$

Since $g(x_\star) = f(X_\star)$ it follows that

$$\mathbb{E}[\text{sReg}_n] \leq 2(d+1)\sqrt{\frac{d}{n}}. \qquad \square$$

So what has been achieved? Algorithm 13.1 is computationally practical and has excellent simple regret when $\gamma = 1$. On the other hand, the dependence of its regret on n is suboptimal, though in some regimes it is theoretically superior to Algorithm 11.3 in the adversarial setting and its analysis and implementation are much simpler than Algorithm 10.2 in the stochastic setting.

13.4 Notes

13.i There are many resources for studying submodular functions and optimisation; for example, the book by Bach (2013) or the wonderful short survey by Bilmes (2022).

13.ii Algorithm 13.1 is due to Hazan and Kale (2012), though the elementary simple regret analysis is new.

13.iii Bandit submodular *maximisation* is another topic altogether and has its own rich literature (Gabillon et al., 2013; Zhang et al., 2019; Foster and Rakhlin, 2021; Chen et al., 2017; Takemori et al., 2020; Tajdini et al., 2024; Niazadeh et al., 2021). Even in the classical optimisation setting without noise, exact submodular maximisation is computationally intractable. Approximately maximising submodular functions is often possible, however, at least provided the constraints are reasonably well behaved. Because of this the standard approach in bandit submodular maximisation is to prove that

$$\sum_{t=1}^n f_t(X_t) \geq \alpha \max_{X \in \mathscr{C}} \sum_{t=1}^n f_t(X) + o(n),$$

where $\alpha \in (0, 1)$ is the approximation ratio, which depends on the constraints $\mathscr{C}$ and assumptions on the functions (f_t). For example, when the functions (f_t) are assumed to be submodular and monotone and $\mathscr{C} = \{X \subset [d]: |X| \leq k\}$, then Niazadeh et al. (2021) design an efficient algorithm such that

$$\left(1 - \frac{1}{e}\right) \max_{X \in \mathscr{C}} \sum_{t=1}^{n} f_t(X) - \mathbb{E}\left[\sum_{t=1}^{n} f_t(X_t)\right] = \tilde{O}(kd^{2/3}n^{2/3}).$$

In the stochastic setting the regret can be improved to $\tilde{O}(kd^{1/3}n^{2/3})$, which is essentially the best achievable (Tajdini et al., 2024).

13.iv The Lovász extension is due to Lovász (1983) and provides the interface between submodular bandits and convex bandits but introduces additional noise. This is one justification for ensuring your algorithm can handle additional noise, even in the adversarial setting.

13.v The complexity of minimising a submodular functions f without noise is still an active area of research. Let g be the Lovász extension of f and $f_\star = \min_{x \in \{0,1\}^d} g(x)$. By Proposition 13.5 a subgradient of g can be computed with $O(d)$ queries to the f. Combining this with cutting plane methods (Bach, 2013; Bubeck, 2015) shows that with $O(d^2 \log(d/\varepsilon))$ queries to f one can find an $\widehat{x} \in [0, 1]^d$ such that $g(\widehat{x}) \leq f_\star + \varepsilon$. Then let

$$\widehat{S} = \arg\min\{S(k|\widehat{x}): 0 \leq k \leq d\},$$

which can be evaluated with another $O(d)$ queries to the loss function f and satisfies $f(\widehat{S}) \leq f_\star + \varepsilon$. The discrete structure of submodular optimisation means you can even achieve exact minimisation (Jiang, 2022).

14
Outlook

The tool-chest for convex bandits and zeroth-order optimisation has been steadily growing in recent decades. Nevertheless, there are many intriguing open questions, both theoretical and practical. The purpose of this short chapter is to highlight some of the most important (in the author's view, of course) open problems.

14.i The most fundamental problem is to understand the minimax regret for $\mathscr{F}_b$. The lower bound is $\Omega(d\sqrt{n})$ and the upper bound is $\tilde{O}(d^{1.5}\sqrt{n})$ in the stochastic setting and $\tilde{O}(d^{2.5}\sqrt{n})$ in the adversarial setting.

14.ii From a practical perspective the situation is still relatively dire for $d > 1$. The algorithms that are simple and efficient to implement have slow convergence rates without smoothness and strong convexity. Algorithms with fast convergence rates have awkward assumptions. For example, online Newton step learns fast for $\mathscr{F}_b^s$ and is difficult to tune. Is there a simple algorithm that works well in practice without too much tuning and obtains the fast rate?

14.iii Algorithms that manage $\tilde{O}(\text{poly}(d)\sqrt{n})$ regret without smoothness and strong convexity all estimate some kind of curvature or use continuous exponential weights. In particular, they use $\Omega(d^2)$ memory. Can you prove this is necessary?

14.iv In the stochastic setting both the range of the loss function and the Orlicz norm (or maybe variance) of the noise should appear in the regret. This is hidden throughout because in most places we (questionably) opted to fix the range to $[0, 1]$ and the Orlicz norm of the noise to 1. If you repeat the analysis naively for most settings you will find that for losses bounded in $[0, B]$ and Orlicz norm bound of σ, the leading term in the regret is $B + \sigma$. For example, for online Newton step with K in Löwner's position we would have a regret of $\tilde{O}((B+\sigma)d^{1.5}\sqrt{n})$. Really, however, the range of the losses should appear in a lower-order term, since over time an algorithm with sublinear regret will play in a region where the range of the losses is small (otherwise it would have high regret). Handling this properly in the analysis is probably quite complicated and maybe not fundamentally that interesting. But it could lead to practical improvements in many cases. Note, we did things properly in Chapter 4 where the loss was not assumed to be bounded and also in Section 6.6. The techniques developed there may be adaptable to other algorithms, including cutting plane methods and online Newton step.

14.v More adaptive algorithms are needed. We have seen a plethora of results for this algorithm or that with such-and-such assumptions. But what if you don't know what class the losses lie in. Can you adapt? What is the price? Very few works consider this or have serious limitations. A good place to start is the paper by Luo et al. (2022). We have also assumed that n is known upfront and used this to tune learning rates or other parameters. You can always use a doubling trick (Besson and Kaufmann, 2018), but generally speaking you would expect better practical performance by using a decaying learning rate. We would not expect to encounter too many challenges implementing this idea, but the devil may be in the details. For example, the set K_ε usually depends on n via ε in many algorithms. And in the analysis of online Newton step the definition of the extended loss would become time-dependent.

14.vi There is scope to refine the algorithms and analysis in this text to the non-convex case; of course, proving bounds relative to a stationary point rather than a global minimum. Someone should push this program through. Alternatively, one may still focus on finding the global minimum but with weaker assumptions such as quasi-convexity or losses that satisfy the Polyak–Lojasiewicz condition (Polyak, 1963; Karimi et al., 2016; Akhavan et al., 2024b). Note that these function classes are not closed under addition and hence are not amenable to the adversarial setting.

14.vii Almost all of the properties we proved for the optimistic surrogate relied on Gaussianity of the exploration distribution. Two properties that do not rely on this, however, are optimism and convexity. This leaves hope that something may be possible using an exponential weights distribution rather than a Gaussian and this may interact better with the geometry of the constraint set. This seems to have been the original plan of Bubeck et al. (2017) before they resorted to approximating exponential weights distributions by Gaussians. Perhaps you can make it work.

14.viii Suggala et al. (2021) and Bubeck et al. (2017) both handle adversarial problems by some sort of test to see if the adversary is moving the minimum

14 Outlook

and proving that if this occurs, then the regret must be negative and it is safe to restart the algorithm. One might wonder if there is some black-box procedure to implement this program so that any algorithm designed for the stochastic setting can be used in the adversarial setting.

14.ix It would be fascinating to gain a better understanding of Algorithm 8.3. What loss estimators does it use? Maybe you can somehow implement this algorithm when $d = 1$ or derive analytically what the estimators look like for special cases.

14.x There is potential to unify the algorithms and analysis from stochastic approximation and bandit convex optimisation. The former are generally focused on precise asymptotics while the latter concentrate on minimax finite-time regret. At the moment there is very little integration between these fields, even though many of the ideas are the same.

14.xi You could spend a huge amount of time generalising the conditions on the noise; for example, to heavy-tailed distributions. This has been widely explored in the multi-armed bandit setting (Bubeck et al., 2013, and citations to/from). Probably this should only be done if you have a particular application in mind. Alternatively, you could investigate heteroscedastic or multiplicative noise, with an initial foray by Jingxin et al. (2025).

14.xii When $d = 1$ the best bound on the cumulative regret for losses in $\mathscr{F}_b$ is $O(\sqrt{n}\log(n))$ while the lower bound is $\Omega(\sqrt{n})$. Maybe this setting is the best place to start trying to understand whether or not the logarithmic factors are necessary.

14.xiii This entire book is about bandit convex optimisation on subsets of euclidean space. Convexity and the convex bandit problem can be generalised to Riemannian manifolds. Ao et al. (2025) start this program by constructing the Riemannian analogue of Algorithm 6.2 and proving that under appropriate smoothness conditions its regret is $O(n^{2/3})$. The extent to which other algorithms and analyses in this book can be generalised to the non-euclidean setting is probably quite a fascinating question.

Appendix A
Miscellaneous

A.1 Identities

Proposition A.1 (§4.9.1.4, Zwillinger 2018) *Let $\Gamma(\cdot)$ be Euler's gamma function. Then:*
(1) $\operatorname{vol}(\mathbb{B}_r^d) = \frac{r^d \pi^{d/2}}{\Gamma(\frac{d}{2}+1)}$.
(2) $\operatorname{vol}(\mathbb{S}_r^{d-1}) = \frac{d}{r}\operatorname{vol}(\mathbb{B}_r^d)$.

The next proposition is the standard formula for integration in spherical coordinates, which follows from the co-area formula (Evans, 2018, Appendix C) or by direct proof.

Proposition A.2 *Suppose that $f\colon \mathbb{R}^d \to \mathbb{R}$ satisfies $f(x) = g(\|x\|)$ for some $g\colon \mathbb{R}^d \to \mathbb{R}$. Then, as long as either the left-hand or right-hand side below is well-defined,*

$$\int_{\mathbb{B}_r^d} f(x)\,dx = d\operatorname{vol}(\mathbb{B}_1^d) \int_0^r s^{d-1} g(s)\,ds\,.$$

Proposition A.3 *Suppose that W has law $\mathcal{N}(0, \Sigma)$. Then:*
(1) $\mathbb{E}[\|W\|^2] = \operatorname{tr}(\Sigma)$.
(2) $\mathbb{E}[\|W\|^4] = \operatorname{tr}(\Sigma)^2 + 2\operatorname{tr}(\Sigma^2)$.
(3) $\mathbb{E}[\exp(\langle W, a\rangle)] = \exp\left(\frac{1}{2}\|a\|_\Sigma^2\right)$.

Proof Let Z have law $\mathcal{N}(0, \mathbb{1})$. Then W and $\Sigma^{1/2}Z$ have the same law. Therefore $\mathbb{E}[\|W\|^2] = \mathbb{E}[\|\Sigma^{1/2}Z\|^2] = \mathbb{E}[Z^\top \Sigma Z] = \mathbb{E}[\operatorname{tr}(ZZ^\top \Sigma)] = \operatorname{tr}(\Sigma)$. For the second part, since the euclidean norm is rotationally invariant we can assume without loss of generality that Σ is diagonal. Then write $\|W\|^2$ as a sum, expand the square $\mathbb{E}[\|W\|^4] = \mathbb{E}[\|W\|^2 \|W\|^2]$ and use the fact that $\mathbb{E}[Z_k^4] = 3$. Finally, note that $X = \langle W, a\rangle$ has law $\mathcal{N}(0, \|a\|_\Sigma^2)$, which has moment-generating function $M_X(\lambda) \triangleq \mathbb{E}[\exp(\lambda X)] = \exp(\lambda^2 \|a\|_\Sigma^2 / 2)$; the result follows by substituting $\lambda = 1$. □

Proposition A.4 *Suppose that X has law $\mathscr{U}(\mathbb{B}_1^d)$. Then $\mathbb{E}[\|X\|] = \frac{d}{d+1}$.*

Proof By Proposition A.2,

$$\mathbb{E}[\|X\|] = \frac{1}{\text{vol}(\mathbb{B}_1^d)} \int_{\mathbb{B}_1^d} \|x\| \, dx = d \int_0^1 r^d \, dr = \frac{d}{d+1}.$$ □

A.2 Moore–Penrose Pseudoinverse

Given a matrix $A \in \mathbb{R}^{m \times n}$, the Moore–Penrose pseudoinverse is a matrix $A^+ \in \mathbb{R}^{n \times m}$ such that all of the following hold:
(1) $AA^+A = A$.
(2) $A^+AA^+ = A^+$.
(3) $(AA^+)^\top = AA^+$.
(4) $(A^+A)^\top = A^+A$.

Proposition A.5 *The Moore–Penrose pseudoinverse of any $A \in \mathbb{R}^{m \times n}$ exists and is unique.*

Proof Let $A = UDV^\top$ be the singular value decomposition of A, which means that D is diagonal and U and V have orthonormal columns. A straightforward calculation shows that if D has diagonal $\lambda_1, \ldots, \lambda_k$, then D^+ is the diagonal matrix with diagonal $\rho_1, \ldots, \rho_k$ and $\rho_i = 1/\lambda_i$ for $\lambda_i \neq 0$ and 0 otherwise. Then $A^+ = VD^+U^\top$ straightforwardly satisfies the conditions of being a pseudoinverse. For uniqueness, let B and C be two matrices satisfying the conditions. Then

$$AB = ACAB = (AC)^\top (AB)^\top = C^\top A^\top B^\top A^\top = C^\top (ABA)^\top = C^\top A^\top = AC.$$

Similarly, $BA = CA$. Therefore $B = BAB = BAC = CAC = C$. □

Fact A.6 *Suppose that $A \in \mathbb{R}^{m \times n}$ is a matrix and $y \in \text{im}(A^\top)$ and $\theta \in \mathbb{R}^n$. Then $\langle y, A^+A\theta \rangle = \langle y, \theta \rangle$.*

Proof By assumption there exists a w such that $y = A^\top w$ and so $\langle y, A^+A\theta \rangle = \langle A^\top w, A^+A\theta \rangle = \langle w, AA^+A\theta \rangle = \langle w, A\theta \rangle = \langle A^\top w, \theta \rangle = \langle y, \theta \rangle$. □

Fact A.7 *Suppose that A, B are positive semidefinite and $A \succeq B$. Then $A^+ \preceq B^+$ if and only if $\ker(A) = \ker(B)$.*

Fact A.8 *Suppose that $A \in \mathbb{R}^{m \times n}$. Then $\text{tr}(AA^+) = \text{tr}(A^+A) = \text{rank}(A)$.*

Proof Let $A = UDV^\top$ be the singular value decomposition of A so that U and V have orthonormal columns and D is diagonal with $\text{rank}(A)$ nonzero entries. Then

$$\text{tr}(AA^+) = \text{tr}(UDD^+U^\top) = \text{tr}(DD^+) = \text{rank}(A).$$

Moreover, $\text{tr}(A^+A) = \text{tr}(D^+D) = \text{tr}(DD^+) = \text{rank}(A)$. □

A.3 Technical Inequalities

Lemma A.9 *Suppose that A is positive definite and $A \preceq \mathbb{1}$. Then $\text{tr}(A) \leq 2\log\det(\mathbb{1} + A)$.*

Proof Use the facts that the trace is the sum of the eigenvalues and the determinant is the product, and that $x \leq 2\log(1+x)$ for $x \in [0, 1]$. □

Lemma A.10 *Suppose $x, y > 0$ and $x\mathbb{1} \preceq A \in \mathbb{S}_+^d$. Then $\log\det(A + y\mathbb{1}) \leq \log\det(A) + \frac{dy}{x}$.*

Proof Let $(\lambda_k)_{k=1}^d$ be the eigenvalues of A. The eigenvalues of $A + y\mathbb{1}$ are $(\lambda_k + y)_{k=1}^d$ and by concavity of the logarithm,

$$\log\det(A + y\mathbb{1}) = \sum_{k=1}^d \log(\lambda_k + y\mathbb{1})$$

$$\leq \sum_{k=1}^d \left(\log(\lambda_k) + \frac{y}{\lambda_k}\right)$$

$$\leq \sum_{k=1}^d \log(\lambda_k) + \frac{dy}{x}$$

$$= \log\det(A) + \frac{dy}{x}.$$
□

Lemma A.11 *Suppose that $f(x) = \|x - y\|_A^2$ and $g(x) = \|x - z\|_B^2$ with $A, B \in \mathbb{S}_{++}^d$. Then*

$$\min_{x \in \mathbb{R}^d}(f(x) + g(x)) = \|z - y\|_{A - A(A+B)^{-1}A}^2.$$

Proof Let $h(x) = f(x) + g(x)$. Then h is quadratic and strictly convex and hence has a unique minimiser at $x \in \mathbb{R}^d$ with

$$0 = h'(x) = 2A(x - y) + 2B(x - z).$$

A.3 Technical Inequalities

Solving shows that $x = (A+B)^{-1}(Ay + Bz)$ and therefore

$$\min_{x \in \mathbb{R}^d} h(x) = \left\| (A+B)^{-1}(Ay+Bz) - y \right\|_A^2 + \left\| (A+B)^{-1}(Ay+Bz) - z \right\|_B^2$$
$$= \left\| (A+B)^{-1}(Bz - By) \right\|_A^2 + \left\| (A+B)^{-1}(Ay - Az) \right\|_B^2$$
$$= \|z - y\|_H^2 ,$$

where

$$H = B(A+B)^{-1}A(A+B)^{-1}B + A(A+B)^{-1}B(A+B)^{-1}A$$
$$= A(A+B)^{-1}B + A(A+B)^{-1}\left[-A(A+B)^{-1}B + B(A+B)^{-1}A\right]$$
$$= A(A+B)^{-1}B$$
$$= A - A(A+B)^{-1}A . \qquad \square$$

Appendix B
Concentration

B.1 Orlicz Norms

Given a random variable X and $k \in \{1, 2\}$ let

$$\|X\|_{\psi_k} = \inf\left\{t > 0 \colon \mathbb{E}\left[\exp\left(|X/t|^k\right)\right] \leq 2\right\}.$$

The random variable X is called subgaussian if $\|X\|_{\psi_2} < \infty$ and subexponential if $\|X\|_{\psi_1} < \infty$. As explained in detail by Vershynin (2018), this definition is equivalent except for universal constants to the definitions based on moments or the moment generating function, which appear, for example, in the book by Boucheron et al. (2013). See also Proposition B.10.

Fact B.1 For $k \in \{1, 2\}$, $\|\cdot\|_{\psi_k}$ is a norm on the corresponding Orlicz space, which is the subset of measurable functions f such that $\|f\|_{\psi_k} < \infty$ and where functions that agree $\mathbb{P}$-almost everywhere are identified. In particular:
(1) $\|X + Y\|_{\psi_k} \leq \|X\|_{\psi_k} + \|Y\|_{\psi_k}$.
(2) $\|aX\|_{\psi_k} = a \|X\|_{\psi_k}$ for all $a \geq 0$.
(3) $\|X\|_{\psi_k} = 0$ implies that $X = 0$ with probability 1.

Regrettably, the Orlicz norms of constant functions do not behave exactly as you might expect:

$$\|1\|_{\psi_1} = \frac{1}{\log(2)} \quad \text{and} \quad \|1\|_{\psi_2} = \frac{1}{\sqrt{\log(2)}}. \tag{B.1}$$

More generally, for bounded random variables:

Lemma B.2 Suppose that $|X| \leq B$. Then
(1) $\|X\|_{\psi_1} \leq \frac{B}{\log(2)}$,
(2) $\|X\|_{\psi_2} \leq \frac{B}{\sqrt{\log(2)}}$.

B.1 Orlicz Norms

Proof Substitute the definitions. □

Lemma B.3 *Given any random variable X and $t > 0$,*
(1) $\mathbb{P}(|X| \geq t) \leq 2\exp\left(-\frac{t}{\|X\|_{\psi_1}}\right)$,
(2) $\mathbb{P}(|X| \geq t) \leq 2\exp\left(-\frac{t^2}{\|X\|_{\psi_2}^2}\right)$.

Proof Both results follow from a standard method. For (1),

$$\mathbb{P}(|X| \geq t) = \mathbb{P}\left(\exp\left(\frac{|X|}{\|X\|_{\psi_1}}\right) \geq \exp\left(\frac{t}{\|X\|_{\psi_1}}\right)\right)$$
$$\leq 2\exp\left(-\frac{t}{\|X\|_{\psi_1}}\right). \qquad \text{Markov's inequality}$$

Part (2) is left as an exercise. □

Lemma B.4 *Let $\Gamma(\cdot)$ be the Gamma function. Given any random variable X and $k \geq 1$,*
(1) $\mathbb{E}[|X|^k] \leq 2\Gamma(1+k)\|X\|_{\psi_1}^k$,
(2) $\mathbb{E}[|X|^k] \leq 2\Gamma(1+k/2)\|X\|_{\psi_2}^k$.

Proof Since $|X|$ is non-negative,

$$\mathbb{E}[|X|^k] = \int_0^\infty \mathbb{P}(|X|^k \geq t)\,dt$$
$$= \int_0^\infty \mathbb{P}(|X| \geq t^{1/k})\,dt$$
$$\leq \int_0^\infty 2\exp\left(-\frac{t^{1/k}}{\|X\|_{\psi_1}}\right)dt$$
$$= 2\Gamma(1+k)\|X\|_{\psi_1}^k.$$

Part (2) follows by the same argument. □

Lemma B.4 can be refined when $k = 1$.

Lemma B.5 *Given any random variable X,*
(1) $\mathbb{E}[|X|] \leq \|X\|_{\psi_1}$,
(2) $\mathbb{E}[|X|] \leq \sqrt{\frac{1}{\log(2)}} \|X\|_{\psi_2}$.

Proof For (1) assume without loss of generality that $\|X\|_{\psi_1} = 1$. Using the inequality $x \leq \exp(x) - 1$,

$$\mathbb{E}[|X|] \leq \mathbb{E}[\exp(|X|)] - 1 \leq 1.$$

For (2) assume without loss of generality that $\|X\|_{\psi_2} = 1$. Then, by Proposition B.12 and (B.1),

$$\mathbb{E}[|X|] \leq \|X\|_{\psi_1} \leq \|X\|_{\psi_2} \|1\|_{\psi_2} = \frac{1}{\sqrt{\log(2)}} \approx 1.2011\ldots. \qquad \square$$

Lemma B.6 *Given a random variable X,*
(1) $\|X - \mathbb{E}[X]\|_{\psi_1} \leq (1 + \frac{1}{\log(2)}) \|X\|_{\psi_1}$,
(2) $\|X - \mathbb{E}[X]\|_{\psi_2} \leq (1 + \frac{1}{\log(2)}) \|X\|_{\psi_2}$.

Proof By the triangle inequality (Fact B.1),

$$\|X - \mathbb{E}[X]\|_{\psi_1} \leq \|X\|_{\psi_1} + \|\mathbb{E}[X]\|_{\psi_1}$$

$$\leq \|X\|_{\psi_1} + \frac{1}{\log(2)} |\mathbb{E}[X]| \qquad \text{Lemma B.2}$$

$$\leq \|X\|_{\psi_1} + \frac{1}{\log(2)} \mathbb{E}[|X|] \qquad \text{Jensen's inequality}$$

$$\leq \|X\|_{\psi_1} + \frac{1}{\log(2)} \|X\|_{\psi_1}. \qquad \text{By Lemma B.5}$$

Part (2) follows using the same argument. $\qquad \square$

Lemma B.7 *Suppose that X is a non-negative random variable with $\mathbb{E}[X] = 1$. Then $\mathbb{E}[X \log X] \leq \log \mathbb{E}[X^2]$.*

Proof Let ρ be the law of X and define a measure ν by $\nu(A) = \mathbb{E}[X \mathbf{1}_A(X)]$, which is a probability measure by the assumption that $\mathbb{E}[X] = 1$. By construction $\frac{d\nu}{d\rho}(x) = x$ so that

$$\int_{\mathbb{R}} x \log(x) \, d\rho(x) = \int_{\mathbb{R}} \log(x) \, d\nu(x)$$

$$\leq \log \left(\int_{\mathbb{R}} x \, d\nu(x) \right)$$

$$= \log \left(\int_{\mathbb{R}} x^2 \, d\rho(x) \right)$$

$$= \log \mathbb{E}[X^2],$$

where the inequality follows from concavity of the logarithm. $\qquad \square$

Lemma B.8 *Let $\log_+(x) = \log(\max(1, x))$. There exist absolute constants $(C_k)_{k=1}^{\infty}$ depending only on k and with $C_1 = 1$ such that for any non-negative*

B.1 Orlicz Norms

random variables X and Y with $\mathbb{E}[X^2] < \infty$ and $\|Y^{1/k}\|_{\psi_1} < \infty$, it holds that

$$\mathbb{E}[XY] \leq C_k \mathbb{E}[X] \|Y^{1/k}\|_{\psi_1}^k \left(1 + \left(\log \frac{\mathbb{E}[X^2]}{\mathbb{E}[X]^2}\right)^k\right) \quad \text{and}$$

$$E[XY] \leq C_k \|Y^{1/k}\|_{\psi_1}^k \left(\mathbb{E}[X] + \mathbb{E}[X]\left(\log_+ \frac{\mathbb{E}[X^2]}{\xi^2}\right)^k + \xi\right) \quad \text{for all } \xi > 0.$$

Proof Suppose that $k = 1$. The result is immediate if $\mathbb{E}[X]$ or $\mathbb{E}[Y]$ vanish. Hence, by normalising it suffices to consider the case where $\mathbb{E}[X] = 1$ and $\|Y\|_{\psi_1} = 1$. Let $f(y) = \exp(y)$ which has convex conjugate $f^*(x) = x \log x - x$. By the Fenchel–Young inequality,

$$\begin{aligned}
\mathbb{E}[XY] &\leq \mathbb{E}[f^*(X) + f(Y)] && \text{Fenchel–Young} \\
&= \mathbb{E}[X \log X + \exp(Y)] - 1 \\
&\leq \mathbb{E}[X \log X] + 1 && \text{since } \|Y\|_{\psi_1} = 1 \\
&\leq 1 + \log \mathbb{E}[X^2]. && \text{by Lemma B.7}
\end{aligned}$$

The second part follows since

$$\begin{aligned}
\mathbb{E}[X] \log\left(\frac{\mathbb{E}[X^2]}{\mathbb{E}[X]^2}\right) &= \mathbb{E}[X] \log\left(\frac{\mathbb{E}[X^2]}{\xi^2}\right) + \mathbb{E}[X] \log\left(\frac{\xi^2}{\mathbb{E}[X]^2}\right) \\
&\leq \mathbb{E}[X] \log\left(\frac{\mathbb{E}[X^2]}{\xi^2}\right) + \xi,
\end{aligned}$$

where the inequality follows because $\log(x) \leq \sqrt{x}$ for all $x > 0$. The argument for $k > 1$ follows from the same high-level idea using the (non-convex) function $f(y) = \exp(y^{1/k})$ and is left as an exercise. □

Exercise B.9 ★ Prove Lemma B.8 with $k > 1$.

The definition of subgaussianity based on moment generating functions is as follows. Given a random variable X, let $M_X(\lambda) = \mathbb{E}[\exp(\lambda X)]$ be its moment generating function. The set of subgaussian random variables with variance proxy σ^2 is

$$\mathscr{G}(\sigma) = \{X : M_X(\lambda) \leq \exp(\sigma^2 \lambda^2 / 2) \text{ for all } \lambda \in \mathbb{R}\}.$$

The next proposition connects $\mathscr{G}(\sigma)$ to $\{X : \mathbb{E}[X] = 0, \|X\|_{\psi_2} \leq \sigma\}$. Similar results with slightly larger constants are given by Boucheron et al. (2013); Vershynin (2018); Zhang and Chen (2021).

Proposition B.10 *Suppose that $\mathbb{E}[X] = 0$. Then:*
(1) *If $X \in \mathscr{G}(\sigma)$, then $\|X\|_{\psi_2} \leq \sqrt{8/3}\sigma$.*

(2) If $\|X\|_{\psi_2} \leq \sigma$, then $X \in \mathcal{G}(\sqrt{2}\sigma)$.

Remark B.11 When X has law $\mathcal{N}(0, 1)$, then Proposition B.10(1) holds with equality.

Proof In both parts assume without loss of generality that $\sigma = 1$. For (1), let $a = \sqrt{8/3}$. Then

$$\mathbb{E}[\exp((X/a)^2)] = \mathbb{E}\left[\frac{1}{\sqrt{\pi}} \int_{-\infty}^{\infty} \exp\left(-t^2 + \frac{2tX}{a}\right) dt\right]$$

$$= \frac{1}{\sqrt{\pi}} \int_{-\infty}^{\infty} \mathbb{E}\left[\exp\left(-t^2 + \frac{2tX}{a}\right)\right] dt$$

$$\leq \frac{1}{\sqrt{\pi}} \int_{-\infty}^{\infty} \exp\left(-t^2 + \frac{2t^2}{a^2}\right) dt$$

$$= 2.$$

Therefore $\|X\|_{\psi_2} \leq a$. Moving now to (2), suppose that $|\lambda| \leq 1$. Then,

$$\mathbb{E}[\exp(\lambda X)] \stackrel{(a)}{\leq} \mathbb{E}[\exp(\lambda^2 X^2) + \lambda X]$$

$$\stackrel{(b)}{\leq} \lambda^2 \mathbb{E}[\exp(X^2)] + 1 - \lambda^2$$

$$\stackrel{(c)}{\leq} 1 + \lambda^2$$

$$\stackrel{(d)}{\leq} \exp(\lambda^2),$$

where (a) follows from the fact that $\exp(x) \leq x + \exp(x^2)$ for all $x \in \mathbb{R}$, (b) since $\mathbb{E}[X] = 0$ and by convexity of $\lambda^2 \mapsto \exp(x^2 \lambda^2)$, (c) since by assumption $\mathbb{E}[\exp(X^2)] \leq 2$ and (d) since $1 + x \leq \exp(x)$ for all $x \in \mathbb{R}$. On the other hand, if $|\lambda| \geq 1$, then

$$\mathbb{E}[\exp(\lambda X)] = \mathbb{E}\left[\exp\left(\frac{\lambda}{\sqrt{2}} \sqrt{2} X\right)\right]$$

$$\stackrel{(a)}{\leq} \mathbb{E}\left[\exp\left(\frac{\lambda^2}{8} + X^2\right)\right]$$

$$\stackrel{(b)}{\leq} 2 \exp(\lambda^2/8)$$

$$\stackrel{(c)}{\leq} \exp(\lambda^2),$$

where (a) follows from the Fenchel–Young inequality: $xy \leq x^2/2 + y^2/2$ for all $x, y \in \mathbb{R}$, (b) since $\mathbb{E}[\exp(X^2)] \leq 2$ by assumption and (c) from the assumption that $|\lambda| \geq 1$. □

Proposition B.12 (Lemma 2.7.7, Vershynin 2018) *Let X and Y be any random variables. Then $\|XY\|_{\psi_1} \leq \|X\|_{\psi_2} \|Y\|_{\psi_2}$.*

All the results in the next proposition can be found somewhere in the book by Vershynin (2018) but with non-explicit constants. The referenced paper gives the explicit constant but is probably not the first to do so.

Proposition B.13 (Lattimore and György 2023) *Suppose that W is a standard Gaussian random variable in $\mathbb{R}^d$. Then:*
(1) $\|\langle x, W\rangle\|_{\psi_2} = 2\sqrt{2/3}\,\|x\|$.
(2) $\|\mathrm{tr}(AWW^\top)\|_{\psi_1} \leq 3\,\mathrm{tr}(A)$.
(3) $\big\|\|W\|^2\big\|_{\psi_1} \leq 8d/3$.
(4) $\big\|\|WW^\top - \mathbb{1}\|\big\|_{\psi_1} \leq 5d$.

Lastly we give a bound on the Orlicz norm of $\langle U, \eta\rangle$ where U is uniformly distributed on the sphere. Morally this is comparable to the case where U is $\mathcal{N}(0, \tfrac{1}{d}\mathbb{1})$, as the bound shows.

Proposition B.14 *Let $X = \langle U, \eta\rangle$ where U has law $\mathscr{U}(\mathbb{S}_1^{d-1})$ and $\eta \in \mathbb{R}^d$. Then*

$$\|X\|_{\psi_2} \leq \|\eta\|\sqrt{\frac{4}{3(d+1)}}\,.$$

Proof Assume without loss of generality that $\|\eta\| = 1$. Let Y be beta distributed with parameters $\alpha = \beta = d/2$, which has mean $1/2$. Then $X/2 + 1/2$ has the same law as Y and Marchal and Arbel (2017) prove that for all $\lambda \in \mathbb{R}$,

$$\mathbb{E}[\exp(\lambda(Y - \mathbb{E}[Y]))] \leq \exp\left(-\frac{\lambda^2}{8(d+1)}\right).$$

Therefore

$$\mathbb{E}[\exp(\lambda X)] = \mathbb{E}[\exp((2\lambda)(Y - \mathbb{E}[Y]))] \leq \exp\left(-\frac{\lambda^2}{4(d+1)}\right) = \exp\left(-\frac{\lambda^2 \sigma^2}{2}\right),$$

where $\sigma^2 = \frac{1}{2(d+1)}$. The result follows from Proposition B.10. □

B.2 Concentration

The following are classical:

Theorem B.15 (Duembgen 2010) *Suppose that X has law $\mathcal{N}(0, 1)$. Then, for any $x \geq 0$,*

$$\mathbb{P}(X \geq x) \leq \frac{1}{2}\exp\left(-\frac{x^2}{2}\right).$$

Theorem B.16 (Boucheron et al. 2013, Theorem 5.6) *Suppose that $f : \mathbb{R}^d \to \mathbb{R}$ and X has law $\mathcal{N}(\mu, \Sigma)$. Then, for any $\delta \in (0, 1)$,*

$$\mathbb{P}\left(|\mathbb{E}[f(X)] - f(X)| \geq \mathrm{lip}(f)\sqrt{2\,\|\Sigma\|\log(2/\delta)}\right) \leq \delta.$$

Furthermore, $\|f(X) - \mathbb{E}[f(X)]\|_{\psi_2} \leq \mathrm{lip}(f)\sqrt{6\,\|\Sigma\|}$.

The next two theorems are versions of Hoeffding's and Bernstein's inequalities in terms of Orlicz norms. The constant 4 appearing in Hoeffding's inequality follows by combining the bound using the definition of subgaussianity based on the moment generating function (Boucheron et al., 2013) and Proposition B.10.

Theorem B.17 (Hoeffding's inequality) *Let $X_1, \ldots, X_n$ be a sequence of independent random variables with $\|X_t\|_{\psi_2} \leq \sigma$ and $\mathbb{E}[X_t] = 0$. Then, for any $\delta \in (0, 1)$,*

$$\mathbb{P}\left(\left|\frac{1}{n}\sum_{t=1}^{n} X_t\right| \geq \sigma\sqrt{\frac{4\log(2/\delta)}{n}}\right) \leq \delta.$$

Theorem B.18 (Bernstein's inequality, Pinelis 2022) *Let $X_1, \ldots, X_n$ be a sequence of independent random variables with $\|X_t\|_{\psi_1} \leq \sigma$ and $\mathbb{E}[X_t] = 0$ for all $1 \leq t \leq n$. Then, for any $\delta \in (0, 1)$,*

$$\mathbb{P}\left(\left|\frac{1}{n}\sum_{t=1}^{n} X_t\right| \geq \max\left(\sqrt{\frac{4\sigma^2 \log(2/\delta)}{n}},\, \frac{2\sigma \log(2/\delta)}{n}\right)\right) \leq \delta.$$

Theorem B.19 (Azuma's inequality) *Let $X_0, X_1, \ldots, X_n$ be a martingale with $|X_t - X_{t-1}| \leq c_t$ almost surely. Then, with probability at least $1 - \delta$,*

$$X_n \leq X_0 + \sqrt{2\sum_{t=1}^{n} c_t^2 \log(1/\delta)}.$$

The next theorem is a strengthened version of Freedman's inequality due to Zimmert and Lattimore (2022).

Theorem B.20 *Let $X_1, \ldots, X_n$ be a sequence of random variables adapted to filtration $(\mathcal{F}_t)$ and τ be a stopping time with respect to $(\mathcal{F}_t)_{t=1}^n$ with $\tau \leq n$ almost surely. Let $\mathbb{E}_t[\cdot] = \mathbb{E}[\cdot|\mathcal{F}_t]$ and assume that $\mathbb{E}_{t-1}[X_t] = 0$ almost surely for all $t \leq \tau$. Then, with probability at least $1 - \delta$,*

$$\left|\sum_{t=1}^{\tau} X_t\right| \leq 3\sqrt{V_\tau \log\left(\frac{2\max(B, \sqrt{V_\tau})}{\delta}\right)} + 2B \log\left(\frac{2\max(B, \sqrt{V_\tau})}{\delta}\right),$$

where $V_\tau = \sum_{t=1}^\tau \mathbb{E}_{t-1}[X_t^2]$ is the sum of the predictable variations and $B = \max(1, \max_{1 \leq t \leq \tau} |X_t|)$.

The next theorem is a folklore result. A version without stopping times appears as Exercise 5.15 in the book by Lattimore and Szepesvári (2020).

Theorem B.21 *Let $X_1, \ldots, X_n$ be a sequence of random variables adapted to filtration $(\mathscr{F}_t)_{t=1}^n$ and τ be a stopping time with respect to the same filtration. Suppose that $\alpha |X_t| \leq 1$ almost surely for all $t \leq \tau$ with $\alpha \geq 0$. Then, with probability at least $1 - \delta$,*

$$\sum_{t=1}^\tau (X_t - \mathbb{E}_{t-1}[X_t]) \leq \alpha \sum_{t=1}^\tau \mathbb{E}_{t-1}[X_t^2] + \frac{\log(1/\delta)}{\alpha},$$

where $\mathbb{E}_t[\cdot] = \mathbb{E}[\cdot | \mathscr{F}_t]$.

Proof Let $\Delta_t = X_t - \mathbb{E}_{t-1}[X_t]$ and $S_\tau = \sum_{t=1}^\tau \Delta_t$ and $V_\tau = \sum_{t=1}^\tau \mathbb{E}_{t-1}[X_t^2]$. By Markov's inequality,

$$\mathbb{P}\left(S_\tau \geq \alpha V_\tau + \frac{\log(1/\delta)}{\alpha}\right) = \mathbb{P}\left(\exp\left(\alpha S_\tau - \alpha^2 V_\tau\right) \geq \frac{1}{\delta}\right)$$
$$\leq \delta \mathbb{E}\left[\exp\left(\alpha S_\tau - \alpha^2 V_\tau\right)\right]$$
$$= \delta \mathbb{E}[M_\tau],$$

where $M_t = \exp\left(\alpha S_t - \alpha^2 V_t\right)$. Suppose that $t \leq \tau$. Then

$$\mathbb{E}_{t-1}[M_t] = M_{t-1} \mathbb{E}_{t-1}\left[\exp\left(\alpha \Delta_t - \alpha^2 \mathbb{E}_{t-1}[X_t^2]\right)\right]$$
$$= M_{t-1} \exp\left(-\mathbb{E}_{t-1}[\alpha^2 X_t^2 + \alpha X_t]\right) \mathbb{E}_{t-1}[\exp(\alpha X_t)]$$
$$\leq M_{t-1} \exp\left(-\mathbb{E}_{t-1}[\alpha^2 X_t^2 + \alpha X_t]\right) \mathbb{E}_{t-1}\left[1 + \alpha X_t + \alpha^2 X_t^2\right]$$
$$\leq M_{t-1},$$

where in the first inequality we used the fact that for $|x| \leq 1$, $\exp(x) \leq 1 + x + x^2$ and in the last that $1 + x \leq \exp(x)$ for all x. Hence (M_t) is a supermartingale and $M_0 = 1$ is immediate from the definition. Since τ is almost surely bounded, by the optional stopping theorem $\mathbb{E}[M_\tau] \leq M_0 = 1$. Therefore

$$\mathbb{P}\left(S_\tau \geq \alpha V_\tau + \frac{\log(1/\delta)}{\alpha}\right) \leq \delta. \qquad \square$$

The following is an elementary corollary of Theorem B.21.

Theorem B.22 *Let $X_1, \ldots, X_n$ be a sequence of non-negative random variables adapted to filtration $(\mathscr{F}_t)_{t=1}^n$ and τ be a stopping time with respect to the same* *filtration. Suppose that $\alpha X_t \leq 1$ almost surely for all $t \leq \tau$ with $\alpha \geq 0$. Then, with probability at least $1 - \delta$,*

$$\sum_{t=1}^{\tau} X_t \leq 2 \sum_{t=1}^{\tau} \mathbb{E}_{t-1}[X_t] + \frac{\log(1/\delta)}{\alpha},$$

where $\mathbb{E}_t[\cdot] = \mathbb{E}[\cdot|\mathscr{F}_t]$.

Proof Apply Theorem B.21 and bound $\alpha \mathbb{E}_{t-1}[X_t^2] \leq \mathbb{E}_{t-1}[X_t]$. □

Appendix C
Notation

Sets

$\mathbb{R}, \mathbb{Z}$	reals, integers
$\mathbb{R}_{++}, \mathbb{R}_+$	$(0, \infty)$ and $[0, \infty)$
$\mathbb{S}^d_{++}, \mathbb{S}^d_+$	positive definite and positive semidefinite matrices acting on $\mathbb{R}^d$
$\mathbb{B}^d_r$	euclidean ball of radius r in $\mathbb{R}^d$
$\mathbb{S}^{d-1}_r$	euclidean sphere of radius r embedded in $\mathbb{R}^d$
$E(x, A)$	the ellipsoid $\{y\colon \|x - y\|_{A^{-1}} \leq 1\}$
$H(x, \eta)$	the half-space $\{y\colon \langle y - x, \eta \rangle \leq 0\}$
$[x, y]$	convex chord $\{\lambda x + (1 - \lambda)y\colon x \in [0, 1]\}$

Norms

$\|\cdot\|$	euclidean/spectral norm of vector/matrix	
$\|\cdot\|_1$	1-norm, $\|x\|_1 = \sum_k |x_k|$	
$\|\cdot\|_\infty$	∞-norm, $\|x\|_\infty = \max_k |x_k|$	
$\|\cdot\|_{\psi_k}$	Orlicz norms, $k \in \{1, 2\}$	p. 246
$\|\cdot\|_A$	$\|x\|_A = \sqrt{x^\top A x}$ for positive semidefinite A	
$\|\cdot\|_K$	$\|\cdot\|_K = \pi_K(\cdot)$ when K is a symmetric convex body	p. 27

Minkowski Arithmetic

$A + B$	Minkowski addition, $A + B = \{a + b : a \in A, b \in B\}$
$-A$	$-A = \{-a : a \in A\}$
$A - B$	Minkowski subtraction, $A - B = A + (-B)$
$x + A$	abbreviation for $\{x\} + A$
uA	Minkowski multiplication, $uA = \{ua : a \in A\}, u \in \mathbb{R}$

Elementary Relations and Operators

$\subset, \supset$	subset/superset, possibly equal	
$\succeq, \preceq, \succ, \prec$	Löwner order operators	
$\lceil \cdot \rceil, \lfloor \cdot \rfloor$	ceiling/floor functions	
$f * g$	convolution of f and g	
$\langle x, y \rangle$	standard euclidean inner product	
$\langle x, y \rangle_A$	inner product $x^\top A y$ for $A \in \mathbb{S}^d_{++}$	
$\text{int}(K)$	interior of K	p. 10
∂K	boundary of K	p. 10
$\text{diam}(K)$	diameter of K, $\sup_{x,y \in K} \|x - y\|$	p. 29
$\text{vol}(K)$	volume of K	
$N(A, B), \bar{N}(A, B)$	external/internal covering numbers	p. 79

Convex Bandits

$f_1, \ldots, f_n$	loss functions in rounds $t \in 1 \ldots n$	
$\varepsilon_1, \ldots, \varepsilon_n$	noise random variables	p. 6
$X_1, \ldots, X_n$	iterates played by algorithm	p. 4
$Y_1, \ldots, Y_n$	observed losses	p. 4
α and β	smoothness and strong convexity parameters	p. 5

C Notation

Probability

$\mathscr{B}(K)$	Borel σ-algebra on K	
$\Delta(K)$	probability measures on $(K, \mathscr{B}(K))$	
Δ_m	probability distribution on $\{1, \ldots, m\}$	
Δ_m^+	$\Delta_m \cap \mathbb{R}_{++}^m$	
$\mathscr{U}(A)$	uniform probability measure on $A \subset \mathbb{R}^d$	
$\mathscr{F}_t$	natural filtration $\sigma(X_1, Y_1, \ldots, X_t, Y_t)$	p. 11
$\mathbb{P}_t$	conditional probability measure $\mathbb{P}(\cdot \vert \mathscr{F}_t)$	p. 11
$\mathbb{E}_t$	conditional expectation $\mathbb{E}[\cdot \vert \mathscr{F}_t]$	p. 11

Convexity

K	normally a convex set	
K°	the polar of a convex set K	p. 27
π_K	Minkowski functional of K, usually abbreviated to π	p. 26
h_K	support function of K, usually abbreviated to h	p. 27
$\mathrm{ri}(K)$	relative interior of K	p. 10
$\mathrm{conv}(A)$	convex hull of A	
ISO_K	affine map such that $\mathrm{ISO}_K(K)$ is isotropic	p. 33
JOHN_K	affine map such that $\mathrm{JOHN}_K(K)$ is in John's position	p. 40
$\mathrm{SEP}_K, \mathrm{MEM}_K$	separation/membership oracle for K	p. 40

Functions and Calculus

f' / f''	gradient/Hessian of $f: \mathbb{R}^d \to \mathbb{R}$
$\partial f(x)$	subgradients of f at x
$D^k f(x)[\cdots]$	kth directional derivative of f at x
$\mathrm{dom}(f)$	domain of convex f, $\{x \in \mathbb{R}^d : f(x) < \infty\}$
$\mathrm{lip}_K(f)$	Lipschitz constant of f on K with respect to $\|\cdot\|$
$\mathrm{lip}(f)$	$\mathrm{lip}_{\mathrm{dom}(f)}(f)$

References

Abernethy, J. D., Hazan, E., and Rakhlin, A. 2008. Competing in the dark: An efficient algorithm for bandit linear optimization. In: *Proceedings of the 21st Conference on Learning Theory*.

Agarwal, A., Dekel, O., and Xiao, L. 2010. Optimal algorithms for online convex optimization with multi-point bandit feedback. In: *Proceedings of the 23rd Conference on Learning Theory*.

Agarwal, A., Foster, D. P., Hsu, D. J., Kakade, S. M., and Rakhlin, A. 2011. Stochastic convex optimization with bandit feedback. In: *Advances in Neural Information Processing Systems*.

Agarwal, A., Foster, D. P., Hsu, D., Kakade, S. M., and Rakhlin, A. 2013. Stochastic convex optimization with bandit feedback. *SIAM Journal on Optimization*, **23**(1), 213–240.

Akhavan, A., Pontil, M., and Tsybakov, A. 2020. Exploiting higher order smoothness in derivative-free optimization and continuous bandits. In: *Advances in Neural Information Processing Systems*.

Akhavan, A., Lounici, K., Pontil, M., and Tsybakov, A. 2024a. *Contextual continuum bandits: Static versus dynamic regret*. arXiv:2406.05714.

Akhavan, A., Chzhen, E., Pontil, M., and Tsybakov, A. 2024b. Gradient-free optimization of highly smooth functions: Improved analysis and a new algorithm. *Journal of Machine Learning Research*, **25**(370), 1–50.

Ao, R., Hu, H., and Simchi-Levi, D. 2025. *Riemannian online convex optimization with self-concordant barrier*. Available at SSRN 5250625.

Artstein-Avidan, S., Giannopoulos, A., and Milman, V. D. 2015. *Asymptotic geometric analysis, Part I*. American Mathematical Society.

Atkinson, D. S., and Vaidya, P. M. 1995. A cutting plane algorithm for convex programming that uses analytic centers. *Mathematical Programming*, **69**(1), 1–43.

Bach, F. 2013. Learning with submodular functions: A convex optimization perspective. *Foundations and Trends® in Machine Learning*, **6**(2–3), 145–373.

Bach, F., and Perchet, V. 2016. Highly-smooth zero-th order online optimization. In: *Proceedings of the 29th Conference on Learning Theory*.

Bachoc, F., Cesari, T., Colomboni, R., and Paudice, A. 2022. *Regret analysis of dyadic search*. arXiv:2209.00885.

References

Bachoc, F., Cesari, T., Colomboni, R., and Paudice, A. 2024. A theoretical framework for zeroth-order budget convex optimization. *Transactions on Machine Learning Research*.

Bakhtiari, A., Lattimore, T., and Szepesvári, Cs. 2025. Thompson sampling for bandit convex optimisation. In: *Proceedings of the 38th Conference on Learning Theory*.

Balasubramanian, K., and Ghadimi, S. 2022. Zeroth-order nonconvex stochastic optimization: Handling constraints, high dimensionality, and saddle points. *Foundations of Computational Mathematics*, **22**(2), 1–42.

Barthe, F. 1998. An extremal property of the mean width of the simplex. *Mathematische Annalen*, **310**, 685–693.

Bauschke, H., and Borwein, J. 1997. Legendre functions and the method of random Bregman projections. *Journal of Convex Analysis*, **4**(1), 27–67.

Belloni, A., Liang, T., Narayanan, H., and Rakhlin, A. 2015. Escaping the local minima via simulated annealing: Optimization of approximately convex functions. In: *Proceedings of the 28th Conference on Learning Theory*.

Berry, D., Chen, R., Zame, A., Heath, D., and Shepp, L. 1997. Bandit problems with infinitely many arms. *The Annals of Statistics*, **25**(5), 2103–2116.

Bertsimas, D., and Tsitsiklis, J. N. 1997. *Introduction to linear optimization*. Athena Scientific.

Bertsimas, D., and Vempala, S. 2004. Solving convex programs by random walks. *Journal of the ACM (JACM)*, **51**(4), 540–556.

Besson, L., and Kaufmann, E. 2018. *What doubling tricks can and can't do for multi-armed bandits*. arXiv:1803.06971.

Bhatnagar, S., Prasad, H. L., and Prashanth, L. A. 2012. *Stochastic recursive algorithms for optimization: Simultaneous perturbation methods*. Lecture Notes in Control and Information Sciences. Springer.

Bilmes, J. 2022. *Submodularity in machine learning and artificial intelligence*. arXiv:2202.00132.

Blum, J. R. 1954. Multidimensional stochastic approximation methods. *The Annals of Mathematical Statistics*, **25**(4), 737–744.

Boucheron, S., Lugosi, G., and Massart, P. 2013. *Concentration inequalities: A nonasymptotic theory of independence*. Oxford University Press.

Boyd, S., and Vandenberghe, L. 2004. *Convex optimization*. Cambridge University Press.

Bubeck, S. 2015. Convex optimization: Algorithms and complexity. *Foundations and Trends® in Machine Learning*, **8**(3–4), 231–357.

Bubeck, S., and Cesa-Bianchi, N. 2012. Regret analysis of stochastic and nonstochastic multi-armed bandit problems. *Foundations and Trends® in Machine Learning*, **5**(1), 1–122.

Bubeck, S., and Eldan, R. 2015. The entropic barrier: A simple and optimal universal self-concordant barrier. In: *Proceedings of the 28th Conference on Learning Theory*.

Bubeck, S., and Eldan, R. 2018. Exploratory distributions for convex functions. *Mathematical Statistics and Learning*, **1**(1), 73–100.

Bubeck, S., Cesa-Bianchi, N., and Kakade, S. 2012. Towards minimax policies for online linear optimization with bandit feedback. In: *Proceedings of the 25th Conference on Learning Theory*.

Bubeck, S., Cesa-Bianchi, N., and Lugosi, G. 2013. Bandits with heavy tail. *IEEE Transactions on Information Theory*, **59**(11), 7711–7717.

Bubeck, S., Dekel, O., Koren, T., and Peres, Y. 2015. Bandit convex optimization: $\sqrt{T}$ regret in one dimension. In: *Proceedings of the 28th Conference on Learning Theory*.

Bubeck, S., Lee, Y.-T., and Eldan, R. 2017. Kernel-based methods for bandit convex optimization. In: *Proceedings of the 49th Annual ACM SIGACT Symposium on Theory of Computing*.

Bubeck, S., Eldan, R., and Lehec, J. 2018. Sampling from a log-concave distribution with projected Langevin Monte Carlo. *Discrete & Computational Geometry*, **59**, 757–783.

Carpentier, Alexandra. 2025. A simple and improved algorithm for noisy, convex, zeroth-order optimisation. *Mathematical Statistics and Learning*, **8**(3–4), 165–192.

Cesa-Bianchi, N., and Lugosi, G. 2006. *Prediction, learning, and games*. Cambridge University Press.

Chatterji, N., Pacchiano, A., and Bartlett, P. 2019. Online learning with kernel losses. Pages 971–980 of: *Proceedings of the 36th International Conference on Machine Learning*.

Chen, L., Krause, A., and Karbasi, A. 2017. Interactive submodular bandit. In: *Advances in Neural Information Processing Systems*.

Chewi, S. 2023. The entropic barrier is n-self-concordant. In: *Geometric Aspects of Functional Analysis: Israel Seminar*.

Chewi, S. 2024. *Log-concave sampling*.

Conn, A., Scheinberg, K., and Vicente, L. 2009. *Introduction to derivative-free optimization*. Society for Industrial and Applied Mathematics.

Cover, T. M., and Thomas, J. A. 2012. *Elements of information theory*. John Wiley & Sons.

Dani, V., Hayes, T. P., and Kakade, S. M. 2008. Stochastic linear optimization under bandit feedback. In: *Proceedings of the 21st Conference on Learning Theory*.

Drori, Y. 2018. On the properties of convex functions over open sets. arXiv:1812.02419.

Duchi, J., Jordan, M., Wainwright, M., and Wibisono, A. 2015. Optimal rates for zero-order convex optimization: The power of two function evaluations. *IEEE Transactions on Information Theory*, **61**(5), 2788–2806.

Duembgen, L. 2010. Bounding standard gaussian tail probabilities. arXiv:1012.2063.

Evans, L. 2018. *Measure theory and fine properties of functions*. Routledge.

Even-Dar, E., Mannor, S., and Mansour, Y. 2006. Action elimination and stopping conditions for the multi-armed bandit and reinforcement learning problems. *Journal of Machine Learning Research*, **7**, 1079–1105.

Finch, S. 2011. Mean width of a regular simplex. arXiv:1111.4976.

Flaxman, A., Kalai, A., and McMahan, H.B. 2005. Online convex optimization in the bandit setting: Gradient descent without a gradient. In: *Proceedings of the 16th Annual ACM-SIAM Symposium on Discrete Algorithms*.

Fokkema, H., van der Hoeven, D., Lattimore, T., and Mayo, J. 2024. Online Newton method for bandit convex optimisation. In: *Proceedings of the 37th Conference on Learning Theory*.

Foster, D. J., Kakade, S., Qian, J., and Rakhlin, A. 2021. The statistical complexity of interactive decision making. arXiv:2112.13487.

Foster, D. J., Rakhlin, A., Sekhari, A., and Sridharan, K. 2022. On the complexity of adversarial decision making. In: *Advances in Neural Information Processing Systems*.

Foster, D. P., and Rakhlin, A. 2021. *On submodular contextual bandits*. arXiv:2112.02165.

Gabillon, V., Kveton, B., Wen, Z., Eriksson, B., and Muthukrishnan, S. 2013. Adaptive submodular maximization in bandit setting. In: *Advances in Neural Information Processing Systems*.

Galicer, D., Merzbacher, M., and Pinasco, D. 2019. The minimal volume of simplices containing a convex body. *Journal of Geometric Analysis*, **29**, 717–732.

Garber, D., and Kretzu, B. 2022. New projection-free algorithms for online convex optimization with adaptive regret guarantees. In: *Proceedings of the 35th Conference on Learning Theory*.

Ghadimi, S., and Lan, G. 2013. Stochastic first- and zeroth-order methods for nonconvex stochastic programming. *SIAM Journal on Optimization*, **23**(4), 2341–2368.

Giannopoulos, A., and Milman, E. 2014. M-estimates for isotropic convex bodies and their L_q-centroid bodies. In: *Geometric Aspects of Functional Analysis: Israel Seminar*.

Grötschel, M., Lovász, L., and Schrijver, A. 2012. *Geometric algorithms and combinatorial optimization*. Springer Science & Business Media.

Grünbaum, B. 1960. Partitions of mass-distributions and of convex bodies by hyperplanes. *Pacific Journal of Mathematics*, **10**(4), 1257–1261.

Hale, N., Higham, N., and Trefethen, L. 2008. Computing A^α, $\log(A)$ and related matrix functions by contour integrals. *SIAM Journal on Numerical Analysis*, **46**(5), 2505–2523.

Hazan, E. 2016. Introduction to online convex optimization. *Foundations and Trends® in Optimization*, **2**(3–4), 157–325.

Hazan, E., and Kale, S. 2012. Online submodular minimization. *Journal of Machine Learning Research*, **13**(10).

Hazan, E., and Levy, K. 2014. Bandit convex optimization: Towards tight bounds. In: *Advances in Neural Information Processing Systems*.

Hazan, E., and Li, Y. 2016. *An optimal algorithm for bandit convex optimization*. arXiv:1603.04350.

Hazan, E., Agarwal, A., and Kale, S. 2007. Logarithmic regret algorithms for online convex optimization. *Machine Learning*, **69**, 169–192.

Hazan, E., Karnin, Z., and Meka, R. 2016. Volumetric spanners: An efficient exploration basis for learning. *Journal of Machine Learning Research*, **17**(119), 1–34.

Hu, X., Prashanth L. A., György, A., and Szepesvári, Cs. 2016. (Bandit) convex optimization with biased noisy gradient oracles. In: *Proceedings of the 19th International Conference on Artificial Intelligence and Statistics*.

Ito, S. 2020. An optimal algorithm for bandit convex optimization with strongly-convex and smooth loss. In: *Proceedings of the 23rd International Conference on Artificial Intelligence and Statistics*.

Jamieson, K., Nowak, R., and Recht, B. 2012. Query complexity of derivative-free optimization. In: *Advances in Neural Information Processing Systems*.

Jegelka, S., and Bilmes, J. 2011. Online submodular minimization for combinatorial structures. In: *Proceedings of the 28th International Conference on Machine Learning*.

Jiang, H. 2022. Minimizing convex functions with rational minimizers. *Journal of the ACM*, **70**(1), 1–27.

Jiang, S., Song, Z., Weinstein, O., and Zhang, H. 2021. A faster algorithm for solving general LPs. In: *Proceedings of the 53rd Annual ACM SIGACT Symposium on Theory of Computing*.

Jingxin, Z., Yuchen, X., Kaicheng, J., and Zhihua, Z. 2025. *A regularized online Newton method for stochastic convex bandits with linear vanishing noise*. arXiv:2501.11127.

Kaiser, M. J. 1993. The Santaló point of a planar convex set. *Applied Mathematics Letters*, **6**(2), 47–53.

Kannan, R., Lovász, L., and Simonovits, M. 1995. Isoperimetric problems for convex bodies and a localization lemma. *Discrete & Computational Geometry*, **13**, 541–559.

Karimi, H., Nutini, J., and Schmidt, M. 2016. Linear convergence of gradient and proximal-gradient methods under the Polyak-Łojasiewicz condition. In: *Proceedings of the Joint European Conference on Machine Learning and Knowledge Discovery in Databases*.

Karp, R. 1972. Reducibility among combinatorial problems. In: *Proceedings of a Symposium on the Complexity of Computer Computations*.

Khachiyan, L. 1990. An inequality for the volume of inscribed ellipsoids. *Discrete & Computational Geometry*, **5**, 219–222.

Khachiyan, L., and Todd, M. 1993. On the complexity of approximating the maximal inscribed ellipsoid for a polytope. *Mathematical Programming*, **61**(08), 137–159.

Kiefer, J. 1953. Sequential minimax search for a maximum. *Proceedings of the American Mathematical Society*, **4**(3), 502–506.

Kiefer, J., and Wolfowitz, J. 1952. Stochastic estimation of the maximum of a regression function. *The Annals of Mathematical Statistics*, **23**(3), 462–466.

Kiefer, J., and Wolfowitz, J. 1960. The equivalence of two extremum problems. *Canadian Journal of Mathematics*, **12**(5), 363–365.

Kirschner, J. 2021. *Information-directed sampling – frequentist analysis and applications*. Ph.D. thesis, ETH Zurich.

Klartag, B., and Lehec, J. 2024. *Affirmative resolution of Bourgain's slicing problem using Guan's bound*. arXiv:2412.15044.

Kleinberg, R. 2005. Nearly tight bounds for the continuum-armed bandit problem. In: *Advances in Neural Information Processing Systems*.

Larson, J., Menickelly, M., and Wild, S. 2019. Derivative-free optimization methods. *Acta Numerica*, **28**, 287–404.

Lattimore, T. 2020. Improved regret for zeroth-order adversarial bandit convex optimisation. *Mathematical Statistics and Learning*, **2**(3–4), 311–334.

Lattimore, T., and György, A. 2021a. Improved regret for zeroth-order stochastic convex bandits. In: *Proceedings of the 34th Conference on Learning Theory*.

Lattimore, T., and György, A. 2021b. Mirror descent and the information ratio. In: *Proceedings of the 34th Conference on Learning Theory*.

Lattimore, T., and György, A. 2023. A second-order method for stochastic bandit convex optimisation. In: *Proceedings of the 36th Conference on Learning Theory*.

Lattimore, T., and Hao, B. 2021. Bandit phase retrieval. In: *Advances in Neural Information Processing Systems*.

Lattimore, T., and Szepesvári, Cs. 2019. An information-theoretic approach to minimax regret in partial monitoring. In: *Proceedings of the 32nd Conference on Learning Theory*.

Lattimore, T., and Szepesvári, Cs. 2020. *Bandit algorithms*. Cambridge University Press.

Lee, Y.-T., and Yue, M-C. 2021. Universal barrier is n-self-concordant. *Mathematics of Operations Research*, **46**(3), 1129–1148.

Lee, Y.-T., Sidford, A., and Wong, S. 2015. A faster cutting plane method and its implications for combinatorial and convex optimization. In: *IEEE 56th Annual Symposium on Foundations of Computer Science*.

Lee, Y.-T., Sidford, A., and Vempala, S. 2018. Efficient convex optimization with membership oracles. In: *Proceedings of the 31st Conference on Learning Theory*.

Levin, A. 1965. An algorithm for minimizing convex functions. Pages 1244–1247 of: *Doklady Akademii Nauk*, vol. 160. Russian Academy of Sciences.

Liang, T., Narayanan, H., and Rakhlin, A. 2014. *On zeroth-order stochastic convex optimization via random walks*. arXiv:1402.2667.

Liu, S., Chen, P.-Y., Kailkhura, B., Zhang, G., Hero, A. III, and Varshney, P. 2020. A primer on zeroth-order optimization in signal processing and machine learning: Principles, recent advances, and applications. *IEEE Signal Processing Magazine*, **37**(5), 43–54.

Liu, X., Baudry, D., Zimmert, J., Rebeschini, P., and Akhavan, A. 2025. *Non-stationary bandit convex optimization: A comprehensive study*. arXiv:2506.02980.

Lovász, L. 1983. Submodular functions and convexity. Pages 235–257 of: *Mathematical Programming: The State of the Art: Bonn 1982*.

Lovász, L., and Vempala, S. 2006. Simulated annealing in convex bodies and an $O^*(n^4)$ volume algorithm. *Journal of Computer and System Sciences*, **72**(2), 392–417.

Luo, H., Zhang, M., and Zhao, P. 2022. Adaptive bandit convex optimization with heterogeneous curvature. In: *Proceedings of the 25th Conference on Learning Theory*.

Marchal, O., and Arbel, J. 2017. On the sub-Gaussianity of the Beta and Dirichlet distributions. *Electronic Communications in Probability*, **22**(54), 1–14.

McCormick, S. 2005. Submodular function minimization. *Handbooks in Operations Research and Management Science*, **12**, 321–391.

Meyer, M., and Werner, E. 1998. The Santaló-regions of a convex body. *Transactions of the American Mathematical Society*, **350**(11), 4569–4591.

Mhammedi, Z. 2022. Efficient projection-free online convex optimization with membership oracle. In: *Proceedings of the 35th Conference on Learning Theory*.

Milman, E. 2015. On the mean-width of isotropic convex bodies and their associated L p-centroid bodies. *International Mathematics Research Notices*, **2015**(11), 3408–3423.

Motzkin, T., and Straus, G. 1965. Maxima for graphs and a new proof of a theorem of Turán. *Canadian Journal of Mathematics*, **17**, 533–540.

Nemirovski, A. 1996. *Lecture notes: Interior-point polynomial time methods for convex programming*. Georgia Institute of Technology.

Nemirovski, A., Juditsky, A., Lan, G., and Shapiro, A. 2009. Robust stochastic approximation approach to stochastic programming. *SIAM Journal on Optimization*, **19**(4), 1574–1609.

Nemirovsky, A., and Yudin, D. 1983. *Problem complexity and method efficiency in optimization.* John Wiley & Sons.

Nesterov, Y. 1988. Polynomial time methods in linear and quadratic programming. *Izvestija AN SSSR, Tekhnitcheskaya kibernetika.*

Nesterov, Y. 1995. Cutting plane algorithms from analytic centers: efficiency estimates. *Mathematical Programming*, **69**(1), 149–176.

Nesterov, Y. 2018. *Lectures on convex optimization.* Springer.

Nesterov, Y., and Nemirovski, A. 1994. *Interior-point polynomial algorithms in convex programming.* Society for Industrial and Applied Mathematics.

Nesterov, Y., and Nemirovsky, A. 1989. Self-concordant functions and polynomial time methods in convex programming. *USSR Academy of Sciences Central Economic & Mathematical Institute, Moscow.*

Nesterov, Y., and Spokoiny, V. 2017. Random gradient-free minimization of convex functions. *Foundations of Computational Mathematics*, **17**, 527–566.

Newman, D. J. 1965. Location of the maximum on unimodal surfaces. *Journal of the ACM*, **12**(3), 395–398.

Niazadeh, R., Golrezaei, N., Wang, J., Susan, F., and Badanidiyuru, A. 2021. Online learning via offline greedy algorithms: Applications in market design and optimization. In: *Proceedings of the 22nd ACM Conference on Economics and Computation.*

Novitskii, V., and Gasnikov, A. 2021. *Improved exploiting higher order smoothness in derivative-free optimization and continuous bandit.* arXiv:2101.03821.

Orabona, F. 2019. *A modern introduction to online learning.* arXiv:1912.13213.

Orseau, L., and Hutter, M. 2023. *Line search for convex minimization.* arXiv:2307.16560.

Pinelis, I. 2022. Improved concentration bounds for sums of independent sub-exponential random variables. *Statistics & Probability Letters*, **191**, 109666.

Pivovarov, P. 2010. On the volume of caps and bounding the mean-width of an isotropic convex body. *Mathematical Proceedings of the Cambridge Philosophical Society*, **149**(2), 317–331.

Polyak, B. 1963. Gradient methods for minimizing functionals. *Zhurnal Vychislitel'noi Matematiki I Matematicheskoi Fiziki*, **3**(4), 643–653.

Polyak, B. T., and Tsybakov, A. B. 1990. Optimal accuracy orders of stochastic approximation algorithms. *Problemy Peredachi Informatsii*, **26**(2), 45–53.

Prashanth, L. A., and Bhatnagar, S. 2025. Gradient-based algorithms for zeroth-order optimization. *Foundations and Trends® in Optimization*, **8**(1–3), 1–332.

Protasov, V. 1996. Algorithms for approximate calculation of the minimum of a convex function from its values. *Mathematical Notes*, **59**(1), 69–74.

Robbins, H., and Monro, S. 1951. A stochastic approximation method. *The Annals of Mathematical Statistics*, **22**(3), 400–407.

Rockafellar, R. T. 1970. *Convex analysis.* Princeton University Press.

Russo, D., and Van Roy, B. 2014. Learning to optimize via information-directed sampling. In: *Advances in Neural Information Processing Systems.*

Russo, D., and Van Roy, B. 2016. An information-theoretic analysis of Thompson sampling. *Journal of Machine Learning Research*, **17**(1), 2442–2471.

Saha, A., and Tewari, A. 2011. Improved regret guarantees for online smooth convex optimization with bandit feedback. In: *Proceedings of the 14th International Conference on Artificial Intelligence and Statistics.*

Santaló, L. A. 1949. Un invariante afin para los cuerpos convexos del espacio de n dimensiones. *Portugaliae Mathematica*, **8**, 155–161.

Schneider, R. 2013. *Convex bodies: The Brunn–Minkowski theory*. Cambridge University Press.

Shamir, O. 2013. On the complexity of bandit and derivative-free stochastic convex optimization. In: *Proceedings of the 26th Conference on Learning Theory*.

Shamir, O. 2015. On the complexity of bandit linear optimization. In: *Proceedings of the 28th Conference on Learning Theory*.

Shor, N. 1977. Cut-off method with space extension in convex programming problems. *Cybernetics*, **13**(1), 94–96.

Slivkins, A. 2019. Introduction to multi-armed bandits. *Foundations and Trends® in Machine Learning*, **12**(1–2), 1–286.

Spall, J. C. 1992. Multivariate stochastic approximation using a simultaneous perturbation gradient approximation. *IEEE Transactions on Automatic Control*, **37**(3), 332–341.

Spall, J. C. 1994. Developments in stochastic optimization algorithms with gradient approximations based on function measurements. In: *Proceedings of Winter Simulation Conference*.

Suggala, A., Ravikumar, P., and Netrapalli, P. 2021. Efficient bandit convex optimization: Beyond linear losses. In: *Proceedings of the 34th Conference on Learning Theory*.

Suggala, A., Sun, J., Netrapalli, P., and Hazan, E. 2024. Second order methods for bandit optimization and control. In: *Proceedings of the 37th Conference on Learning Theory*.

Tajdini, A., Jain, L., and Jamieson, K. 2024. Nearly minimax optimal submodular maximization with bandit feedback. In: *Advances in Neural Information Processing Systems*.

Takemori, S., Sato, M., Sonoda, T., Singh, J., and Ohkuma, T. 2020. Submodular bandit problem under multiple constraints. In: *Proceedings of the 36th Conference on Uncertainty in Artificial Intelligence*.

Tarasov, S., Khachiyan, L. G., and Erlich, I. I. 1988. The method of inscribed ellipsoids. Pages 226–230 of: *Soviet Mathematics-Doklady*, vol. 37.

Thompson, W. 1933. On the likelihood that one unknown probability exceeds another in view of the evidence of two samples. *Biometrika*, **25**(3–4), 285–294.

Vaidya, P. M. 1996. A new algorithm for minimizing convex functions over convex sets. *Mathematical Programming*, **73**(3), 291–341.

van der Hoeven, D., van Erven, T., and Kotłowski, W. 2018. The many faces of exponential weights in online learning. In: *Proceedings of the 31st Conference on Learning Theory*.

Vershynin, R. 2018. *High-dimensional probability: An introduction with applications in data science*. Cambridge University Press.

Wang, Y. 2023. On adaptivity in nonstationary stochastic optimization with bandit feedback. *Operations Research*, **73**(2), 819–828.

Yudin, D., and Nemirovskii, A. 1976. Informational complexity and efficient methods for the solution of convex extremal problems. *Matekon*, **13**(2), 22–45.

Yudin, D., and Nemirovskii, A. 1977. Evaluation of the informational complexity of mathematical programming problems. *Matekon*, **13**(2), 3–25.

Zhang, H., and Chen, S. 2021. Concentration inequalities for statistical inference. *Communications in Mathematical Research*, **37**(1), 1–85.

Zhang, M., Chen, L., Hassani, H., and Karbasi, A. 2019. Online continuous submodular maximization: From full-information to bandit feedback. In: *Advances in Neural Information Processing Systems*.

Zhao, P., Wang, G., Zhang, L., and Zhou, Z.-H. 2021. Bandit convex optimization in non-stationary environments. *Journal of Machine Learning Research*, **22**(1), 5562–5606.

Zimmert, J., and Lattimore, T. 2019. Connections between mirror descent, Thompson sampling and the information ratio. In: *Advances in Neural Information Processing Systems*.

Zimmert, J., and Lattimore, T. 2022. Return of the bias: Almost minimax optimal high probability bounds for adversarial linear bandits. In: *Proceedings of the 35th Conference on Learning Theory*.

Zinkevich, M. 2003. Online convex programming and generalized infinitesimal gradient ascent. In: *Proceedings of the 20th International Conference on Machine Learning*.

Zwillinger, D. 2018. *CRC standard mathematical tables and formulae*. 33rd edn. Chapman and Hall/CRC.

Index

adaptive, 24, 78, 240
adjacency matrix, 91
affine
 hull, 34
 map, 32, 33, 40, 90, 121, 133, 137, 138, 257
 subset, 6
approximation ratio, 238
Azuma's inequality, 162, 233, 252
bandit
 finite-armed, 49, 117, 120
 Gaussian process, 3
 infinite-armed, 118, 123–127, 142
 kernelised, 92
 linear, 71, 76, 79, 85–89, 117
 phase retrieval, 117
 quadratic, 79, 89–91, 234
 submodular maximisation, 237
 submodular minimisation, 7, 227
Bayesian
 convex bandits, 110
 minimax regret, 110, 112
 stochastic convex bandits, 111
Bernstein's inequality, 132, 217, 252
best arm identification, 8, 127–128, 134, 138
bias, 21
bisection method, 118
 deterministic, 42–43
 stochastic, 43–48
Bregman divergence, 102–104, 106, 115
centre of gravity method, 14, 120, 133–139
concentration, 6, 9, 125, 162, 184, 251
 of surrogate, 212–224
confidence interval, 49, 216
constraint set, 1, 5, 16, 30, 32, 92
continuous exponential weights, 15, 83–86, 92, 95, 239

continuous time, 148, 160
convex body, 5, 26–28, 172
 positions of, 32–33
convex closure, 229
convex hull, 6
covering number, 79–80, 86, 89
curvature, 15, 20, 72, 146, 148, 153, 169, 200, 207, 239
cutting plane methods, 14, 118

decaying online Newton step, 177
diameter, 11, 30
differentiable, 10, 29, 30, 38, 53, 62, 65, 102, 129, 231
Dikin ellipsoid, 62, 73, 153
domain, 11
doubling trick, 240
duality
 Bregman divergence, 115
 information ratio, 16, 117
 minimax, 15, 94, 116

ellipsoid, 10
ellipsoid method, 14, 16, 17, 49, 120, 139–140, 143
 for non-convex optimisation, 196
essentially smooth, 102
essentially strictly convex, 102
exploration by optimisation, 107–110, 117
exponential weights, 81, 85, 94, 104, 108, 147
extension, 34–38, 41, 60, 140, 153

Fenchel–Young inequality, 249
filtration, 11, 161, 214, 252
focus region, 175, 178, 181, 183, 189, 196, 216, 224, 226
follow-the-regularised-leader, 16, 61, 64–65, 104

267

Freedman's inequality, 217, 220, 223, 224, 252
golden section search, 49
Grünbaum's inequality, 120, 133
gradient descent, 14, 50–53, 61, 64, 82
    for non-convex optimisation, 175–177
    for submodular bandits, 234–237
half-space, 10
Hoeffding's inequality, 45, 127, 252
hypercube, 228, 232, 233

information gain, 112
information ratio, 111
information-directed sampling, 15, 116
interior point methods, 4, 62, 76, 138, 182
isotropic position, 32, 150

Jensen's inequality, 130, 152, 201, 207, 248
John's position, 32, 150
John's theorem, 32, 122, 139, 151

Löwner's position, 32, 150, 233
Legendre, 102, 104
linear programming, 14, 62, 230
Lipschitz, 5, 30
local norm, 62
Lovász extension, 228, 238
lower bound, 21, 71, 117

martingale, 4, 217, 233, 252, 253
mean width, 150, 151, 179
measurable, 84, 123, 161, 183, 185, 246
memory, 157, 174, 239
method of inscribed ellipsoid, 137
minimax theorem, 111
Minkowski functional, 26, 28, 35, 62
Minkowski sum, 10
Moore–Penrose pseudoinverse, 81, 243

Newton's method, 49, 148
    damped, 68
noise, 6, 7, 49, 111, 238
    heteroscedastic, 241
    multiplicative, 241
non-constructive, 15, 16, 111, 116
non-convex, 17, 24, 91, 147, 182, 240, 249
non-stationary, 24

online Newton step, 118, 145, 147, 239
optimal design, 80
optimistic, 65, 98, 129, 142, 175, 198
optional stopping theorem, 253
Orlicz norm, 6, 246

perspective, 36
pessimistic, 98, 142
polar, 10, 27, 150

Polyak–Lojasiewicz condition, 240
polytope, 6, 77, 137, 142, 172, 181, 197
posterior, 111, 117
prior, 110, 111, 117
probability kernel, 51, 52, 96, 123
projection, 10, 40, 156, 182
    Bregman divergence, 103
    relative entropy, 147

quadratic programming, 91, 181
quasiconvex, 240

regret, 5
    Bayesian, 15, 110, 111, 117
    minimax, 111
    simple, 7, 235
relative entropy, 84, 104, 147
relative interior, 34
restart, 175, 180, 183, 190, 196, 241
rounded, 32, 149, 175

sample complexity, 7, 22, 24, 59, 118, 134, 143
self-concordant barrier, 16, 62–64, 77, 92, 146
    entropic, 77
    logarithmic, 77
    universal, 77
separation oracle, 32, 40, 60, 92, 139, 140, 143, 172, 197
setting
    adversarial, 7, 15, 111, 175, 227, 238
    deterministic, 16, 49
    full information, 15, 20, 145, 147, 173
    improper, 12, 16, 17, 20, 22, 78
    stochastic, 7, 13, 14, 16, 17, 24, 42, 49, 74, 118, 145, 185, 227, 235, 238, 239
    two-point, 13
    unconstrained, 6, 12, 21, 34, 78
simplex, 91, 119, 121, 133
singular value decomposition, 22, 68, 77, 243
Sion's minimax theorem, 114
slicing conjecture, 33
smooth, 5, 29, 66, 70, 71
smoothing, 38
stochastic approximation, 241
stochastic oracle, 119
Stokes' theorem, 53, 65
stopping time, 161, 183, 214, 252
strongly convex, 5, 29, 66, 71
subexponential, 10, 246
subgaussian, 6, 10, 74, 119, 123, 130, 170, 246
subgradient, 137, 257
    of Lovász extension, 231, 236, 238
    of support function, 28

Index 269

submodular function, 227
support function, 27, 141, 150, 151
surrogate loss, 51, 71, 77, 98
    ellipsoidal, 65, 129
    Gaussian, 154, 175, 198
    kernel, 96
    optimisation, 108
    quadratic, 153
    spherical, 53
suspension cone, 26

Thompson sampling, 117

uniform measure, 11, 33, 40, 53, 66, 97, 132, 150, 228, 251, 257
unimodal, 18, 49
unnormalised negative entropy, 82, 104

Vaidya's method, 119, 142
variance, 6, 16, 21, 72, 74

For EU product safety concerns, contact us at Calle de José Abascal, 56–1º,
28003 Madrid, Spain or eugpsr@cambridge.org.

www.ingramcontent.com/pod-product-compliance
Ingram Content Group UK Ltd.
Pitfield, Milton Keynes, MK11 3LW, UK
UKHW022054120326
468942UK00007B/951